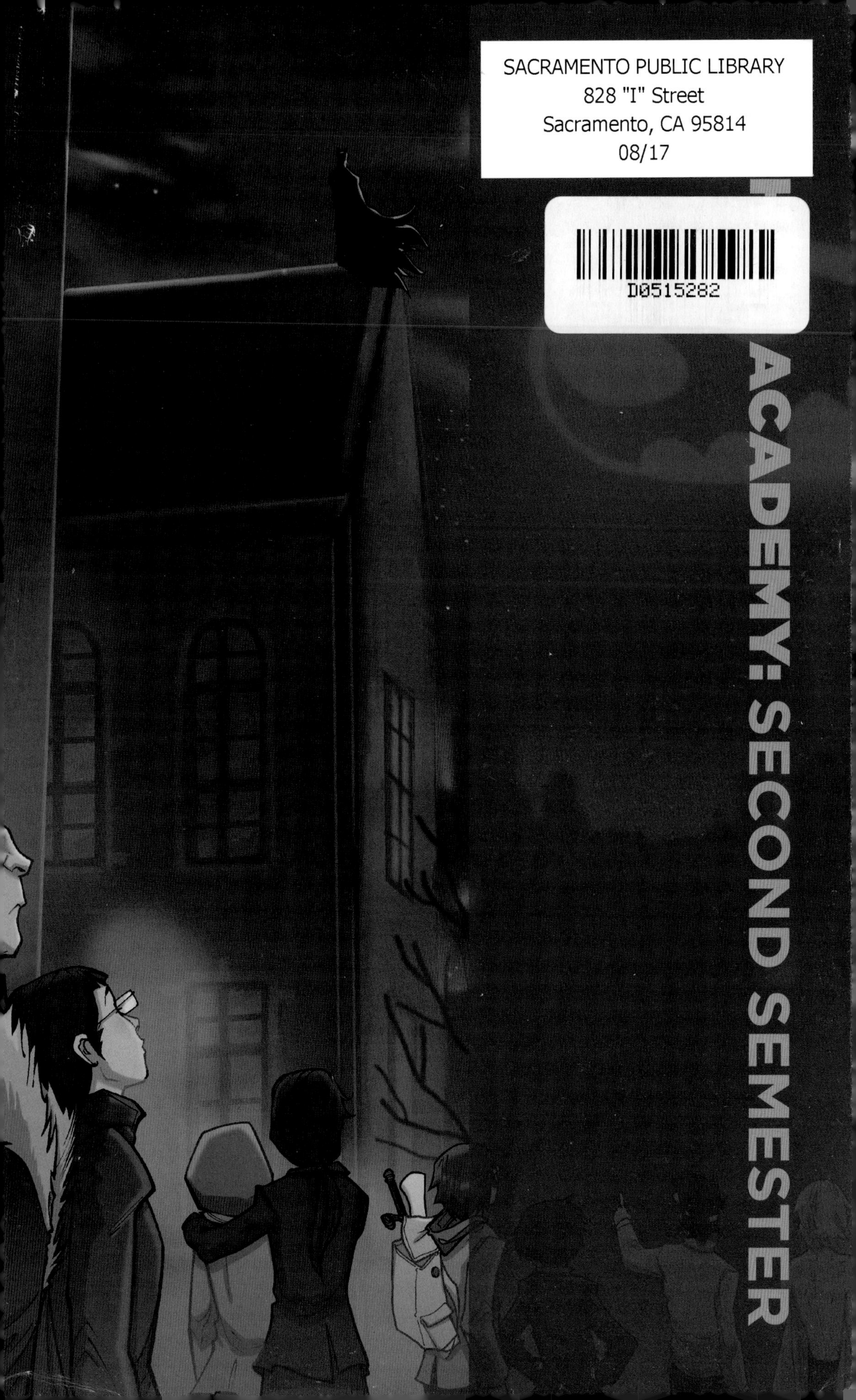
ACADEMY: SECOND SEMESTER

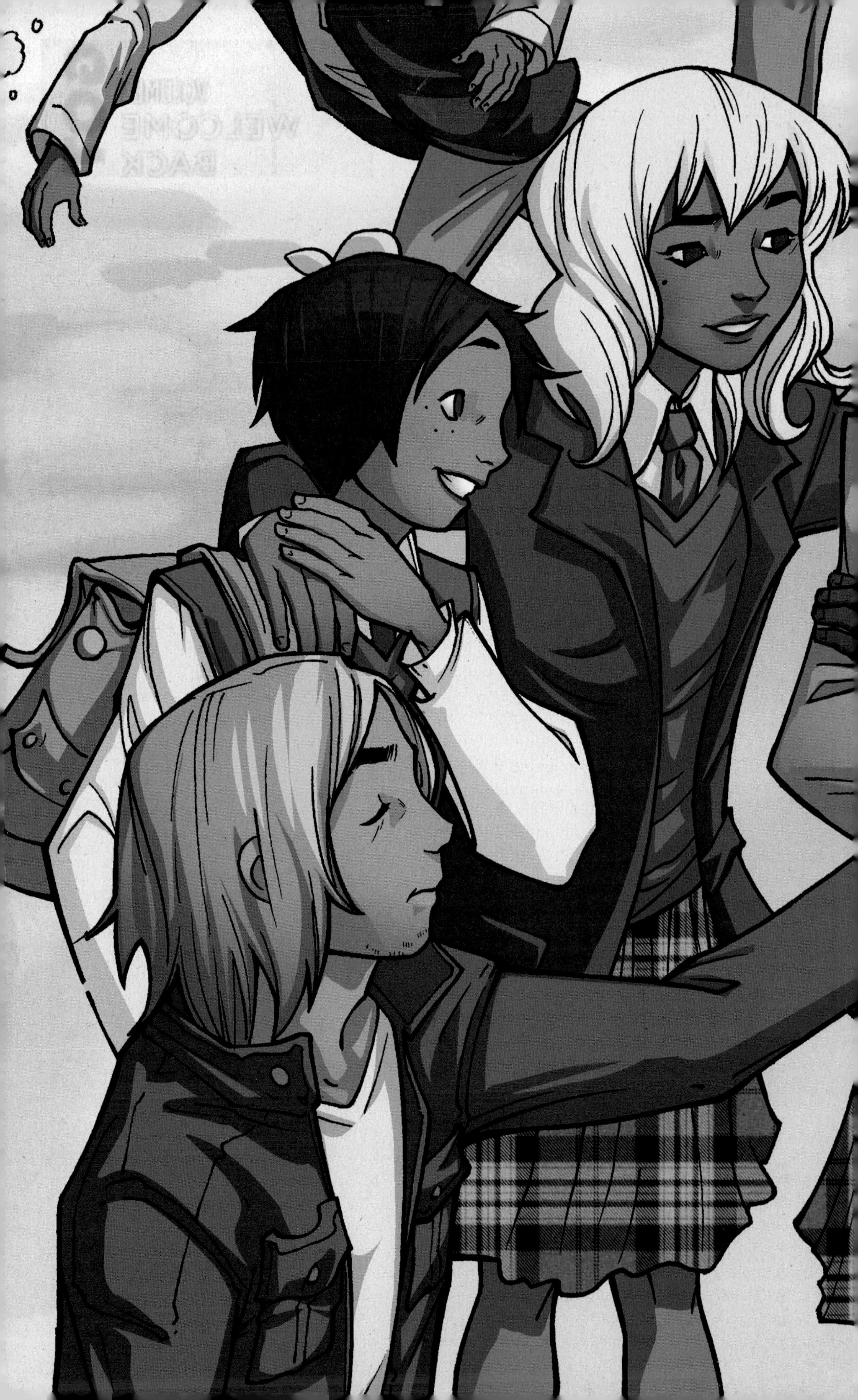

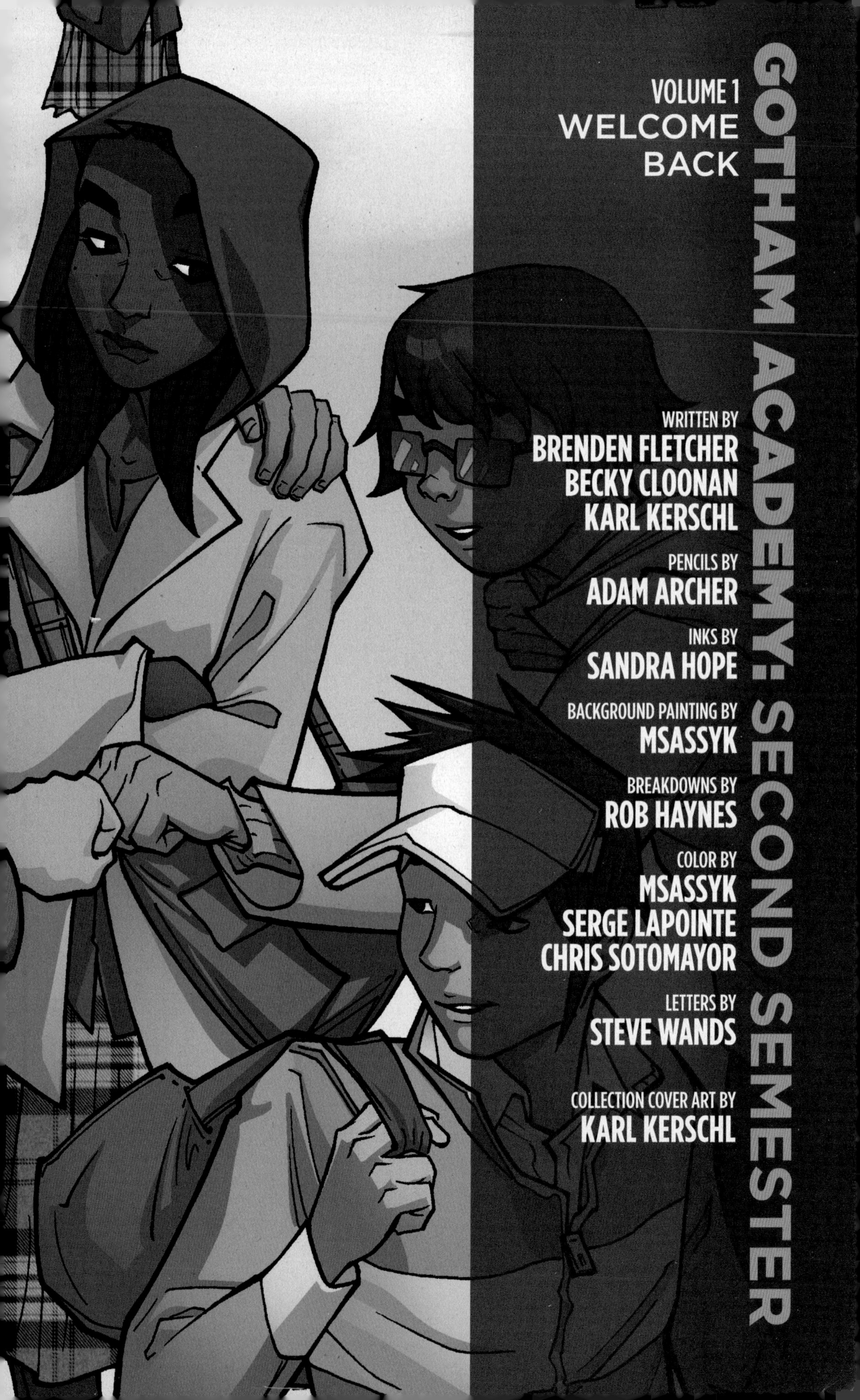

# GOTHAM ACADEMY: SECOND SEMESTER

## VOLUME 1
## WELCOME BACK


WRITTEN BY
**BRENDEN FLETCHER**
**BECKY CLOONAN**
**KARL KERSCHL**

PENCILS BY
**ADAM ARCHER**

INKS BY
**SANDRA HOPE**

BACKGROUND PAINTING BY
**MSASSYK**

BREAKDOWNS BY
**ROB HAYNES**

COLOR BY
**MSASSYK**
**SERGE LAPOINTE**
**CHRIS SOTOMAYOR**

LETTERS BY
**STEVE WANDS**

COLLECTION COVER ART BY
**KARL KERSCHL**

REBECCA TAYLOR  Editor – Original Series
JEB WOODARD  Group Editor – Collected Editions
ROBIN WILDMAN  Editor – Collected Edition
STEVE COOK  Design Director – Books
CURTIS KING JR.  Publication Design

BOB HARRAS  Senior VP – Editor-in-Chief, DC Comics

DIANE NELSON President
DAN DiDIO Publisher
JIM LEE Publisher
GEOFF JOHNS President & Chief Creative Officer
AMIT DESAI Executive VP – Business & Marketing Strategy,
Direct to Consumer & Global Franchise Management
SAM ADES Senior VP – Direct to Consumer
BOBBIE CHASE VP – Talent Development
MARK CHIARELLO Senior VP – Art, Design & Collected Editions
JOHN CUNNINGHAM Senior VP – Sales & Trade Marketing
ANNE DePIES Senior VP – Business Strategy, Finance & Administration
DON FALLETTI VP – Manufacturing Operations
LAWRENCE GANEM VP – Editorial Administration & Talent Relations
ALISON GILL Senior VP – Manufacturing & Operations
HANK KANALZ Senior VP – Editorial Strategy & Administration
JAY KOGAN VP – Legal Affairs
THOMAS LOFTUS VP – Business Affairs
JACK MAHAN VP – Business Affairs
NICK J. NAPOLITANO VP – Manufacturing Administration
EDDIE SCANNELL VP – Consumer Marketing
COURTNEY SIMMONS Senior VP – Publicity & Communications
JIM (SKI) SOKOLOWSKI VP – Comic Book Specialty Sales & Trade Marketing
NANCY SPEARS VP – Mass, Book, Digital Sales & Trade Marketing

**GOTHAM ACADEMY: SECOND SEMESTER VOLUME 1—WELCOME BACK**

DC Comics, 2900 West Alameda Avenue, Burbank, CA 91505
Printed by Solisco Printers, Scott, QC, Canada. 6/16/17. First Printing.
ISBN: 978-1-4012-7119-0

Library of Congress Cataloging-in-Publication Data is available.

PEFC Certified

This product is from
sustainably managed
forests, recycled and
controlled sources

PEFC/26-31-02     www.pefc.org

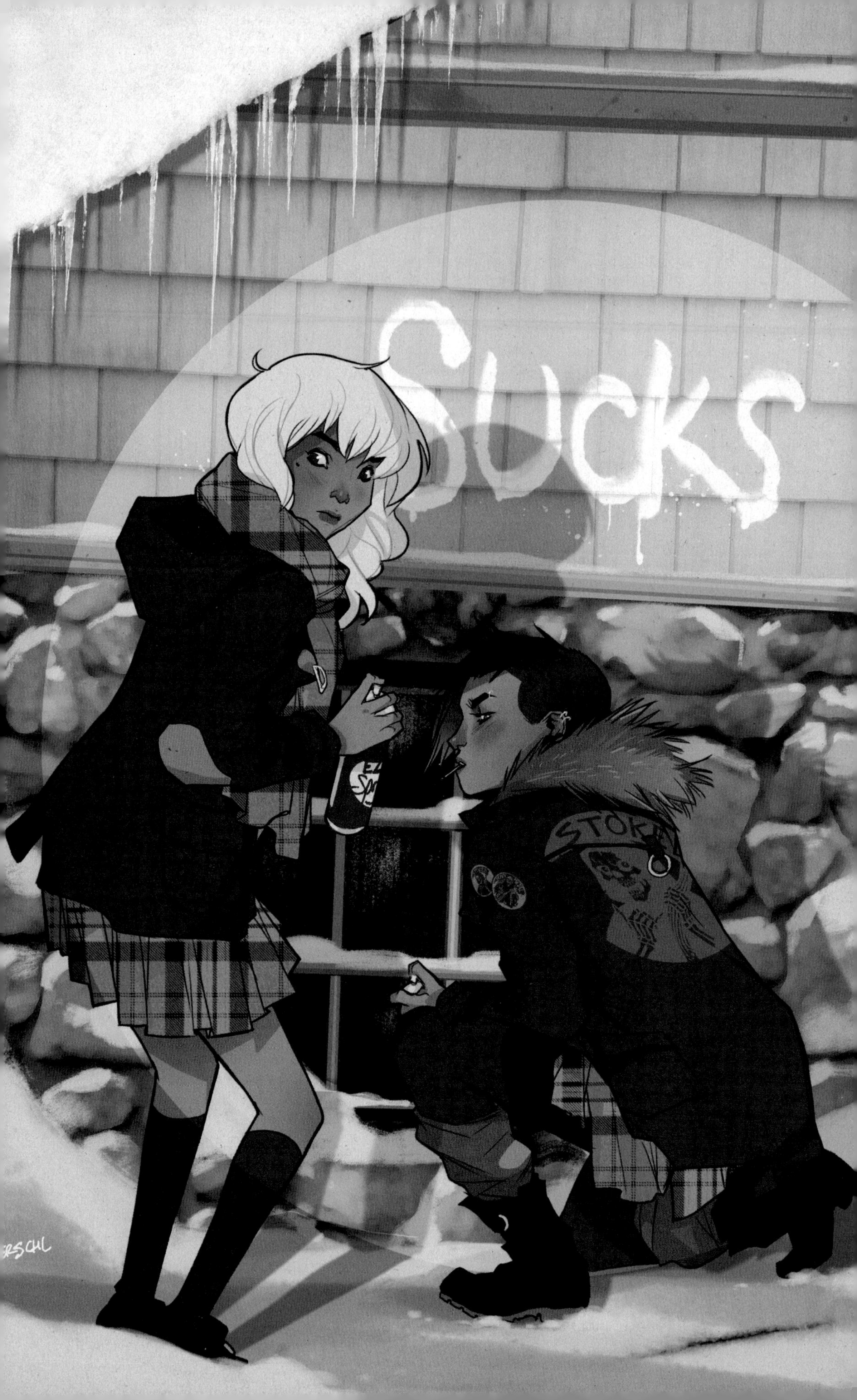
SUCKS

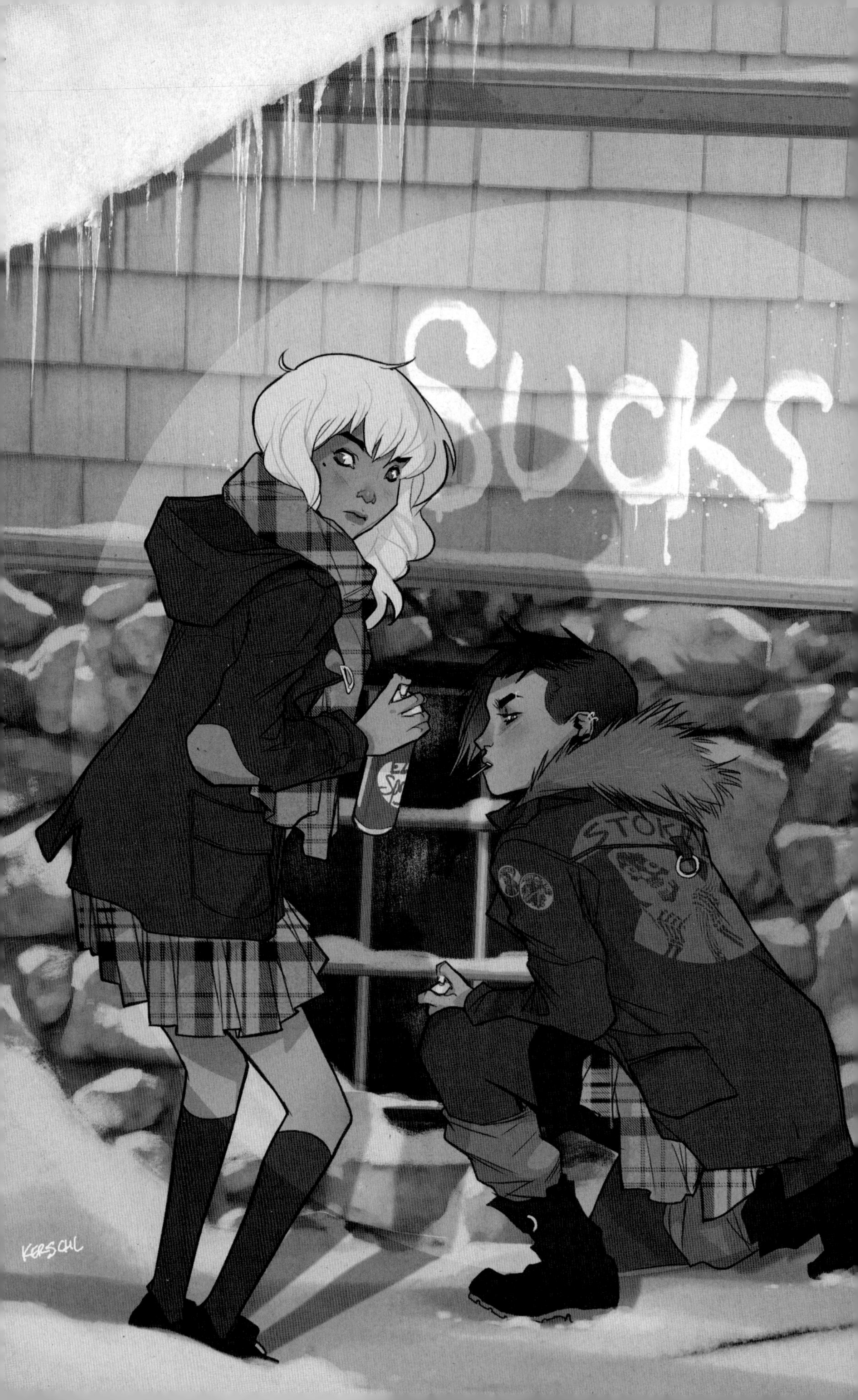
SUCKS
KERSCHL

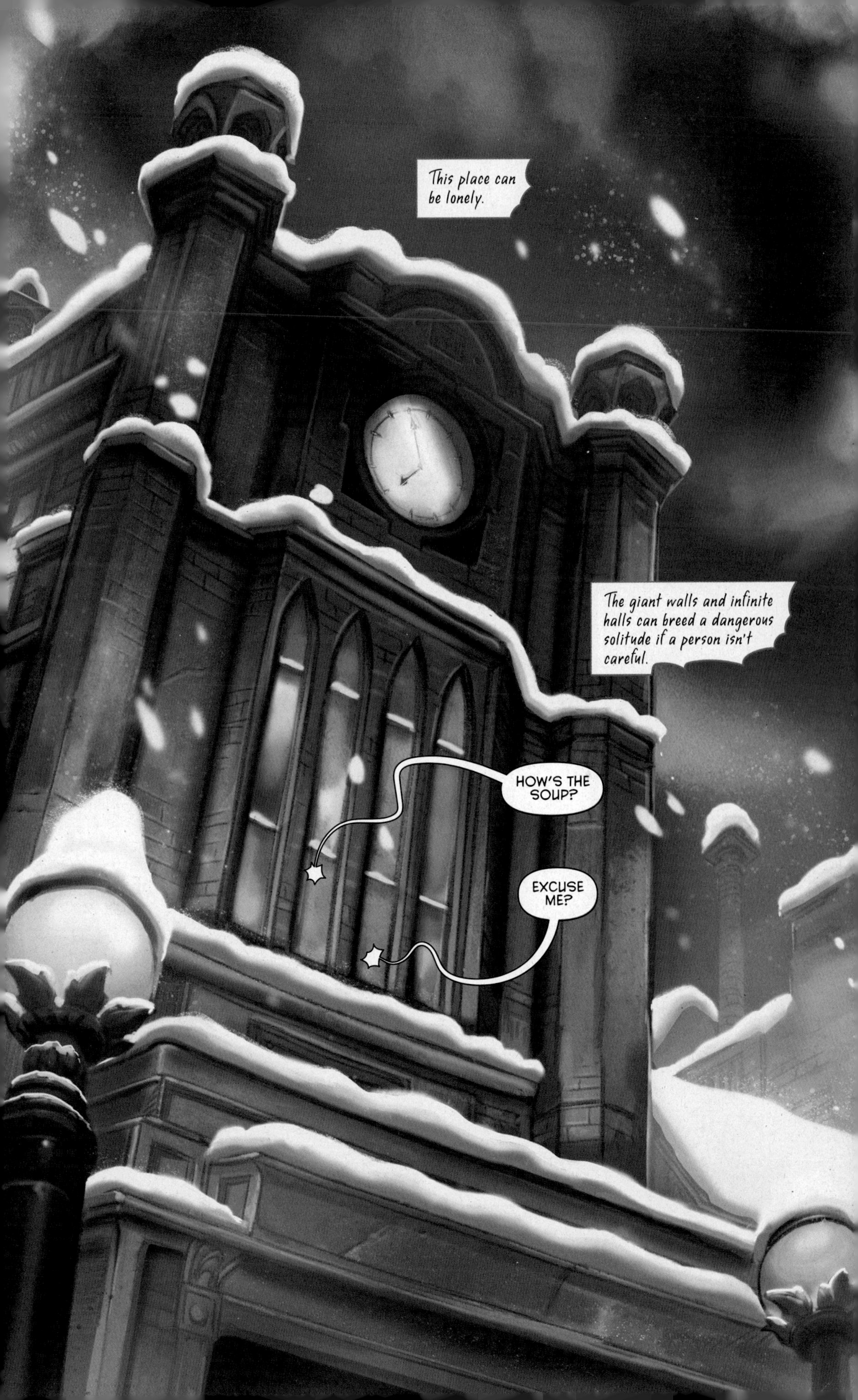
This place can be lonely.
The giant walls and infinite halls can breed a dangerous solitude if a person isn't careful.
HOW'S THE SOUP?
EXCUSE ME?

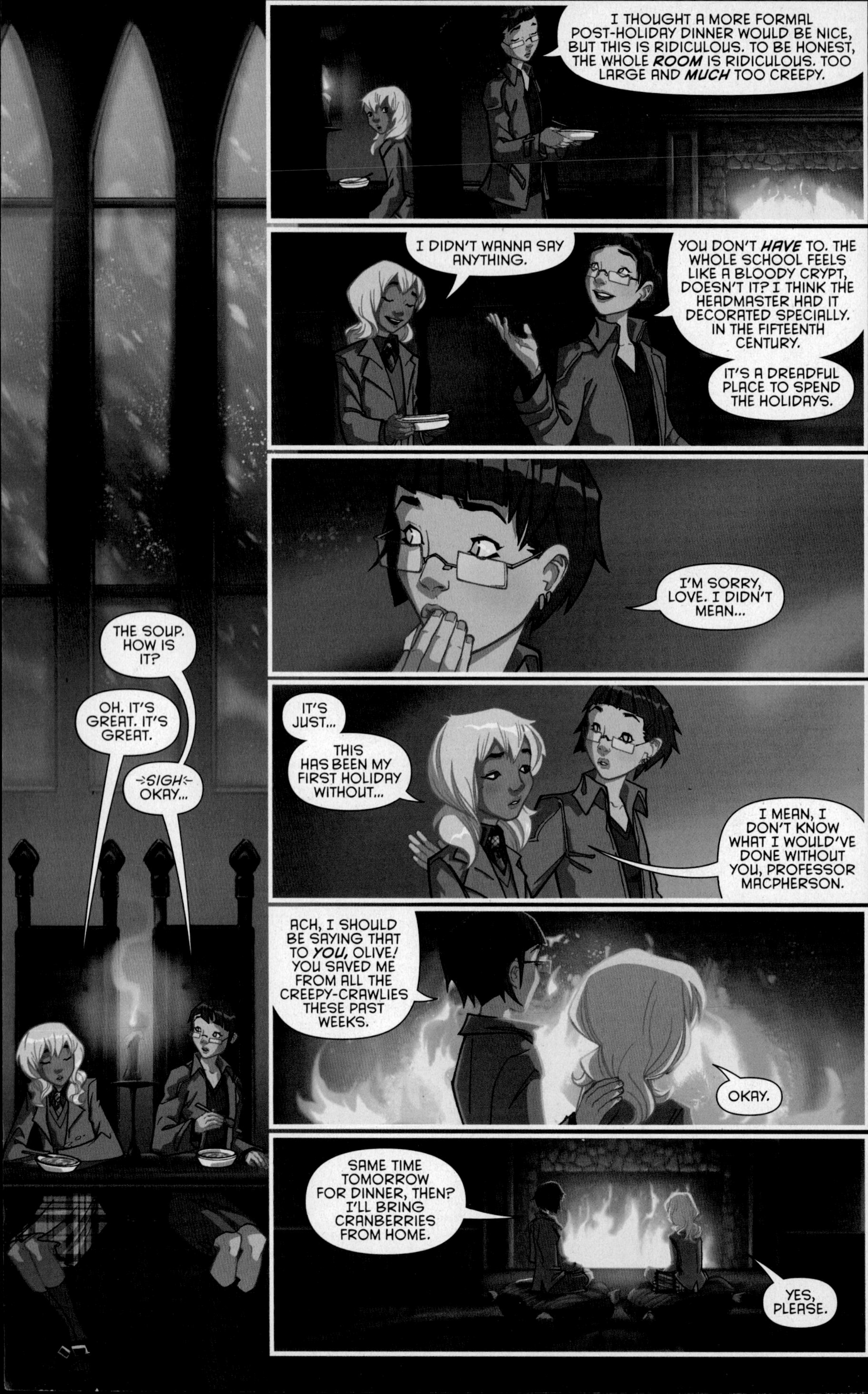

THE SOUP. HOW IS IT?
OH. IT'S GREAT. IT'S GREAT.
⇢SIGH⇠ OKAY...
I THOUGHT A MORE FORMAL POST-HOLIDAY DINNER WOULD BE NICE, BUT THIS IS RIDICULOUS. TO BE HONEST, THE WHOLE ROOM IS RIDICULOUS. TOO LARGE AND MUCH TOO CREEPY.
I DIDN'T WANNA SAY ANYTHING.
YOU DON'T HAVE TO. THE WHOLE SCHOOL FEELS LIKE A BLOODY CRYPT, DOESN'T IT? I THINK THE HEADMASTER HAD IT DECORATED SPECIALLY. IN THE FIFTEENTH CENTURY.
IT'S A DREADFUL PLACE TO SPEND THE HOLIDAYS.
I'M SORRY, LOVE. I DIDN'T MEAN...
IT'S JUST...
THIS HAS BEEN MY FIRST HOLIDAY WITHOUT...
I MEAN, I DON'T KNOW WHAT I WOULD'VE DONE WITHOUT YOU, PROFESSOR MACPHERSON.
ACH, I SHOULD BE SAYING THAT TO YOU, OLIVE! YOU SAVED ME FROM ALL THE CREEPY-CRAWLIES THESE PAST WEEKS.
OKAY.
SAME TIME TOMORROW FOR DINNER, THEN? I'LL BRING CRANBERRIES FROM HOME.
YES, PLEASE.

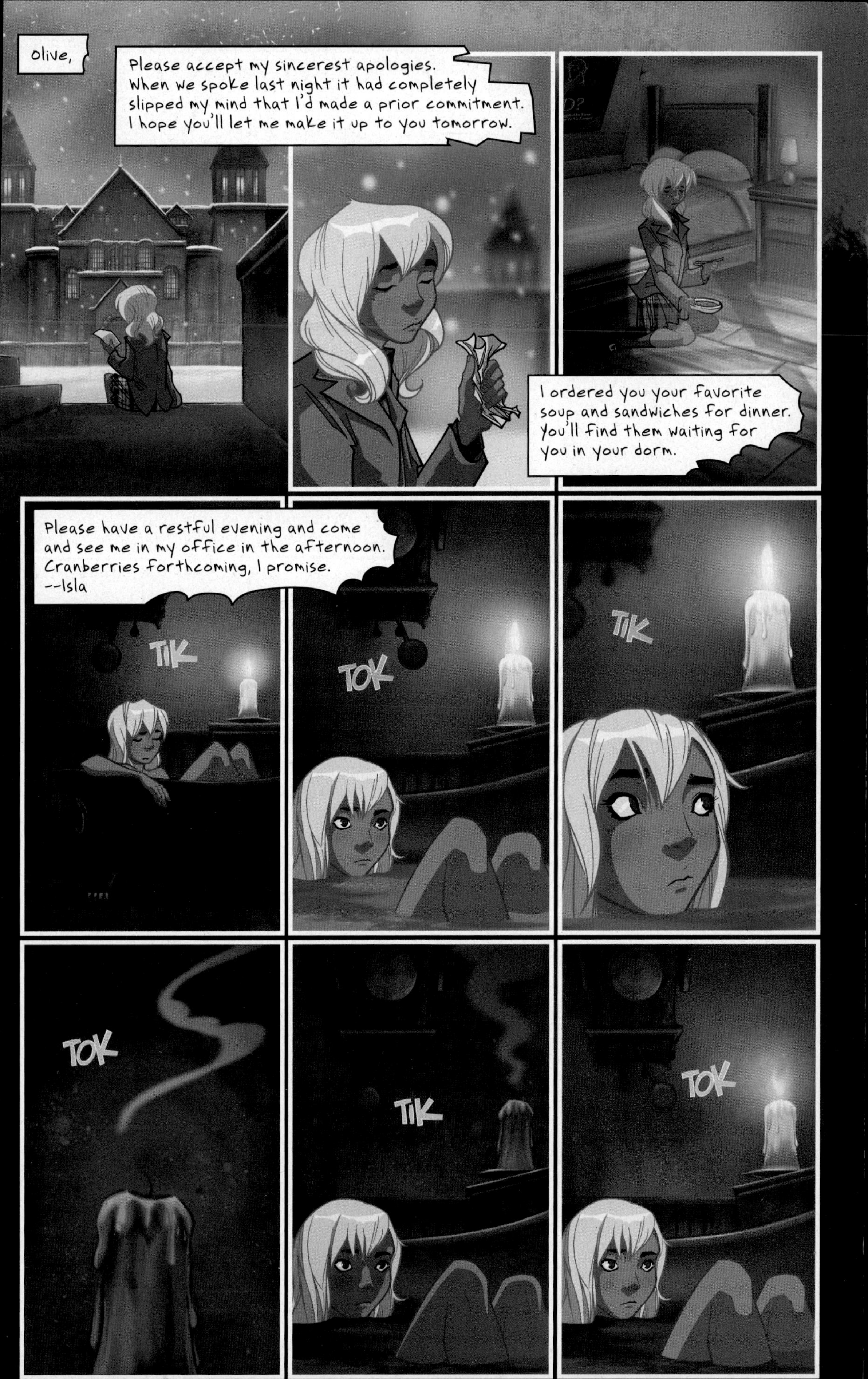
Olive,
Please accept my sincerest apologies. When we spoke last night it had completely slipped my mind that I'd made a prior commitment. I hope you'll let me make it up to you tomorrow.
I ordered you your favorite soup and sandwiches for dinner. You'll find them waiting for you in your dorm.
Please have a restful evening and come and see me in my office in the afternoon. Cranberries forthcoming, I promise. --Isla
TIK
TOK
TIK
TOK
TIK
TOK

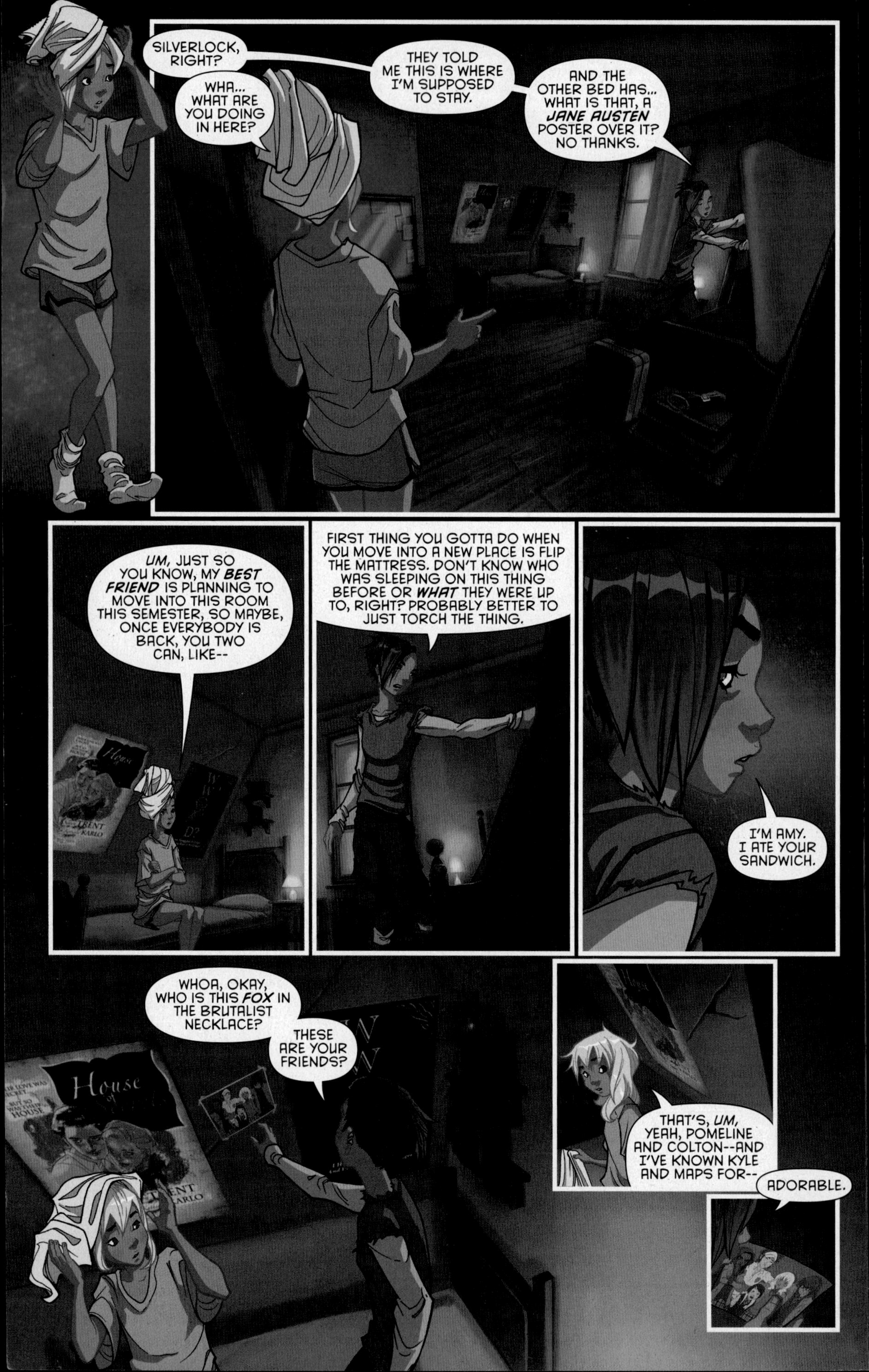
SILVERLOCK, RIGHT?
WHA... WHAT ARE YOU DOING IN HERE?
THEY TOLD ME THIS IS WHERE I'M SUPPOSED TO STAY.
AND THE OTHER BED HAS... WHAT IS THAT, A *JANE AUSTEN* POSTER OVER IT? NO THANKS.
*UM*, JUST SO YOU KNOW, MY *BEST FRIEND* IS PLANNING TO MOVE INTO THIS ROOM THIS SEMESTER, SO MAYBE, ONCE EVERYBODY IS BACK, YOU TWO CAN, LIKE--
FIRST THING YOU GOTTA DO WHEN YOU MOVE INTO A NEW PLACE IS FLIP THE MATTRESS. DON'T KNOW WHO WAS SLEEPING ON THIS THING BEFORE OR *WHAT* THEY WERE UP TO, RIGHT? PROBABLY BETTER TO JUST TORCH THE THING.
I'M AMY. I ATE YOUR SANDWICH.
WHOA, OKAY, WHO IS THIS *FOX* IN THE BRUTALIST NECKLACE?
THESE ARE YOUR FRIENDS?
THAT'S, *UM*, YEAH, POMELINE AND COLTON--AND I'VE KNOWN KYLE AND MAPS FOR--
ADORABLE.

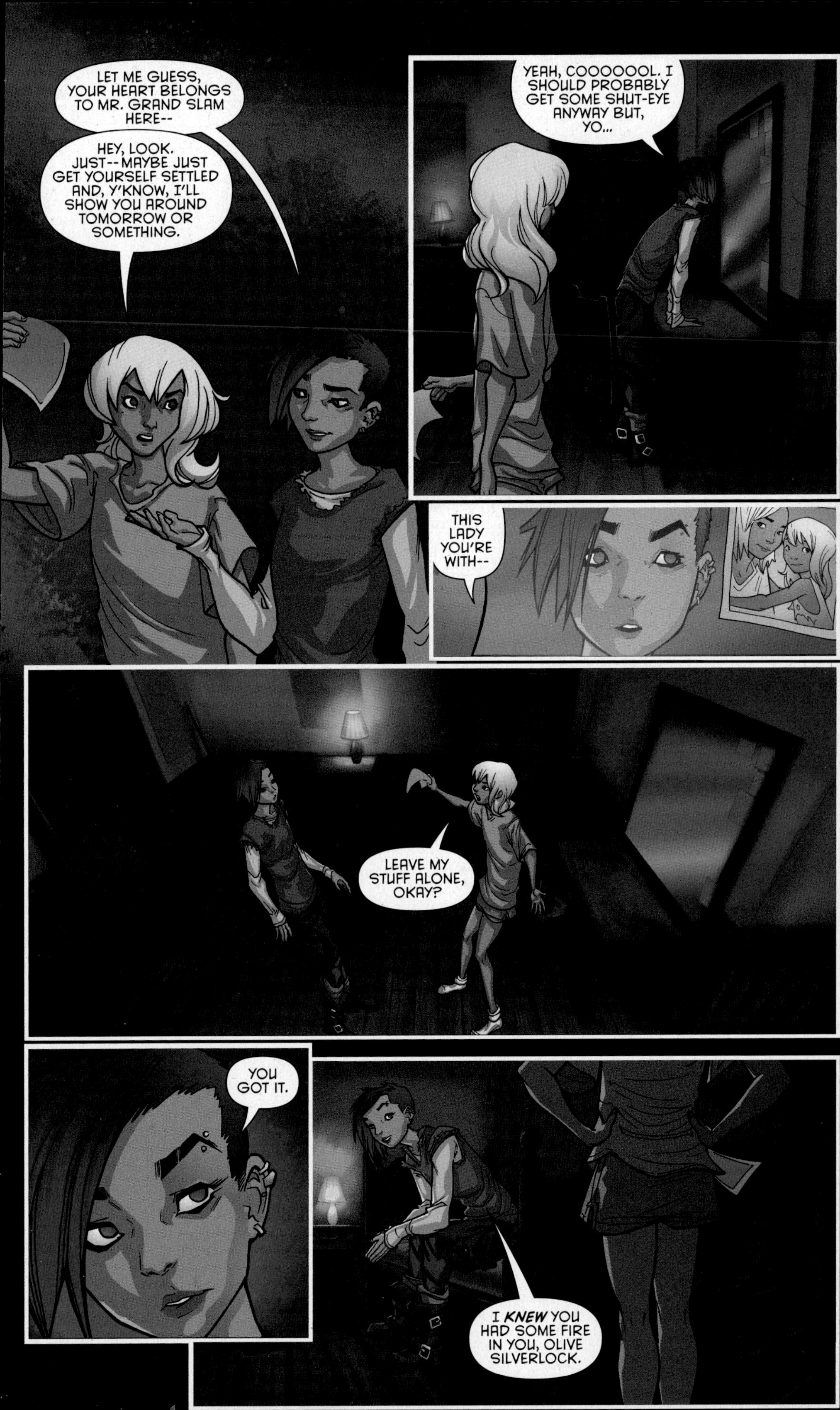
LET ME GUESS, YOUR HEART BELONGS TO MR. GRAND SLAM HERE--
HEY, LOOK. JUST--MAYBE JUST GET YOURSELF SETTLED AND, Y'KNOW, I'LL SHOW YOU AROUND TOMORROW OR SOMETHING.
YEAH, COOOOOOL. I SHOULD PROBABLY GET SOME SHUT-EYE ANYWAY BUT, YO...
THIS LADY YOU'RE WITH--
LEAVE MY STUFF ALONE, OKAY?
YOU GOT IT.
I *KNEW* YOU HAD SOME FIRE IN YOU, OLIVE SILVERLOCK.

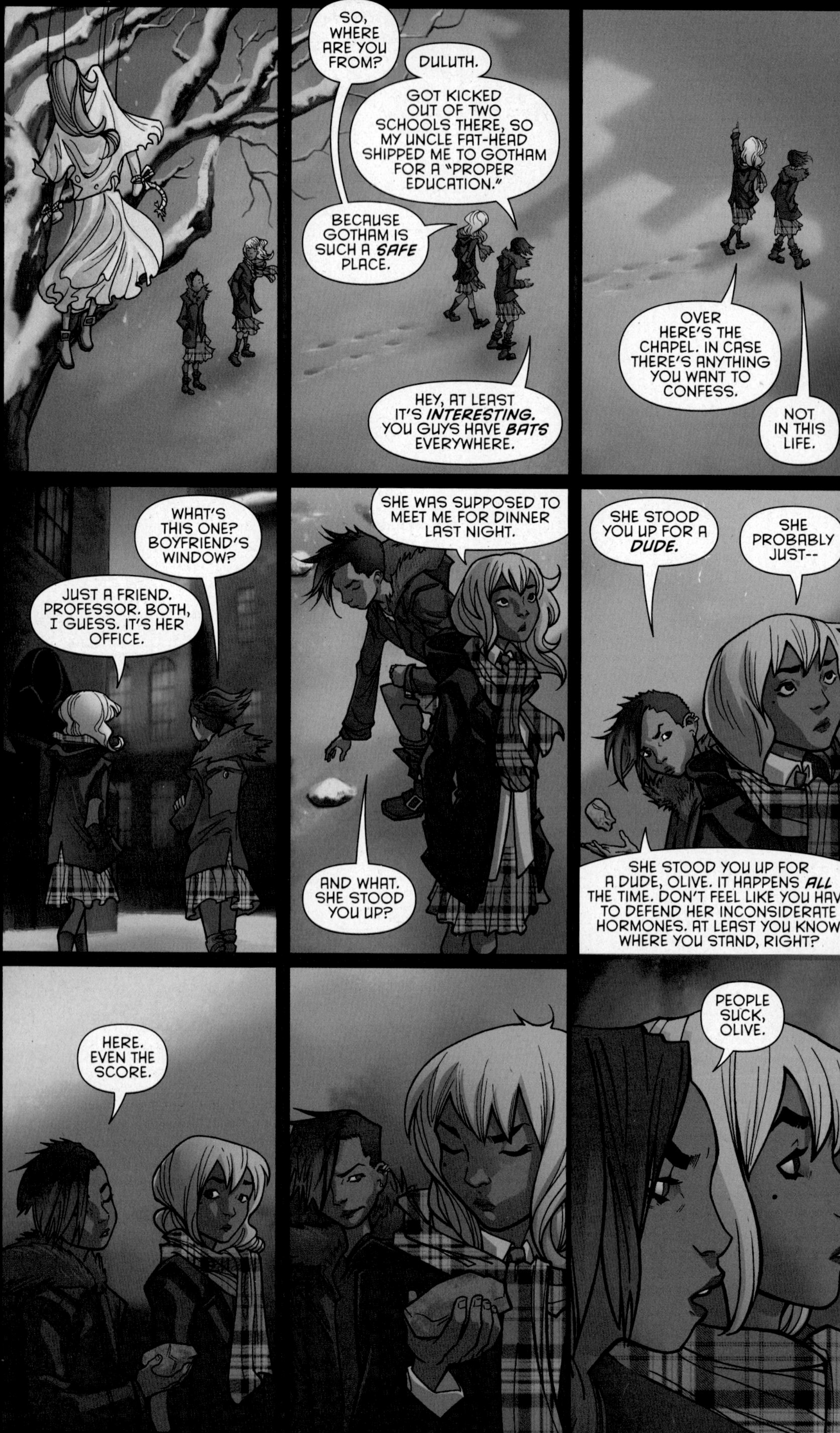
SO, WHERE ARE YOU FROM?
DULUTH.
GOT KICKED OUT OF TWO SCHOOLS THERE, SO MY UNCLE FAT-HEAD SHIPPED ME TO GOTHAM FOR A "PROPER EDUCATION."
BECAUSE GOTHAM IS SUCH A SAFE PLACE.
HEY, AT LEAST IT'S INTERESTING. YOU GUYS HAVE BATS EVERYWHERE.
OVER HERE'S THE CHAPEL. IN CASE THERE'S ANYTHING YOU WANT TO CONFESS.
NOT IN THIS LIFE.
WHAT'S THIS ONE? BOYFRIEND'S WINDOW?
JUST A FRIEND. PROFESSOR. BOTH, I GUESS. IT'S HER OFFICE.
SHE WAS SUPPOSED TO MEET ME FOR DINNER LAST NIGHT.
AND WHAT. SHE STOOD YOU UP?
SHE STOOD YOU UP FOR A DUDE.
SHE PROBABLY JUST--
SHE STOOD YOU UP FOR A DUDE, OLIVE. IT HAPPENS ALL THE TIME. DON'T FEEL LIKE YOU HAVE TO DEFEND HER INCONSIDERATE HORMONES. AT LEAST YOU KNOW WHERE YOU STAND, RIGHT?
HERE. EVEN THE SCORE.
PEOPLE SUCK, OLIVE.

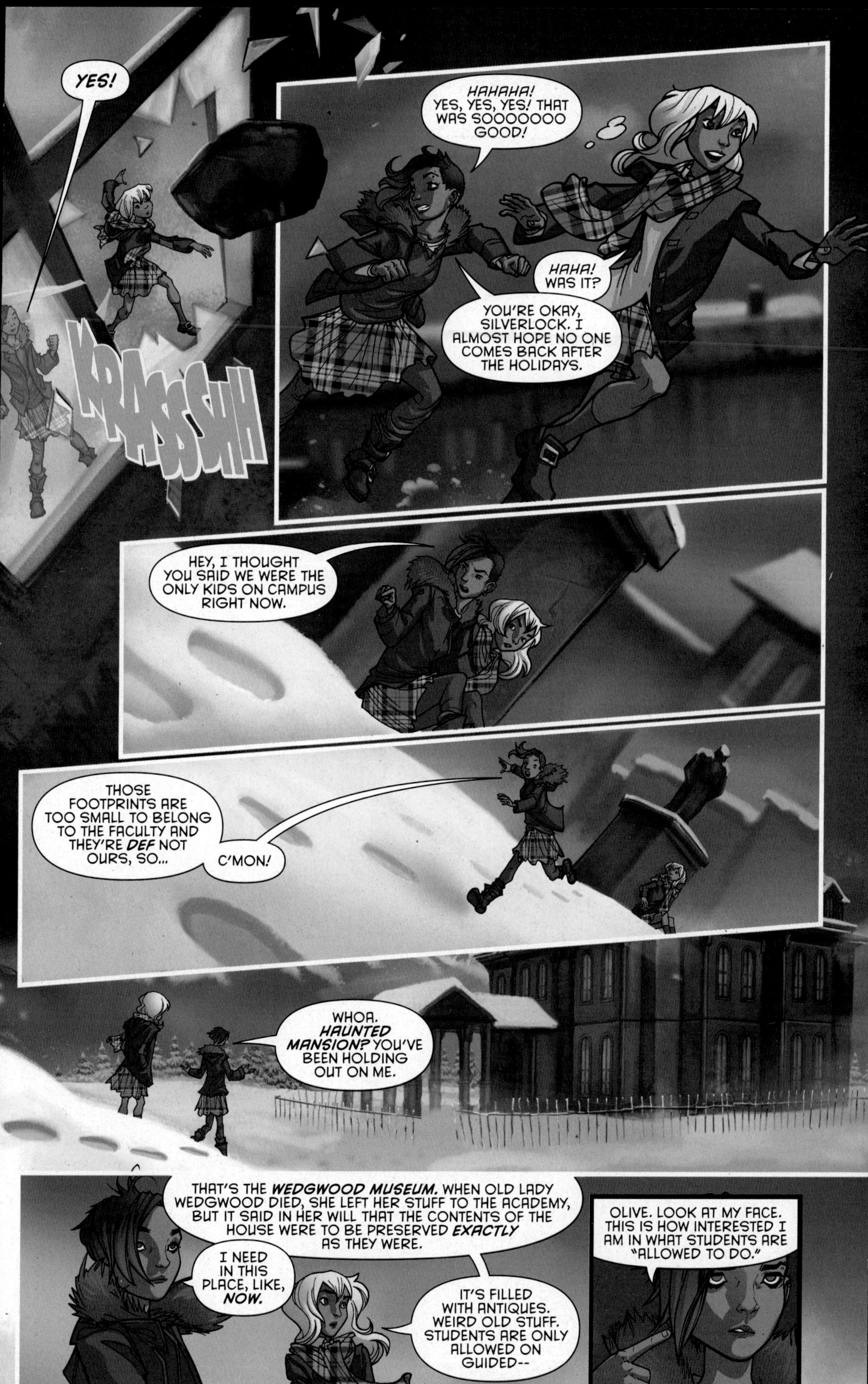
YES!
HAHAHA! YES, YES, YES! THAT WAS SOOOOOOO GOOD!
KRASSSHH
HAHA! WAS IT?
YOU'RE OKAY, SILVERLOCK. I ALMOST HOPE NO ONE COMES BACK AFTER THE HOLIDAYS.
HEY, I THOUGHT YOU SAID WE WERE THE ONLY KIDS ON CAMPUS RIGHT NOW.
THOSE FOOTPRINTS ARE TOO SMALL TO BELONG TO THE FACULTY AND THEY'RE DEF NOT OURS, SO...
C'MON!
WHOA. HAUNTED MANSION? YOU'VE BEEN HOLDING OUT ON ME.
THAT'S THE WEDGWOOD MUSEUM. WHEN OLD LADY WEDGWOOD DIED, SHE LEFT HER STUFF TO THE ACADEMY, BUT IT SAID IN HER WILL THAT THE CONTENTS OF THE HOUSE WERE TO BE PRESERVED EXACTLY AS THEY WERE.
I NEED IN THIS PLACE, LIKE, NOW.
IT'S FILLED WITH ANTIQUES. WEIRD OLD STUFF. STUDENTS ARE ONLY ALLOWED ON GUIDED--
OLIVE. LOOK AT MY FACE. THIS IS HOW INTERESTED I AM IN WHAT STUDENTS ARE "ALLOWED TO DO."

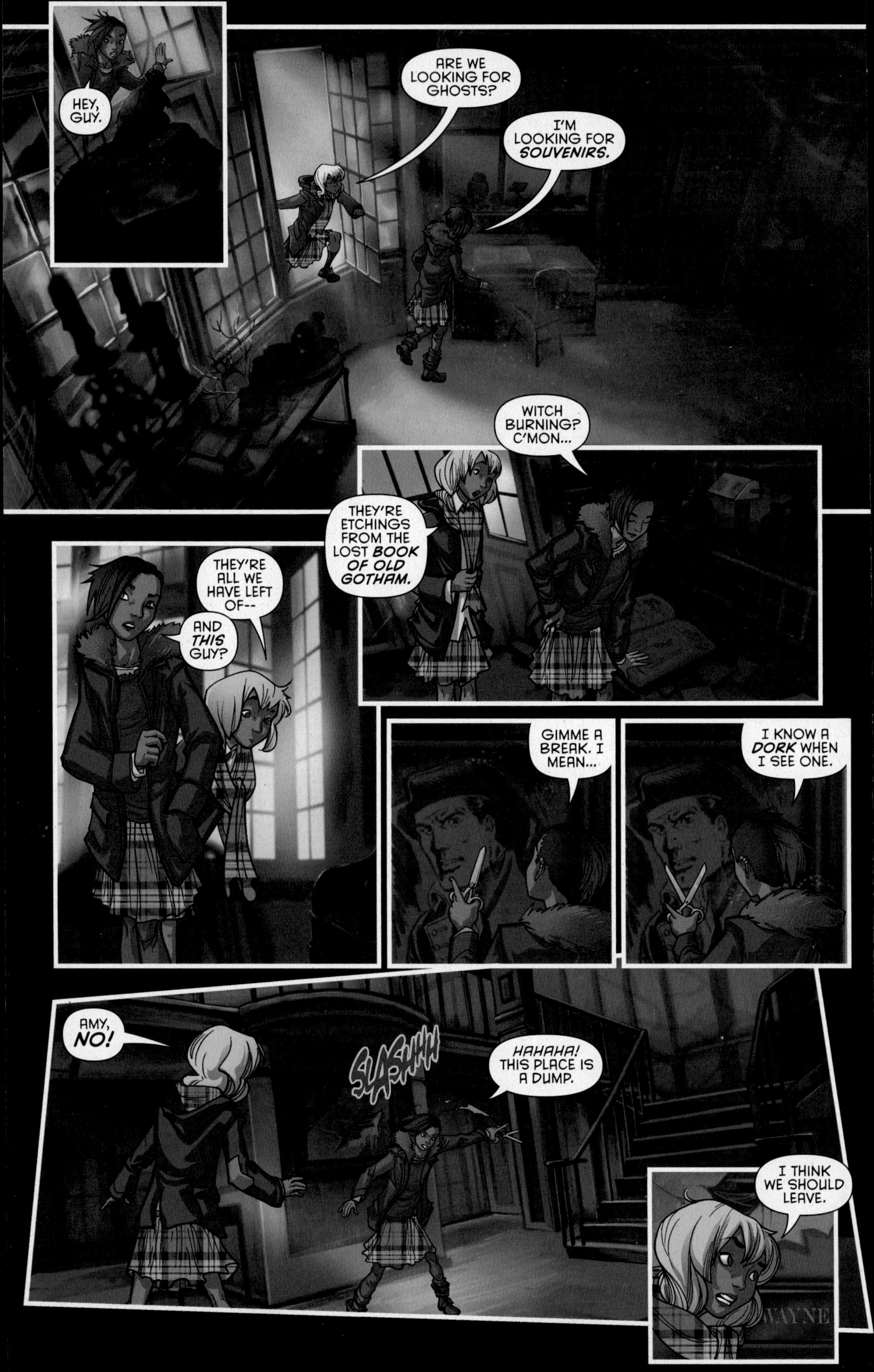
HEY, GUY.
ARE WE LOOKING FOR GHOSTS?
I'M LOOKING FOR SOUVENIRS.
WITCH BURNING? C'MON...
THEY'RE ETCHINGS FROM THE LOST BOOK OF OLD GOTHAM.
THEY'RE ALL WE HAVE LEFT OF--
AND THIS GUY?
GIMME A BREAK. I MEAN...
I KNOW A DORK WHEN I SEE ONE.
AMY, NO!
SLASHHH
HAHAHA! THIS PLACE IS A DUMP.
I THINK WE SHOULD LEAVE.
WAYNE

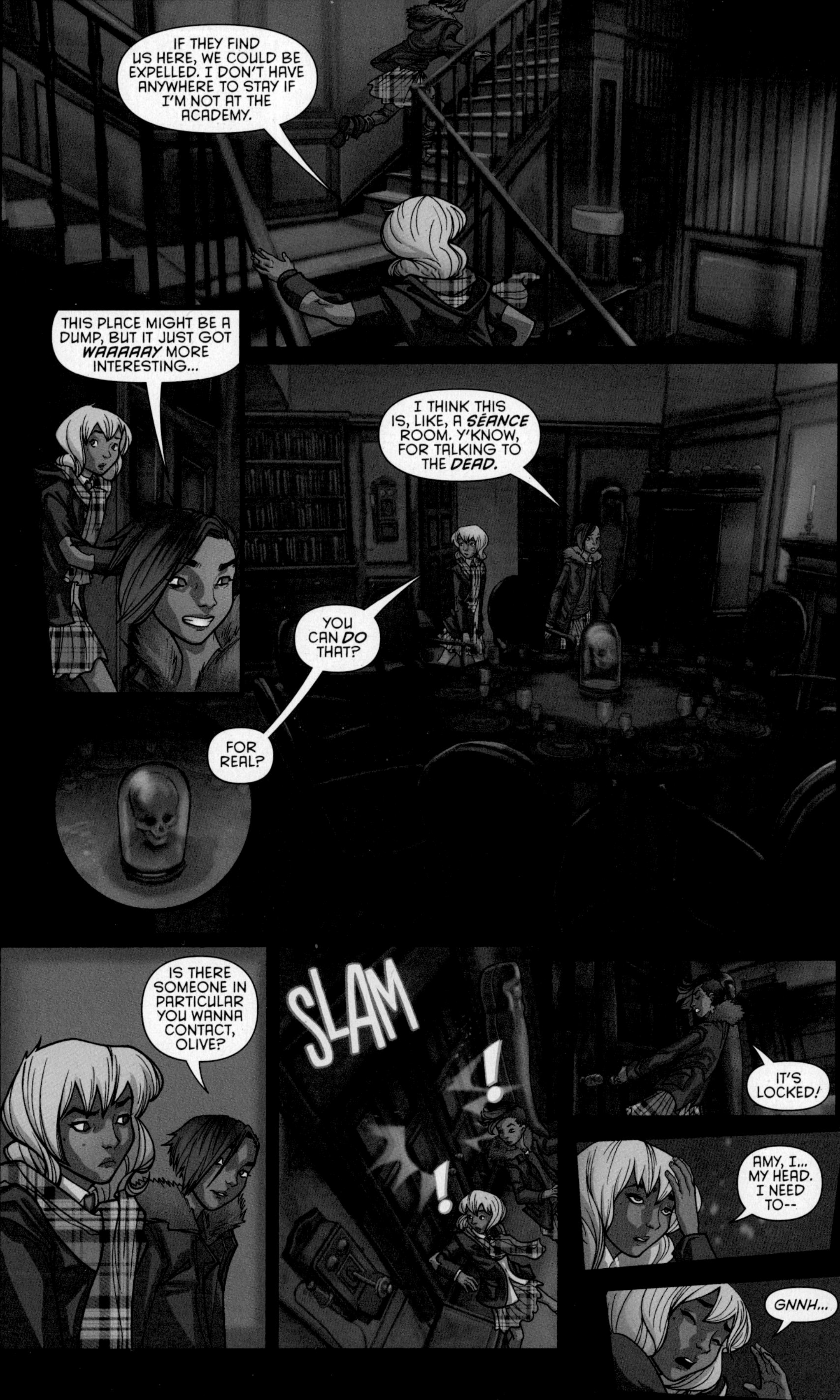

IF THEY FIND US HERE, WE COULD BE EXPELLED. I DON'T HAVE ANYWHERE TO STAY IF I'M NOT AT THE ACADEMY.
THIS PLACE MIGHT BE A DUMP, BUT IT JUST GOT WAAAAAY MORE INTERESTING...
I THINK THIS IS, LIKE, A SÉANCE ROOM. Y'KNOW, FOR TALKING TO THE DEAD.
YOU CAN DO THAT?
FOR REAL?
IS THERE SOMEONE IN PARTICULAR YOU WANNA CONTACT, OLIVE?
SLAM
!
!
IT'S LOCKED!
AMY, I... MY HEAD. I NEED TO--
GNNH...

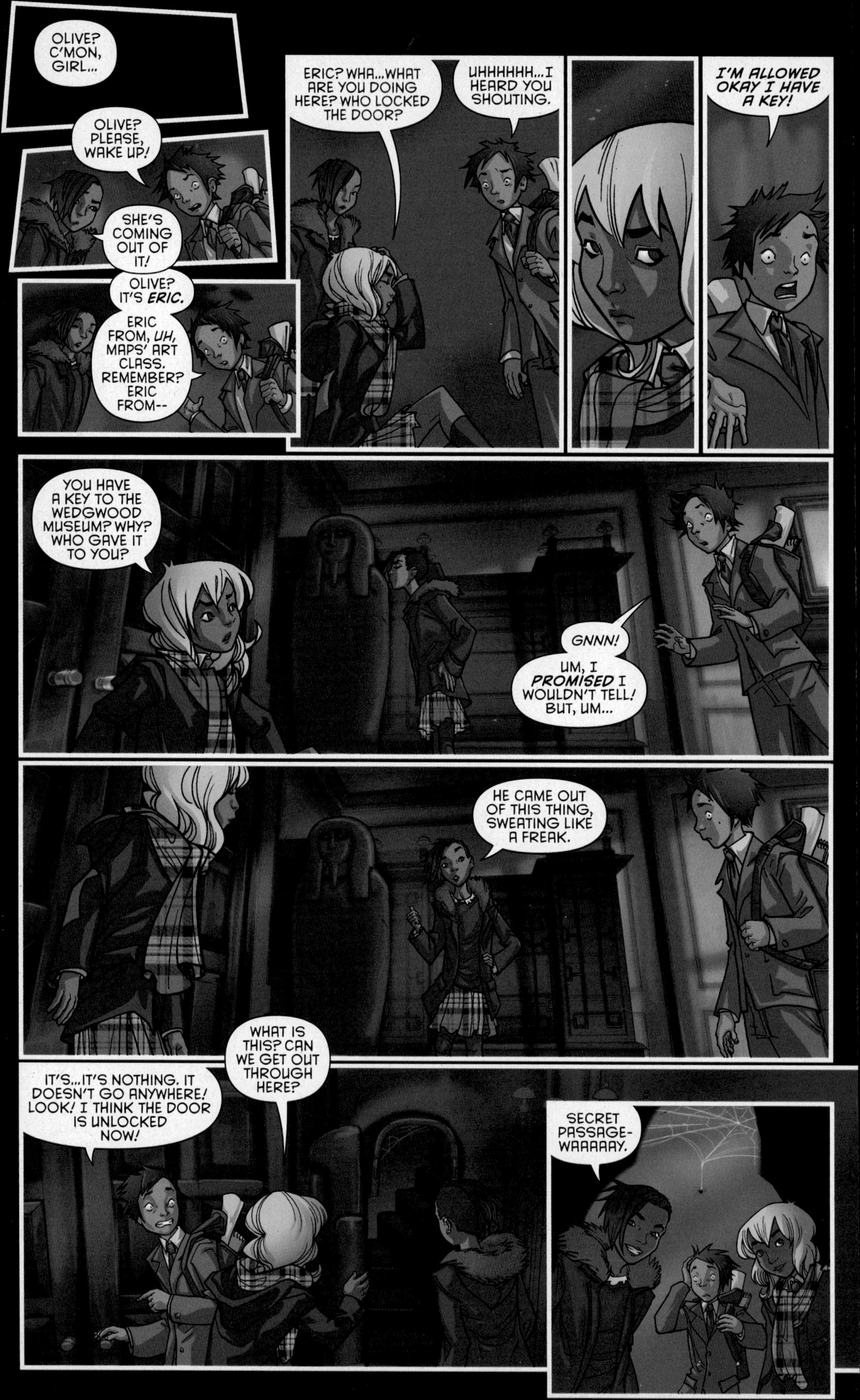
OLIVE? C'MON, GIRL...
OLIVE? PLEASE, WAKE UP!
SHE'S COMING OUT OF IT!
OLIVE? IT'S *ERIC.*
ERIC FROM, *UH,* MAPS' ART CLASS. REMEMBER? ERIC FROM--
ERIC? WHA...WHAT ARE YOU DOING HERE? WHO LOCKED THE DOOR?
UHHHHHH...I HEARD YOU SHOUTING.
*I'M ALLOWED OKAY I HAVE A KEY!*
YOU HAVE A KEY TO THE WEDGWOOD MUSEUM? WHY? WHO GAVE IT TO YOU?
*GNNN!*
UM, I ***PROMISED*** I WOULDN'T TELL! BUT, UM...
HE CAME OUT OF THIS THING, SWEATING LIKE A FREAK.
WHAT IS THIS? CAN WE GET OUT THROUGH HERE?
IT'S...IT'S NOTHING. IT DOESN'T GO ANYWHERE! LOOK! I THINK THE DOOR IS UNLOCKED NOW!
SECRET PASSAGE-WAAAAAY.

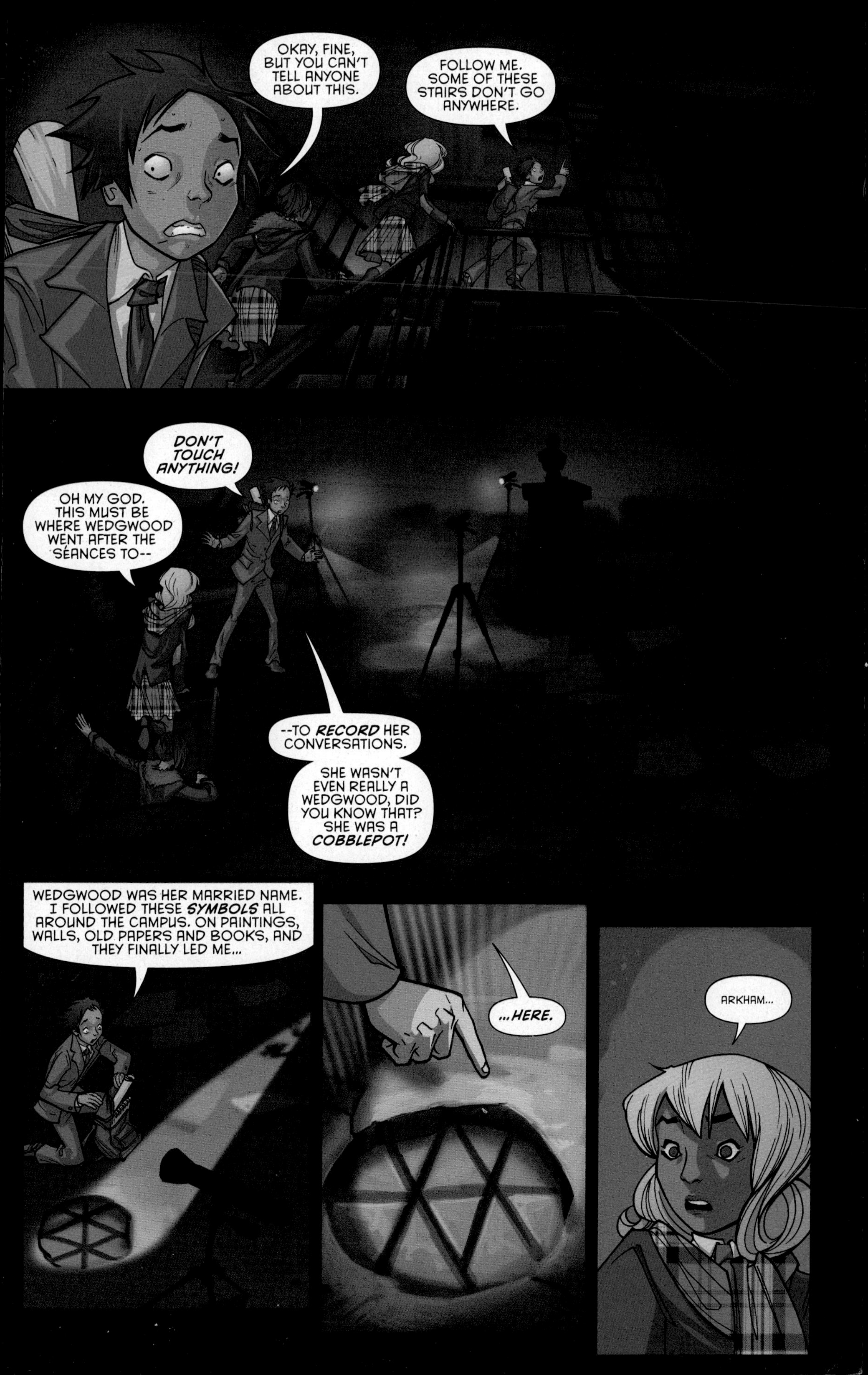
OKAY, FINE, BUT YOU CAN'T TELL ANYONE ABOUT THIS.
FOLLOW ME. SOME OF THESE STAIRS DON'T GO ANYWHERE.
DON'T TOUCH ANYTHING!
OH MY GOD. THIS MUST BE WHERE WEDGWOOD WENT AFTER THE SÉANCES TO--
--TO RECORD HER CONVERSATIONS.
SHE WASN'T EVEN REALLY A WEDGWOOD, DID YOU KNOW THAT? SHE WAS A COBBLEPOT!
WEDGWOOD WAS HER MARRIED NAME. I FOLLOWED THESE SYMBOLS ALL AROUND THE CAMPUS. ON PAINTINGS, WALLS, OLD PAPERS AND BOOKS, AND THEY FINALLY LED ME...
...HERE.
ARKHAM...

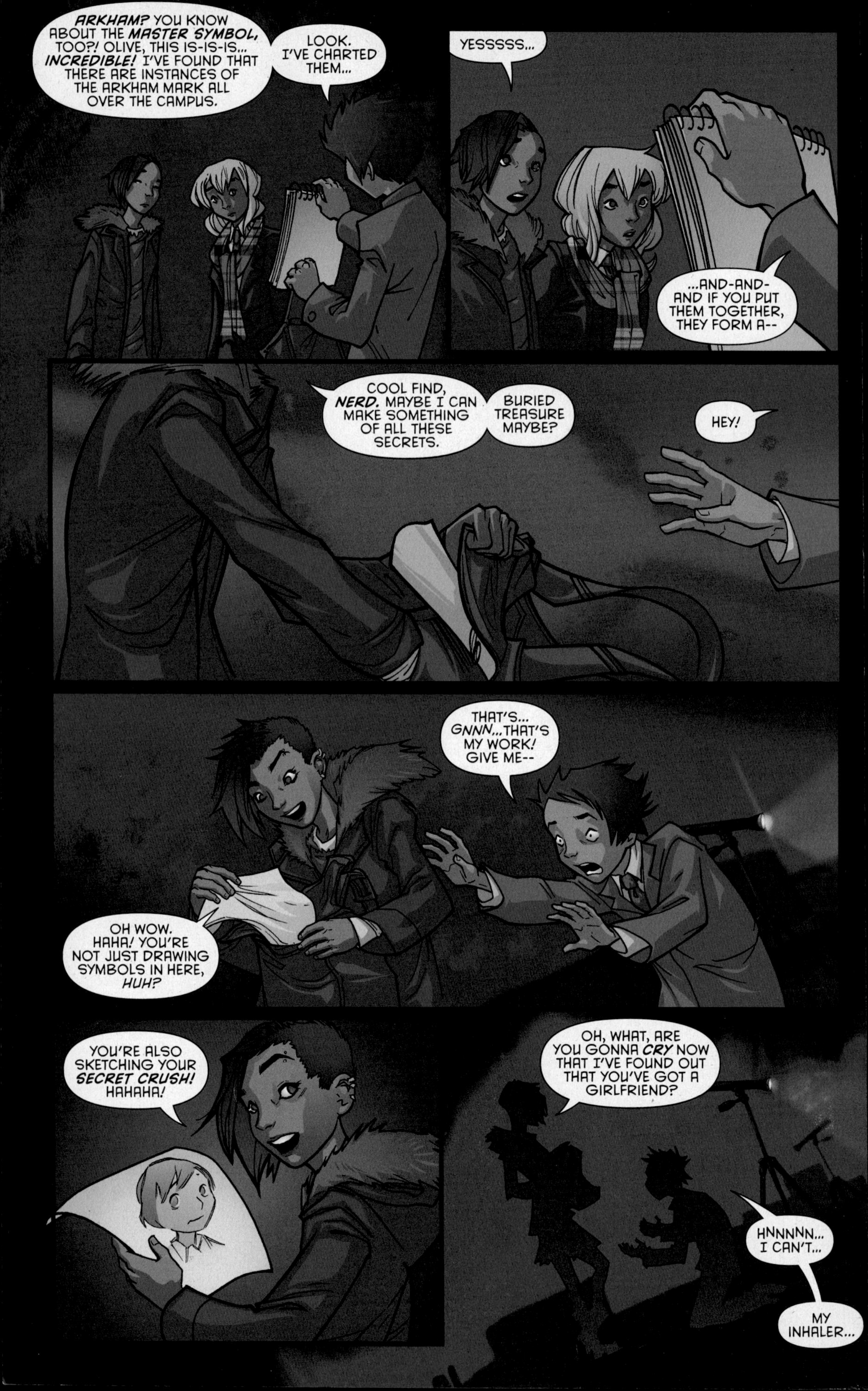
ARKHAM? YOU KNOW ABOUT THE MASTER SYMBOL, TOO?! OLIVE, THIS IS-IS-IS... INCREDIBLE! I'VE FOUND THAT THERE ARE INSTANCES OF THE ARKHAM MARK ALL OVER THE CAMPUS.
LOOK. I'VE CHARTED THEM...
YESSSSS...
...AND-AND-AND IF YOU PUT THEM TOGETHER, THEY FORM A--
COOL FIND, NERD. MAYBE I CAN MAKE SOMETHING OF ALL THESE SECRETS.
BURIED TREASURE MAYBE?
HEY!
THAT'S... GNNN... THAT'S MY WORK! GIVE ME--
OH WOW. HAHA! YOU'RE NOT JUST DRAWING SYMBOLS IN HERE, HUH?
YOU'RE ALSO SKETCHING YOUR SECRET CRUSH! HAHAHA!
OH, WHAT, ARE YOU GONNA CRY NOW THAT I'VE FOUND OUT THAT YOU'VE GOT A GIRLFRIEND?
HNNNNN... I CAN'T...
MY INHALER...

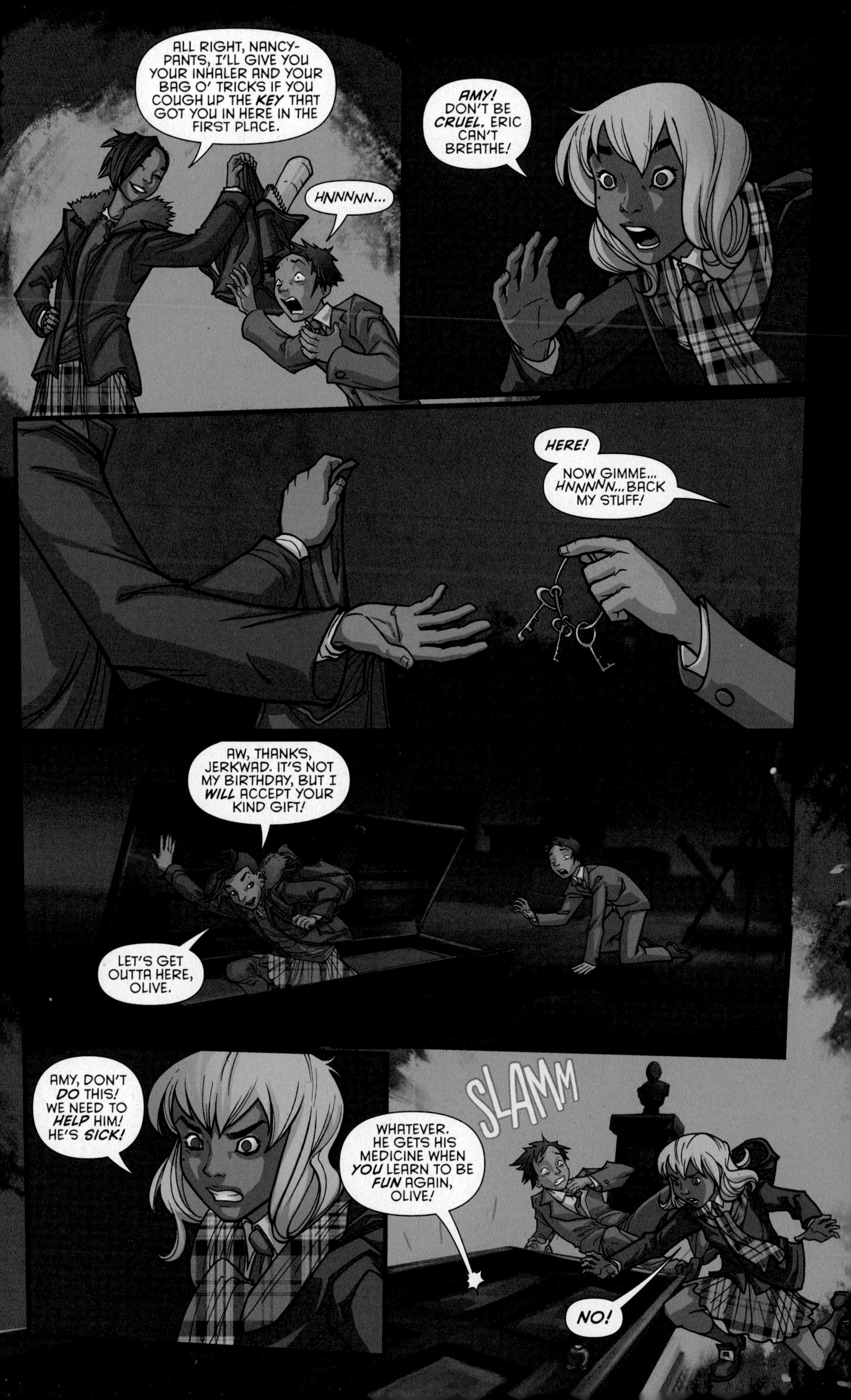
ALL RIGHT, NANCY-PANTS, I'LL GIVE YOU YOUR INHALER AND YOUR BAG O' TRICKS IF YOU COUGH UP THE KEY THAT GOT YOU IN HERE IN THE FIRST PLACE.
HNNNNN...
AMY! DON'T BE CRUEL. ERIC CAN'T BREATHE!
HERE! NOW GIMME... HNNNNN... BACK MY STUFF!
AW, THANKS, JERKWAD. IT'S NOT MY BIRTHDAY, BUT I WILL ACCEPT YOUR KIND GIFT!
LET'S GET OUTTA HERE, OLIVE.
AMY, DON'T DO THIS! WE NEED TO HELP HIM! HE'S SICK!
WHATEVER. HE GETS HIS MEDICINE WHEN YOU LEARN TO BE FUN AGAIN, OLIVE!
SLAMM
NO!

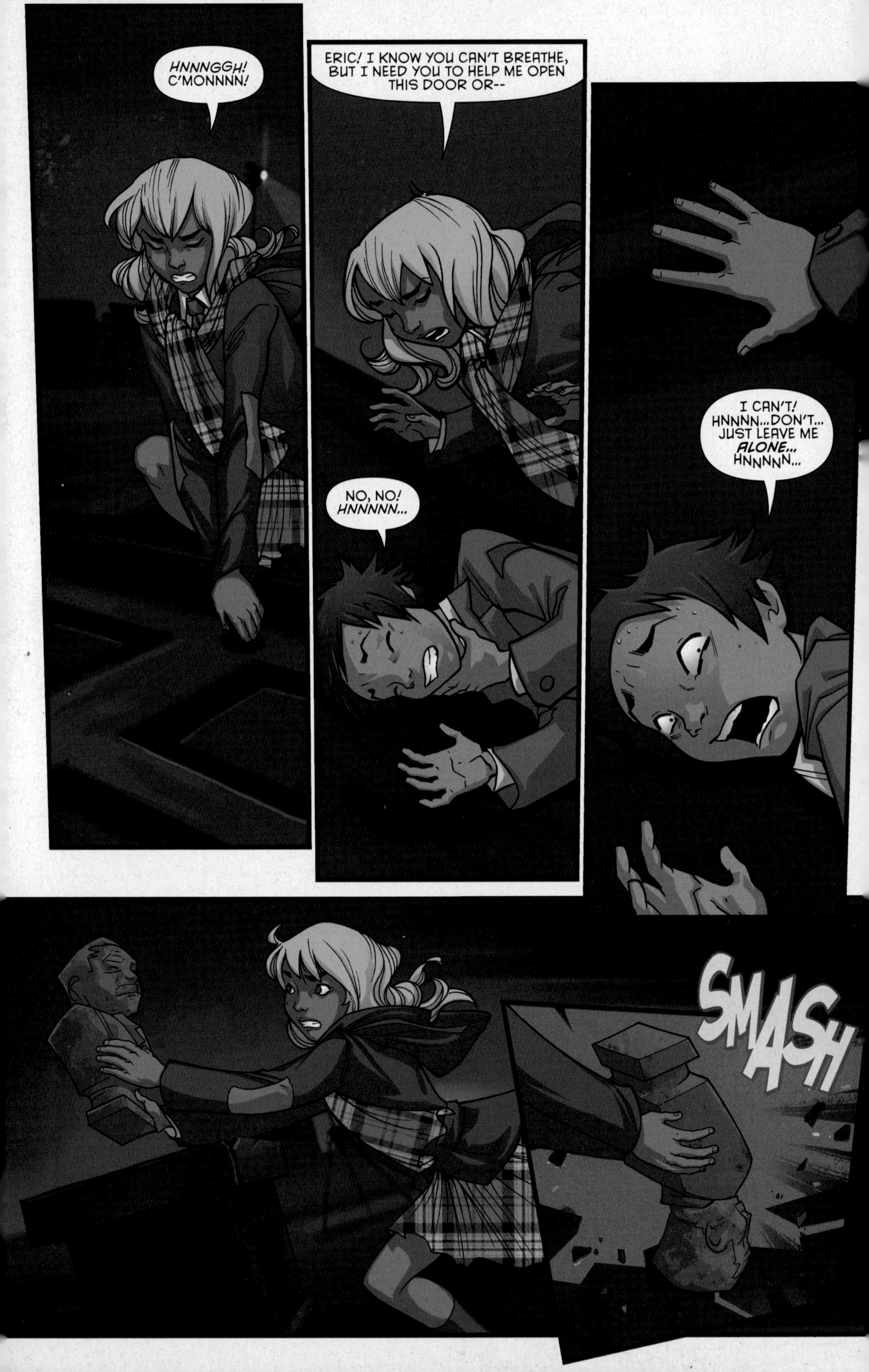
HNNNGGH! C'MONNNN!
ERIC! I KNOW YOU CAN'T BREATHE, BUT I NEED YOU TO HELP ME OPEN THIS DOOR OR--
NO, NO! HNNNNN...
I CAN'T! HNNNN...DON'T... JUST LEAVE ME ALONE... HNNNNN...
SMASH

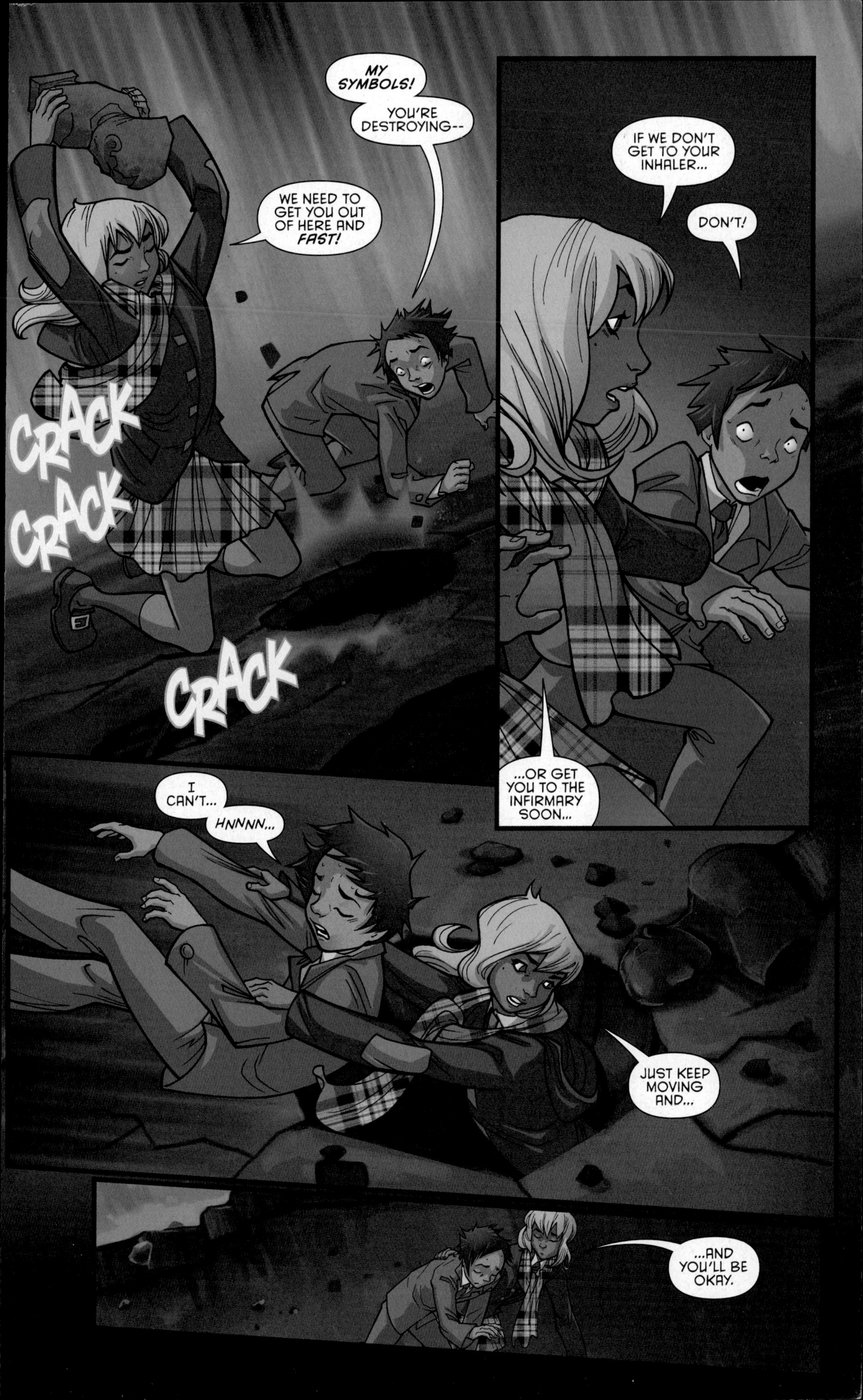

MY SYMBOLS!
YOU'RE DESTROYING--
WE NEED TO GET YOU OUT OF HERE AND FAST!
CRACK
CRACK
CRACK
IF WE DON'T GET TO YOUR INHALER...
DON'T!
...OR GET YOU TO THE INFIRMARY SOON...
I CAN'T...
HNNNN...
JUST KEEP MOVING AND...
...AND YOU'LL BE OKAY.

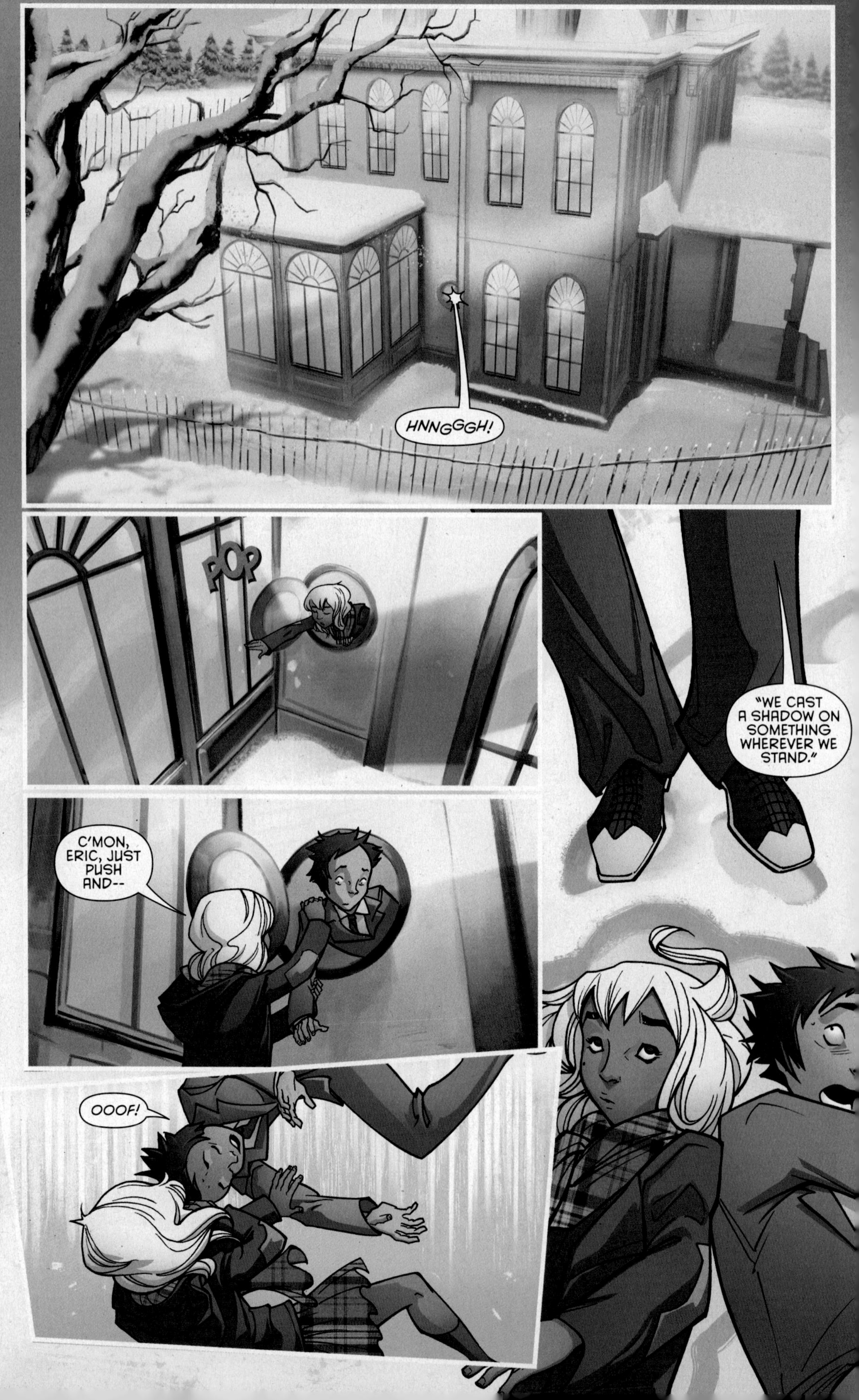
HNNGGGH!
POP
"WE CAST A SHADOW ON SOMETHING WHEREVER WE STAND."
C'MON, ERIC, JUST PUSH AND--
OOOF!

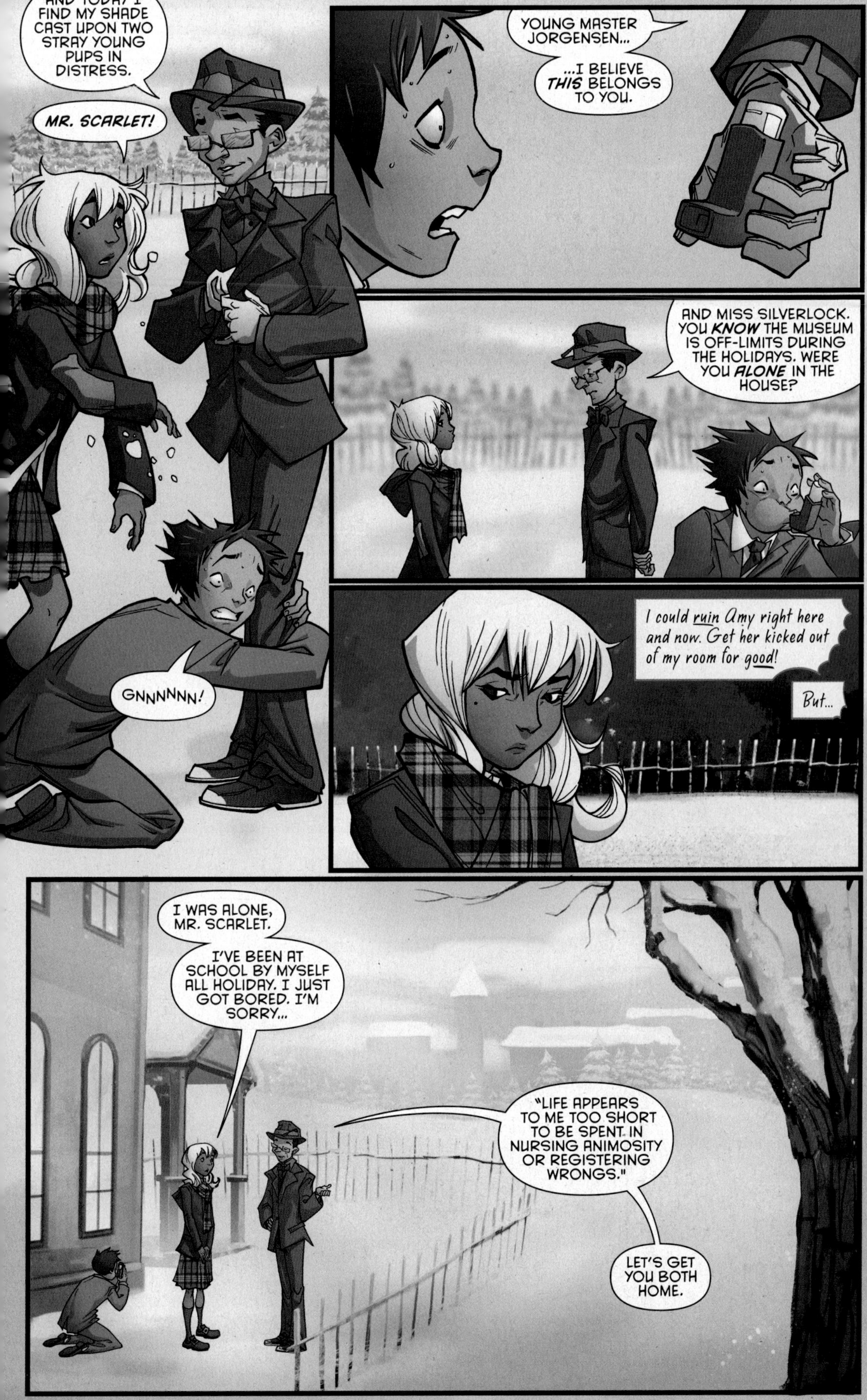
AND TODAY I FIND MY SHADE CAST UPON TWO STRAY YOUNG PUPS IN DISTRESS.
MR. SCARLET!
YOUNG MASTER JORGENSEN...
...I BELIEVE THIS BELONGS TO YOU.
GNNNNNN!
AND MISS SILVERLOCK. YOU KNOW THE MUSEUM IS OFF-LIMITS DURING THE HOLIDAYS. WERE YOU ALONE IN THE HOUSE?
I could ruin Amy right here and now. Get her kicked out of my room for good!
But...
I WAS ALONE, MR. SCARLET.
I'VE BEEN AT SCHOOL BY MYSELF ALL HOLIDAY. I JUST GOT BORED. I'M SORRY...
"LIFE APPEARS TO ME TOO SHORT TO BE SPENT IN NURSING ANIMOSITY OR REGISTERING WRONGS."
LET'S GET YOU BOTH HOME.

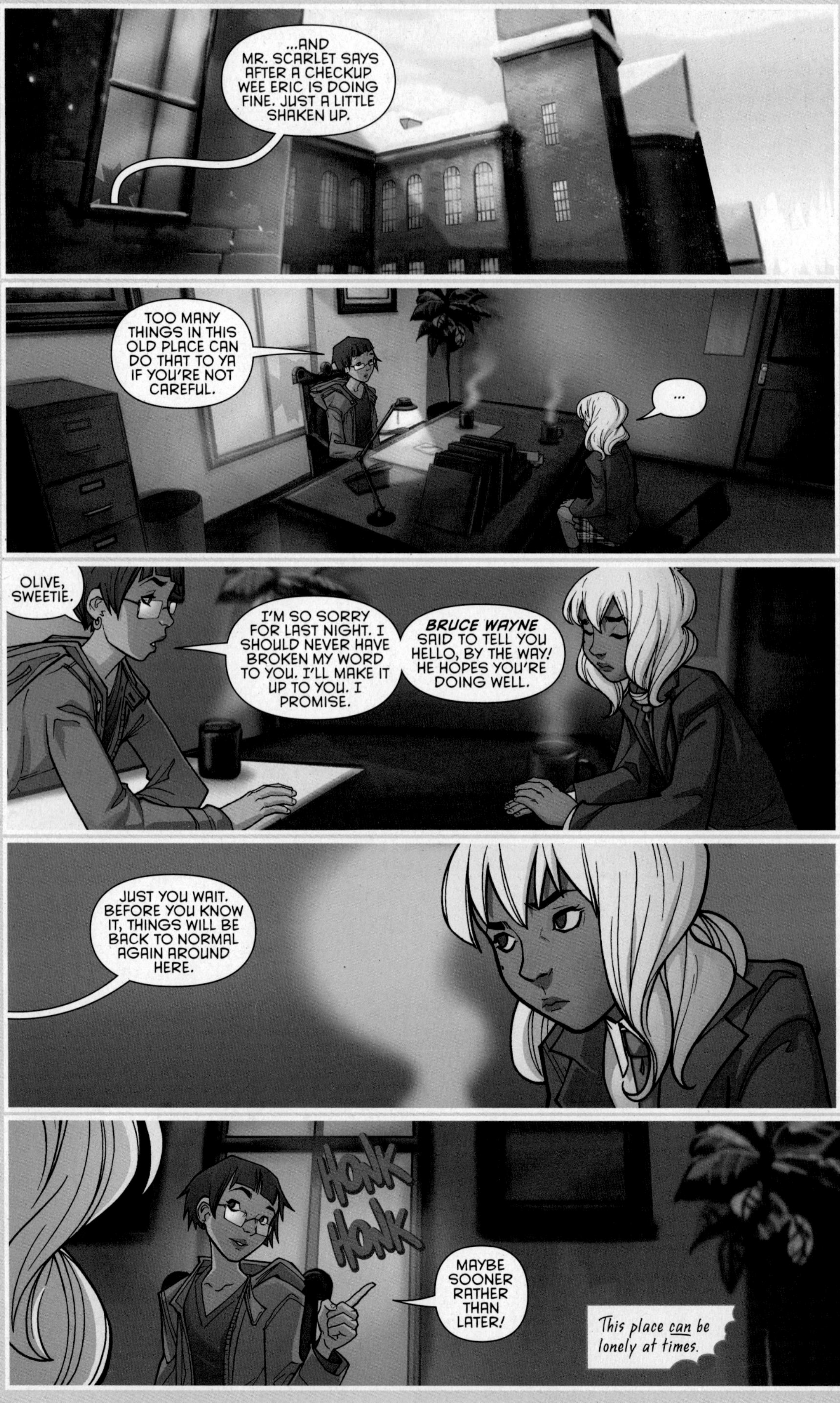
...AND MR. SCARLET SAYS AFTER A CHECKUP WEE ERIC IS DOING FINE. JUST A LITTLE SHAKEN UP.
TOO MANY THINGS IN THIS OLD PLACE CAN DO THAT TO YA IF YOU'RE NOT CAREFUL.
...
OLIVE, SWEETIE.
I'M SO SORRY FOR LAST NIGHT. I SHOULD NEVER HAVE BROKEN MY WORD TO YOU. I'LL MAKE IT UP TO YOU. I PROMISE.
BRUCE WAYNE SAID TO TELL YOU HELLO, BY THE WAY! HE HOPES YOU'RE DOING WELL.
JUST YOU WAIT. BEFORE YOU KNOW IT, THINGS WILL BE BACK TO NORMAL AGAIN AROUND HERE.
HONK HONK
MAYBE SOONER RATHER THAN LATER!
This place can be lonely at times.

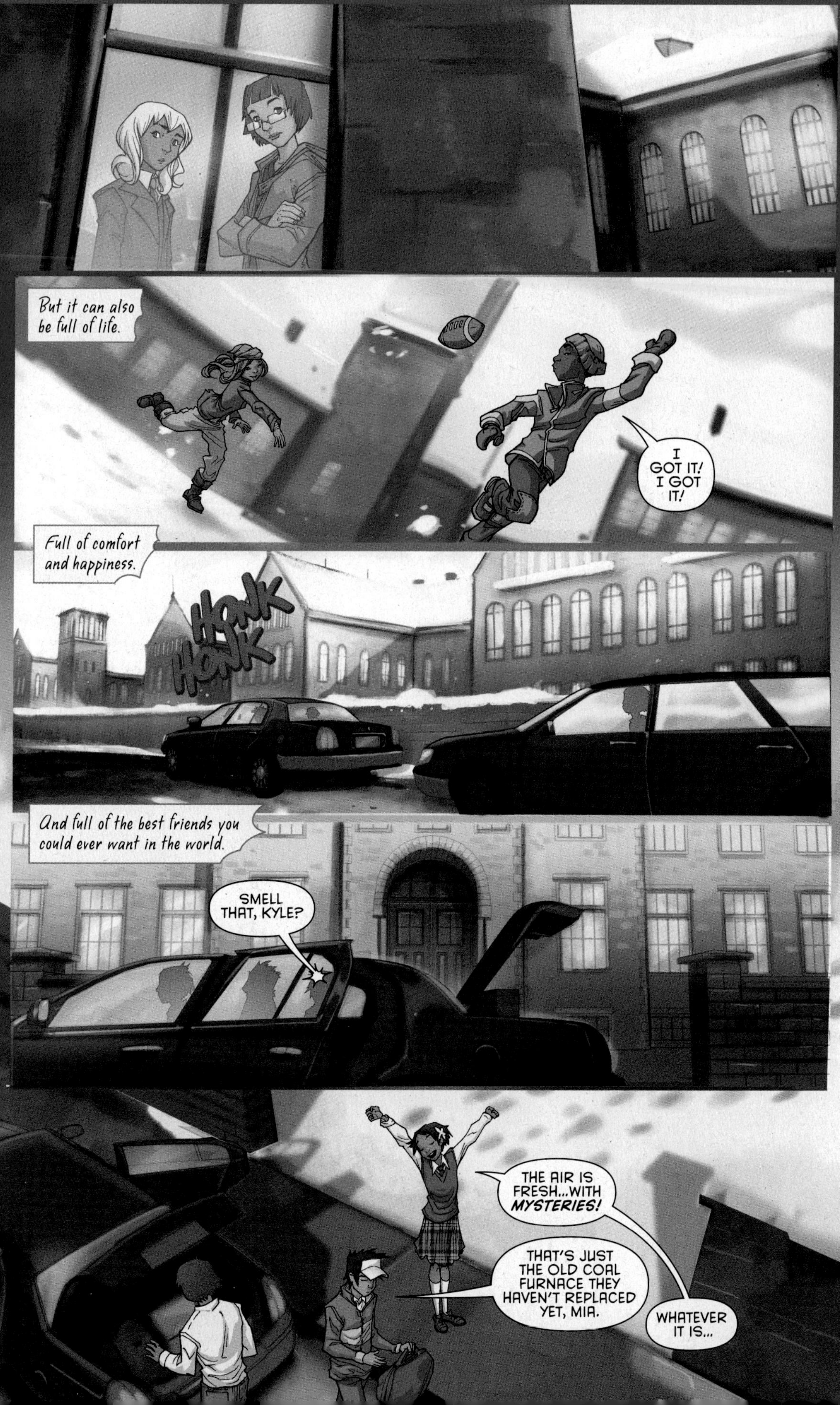
But it can also be full of life.
I GOT IT! I GOT IT!
Full of comfort and happiness.
HONK HONK
And full of the best friends you could ever want in the world.
SMELL THAT, KYLE?
THE AIR IS FRESH...WITH MYSTERIES!
THAT'S JUST THE OLD COAL FURNACE THEY HAVEN'T REPLACED YET, MIA.
WHATEVER IT IS...

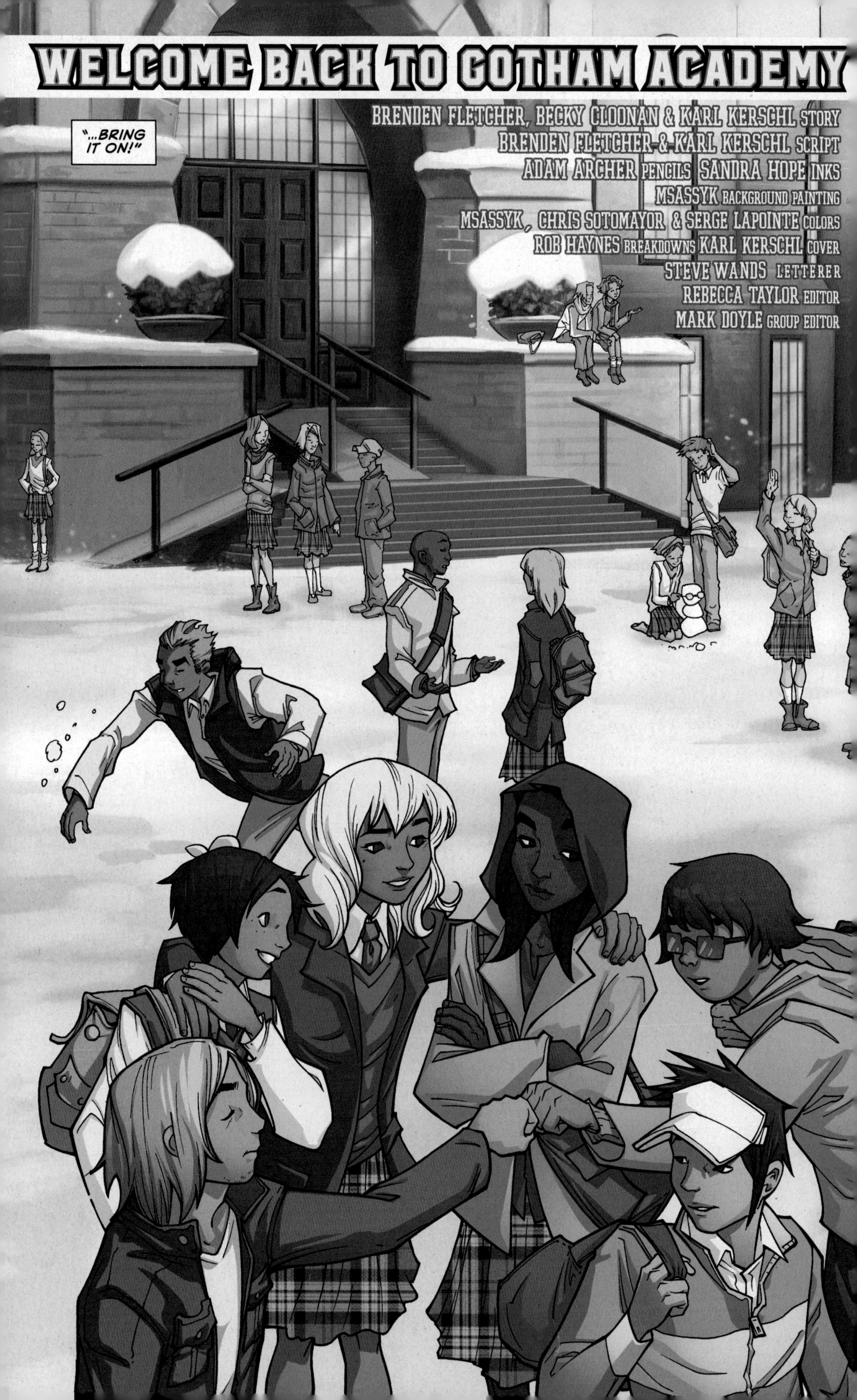
WELCOME BACK TO GOTHAM ACADEMY
BRENDEN FLETCHER, BECKY CLOONAN & KARL KERSCHL STORY
BRENDEN FLETCHER & KARL KERSCHL SCRIPT
ADAM ARCHER PENCILS SANDRA HOPE INKS
MSASSYK BACKGROUND PAINTING
MSASSYK, CHRIS SOTOMAYOR & SERGE LAPOINTE COLORS
ROB HAYNES BREAKDOWNS KARL KERSCHL COVER
STEVE WANDS LETTERER
REBECCA TAYLOR EDITOR
MARK DOYLE GROUP EDITOR
"...BRING IT ON!"

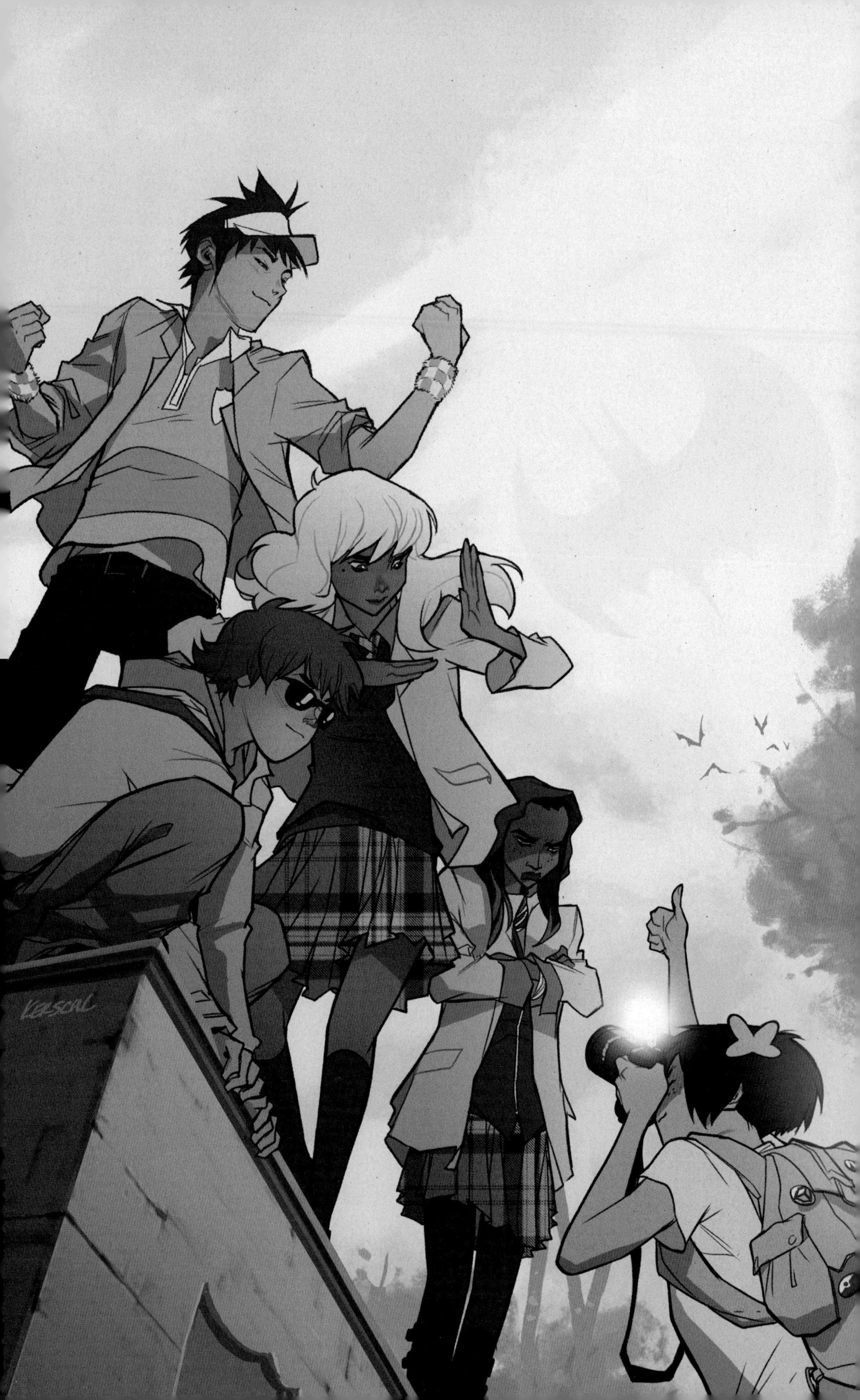

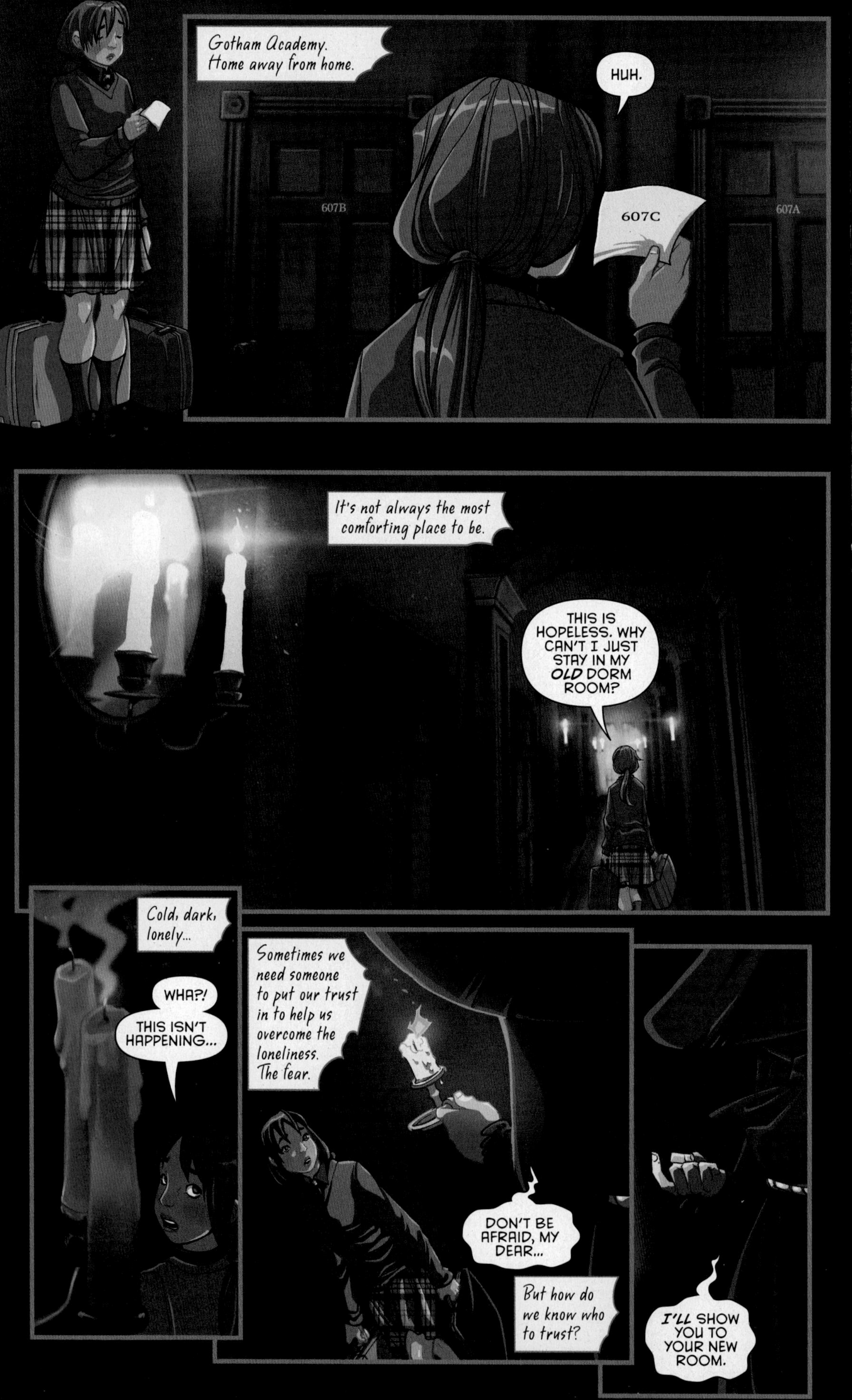
Gotham Academy. Home away from home.
607B
HUH.
607C
607A
It's not always the most comforting place to be.
THIS IS HOPELESS. WHY CAN'T I JUST STAY IN MY OLD DORM ROOM?
Cold, dark, lonely...
WHA?!
THIS ISN'T HAPPENING...
Sometimes we need someone to put our trust in to help us overcome the loneliness. The fear.
DON'T BE AFRAID, MY DEAR...
But how do we know who to trust?
I'LL SHOW YOU TO YOUR NEW ROOM.

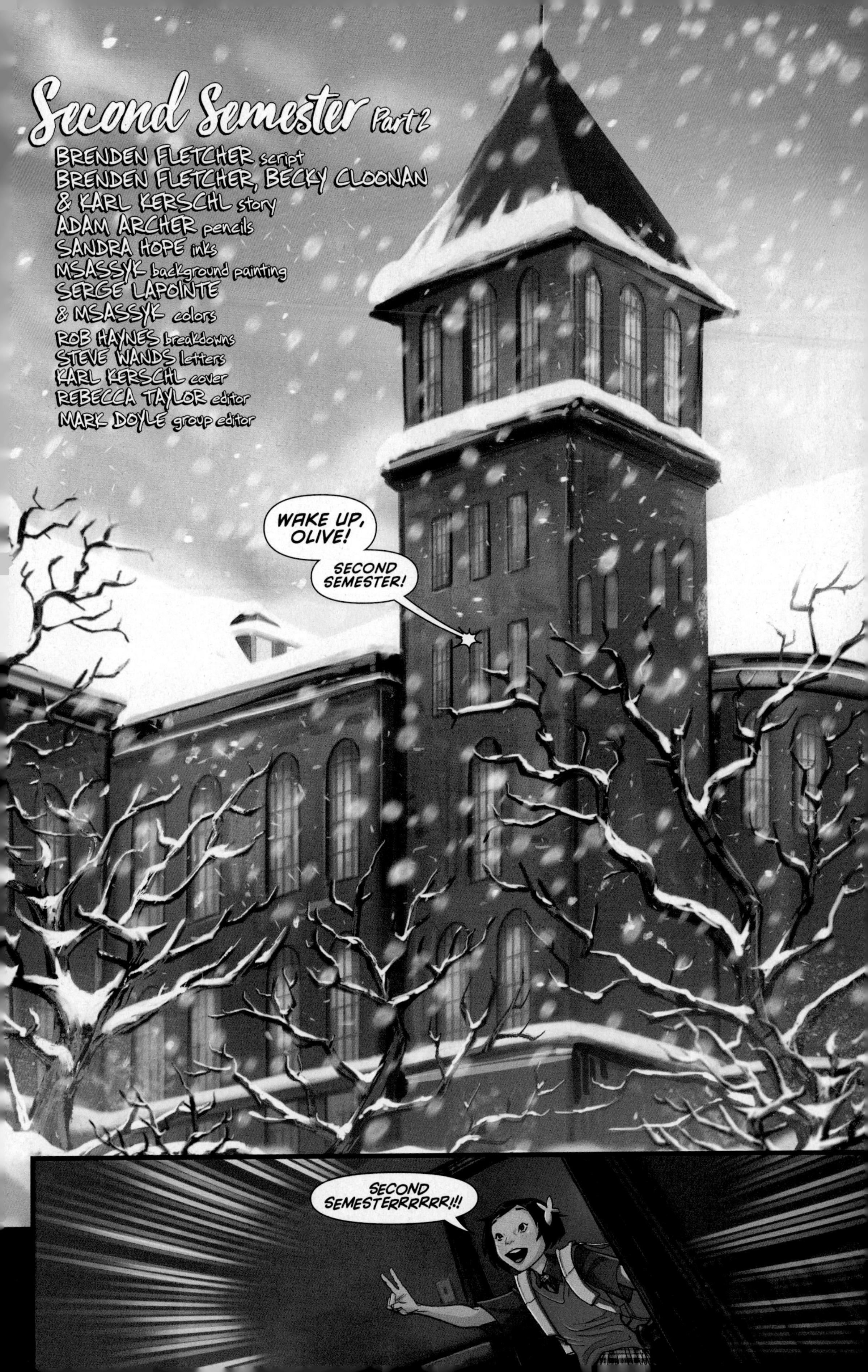
Second Semester Part 2
BRENDEN FLETCHER script
BRENDEN FLETCHER, BECKY CLOONAN
& KARL KERSCHL story
ADAM ARCHER pencils
SANDRA HOPE inks
MSASSYK background painting
SERGE LAPOINTE
& MSASSYK colors
ROB HAYNES breakdowns
STEVE WANDS letters
KARL KERSCHL cover
REBECCA TAYLOR editor
MARK DOYLE group editor
WAKE UP, OLIVE!
SECOND SEMESTER!
SECOND SEMESTERRRRRR!!!

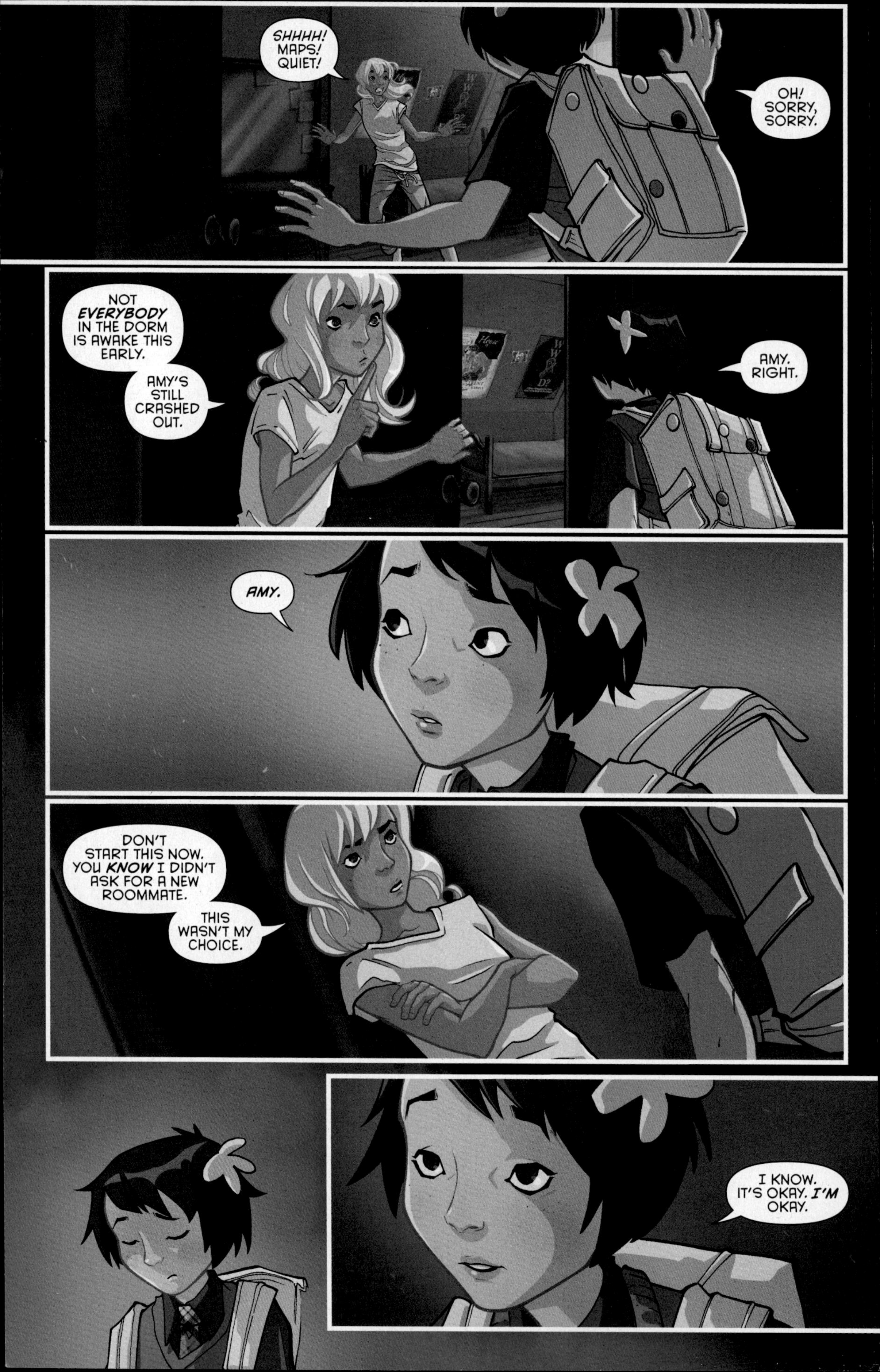
SHHHH! MAPS! QUIET!
OH! SORRY, SORRY.
NOT EVERYBODY IN THE DORM IS AWAKE THIS EARLY.
AMY'S STILL CRASHED OUT.
AMY. RIGHT.
AMY.
DON'T START THIS NOW. YOU KNOW I DIDN'T ASK FOR A NEW ROOMMATE.
THIS WASN'T MY CHOICE.
I KNOW. IT'S OKAY. I'M OKAY.

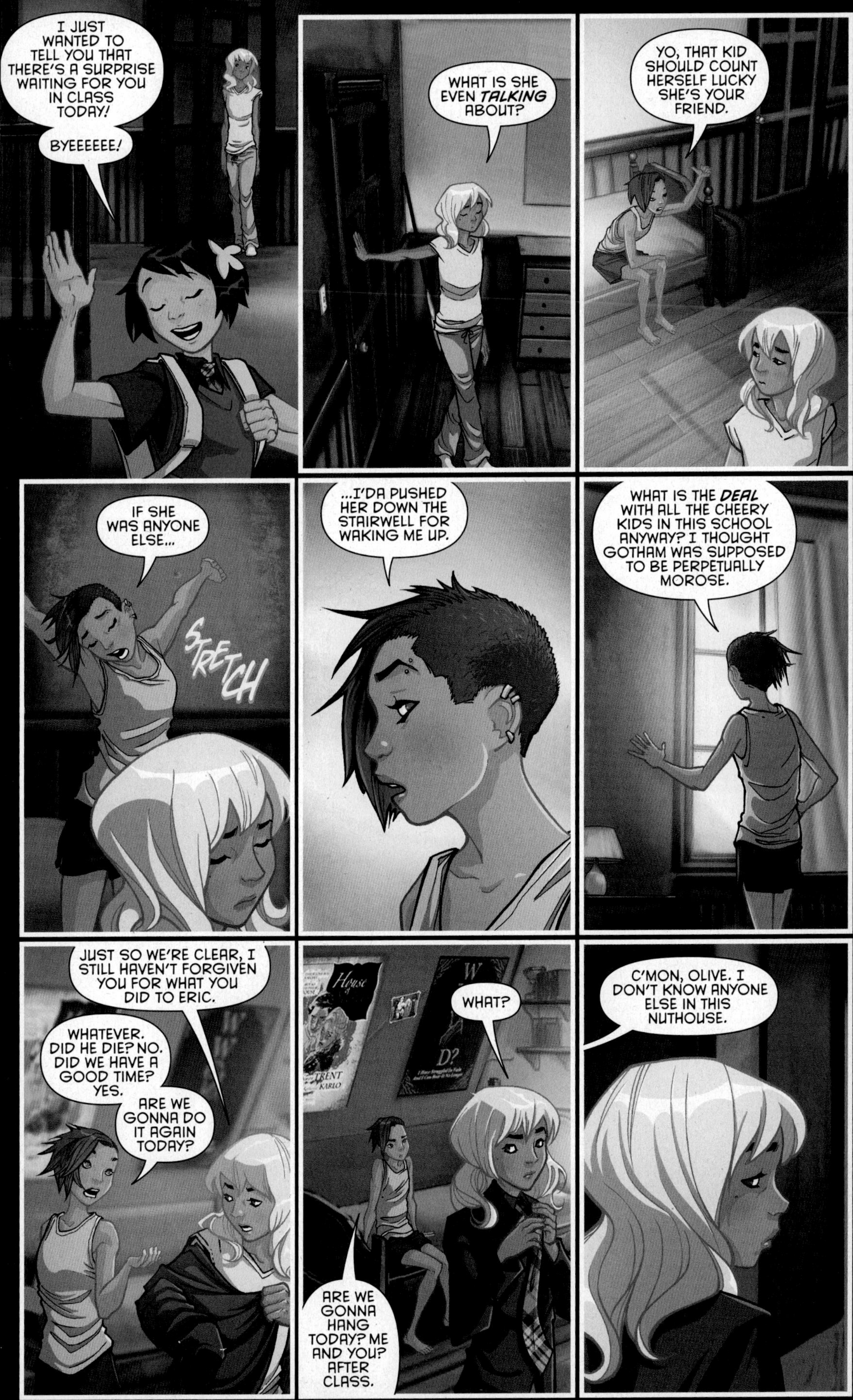
I JUST WANTED TO TELL YOU THAT THERE'S A SURPRISE WAITING FOR YOU IN CLASS TODAY!
BYEEEEEE!
WHAT IS SHE EVEN *TALKING* ABOUT?
YO, THAT KID SHOULD COUNT HERSELF LUCKY SHE'S YOUR FRIEND.
IF SHE WAS ANYONE ELSE...
STRETCH
...I'DA PUSHED HER DOWN THE STAIRWELL FOR WAKING ME UP.
WHAT IS THE *DEAL* WITH ALL THE CHEERY KIDS IN THIS SCHOOL ANYWAY? I THOUGHT GOTHAM WAS SUPPOSED TO BE PERPETUALLY MOROSE.
JUST SO WE'RE CLEAR, I STILL HAVEN'T FORGIVEN YOU FOR WHAT YOU DID TO ERIC.
WHATEVER. DID HE DIE? NO. DID WE HAVE A GOOD TIME? YES.
ARE WE GONNA DO IT AGAIN TODAY?
WHAT?
ARE WE GONNA HANG TODAY? ME AND YOU? AFTER CLASS.
C'MON, OLIVE. I DON'T KNOW ANYONE ELSE IN THIS NUTHOUSE.

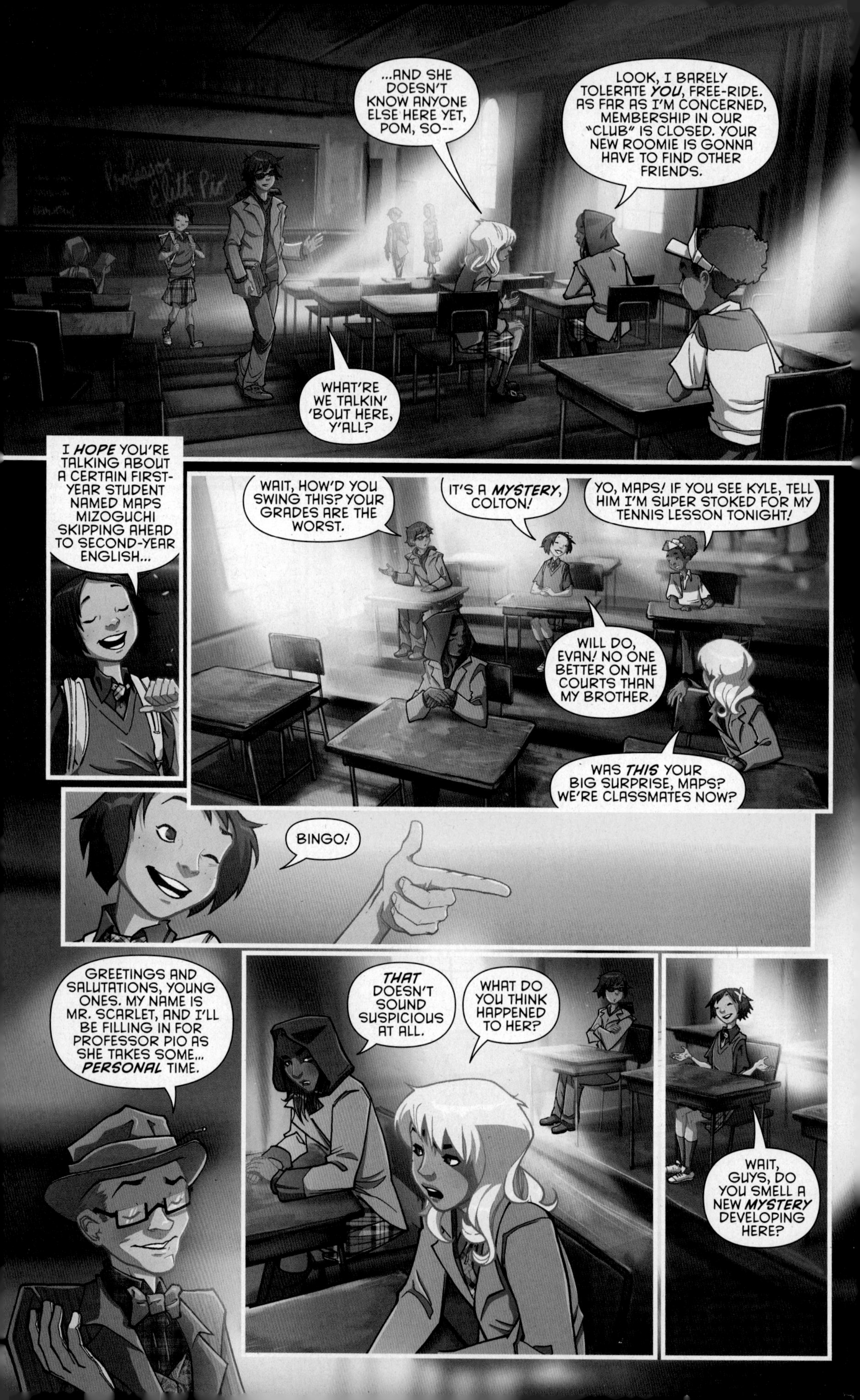
...AND SHE DOESN'T KNOW ANYONE ELSE HERE YET, POM, SO--
LOOK, I BARELY TOLERATE *YOU*, FREE-RIDE. AS FAR AS I'M CONCERNED, MEMBERSHIP IN OUR "CLUB" IS CLOSED. YOUR NEW ROOMIE IS GONNA HAVE TO FIND OTHER FRIENDS.
WHAT'RE WE TALKIN' 'BOUT HERE, Y'ALL?
I *HOPE* YOU'RE TALKING ABOUT A CERTAIN FIRST-YEAR STUDENT NAMED MAPS MIZOGUCHI SKIPPING AHEAD TO SECOND-YEAR ENGLISH...
WAIT, HOW'D YOU SWING THIS? YOUR GRADES ARE THE WORST.
IT'S A *MYSTERY*, COLTON!
YO, MAPS! IF YOU SEE KYLE, TELL HIM I'M SUPER STOKED FOR MY TENNIS LESSON TONIGHT!
WILL DO, EVAN! NO ONE BETTER ON THE COURTS THAN MY BROTHER.
WAS *THIS* YOUR BIG SURPRISE, MAPS? WE'RE CLASSMATES NOW?
BINGO!
GREETINGS AND SALUTATIONS, YOUNG ONES. MY NAME IS MR. SCARLET, AND I'LL BE FILLING IN FOR PROFESSOR PIO AS SHE TAKES SOME... *PERSONAL* TIME.
*THAT* DOESN'T SOUND SUSPICIOUS AT ALL.
WHAT DO YOU THINK HAPPENED TO HER?
WAIT, GUYS, DO YOU SMELL A NEW *MYSTERY* DEVELOPING HERE?

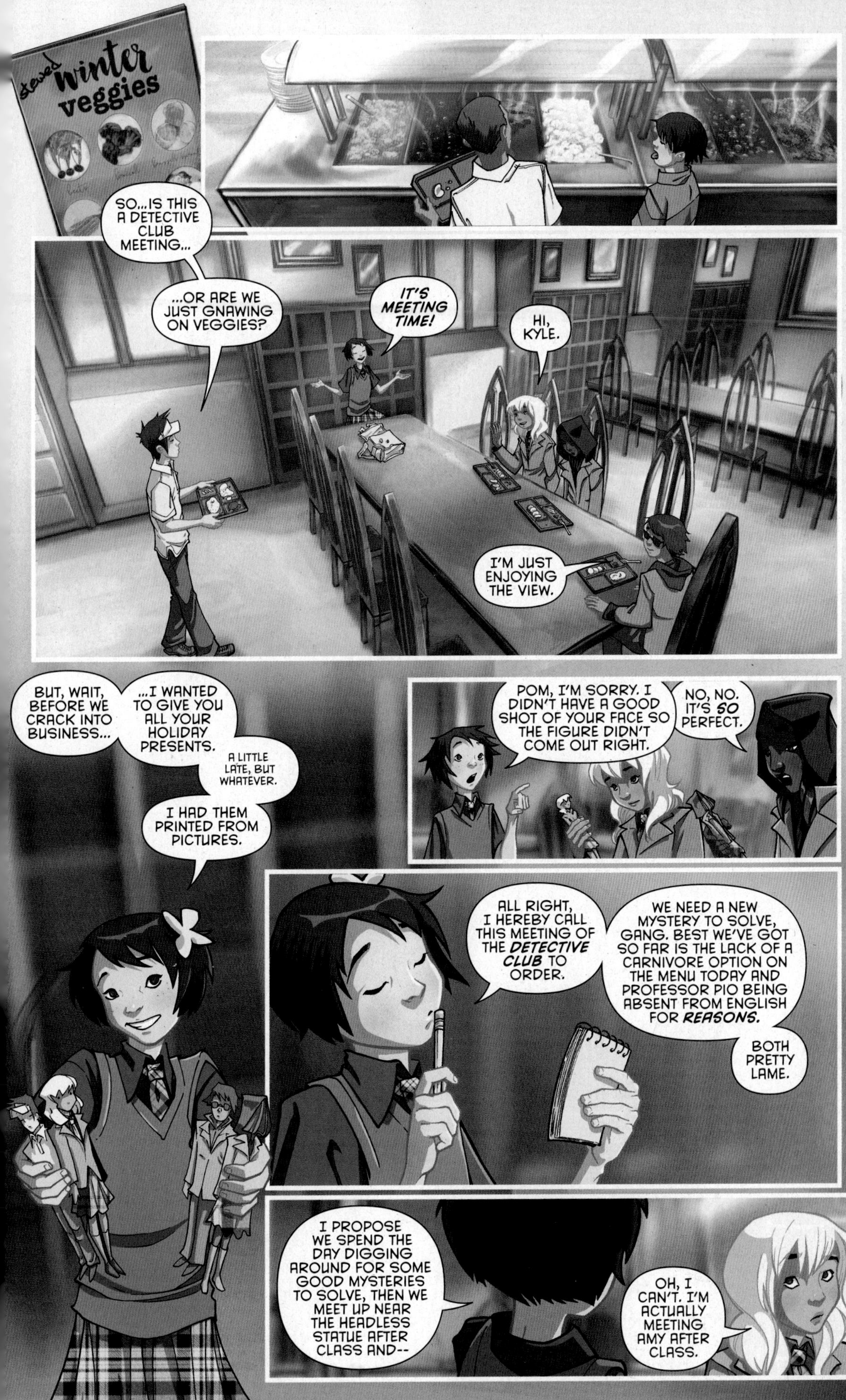
stewed winter veggies
SO...IS THIS A DETECTIVE CLUB MEETING...
...OR ARE WE JUST GNAWING ON VEGGIES?
IT'S MEETING TIME!
HI, KYLE.
I'M JUST ENJOYING THE VIEW.
BUT, WAIT, BEFORE WE CRACK INTO BUSINESS...
...I WANTED TO GIVE YOU ALL YOUR HOLIDAY PRESENTS.
A LITTLE LATE, BUT WHATEVER.
I HAD THEM PRINTED FROM PICTURES.
POM, I'M SORRY. I DIDN'T HAVE A GOOD SHOT OF YOUR FACE SO THE FIGURE DIDN'T COME OUT RIGHT.
NO, NO. IT'S SO PERFECT.
ALL RIGHT, I HEREBY CALL THIS MEETING OF THE DETECTIVE CLUB TO ORDER.
WE NEED A NEW MYSTERY TO SOLVE, GANG. BEST WE'VE GOT SO FAR IS THE LACK OF A CARNIVORE OPTION ON THE MENU TODAY AND PROFESSOR PIO BEING ABSENT FROM ENGLISH FOR REASONS.
BOTH PRETTY LAME.
I PROPOSE WE SPEND THE DAY DIGGING AROUND FOR SOME GOOD MYSTERIES TO SOLVE, THEN WE MEET UP NEAR THE HEADLESS STATUE AFTER CLASS AND--
OH, I CAN'T. I'M ACTUALLY MEETING AMY AFTER CLASS.

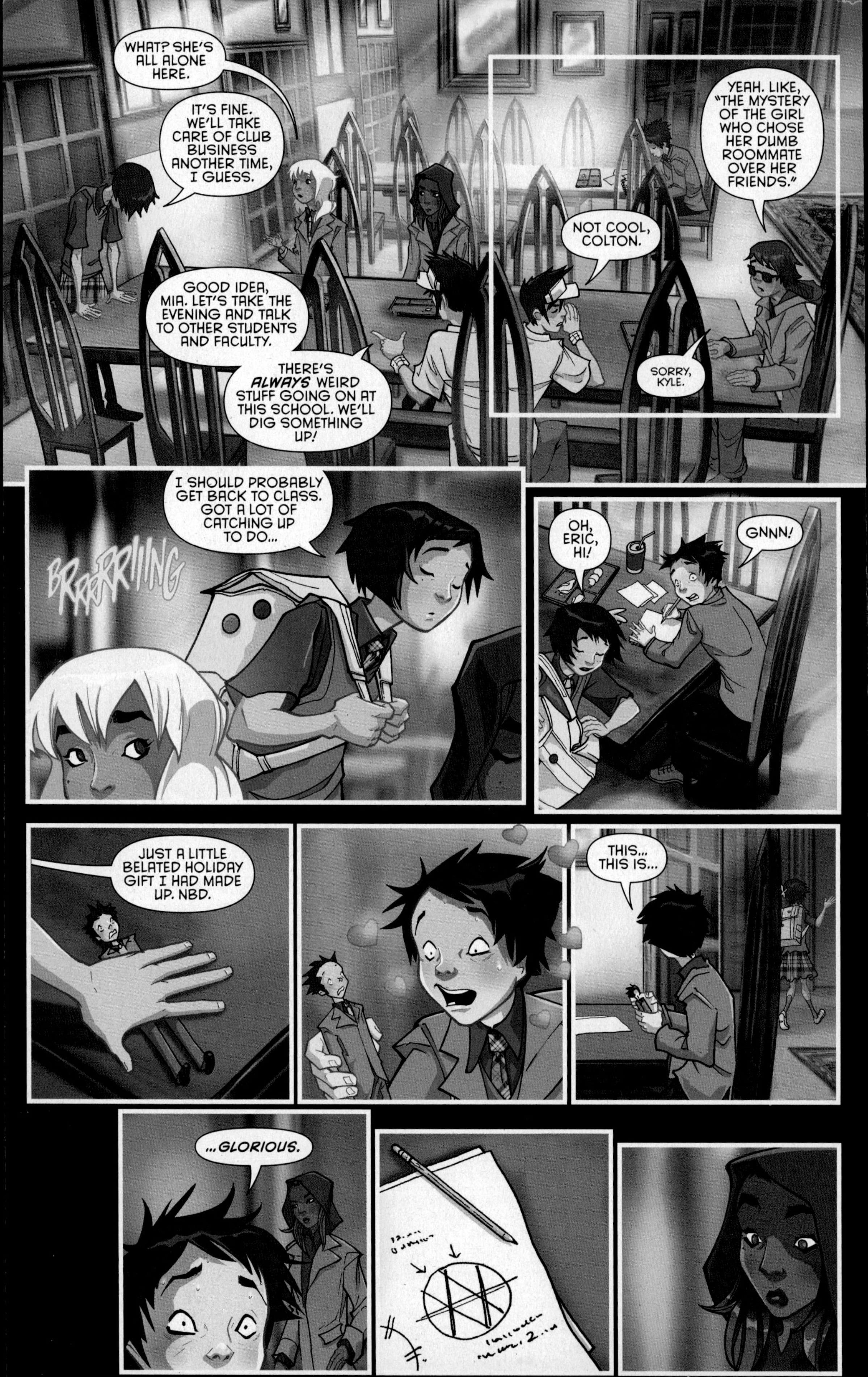
WHAT? SHE'S ALL ALONE HERE.
IT'S FINE. WE'LL TAKE CARE OF CLUB BUSINESS ANOTHER TIME, I GUESS.
GOOD IDEA, MIA. LET'S TAKE THE EVENING AND TALK TO OTHER STUDENTS AND FACULTY.
THERE'S ALWAYS WEIRD STUFF GOING ON AT THIS SCHOOL. WE'LL DIG SOMETHING UP!
YEAH. LIKE, "THE MYSTERY OF THE GIRL WHO CHOSE HER DUMB ROOMMATE OVER HER FRIENDS."
NOT COOL, COLTON.
SORRY, KYLE.
I SHOULD PROBABLY GET BACK TO CLASS. GOT A LOT OF CATCHING UP TO DO...
BRRRRRIIING
OH, ERIC, HI!
GNNN!
JUST A LITTLE BELATED HOLIDAY GIFT I HAD MADE UP. NBD.
THIS... THIS IS...
...GLORIOUS.

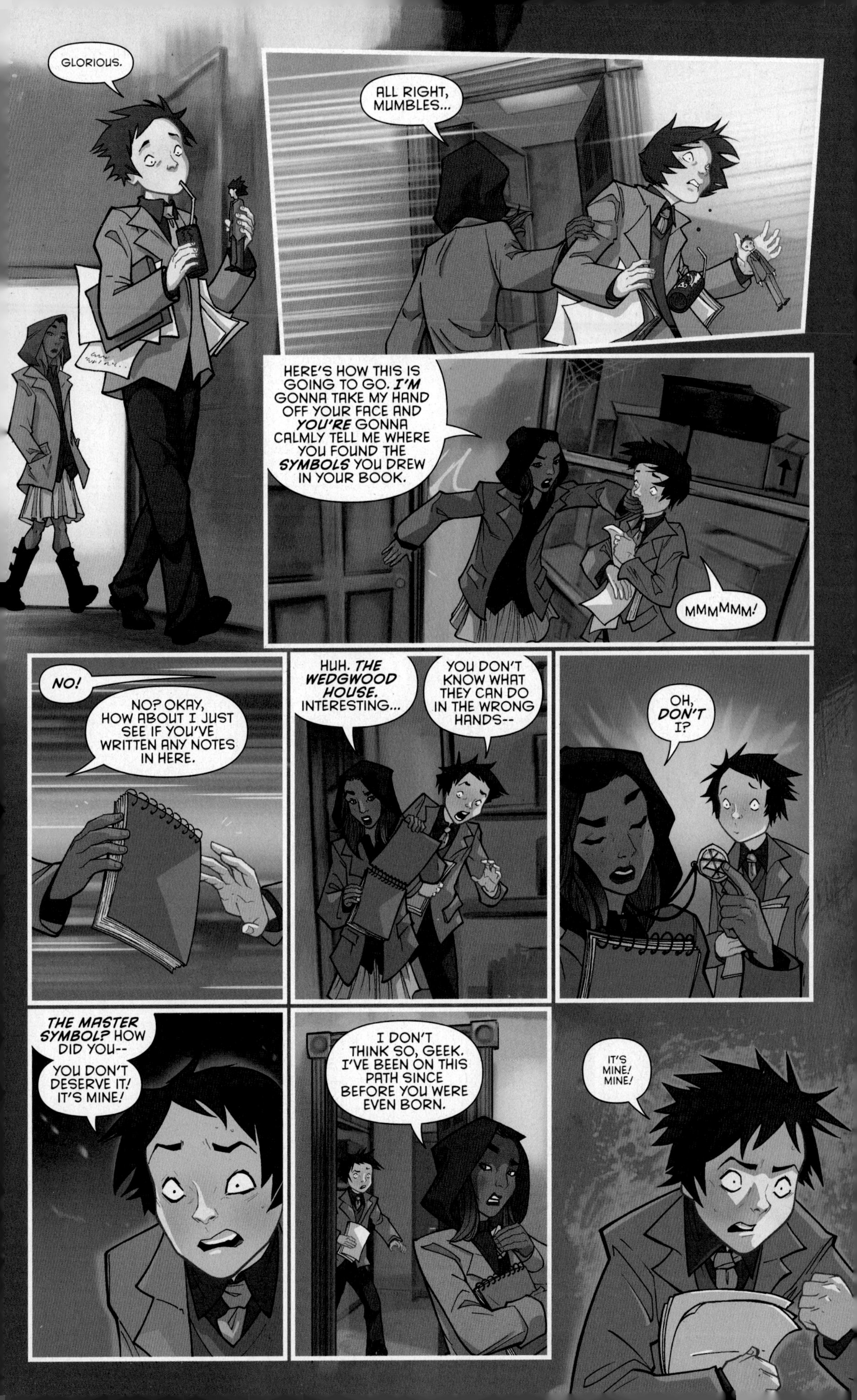
GLORIOUS.
ALL RIGHT, MUMBLES...
HERE'S HOW THIS IS GOING TO GO. *I'M* GONNA TAKE MY HAND OFF YOUR FACE AND *YOU'RE* GONNA CALMLY TELL ME WHERE YOU FOUND THE *SYMBOLS* YOU DREW IN YOUR BOOK.
MMMMMM!
*NO!*
NO? OKAY, HOW ABOUT I JUST SEE IF YOU'VE WRITTEN ANY NOTES IN HERE.
HUH. *THE WEDGWOOD HOUSE.* INTERESTING...
YOU DON'T KNOW WHAT THEY CAN DO IN THE WRONG HANDS--
OH, *DON'T* I?
*THE MASTER SYMBOL?* HOW DID YOU--
YOU DON'T DESERVE IT! IT'S MINE!
I DON'T THINK SO, GEEK. I'VE BEEN ON THIS PATH SINCE BEFORE YOU WERE EVEN BORN.
IT'S MINE! MINE!

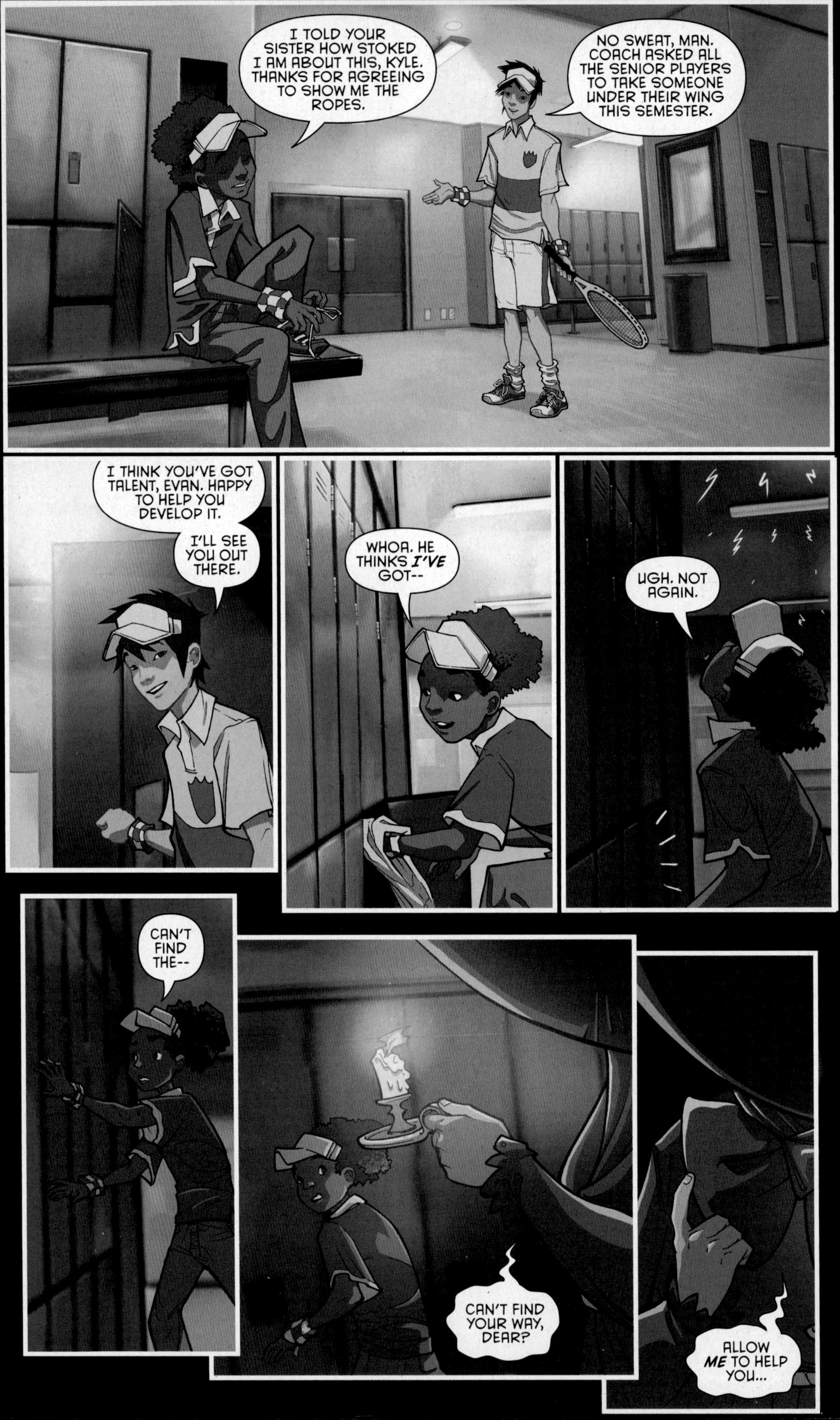
I TOLD YOUR SISTER HOW STOKED I AM ABOUT THIS, KYLE. THANKS FOR AGREEING TO SHOW ME THE ROPES.
NO SWEAT, MAN. COACH ASKED ALL THE SENIOR PLAYERS TO TAKE SOMEONE UNDER THEIR WING THIS SEMESTER.
I THINK YOU'VE GOT TALENT, EVAN. HAPPY TO HELP YOU DEVELOP IT.
I'LL SEE YOU OUT THERE.
WHOA. HE THINKS *I'VE* GOT--
UGH. NOT AGAIN.
CAN'T FIND THE--
CAN'T FIND YOUR WAY, DEAR?
ALLOW *ME* TO HELP YOU...

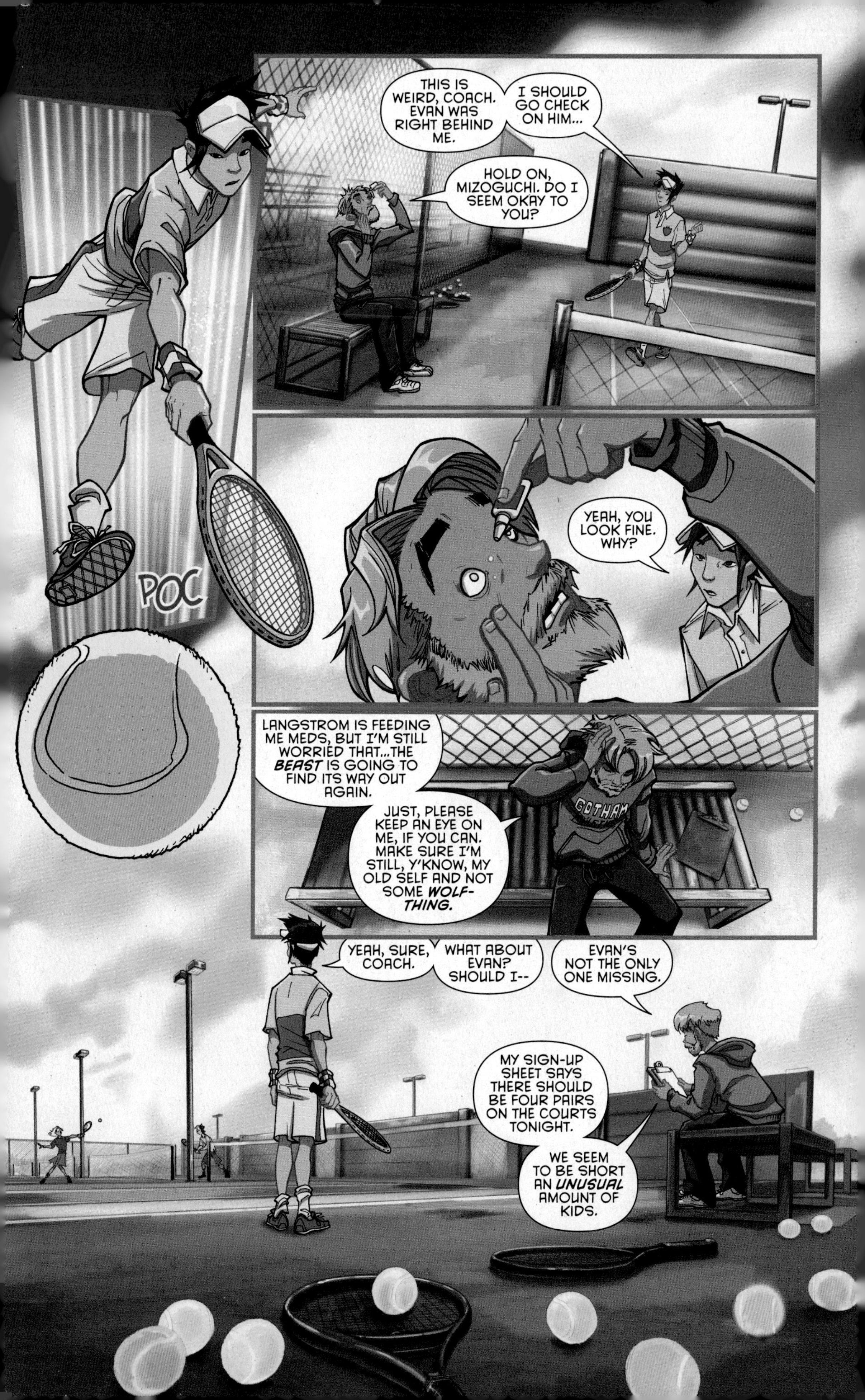
THIS IS WEIRD, COACH. EVAN WAS RIGHT BEHIND ME.
I SHOULD GO CHECK ON HIM...
HOLD ON, MIZOGUCHI. DO I SEEM OKAY TO YOU?
POC
YEAH, YOU LOOK FINE. WHY?
LANGSTROM IS FEEDING ME MEDS, BUT I'M STILL WORRIED THAT...THE *BEAST* IS GOING TO FIND ITS WAY OUT AGAIN.
JUST, PLEASE KEEP AN EYE ON ME, IF YOU CAN. MAKE SURE I'M STILL, Y'KNOW, MY OLD SELF AND NOT SOME *WOLF-THING.*
GOTHAM
YEAH, SURE, COACH.
WHAT ABOUT EVAN? SHOULD I--
EVAN'S NOT THE ONLY ONE MISSING.
MY SIGN-UP SHEET SAYS THERE SHOULD BE FOUR PAIRS ON THE COURTS TONIGHT.
WE SEEM TO BE SHORT AN *UNUSUAL* AMOUNT OF KIDS.

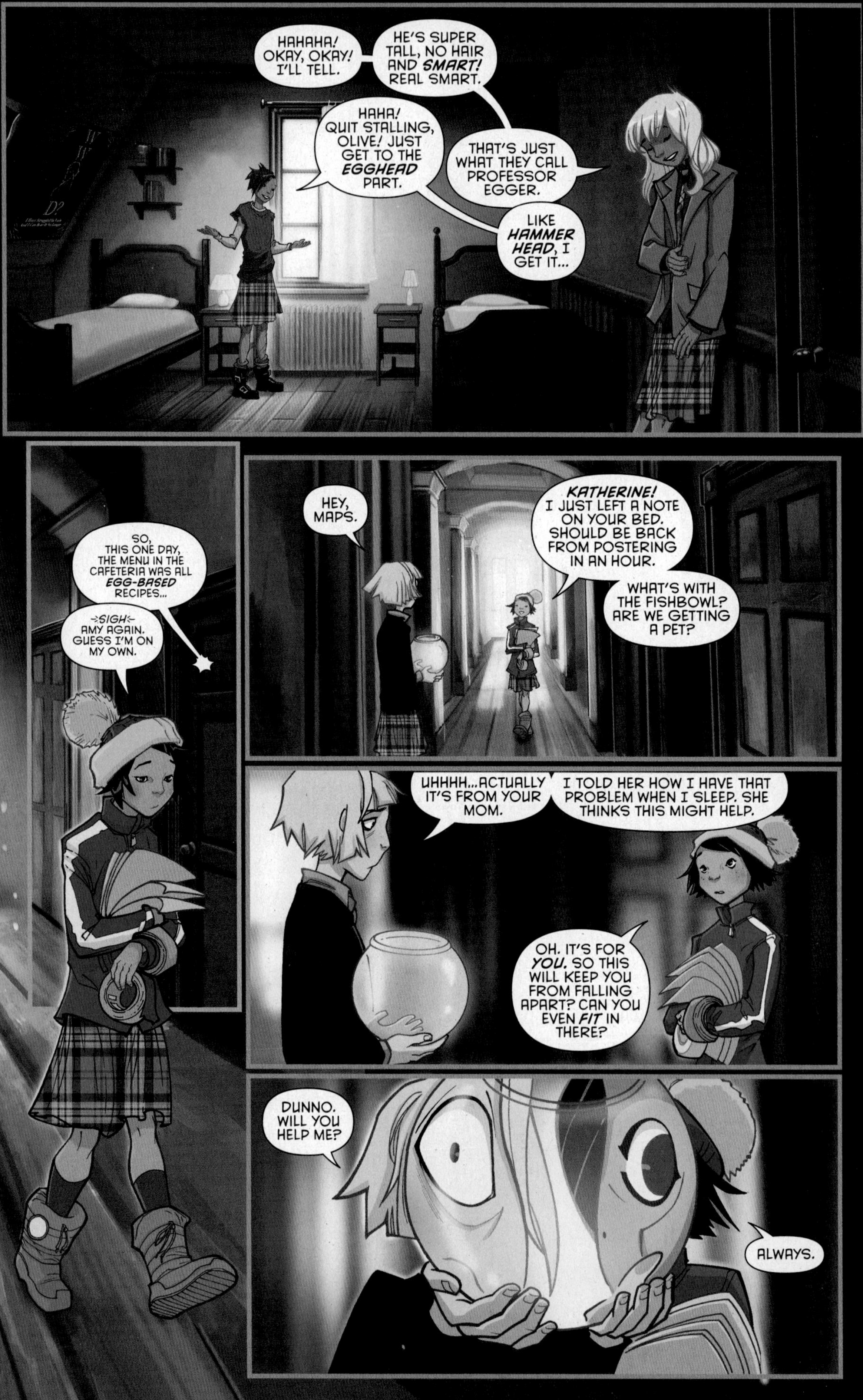
HAHAHA! OKAY, OKAY! I'LL TELL.
HE'S SUPER TALL, NO HAIR AND SMART! REAL SMART.
HAHA! QUIT STALLING, OLIVE! JUST GET TO THE EGGHEAD PART.
THAT'S JUST WHAT THEY CALL PROFESSOR EGGER.
LIKE HAMMER HEAD, I GET IT...
SO, THIS ONE DAY, THE MENU IN THE CAFETERIA WAS ALL EGG-BASED RECIPES...
~SIGH~ AMY AGAIN. GUESS I'M ON MY OWN.
HEY, MAPS.
KATHERINE! I JUST LEFT A NOTE ON YOUR BED. SHOULD BE BACK FROM POSTERING IN AN HOUR.
WHAT'S WITH THE FISHBOWL? ARE WE GETTING A PET?
UHHHH...ACTUALLY IT'S FROM YOUR MOM.
I TOLD HER HOW I HAVE THAT PROBLEM WHEN I SLEEP. SHE THINKS THIS MIGHT HELP.
OH. IT'S FOR YOU. SO THIS WILL KEEP YOU FROM FALLING APART? CAN YOU EVEN FIT IN THERE?
DUNNO. WILL YOU HELP ME?
ALWAYS.

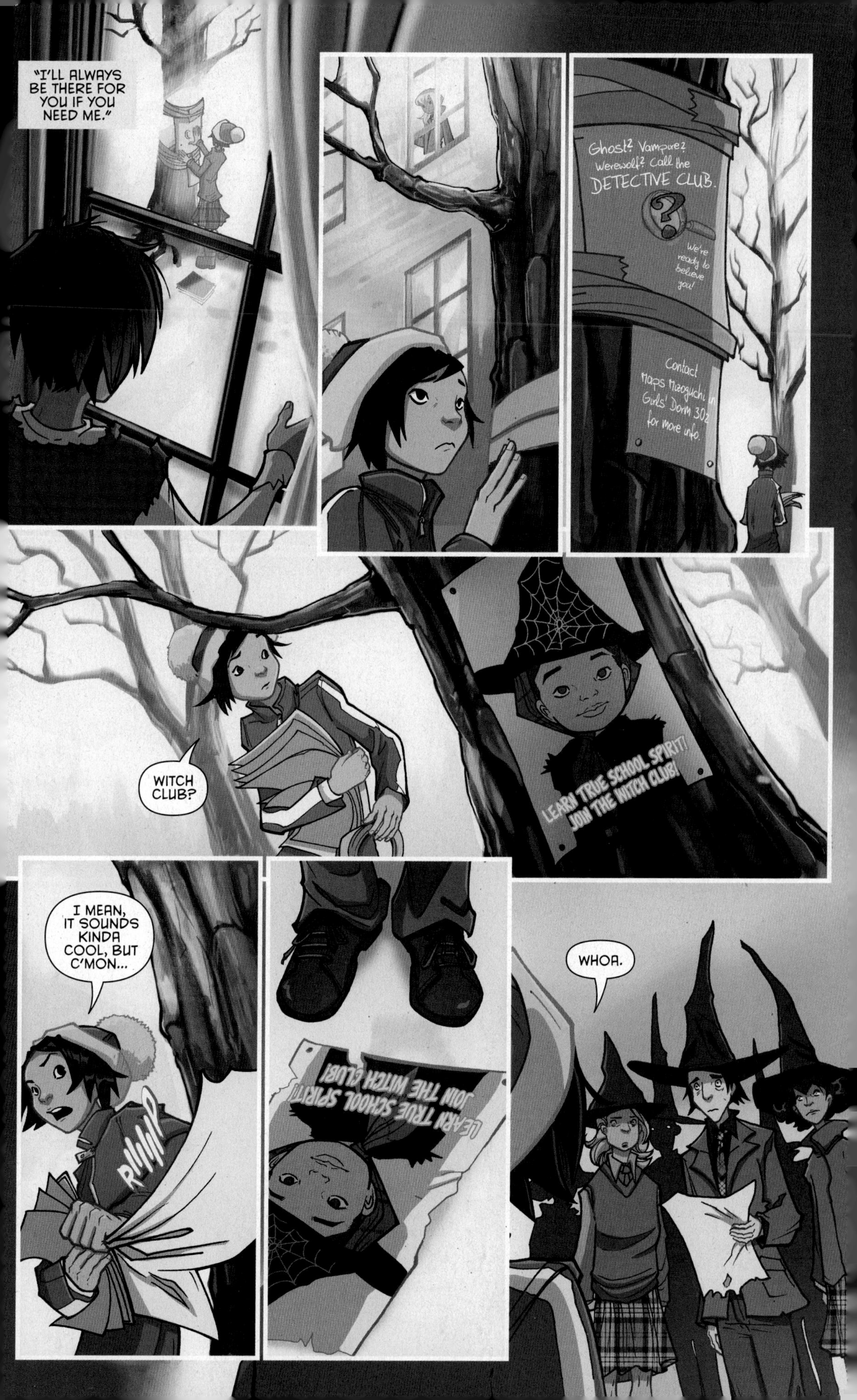
"I'LL ALWAYS BE THERE FOR YOU IF YOU NEED ME."
Ghost? Vampire? Werewolf? Call the DETECTIVE CLUB.
We're ready to believe you!
Contact Maps Mizoguchi in Girls' Dorm 302 for more info.
WITCH CLUB?
LEARN TRUE SCHOOL SPIRIT! JOIN THE WITCH CLUB!
I MEAN, IT SOUNDS KINDA COOL, BUT C'MON...
LEARN TRUE SCHOOL SPIRIT! JOIN THE WITCH CLUB!
WHOA.

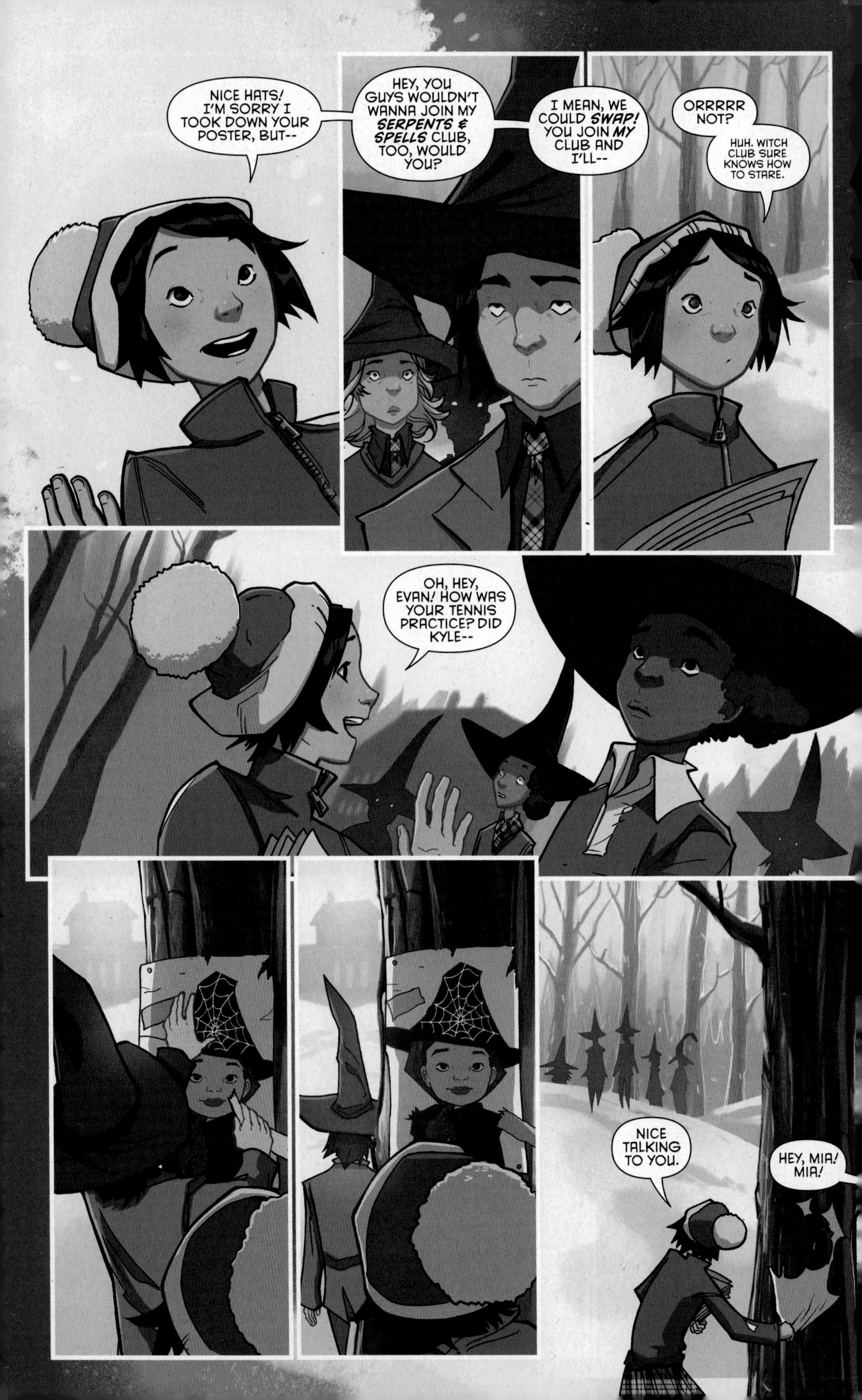
NICE HATS! I'M SORRY I TOOK DOWN YOUR POSTER, BUT--
HEY, YOU GUYS WOULDN'T WANNA JOIN MY *SERPENTS & SPELLS* CLUB, TOO, WOULD YOU?
I MEAN, WE COULD *SWAP!* YOU JOIN *MY* CLUB AND I'LL--
ORRRRR NOT?
HUH. WITCH CLUB SURE KNOWS HOW TO STARE.
OH, HEY, EVAN! HOW WAS YOUR TENNIS PRACTICE? DID KYLE--
NICE TALKING TO YOU.
HEY, MIA! MIA!

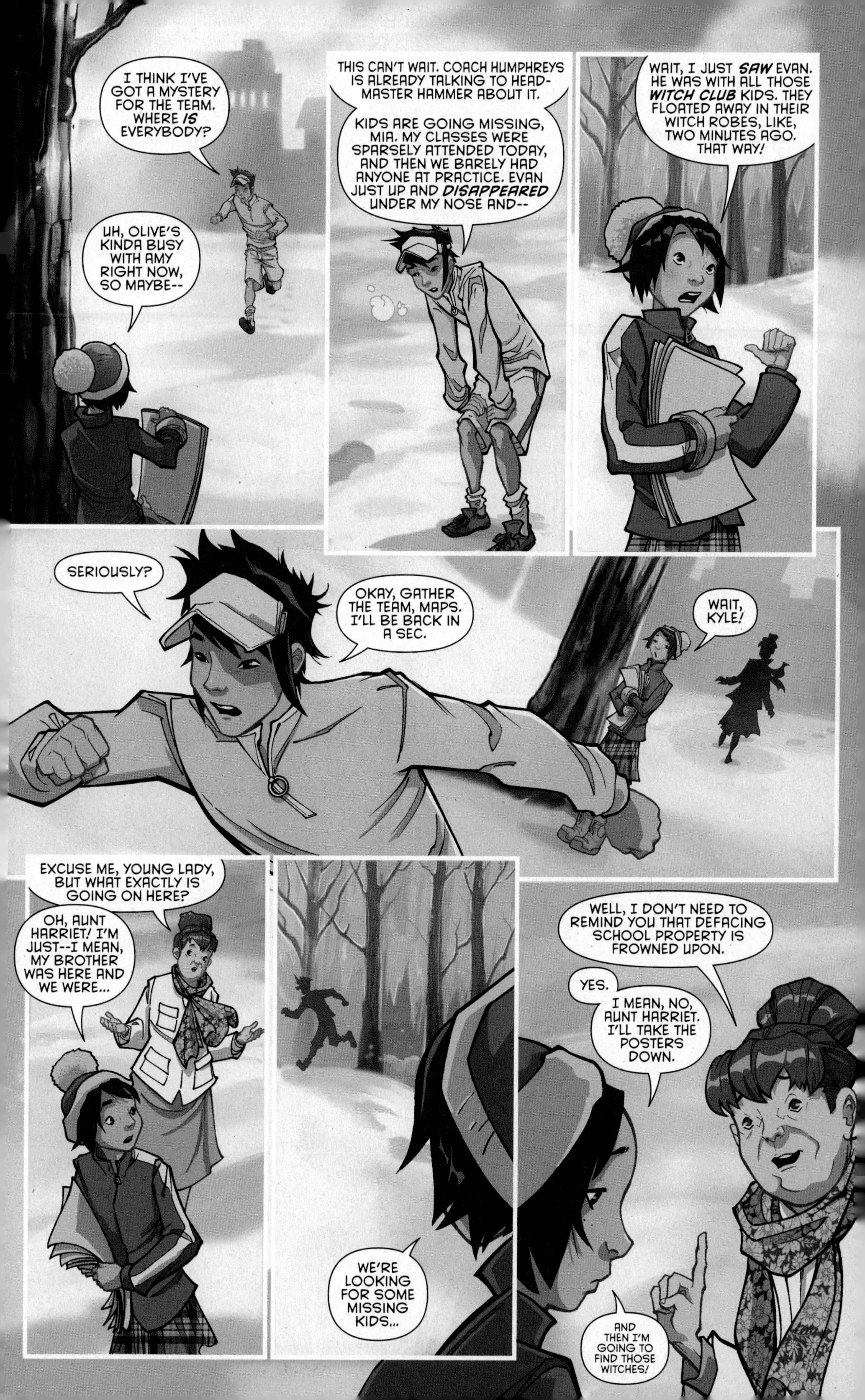
I THINK I'VE GOT A MYSTERY FOR THE TEAM. WHERE *IS* EVERYBODY?
UH, OLIVE'S KINDA BUSY WITH AMY RIGHT NOW, SO MAYBE--
THIS CAN'T WAIT. COACH HUMPHREYS IS ALREADY TALKING TO HEAD-MASTER HAMMER ABOUT IT.
KIDS ARE GOING MISSING, MIA. MY CLASSES WERE SPARSELY ATTENDED TODAY, AND THEN WE BARELY HAD ANYONE AT PRACTICE. EVAN JUST UP AND *DISAPPEARED* UNDER MY NOSE AND--
WAIT, I JUST *SAW* EVAN. HE WAS WITH ALL THOSE *WITCH CLUB* KIDS. THEY FLOATED AWAY IN THEIR WITCH ROBES, LIKE, TWO MINUTES AGO. THAT WAY!
SERIOUSLY?
OKAY, GATHER THE TEAM, MAPS. I'LL BE BACK IN A SEC.
WAIT, KYLE!
EXCUSE ME, YOUNG LADY, BUT WHAT EXACTLY IS GOING ON HERE?
OH, AUNT HARRIET! I'M JUST--I MEAN, MY BROTHER WAS HERE AND WE WERE...
WE'RE LOOKING FOR SOME MISSING KIDS...
WELL, I DON'T NEED TO REMIND YOU THAT DEFACING SCHOOL PROPERTY IS FROWNED UPON.
YES.
I MEAN, NO, AUNT HARRIET. I'LL TAKE THE POSTERS DOWN.
AND THEN I'M GOING TO FIND THOSE WITCHES!

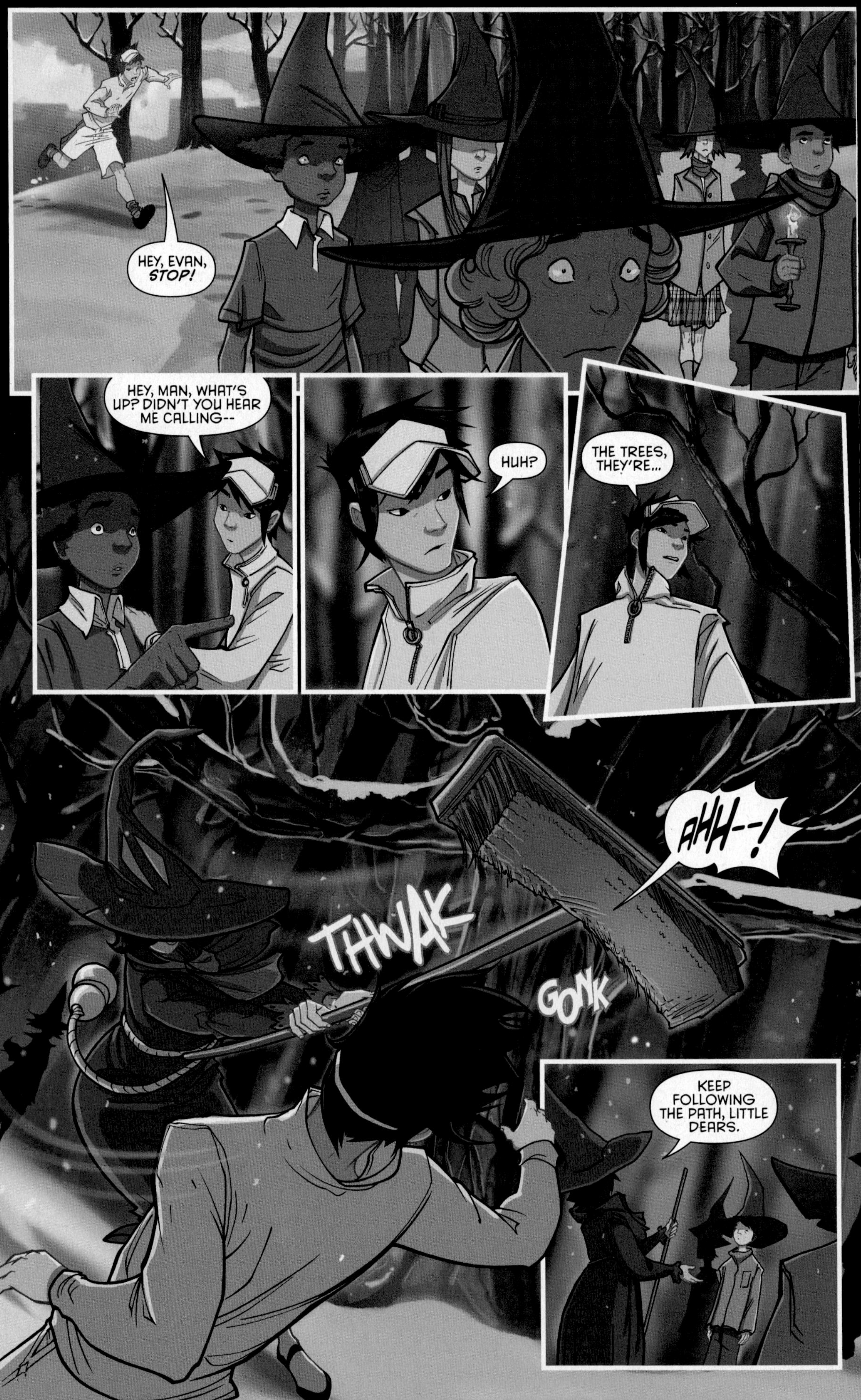
HEY, EVAN, STOP!
HEY, MAN, WHAT'S UP? DIDN'T YOU HEAR ME CALLING--
HUH?
THE TREES, THEY'RE...
AHH--!
THWAK
GONK
KEEP FOLLOWING THE PATH, LITTLE DEARS.

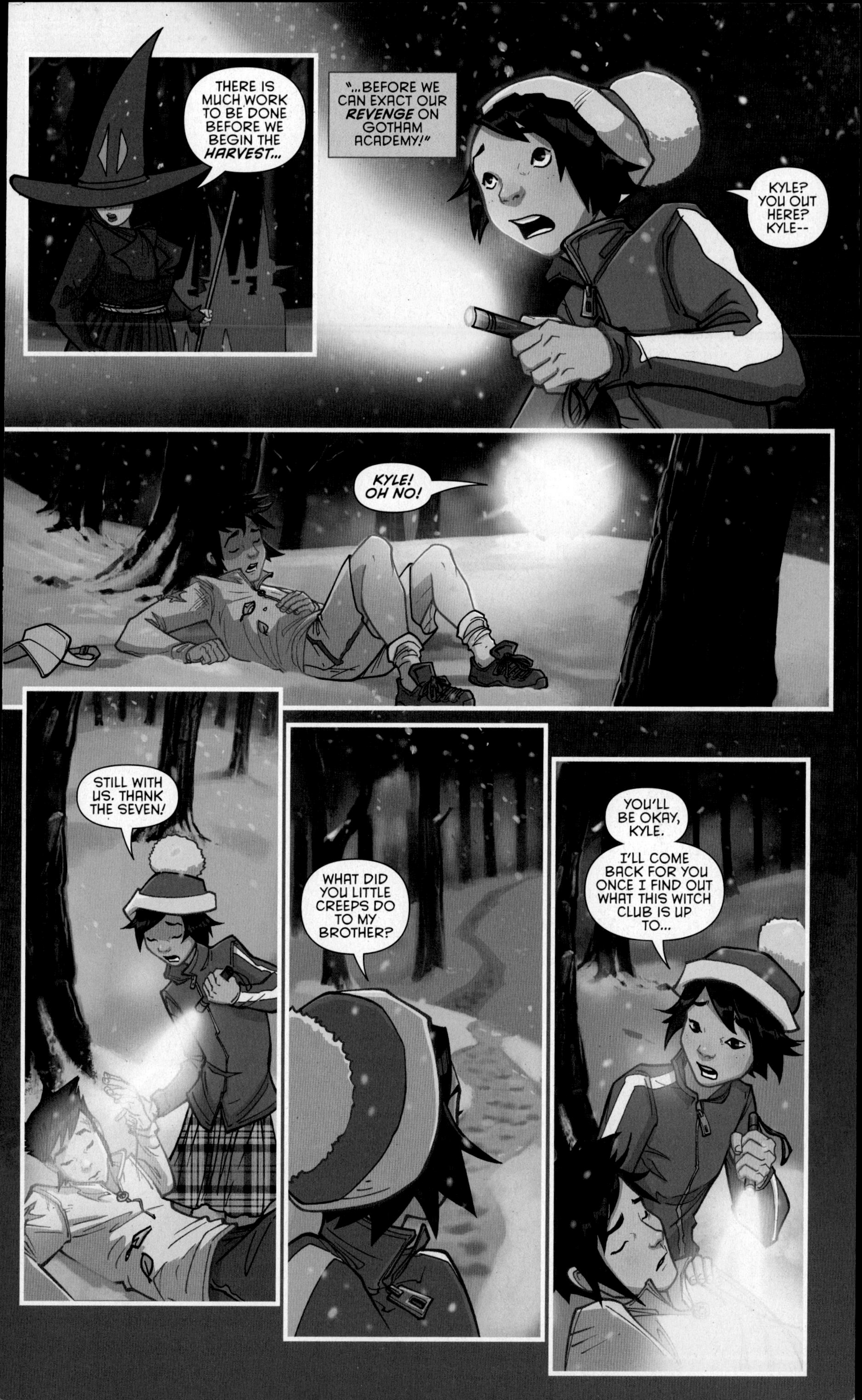
THERE IS MUCH WORK TO BE DONE BEFORE WE BEGIN THE *HARVEST*...
"...BEFORE WE CAN EXACT OUR *REVENGE* ON GOTHAM ACADEMY!"
KYLE? YOU OUT HERE? KYLE--
*KYLE! OH NO!*
STILL WITH US. THANK THE SEVEN!
WHAT DID YOU LITTLE CREEPS DO TO MY BROTHER?
YOU'LL BE OKAY, KYLE.
I'LL COME BACK FOR YOU ONCE I FIND OUT WHAT THIS WITCH CLUB IS UP TO...

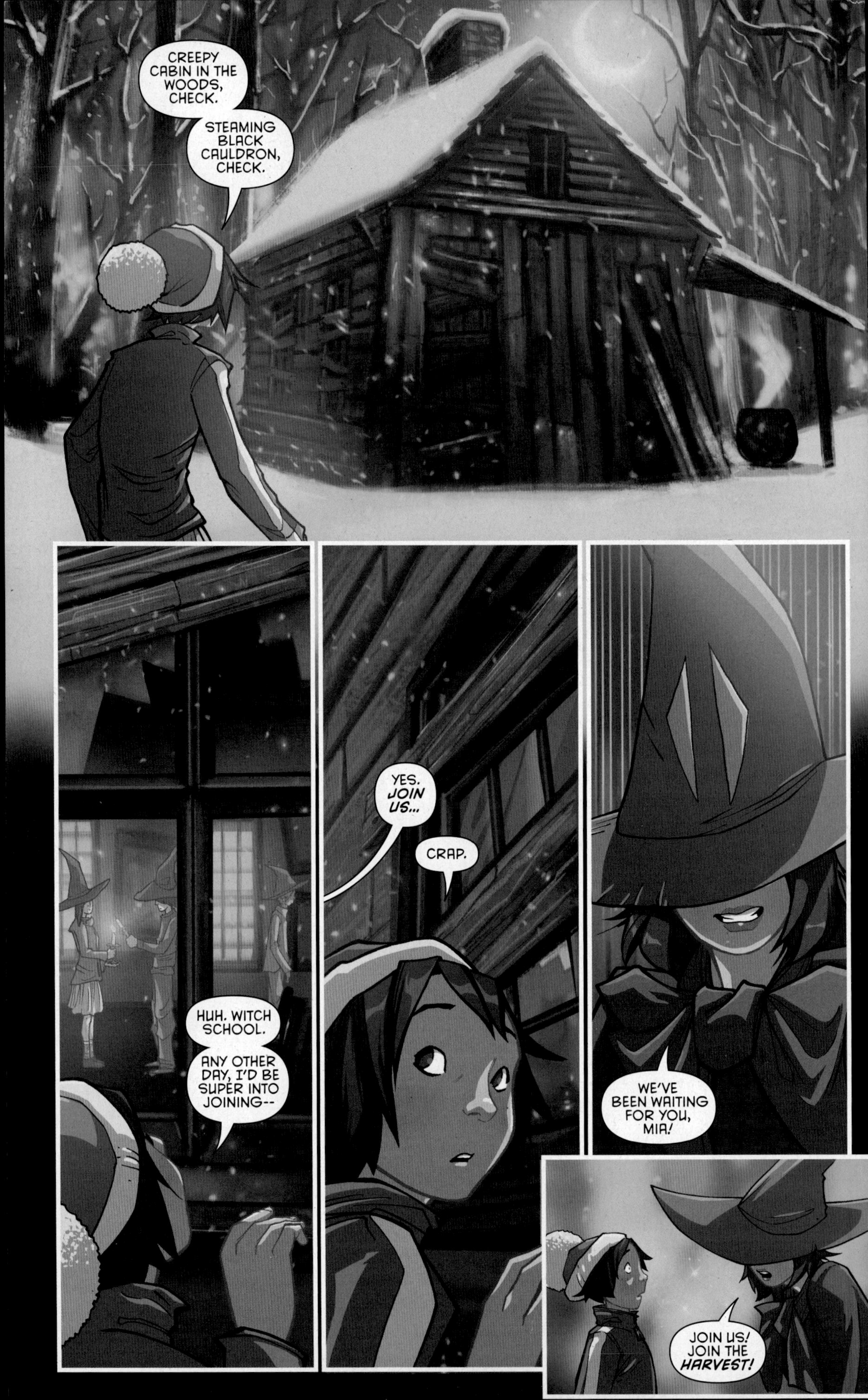
CREEPY CABIN IN THE WOODS, CHECK.
STEAMING BLACK CAULDRON, CHECK.
HUH. WITCH SCHOOL.
ANY OTHER DAY, I'D BE SUPER INTO JOINING--
YES. *JOIN US...*
CRAP.
WE'VE BEEN WAITING FOR YOU, MIA!
JOIN US! JOIN THE *HARVEST!*

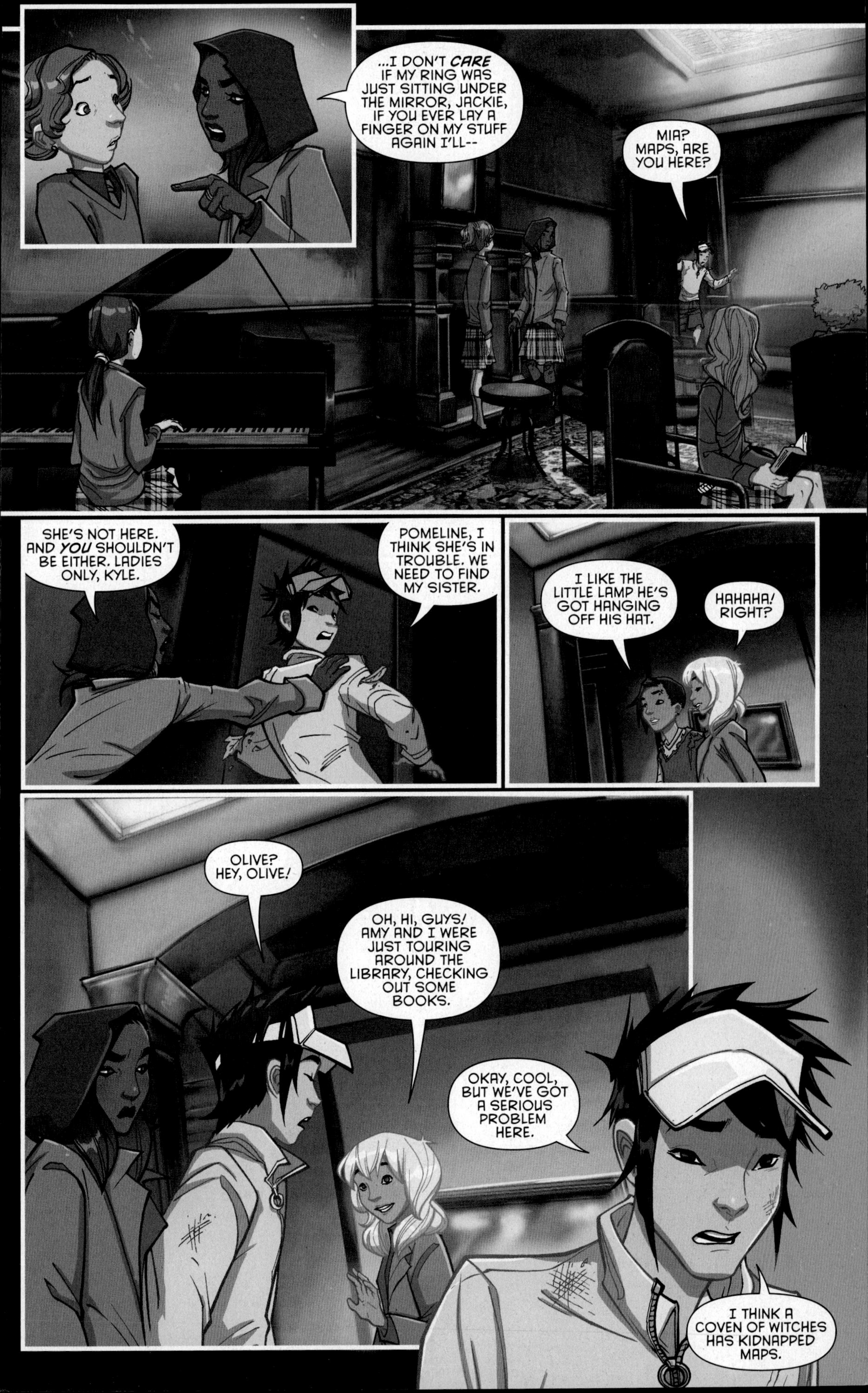
...I DON'T *CARE* IF MY RING WAS JUST SITTING UNDER THE MIRROR, JACKIE, IF YOU EVER LAY A FINGER ON MY STUFF AGAIN I'LL--
MIA? MAPS, ARE YOU HERE?
SHE'S NOT HERE. AND *YOU* SHOULDN'T BE EITHER. LADIES ONLY, KYLE.
POMELINE, I THINK SHE'S IN TROUBLE. WE NEED TO FIND MY SISTER.
I LIKE THE LITTLE LAMP HE'S GOT HANGING OFF HIS HAT.
HAHAHA! RIGHT?
OLIVE? HEY, OLIVE!
OH, HI, GUYS! AMY AND I WERE JUST TOURING AROUND THE LIBRARY, CHECKING OUT SOME BOOKS.
OKAY, COOL, BUT WE'VE GOT A SERIOUS PROBLEM HERE.
I THINK A COVEN OF WITCHES HAS KIDNAPPED MAPS.

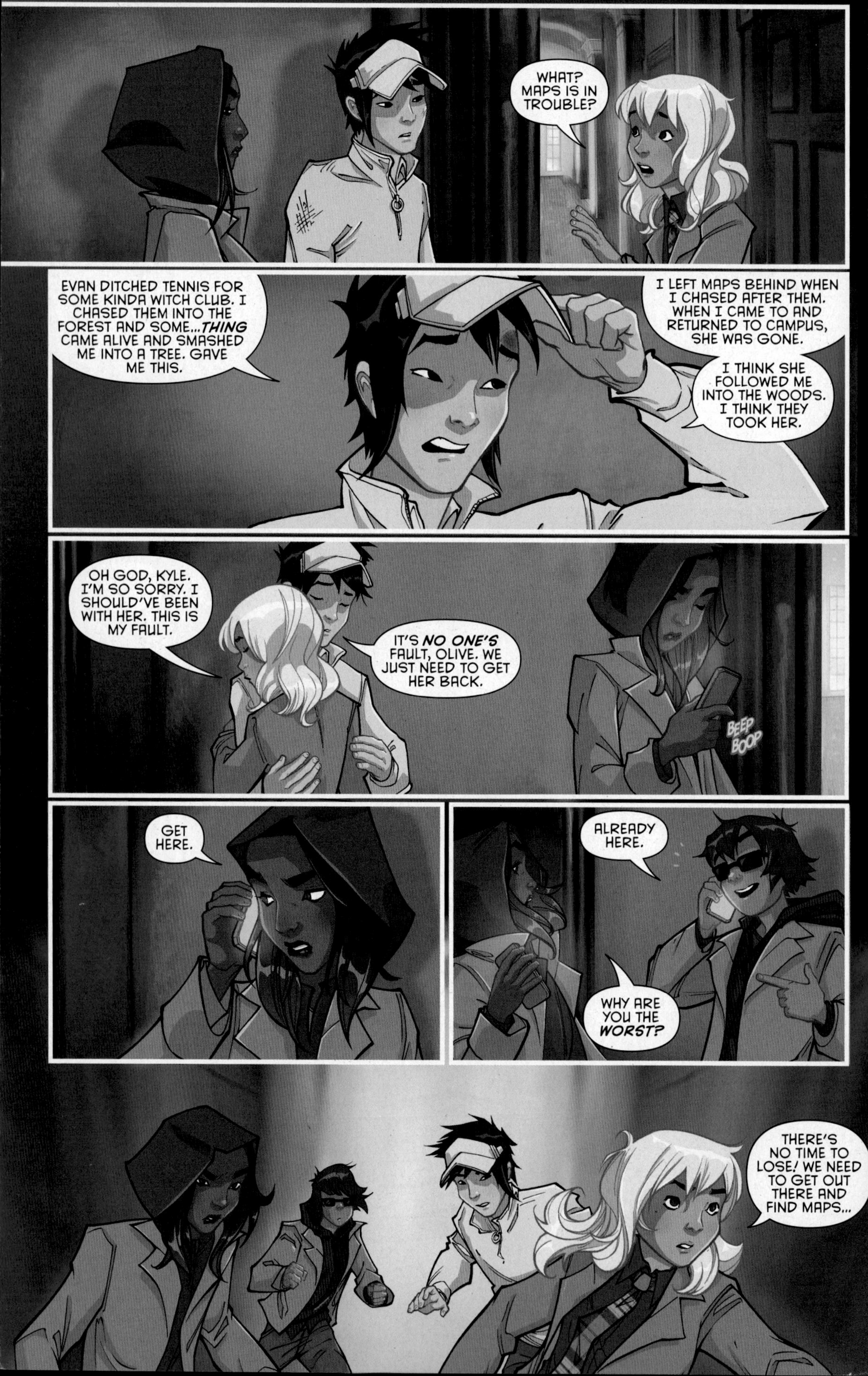
WHAT? MAPS IS IN TROUBLE?
EVAN DITCHED TENNIS FOR SOME KINDA WITCH CLUB. I CHASED THEM INTO THE FOREST AND SOME...*THING* CAME ALIVE AND SMASHED ME INTO A TREE. GAVE ME THIS.
I LEFT MAPS BEHIND WHEN I CHASED AFTER THEM. WHEN I CAME TO AND RETURNED TO CAMPUS, SHE WAS GONE.
I THINK SHE FOLLOWED ME INTO THE WOODS. I THINK THEY TOOK HER.
OH GOD, KYLE. I'M SO SORRY. I SHOULD'VE BEEN WITH HER. THIS IS MY FAULT.
IT'S ***NO ONE'S*** FAULT, OLIVE. WE JUST NEED TO GET HER BACK.
BEEP BOOP
GET HERE.
ALREADY HERE.
WHY ARE YOU THE ***WORST?***
THERE'S NO TIME TO LOSE! WE NEED TO GET OUT THERE AND FIND MAPS...

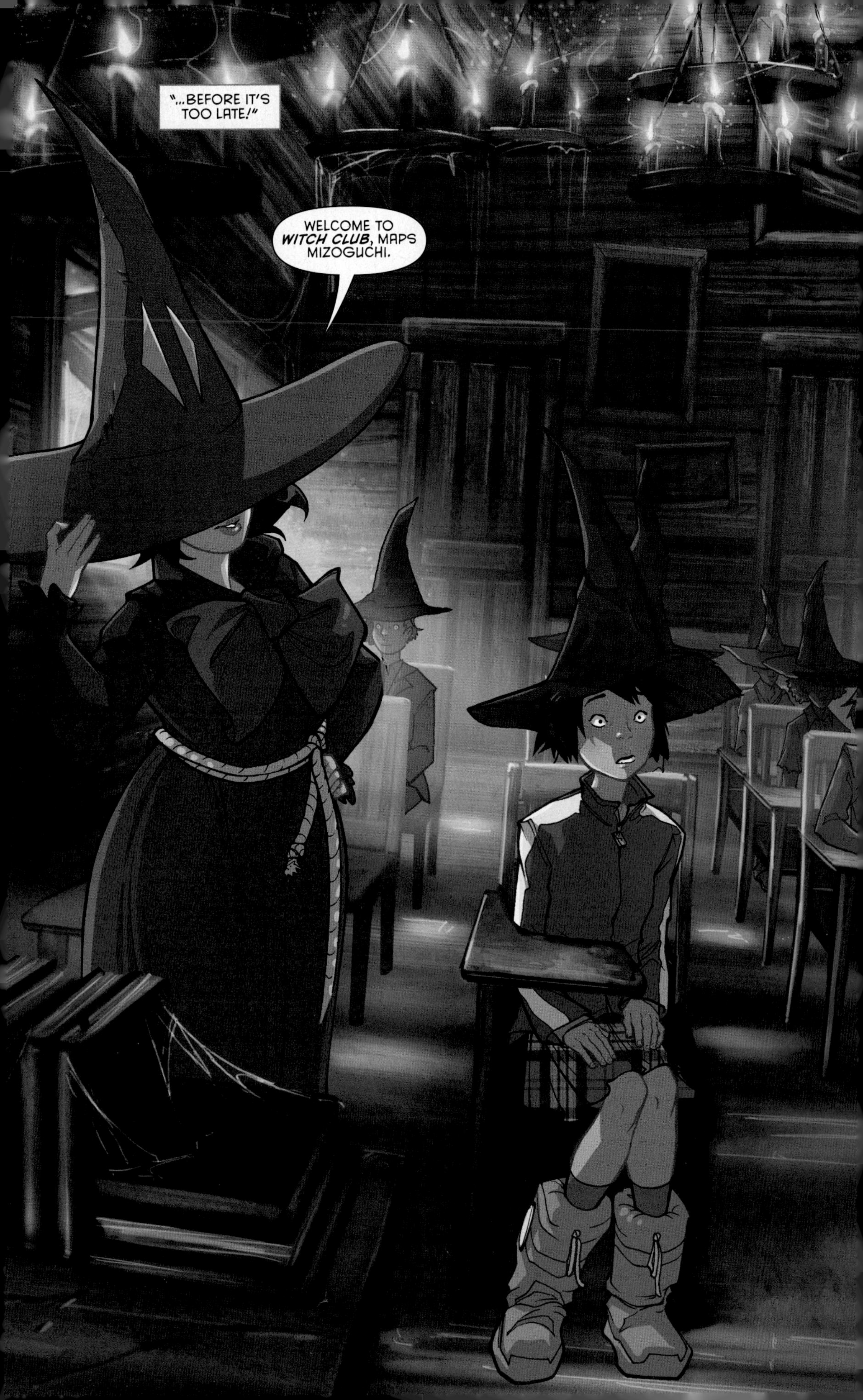
"...BEFORE IT'S TOO LATE!"
WELCOME TO *WITCH CLUB*, MAPS MIZOGUCHI.

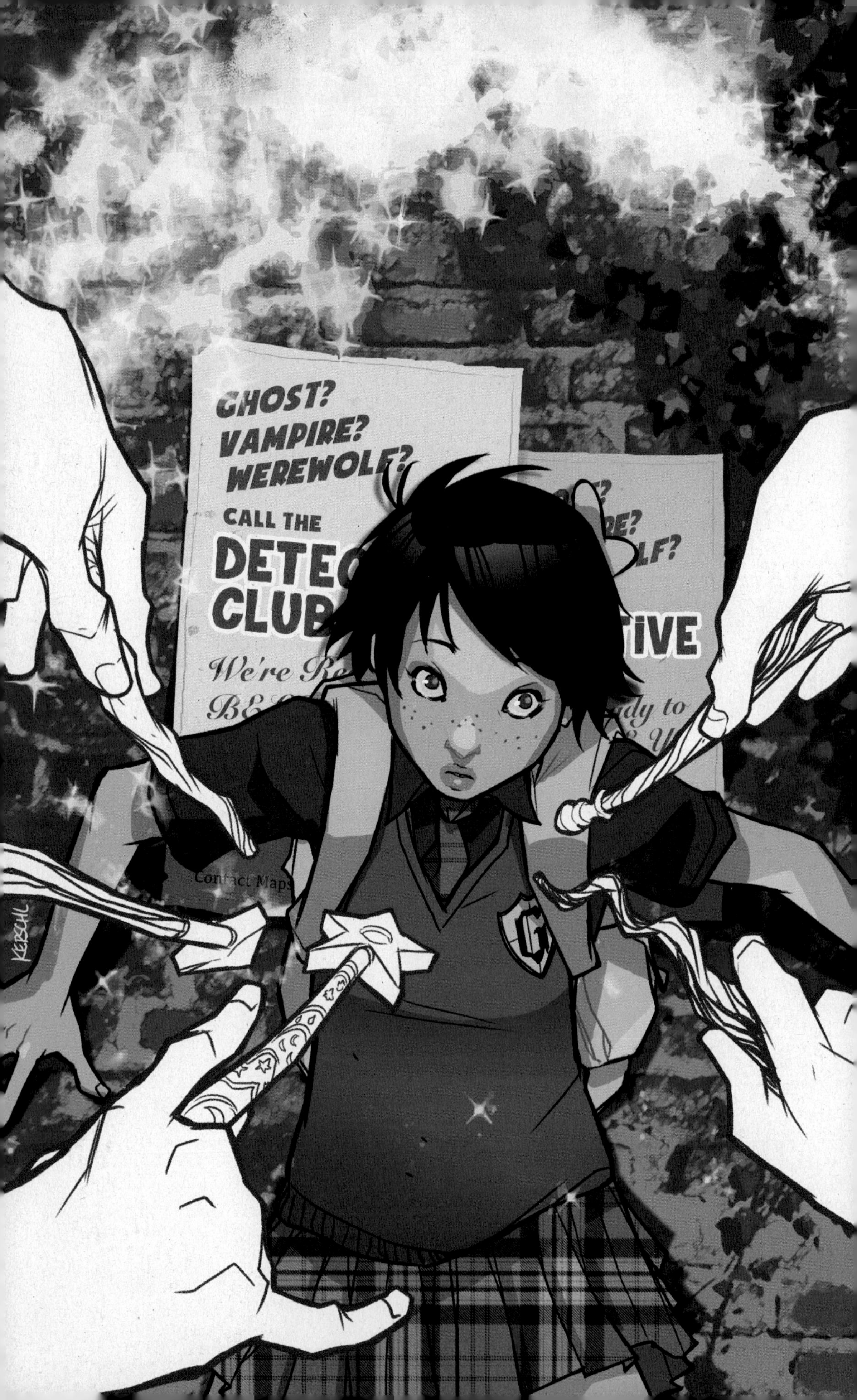
GHOST?
VAMPIRE?
WEREWOLF?
CALL THE
DETEC
CLUB
We're Re
BE
Contact Maps
TIVE
KERSCHL

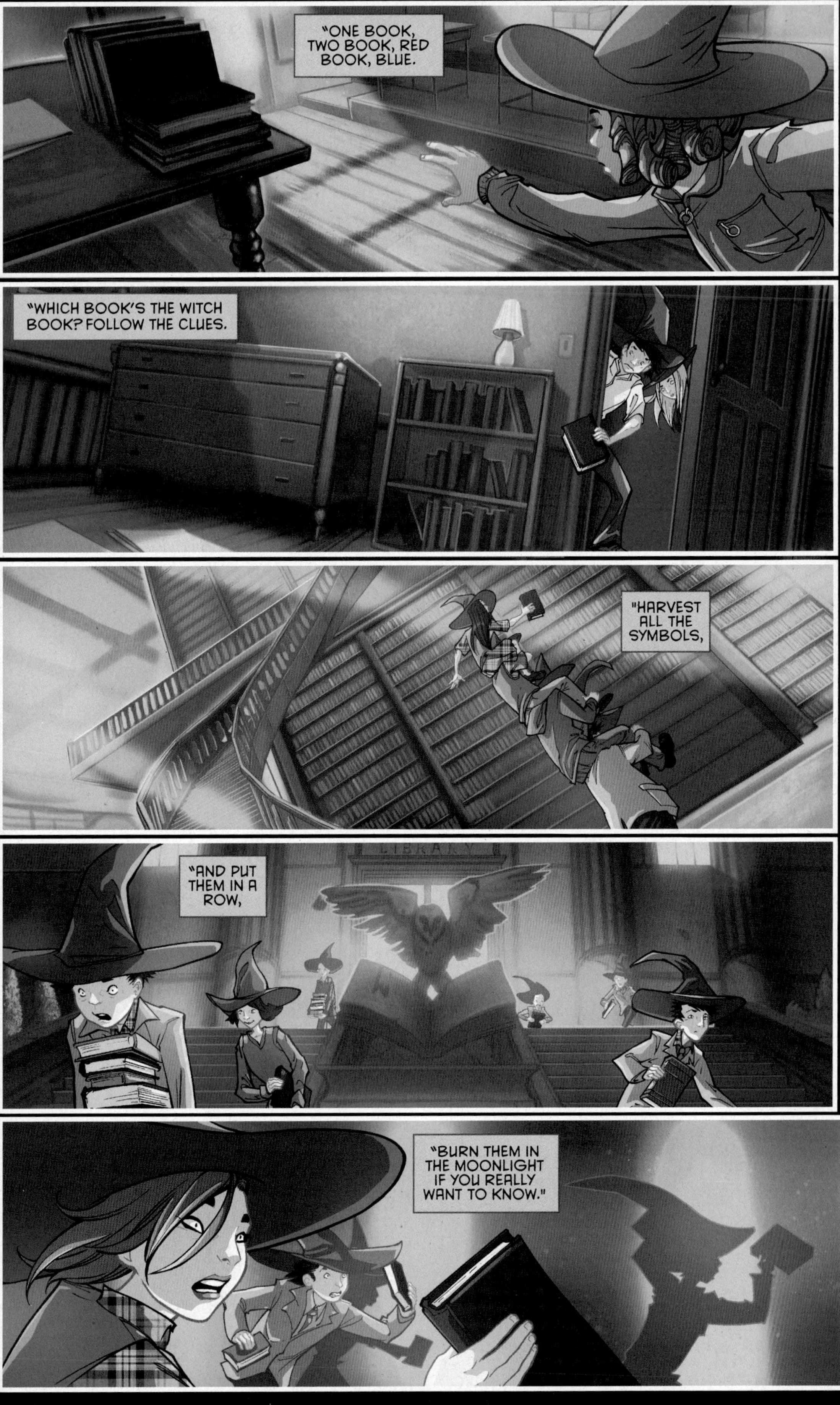
"ONE BOOK, TWO BOOK, RED BOOK, BLUE.
"WHICH BOOK'S THE WITCH BOOK? FOLLOW THE CLUES.
"HARVEST ALL THE SYMBOLS,
LIBRARY
"AND PUT THEM IN A ROW,
"BURN THEM IN THE MOONLIGHT IF YOU REALLY WANT TO KNOW."

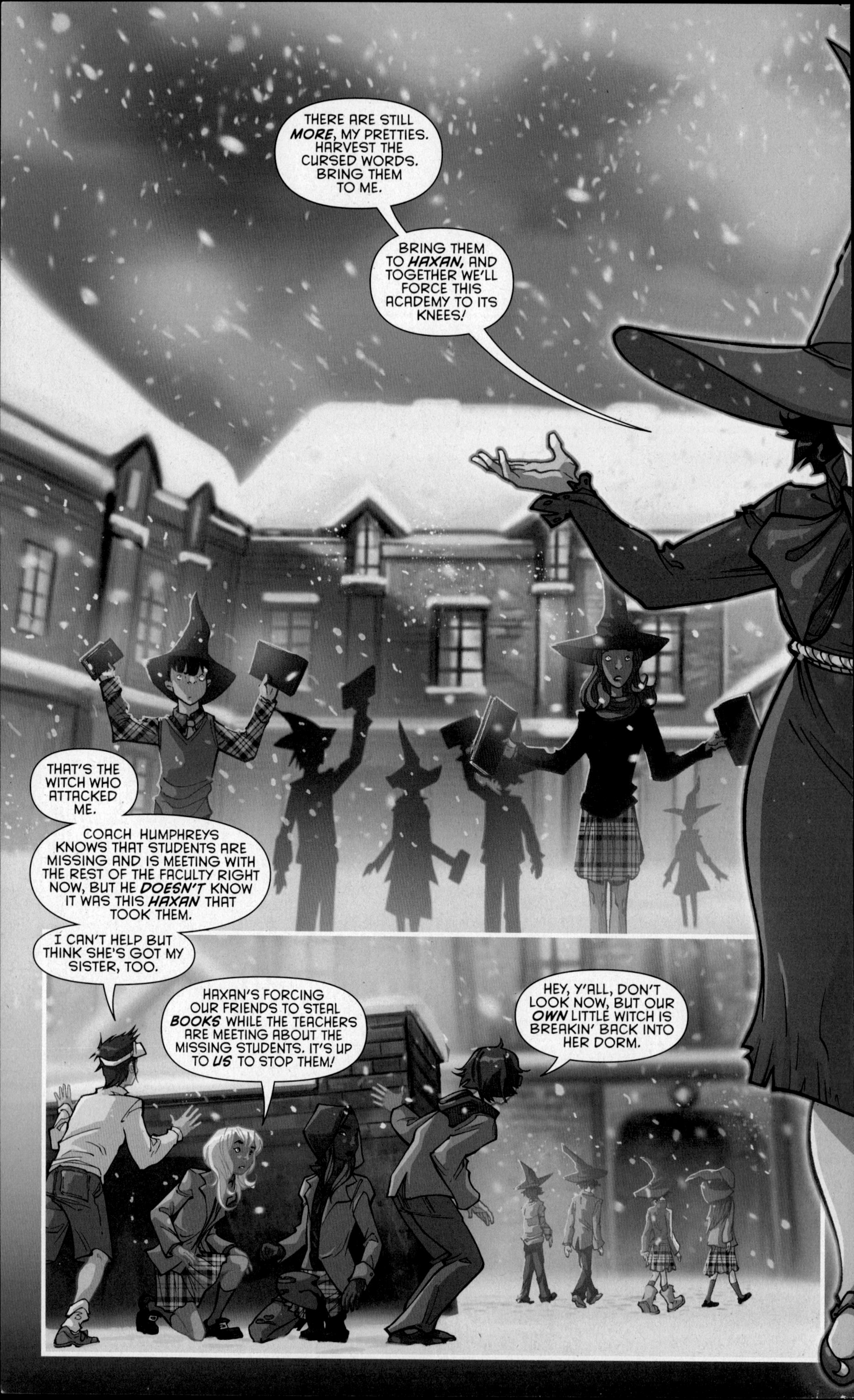
THERE ARE STILL MORE, MY PRETTIES. HARVEST THE CURSED WORDS. BRING THEM TO ME.
BRING THEM TO HAXAN, AND TOGETHER WE'LL FORCE THIS ACADEMY TO ITS KNEES!
THAT'S THE WITCH WHO ATTACKED ME.
COACH HUMPHREYS KNOWS THAT STUDENTS ARE MISSING AND IS MEETING WITH THE REST OF THE FACULTY RIGHT NOW, BUT HE DOESN'T KNOW IT WAS THIS HAXAN THAT TOOK THEM.
I CAN'T HELP BUT THINK SHE'S GOT MY SISTER, TOO.
HAXAN'S FORCING OUR FRIENDS TO STEAL BOOKS WHILE THE TEACHERS ARE MEETING ABOUT THE MISSING STUDENTS. IT'S UP TO US TO STOP THEM!
HEY, Y'ALL, DON'T LOOK NOW, BUT OUR OWN LITTLE WITCH IS BREAKIN' BACK INTO HER DORM.

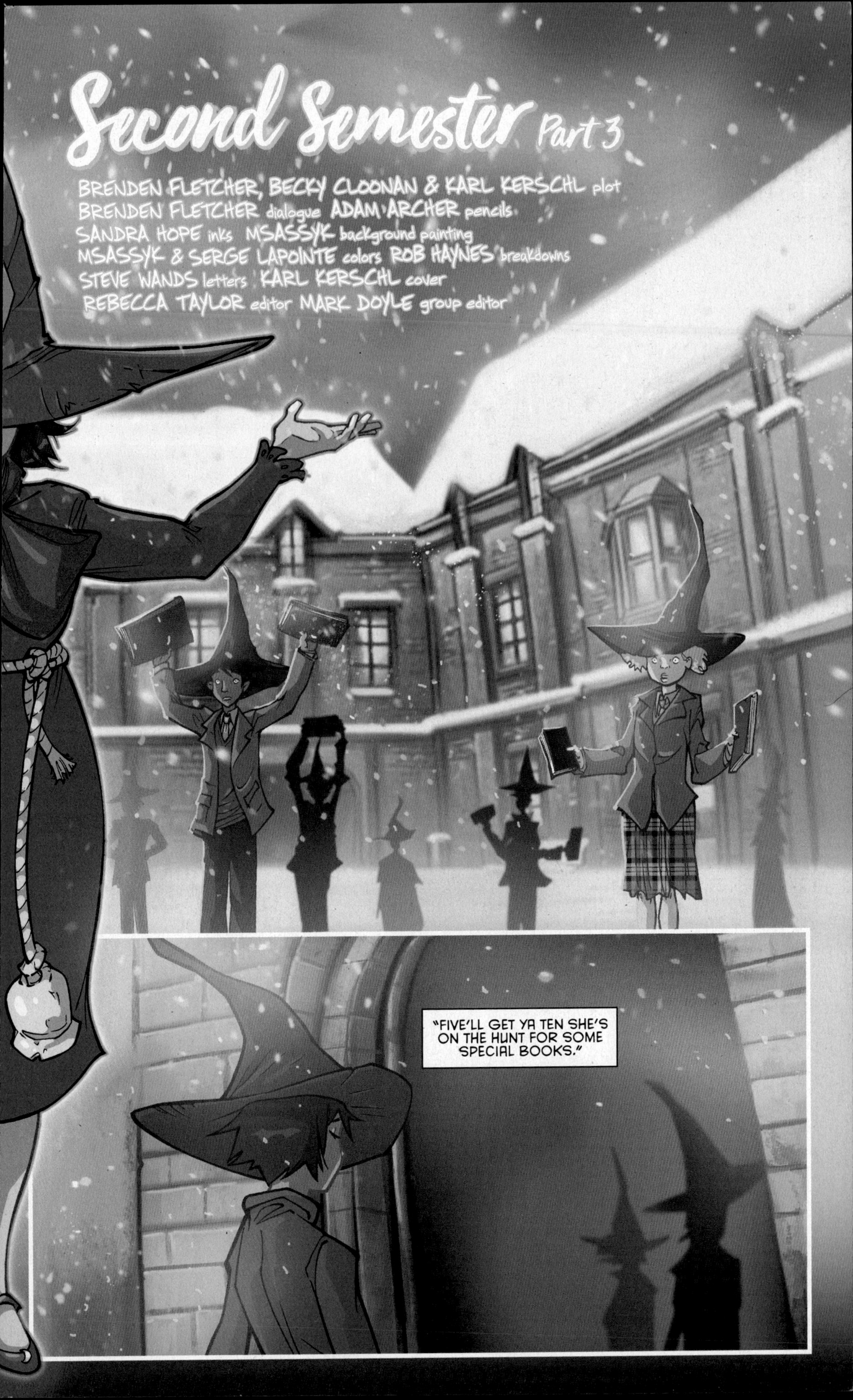
Second Semester Part 3
BRENDEN FLETCHER, BECKY CLOONAN & KARL KERSCHL plot
BRENDEN FLETCHER dialogue ADAM ARCHER pencils
SANDRA HOPE inks MSASSYK background painting
MSASSYK & SERGE LAPOINTE colors ROB HAYNES breakdowns
STEVE WANDS letters KARL KERSCHL cover
REBECCA TAYLOR editor MARK DOYLE group editor
"FIVE'LL GET YA TEN SHE'S ON THE HUNT FOR SOME SPECIAL BOOKS."

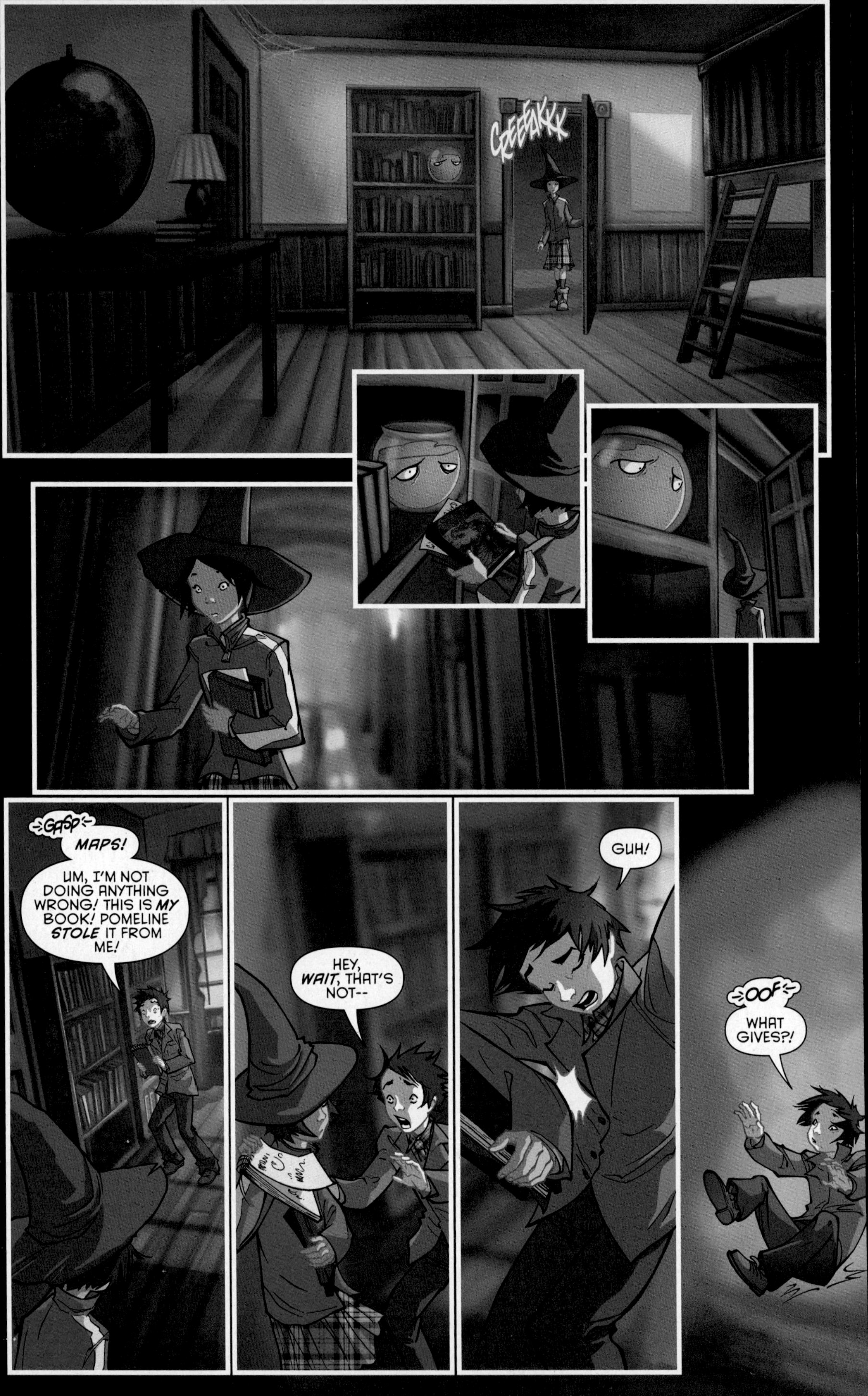
CREEEAKKK
-GASP-
MAPS!
UM, I'M NOT DOING ANYTHING WRONG! THIS IS MY BOOK! POMELINE STOLE IT FROM ME!
HEY, WAIT, THAT'S NOT--
GUH!
-OOF-
WHAT GIVES?!

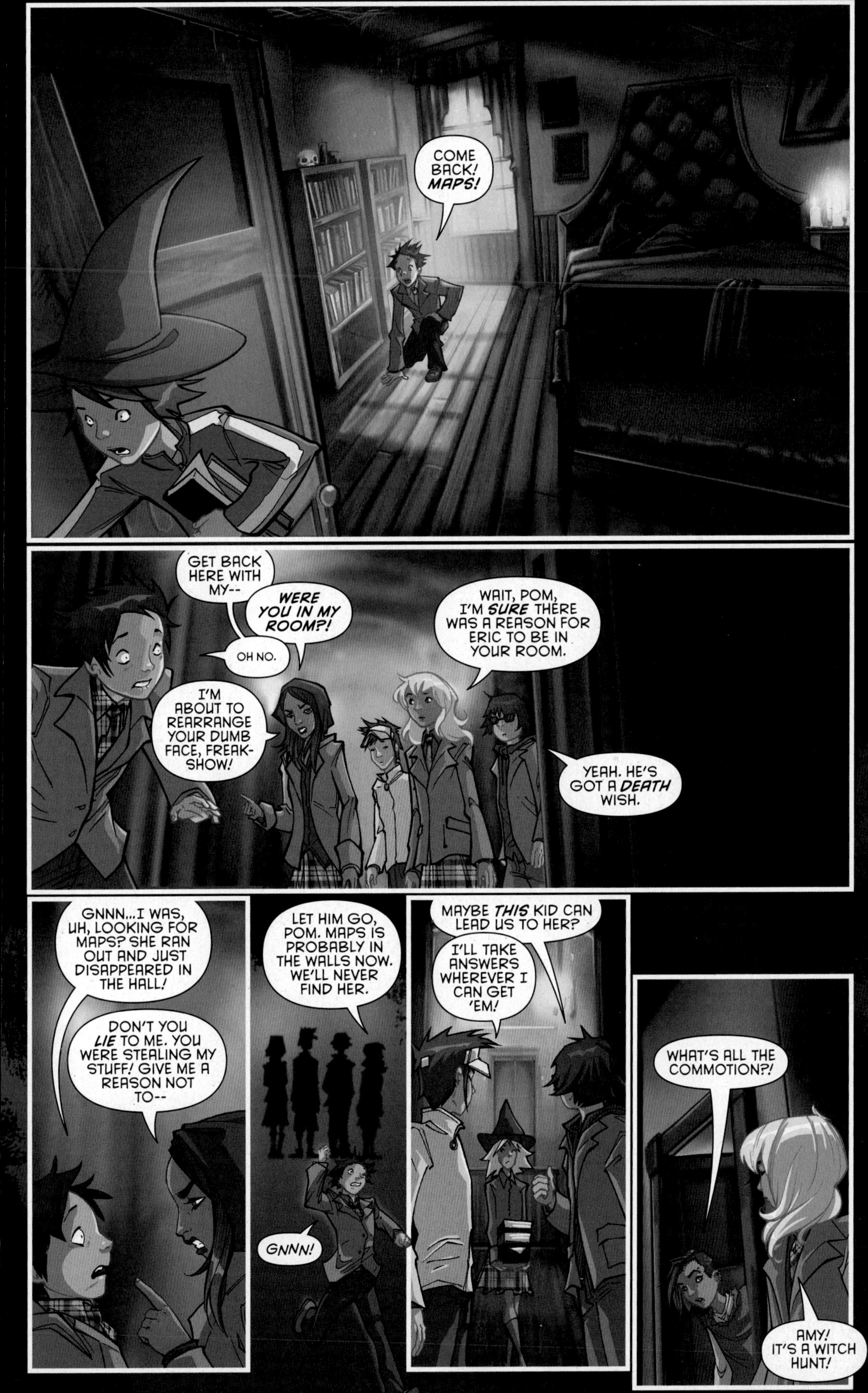
COME BACK! MAPS!
GET BACK HERE WITH MY--
WERE YOU IN MY ROOM?!
OH NO.
I'M ABOUT TO REARRANGE YOUR DUMB FACE, FREAK-SHOW!
WAIT, POM, I'M SURE THERE WAS A REASON FOR ERIC TO BE IN YOUR ROOM.
YEAH. HE'S GOT A DEATH WISH.
GNNN...I WAS, UH, LOOKING FOR MAPS? SHE RAN OUT AND JUST DISAPPEARED IN THE HALL!
DON'T YOU LIE TO ME. YOU WERE STEALING MY STUFF! GIVE ME A REASON NOT TO--
LET HIM GO, POM. MAPS IS PROBABLY IN THE WALLS NOW. WE'LL NEVER FIND HER.
GNNN!
MAYBE THIS KID CAN LEAD US TO HER?
I'LL TAKE ANSWERS WHEREVER I CAN GET 'EM!
WHAT'S ALL THE COMMOTION?!
AMY! IT'S A WITCH HUNT!

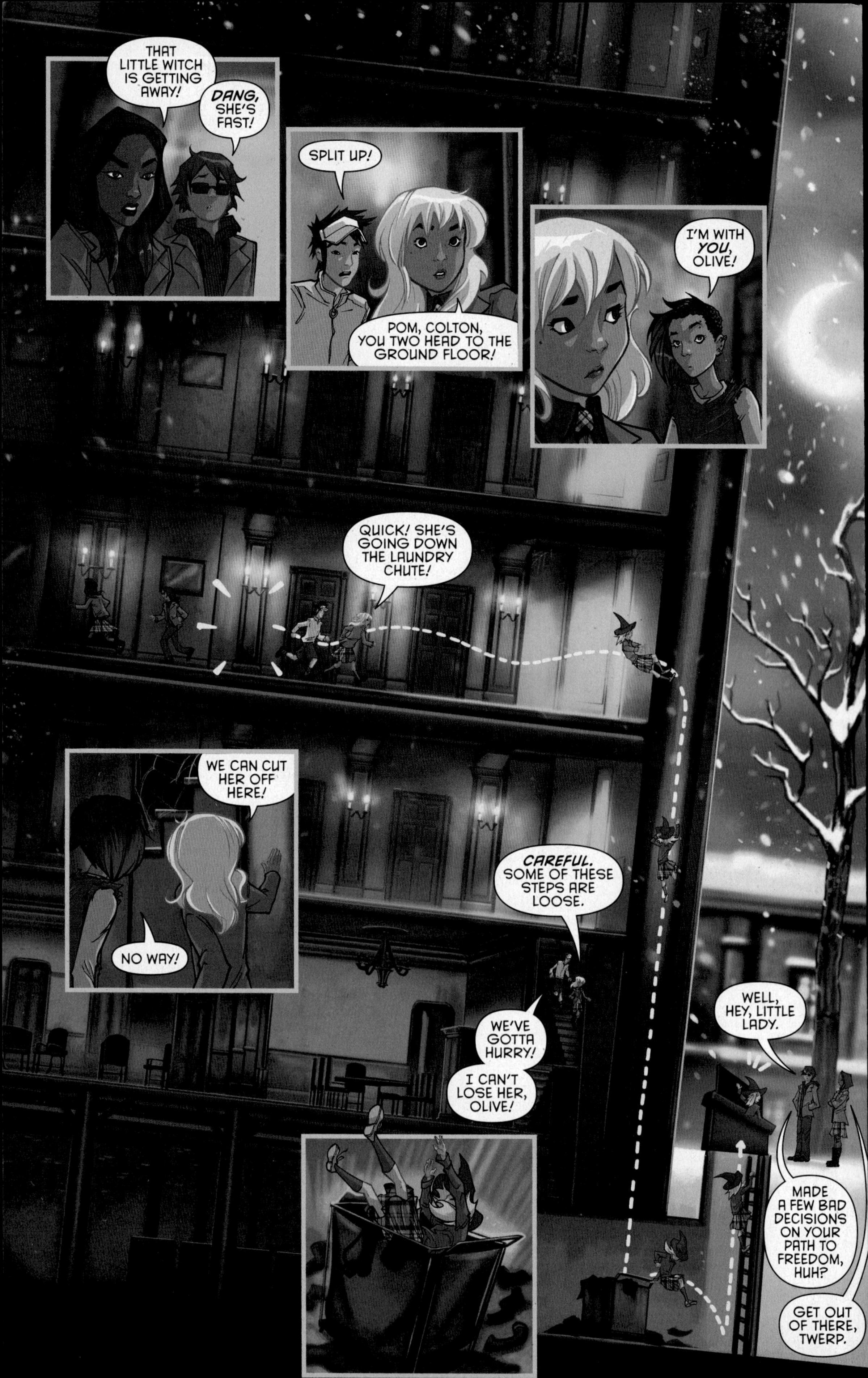
THAT LITTLE WITCH IS GETTING AWAY!
DANG, SHE'S FAST!
SPLIT UP!
POM, COLTON, YOU TWO HEAD TO THE GROUND FLOOR!
I'M WITH YOU, OLIVE!
QUICK! SHE'S GOING DOWN THE LAUNDRY CHUTE!
WE CAN CUT HER OFF HERE!
NO WAY!
CAREFUL. SOME OF THESE STEPS ARE LOOSE.
WE'VE GOTTA HURRY!
I CAN'T LOSE HER, OLIVE!
WELL, HEY, LITTLE LADY.
MADE A FEW BAD DECISIONS ON YOUR PATH TO FREEDOM, HUH?
GET OUT OF THERE, TWERP.

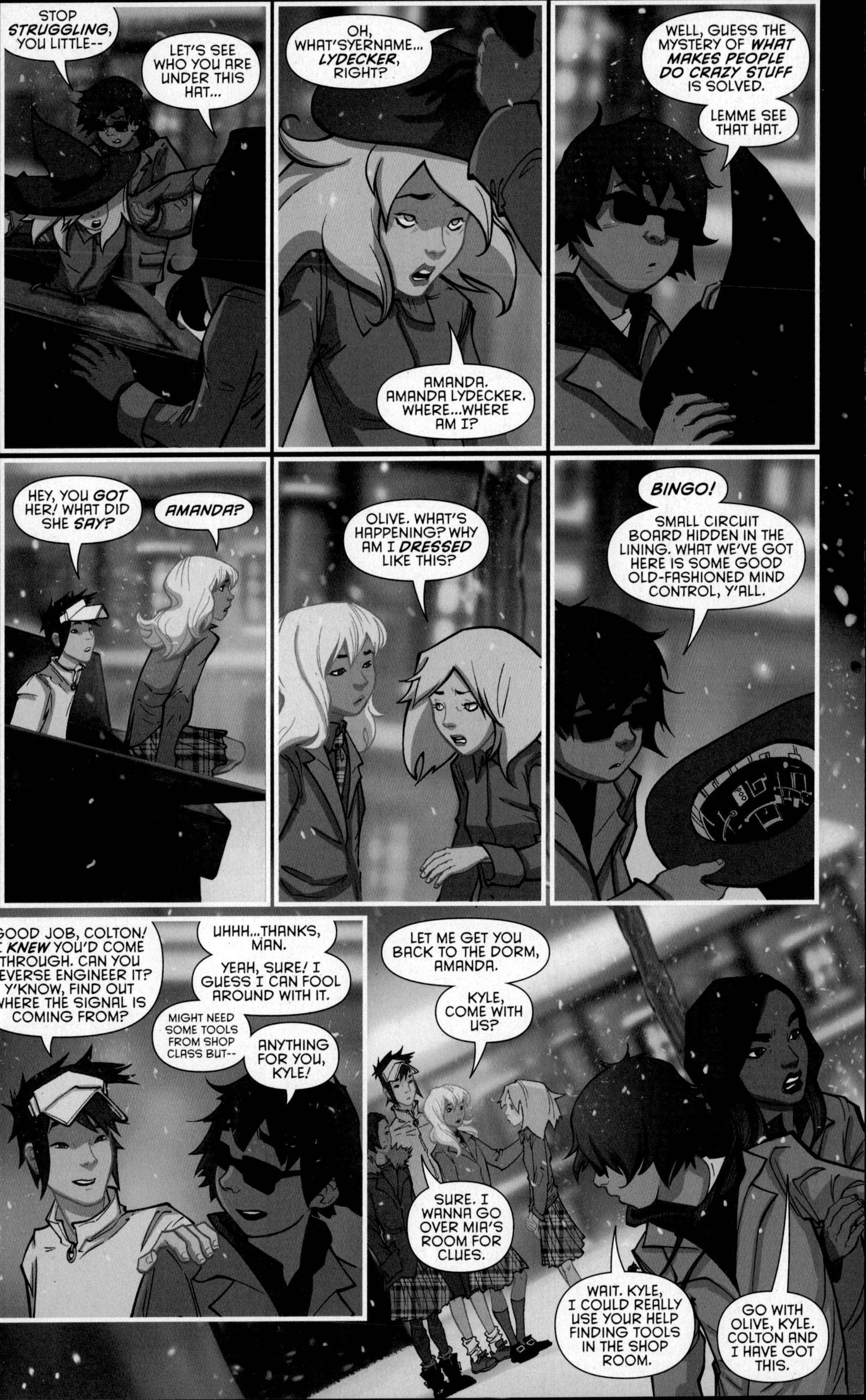
STOP *STRUGGLING*, YOU LITTLE--
LET'S SEE WHO YOU ARE UNDER THIS HAT...
OH, WHAT'SYERNAME... *LYDECKER*, RIGHT?
AMANDA. AMANDA LYDECKER. WHERE...WHERE AM I?
WELL, GUESS THE MYSTERY OF *WHAT MAKES PEOPLE DO CRAZY STUFF* IS SOLVED.
LEMME SEE THAT HAT.
HEY, YOU *GOT* HER! WHAT DID SHE *SAY*?
*AMANDA?*
OLIVE. WHAT'S HAPPENING? WHY AM I *DRESSED* LIKE THIS?
*BINGO!*
SMALL CIRCUIT BOARD HIDDEN IN THE LINING. WHAT WE'VE GOT HERE IS SOME GOOD OLD-FASHIONED MIND CONTROL, Y'ALL.
GOOD JOB, COLTON! I *KNEW* YOU'D COME THROUGH. CAN YOU REVERSE ENGINEER IT? Y'KNOW, FIND OUT WHERE THE SIGNAL IS COMING FROM?
UHHH...THANKS, MAN.
YEAH, SURE! I GUESS I CAN FOOL AROUND WITH IT.
MIGHT NEED SOME TOOLS FROM SHOP CLASS BUT--
ANYTHING FOR YOU, KYLE!
LET ME GET YOU BACK TO THE DORM, AMANDA.
KYLE, COME WITH US?
SURE. I WANNA GO OVER MIA'S ROOM FOR CLUES.
WAIT. KYLE, I COULD REALLY USE YOUR HELP FINDING TOOLS IN THE SHOP ROOM.
GO WITH OLIVE, KYLE. COLTON AND I HAVE GOT THIS.

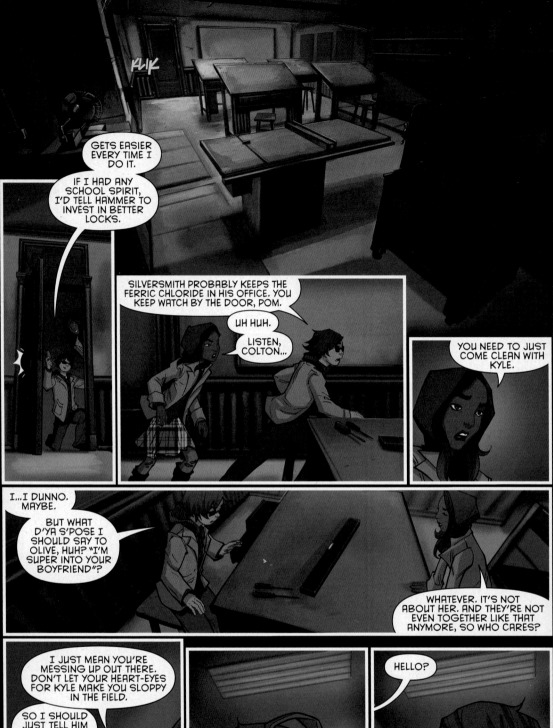

GETS EASIER EVERY TIME I DO IT.

IF I HAD ANY SCHOOL SPIRIT, I'D TELL HAMMER TO INVEST IN BETTER LOCKS.

SILVERSMITH PROBABLY KEEPS THE FERRIC CHLORIDE IN HIS OFFICE. YOU KEEP WATCH BY THE DOOR, POM.

UH HUH.

LISTEN, COLTON...

YOU NEED TO JUST COME CLEAN WITH KYLE.

I...I DUNNO. MAYBE.

BUT WHAT D'YA S'POSE I SHOULD SAY TO OLIVE, HUH? "I'M SUPER INTO YOUR BOYFRIEND"?

WHATEVER. IT'S NOT ABOUT HER. AND THEY'RE NOT EVEN TOGETHER LIKE THAT ANYMORE, SO WHO CARES?

I JUST MEAN YOU'RE MESSING UP OUT THERE. DON'T LET YOUR HEART-EYES FOR KYLE MAKE YOU SLOPPY IN THE FIELD.

SO I SHOULD JUST TELL HIM AND *WHAT?* MOVE ON?

MAYBE.

IT'LL HAVE TO WAIT. NO FC HERE, BUT THESE BAD BOYS WILL LET ME WORK ON THE WITCH CIRCUITRY AND--

HELLO?

CRAP. TEACHER ALERT! HIDE!

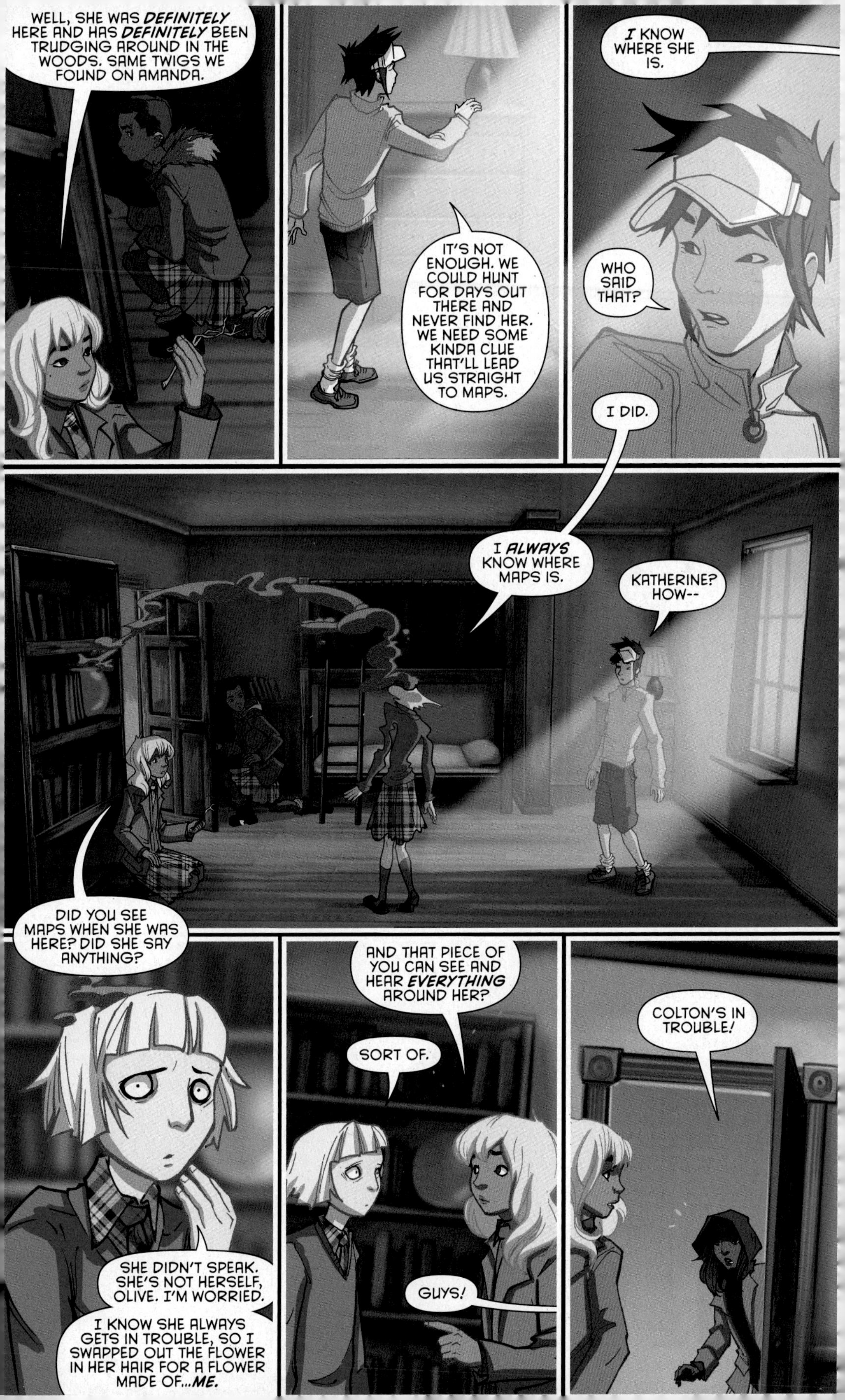
WELL, SHE WAS DEFINITELY HERE AND HAS DEFINITELY BEEN TRUDGING AROUND IN THE WOODS. SAME TWIGS WE FOUND ON AMANDA.
IT'S NOT ENOUGH. WE COULD HUNT FOR DAYS OUT THERE AND NEVER FIND HER. WE NEED SOME KINDA CLUE THAT'LL LEAD US STRAIGHT TO MAPS.
I KNOW WHERE SHE IS.
WHO SAID THAT?
I DID.
I ALWAYS KNOW WHERE MAPS IS.
KATHERINE? HOW--
DID YOU SEE MAPS WHEN SHE WAS HERE? DID SHE SAY ANYTHING?
SHE DIDN'T SPEAK. SHE'S NOT HERSELF, OLIVE. I'M WORRIED.
I KNOW SHE ALWAYS GETS IN TROUBLE, SO I SWAPPED OUT THE FLOWER IN HER HAIR FOR A FLOWER MADE OF...ME.
AND THAT PIECE OF YOU CAN SEE AND HEAR EVERYTHING AROUND HER?
SORT OF.
GUYS!
COLTON'S IN TROUBLE!

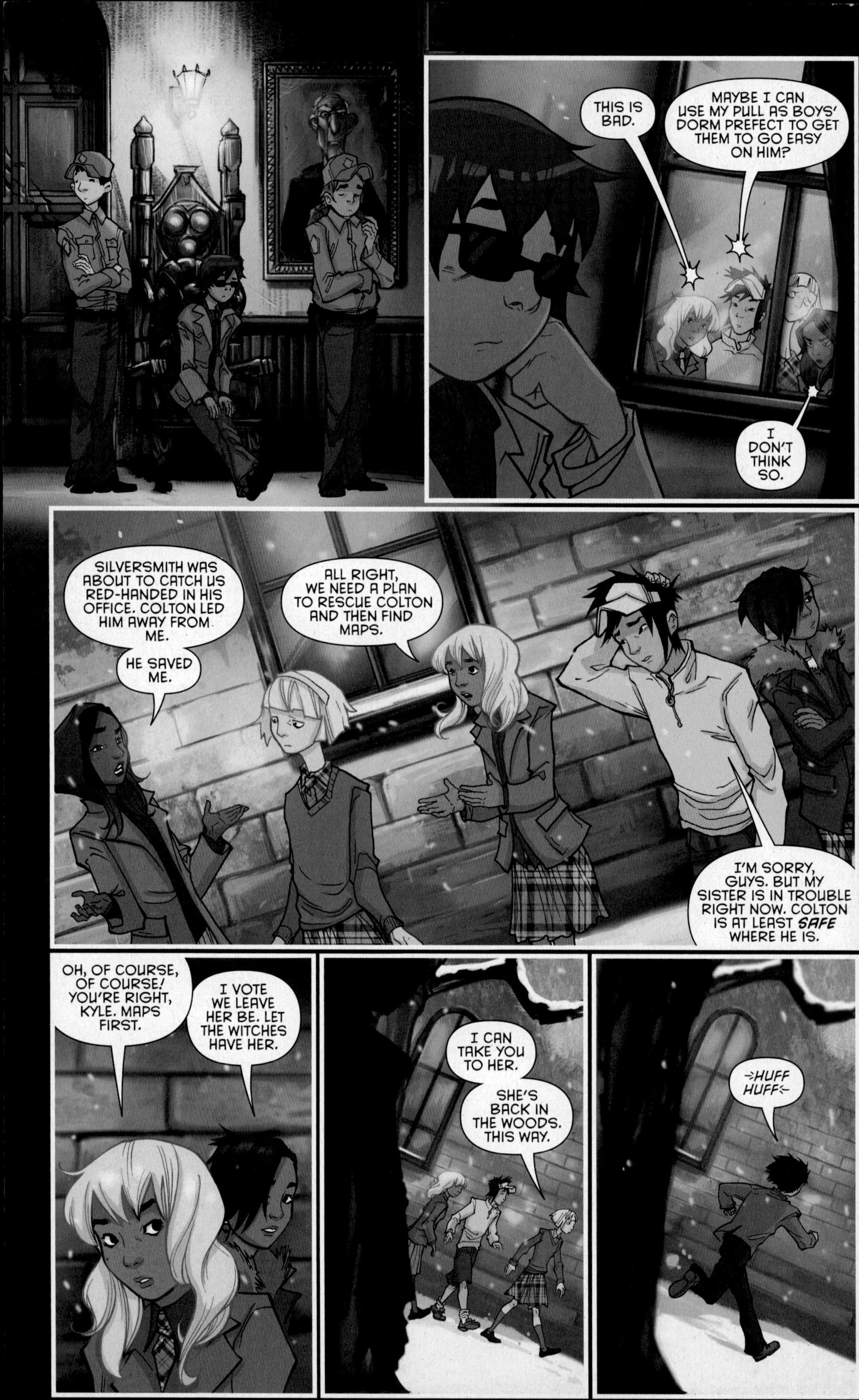
THIS IS BAD.
MAYBE I CAN USE MY PULL AS BOYS' DORM PREFECT TO GET THEM TO GO EASY ON HIM?
I DON'T THINK SO.
SILVERSMITH WAS ABOUT TO CATCH US RED-HANDED IN HIS OFFICE. COLTON LED HIM AWAY FROM ME.
HE SAVED ME.
ALL RIGHT, WE NEED A PLAN TO RESCUE COLTON AND THEN FIND MAPS.
I'M SORRY, GUYS. BUT MY SISTER IS IN TROUBLE RIGHT NOW. COLTON IS AT LEAST SAFE WHERE HE IS.
OH, OF COURSE, OF COURSE! YOU'RE RIGHT, KYLE. MAPS FIRST.
I VOTE WE LEAVE HER BE. LET THE WITCHES HAVE HER.
I CAN TAKE YOU TO HER.
SHE'S BACK IN THE WOODS. THIS WAY.
HUFF HUFF

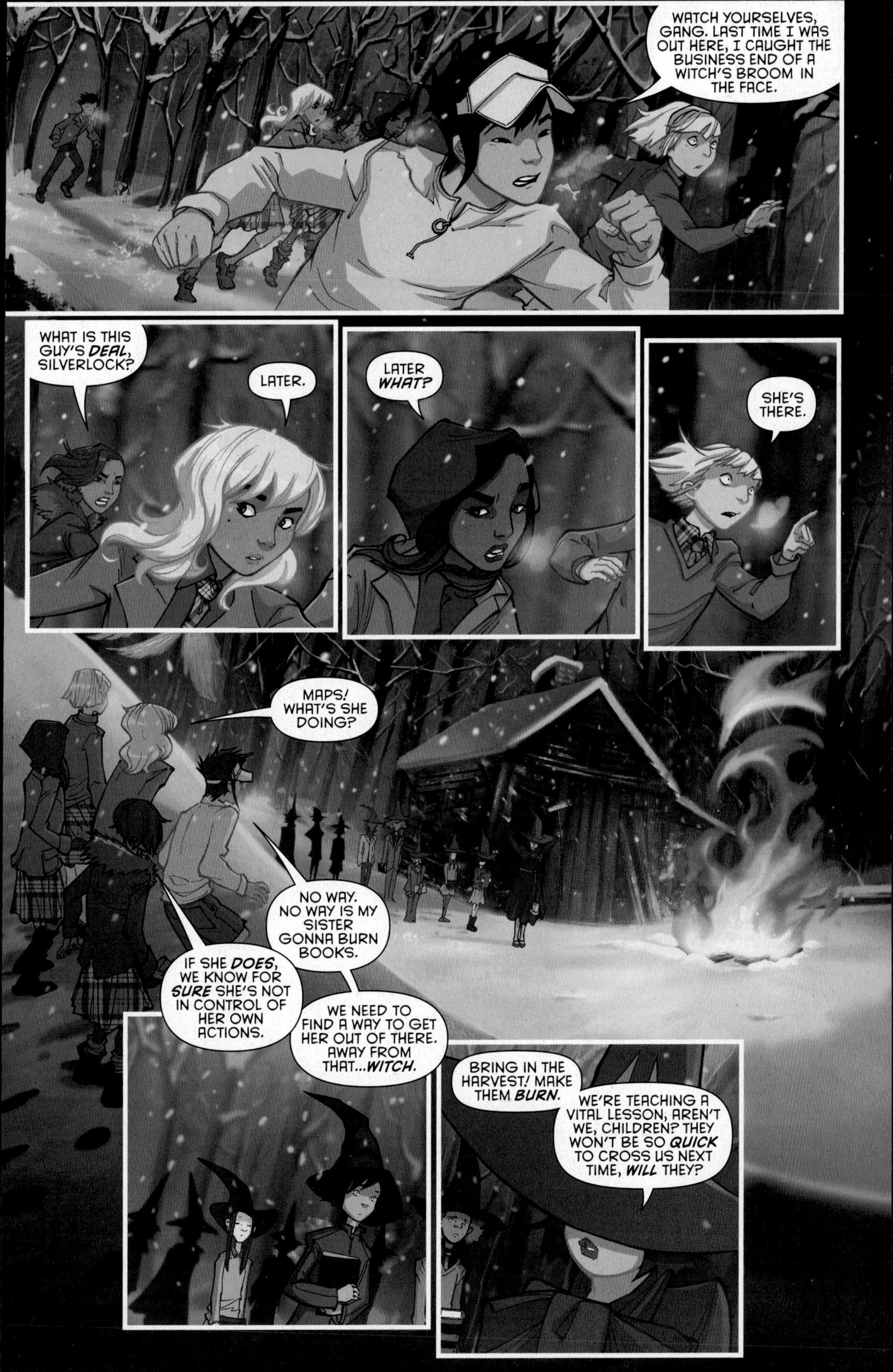

WATCH YOURSELVES, GANG. LAST TIME I WAS OUT HERE, I CAUGHT THE BUSINESS END OF A WITCH'S BROOM IN THE FACE.
WHAT IS THIS GUY'S *DEAL*, SILVERLOCK?
LATER.
LATER *WHAT?*
SHE'S THERE.
MAPS! WHAT'S SHE DOING?
NO WAY. NO WAY IS MY SISTER GONNA BURN BOOKS.
IF SHE *DOES*, WE KNOW FOR *SURE* SHE'S NOT IN CONTROL OF HER OWN ACTIONS.
WE NEED TO FIND A WAY TO GET HER OUT OF THERE. AWAY FROM THAT...*WITCH*.
BRING IN THE HARVEST! MAKE THEM *BURN*.
WE'RE TEACHING A VITAL LESSON, AREN'T WE, CHILDREN? THEY WON'T BE SO *QUICK* TO CROSS US NEXT TIME, *WILL* THEY?

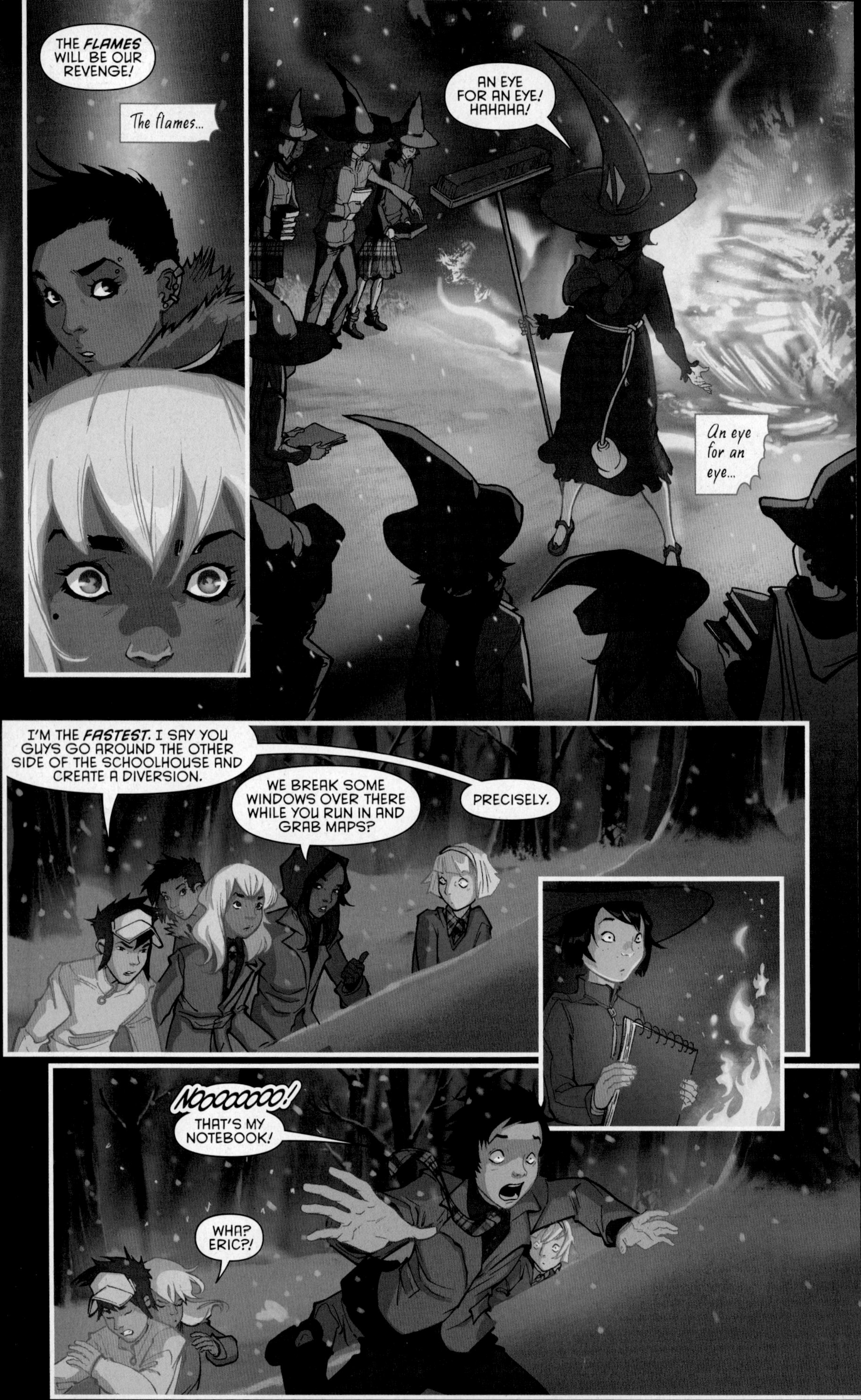
THE FLAMES WILL BE OUR REVENGE!
The flames...
AN EYE FOR AN EYE! HAHAHA!
An eye for an eye...
I'M THE FASTEST. I SAY YOU GUYS GO AROUND THE OTHER SIDE OF THE SCHOOLHOUSE AND CREATE A DIVERSION.
WE BREAK SOME WINDOWS OVER THERE WHILE YOU RUN IN AND GRAB MAPS?
PRECISELY.
NOOOOOOO! THAT'S MY NOTEBOOK!
WHA? ERIC?!

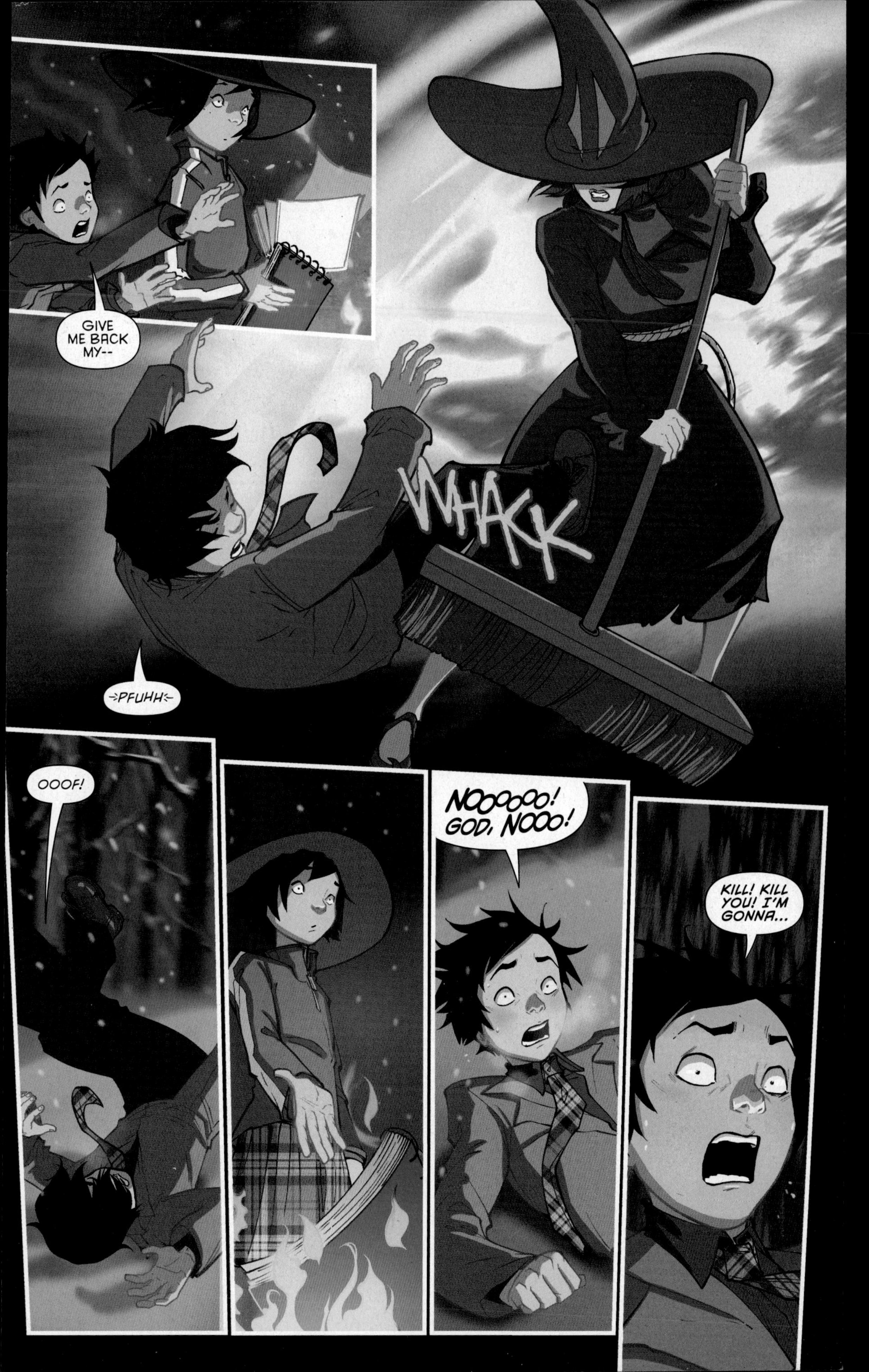
GIVE ME BACK MY--
WHACK
PFUHH
OOOF!
NOOOOOO! GOD, NOOO!
KILL! KILL YOU! I'M GONNA...

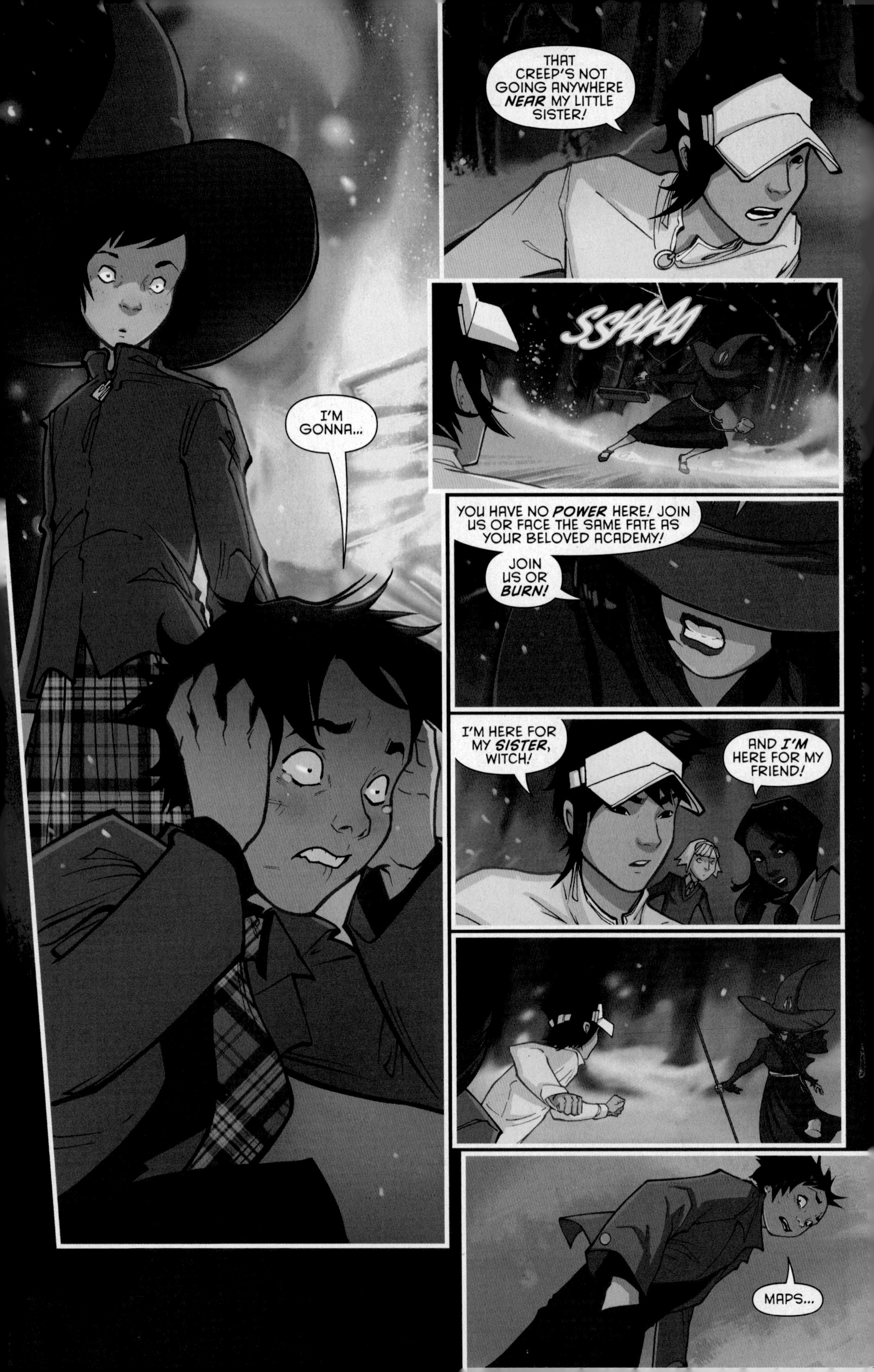
THAT CREEP'S NOT GOING ANYWHERE NEAR MY LITTLE SISTER!
SSHAAA
I'M GONNA...
YOU HAVE NO POWER HERE! JOIN US OR FACE THE SAME FATE AS YOUR BELOVED ACADEMY!
JOIN US OR BURN!
I'M HERE FOR MY SISTER, WITCH!
AND I'M HERE FOR MY FRIEND!
MAPS...

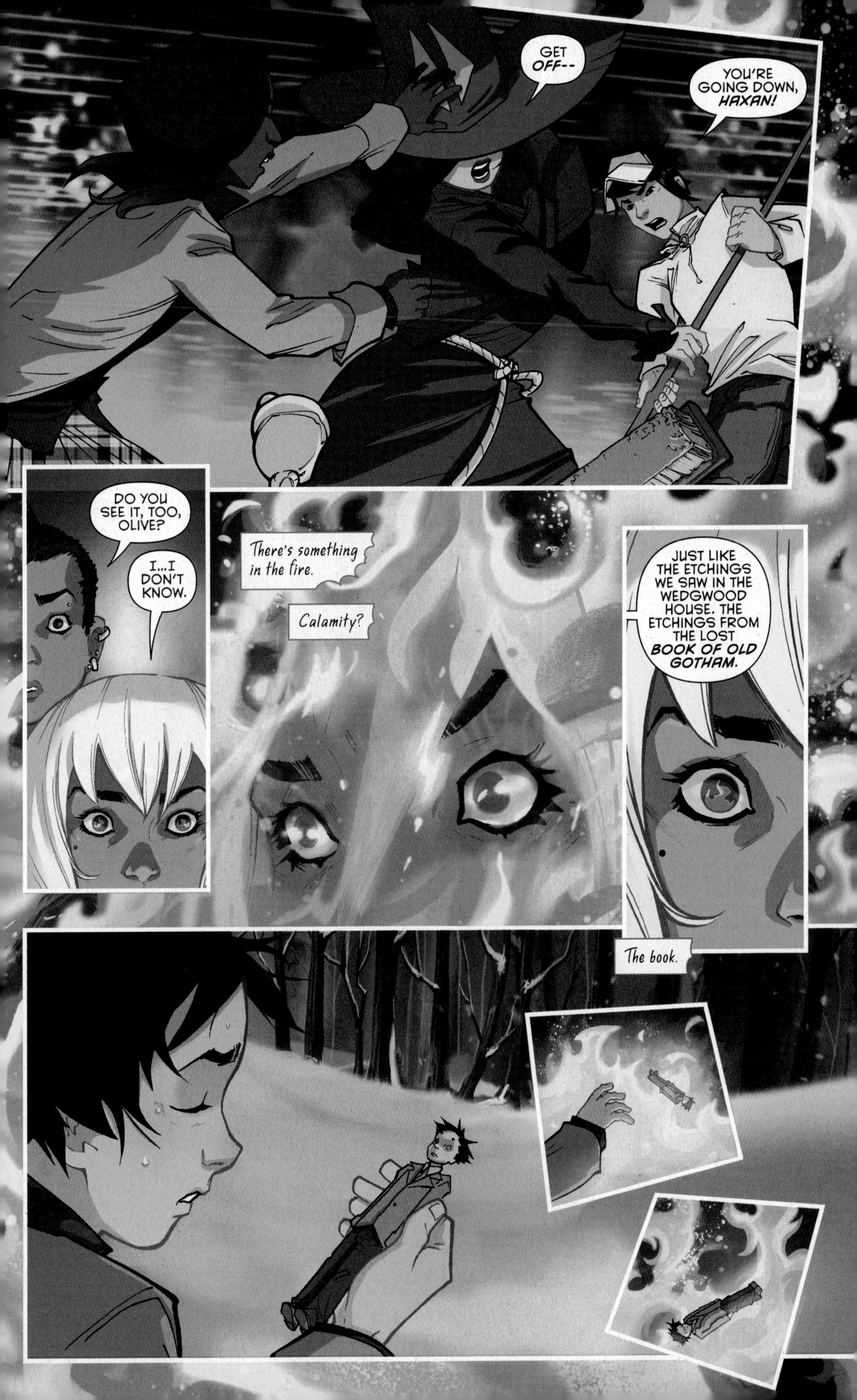
GET OFF--
YOU'RE GOING DOWN, HAXAN!
DO YOU SEE IT, TOO, OLIVE?
I...I DON'T KNOW.
There's something in the fire.
Calamity?
JUST LIKE THE ETCHINGS WE SAW IN THE WEDGWOOD HOUSE. THE ETCHINGS FROM THE LOST BOOK OF OLD GOTHAM.
The book.

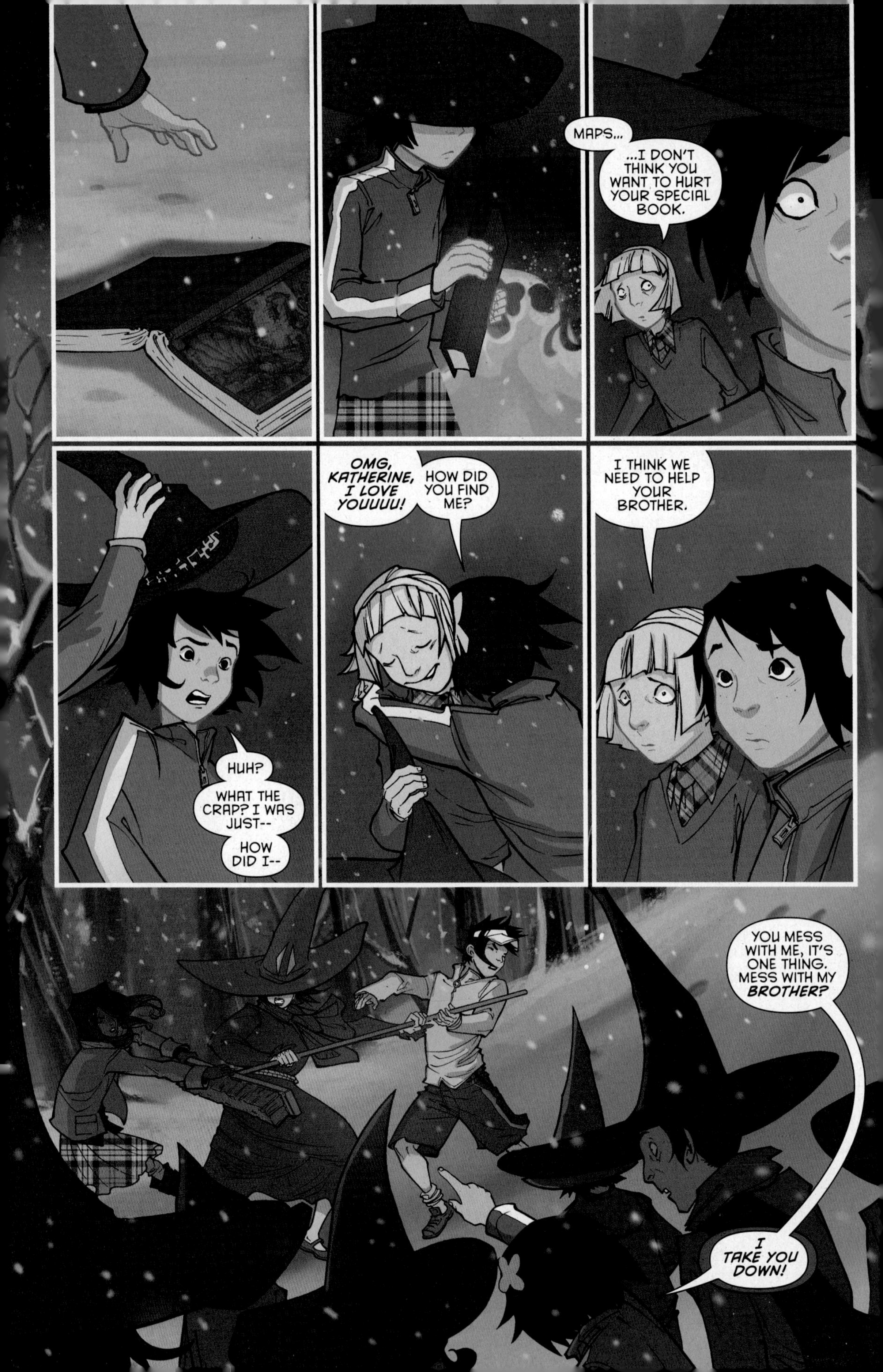
MAPS...
...I DON'T THINK YOU WANT TO HURT YOUR SPECIAL BOOK.
HUH?
WHAT THE CRAP? I WAS JUST--
HOW DID I--
OMG, KATHERINE, I LOVE YOUUUU!
HOW DID YOU FIND ME?
I THINK WE NEED TO HELP YOUR BROTHER.
YOU MESS WITH ME, IT'S ONE THING. MESS WITH MY BROTHER?
I TAKE YOU DOWN!

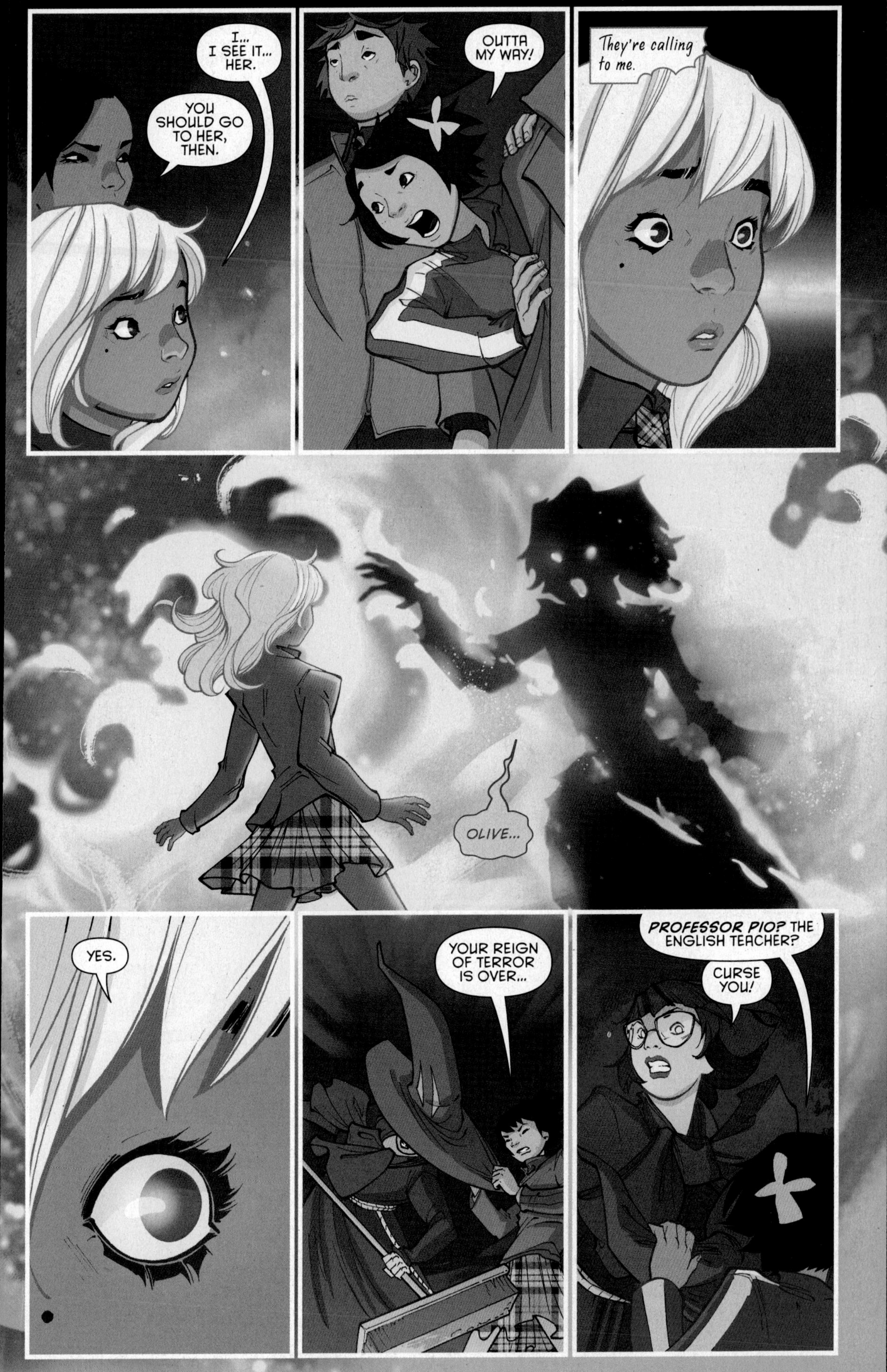
I... I SEE IT... HER.
YOU SHOULD GO TO HER, THEN.
OUTTA MY WAY!
They're calling to me.
OLIVE...
YES.
YOUR REIGN OF TERROR IS OVER...
PROFESSOR PIO? THE ENGLISH TEACHER?
CURSE YOU!

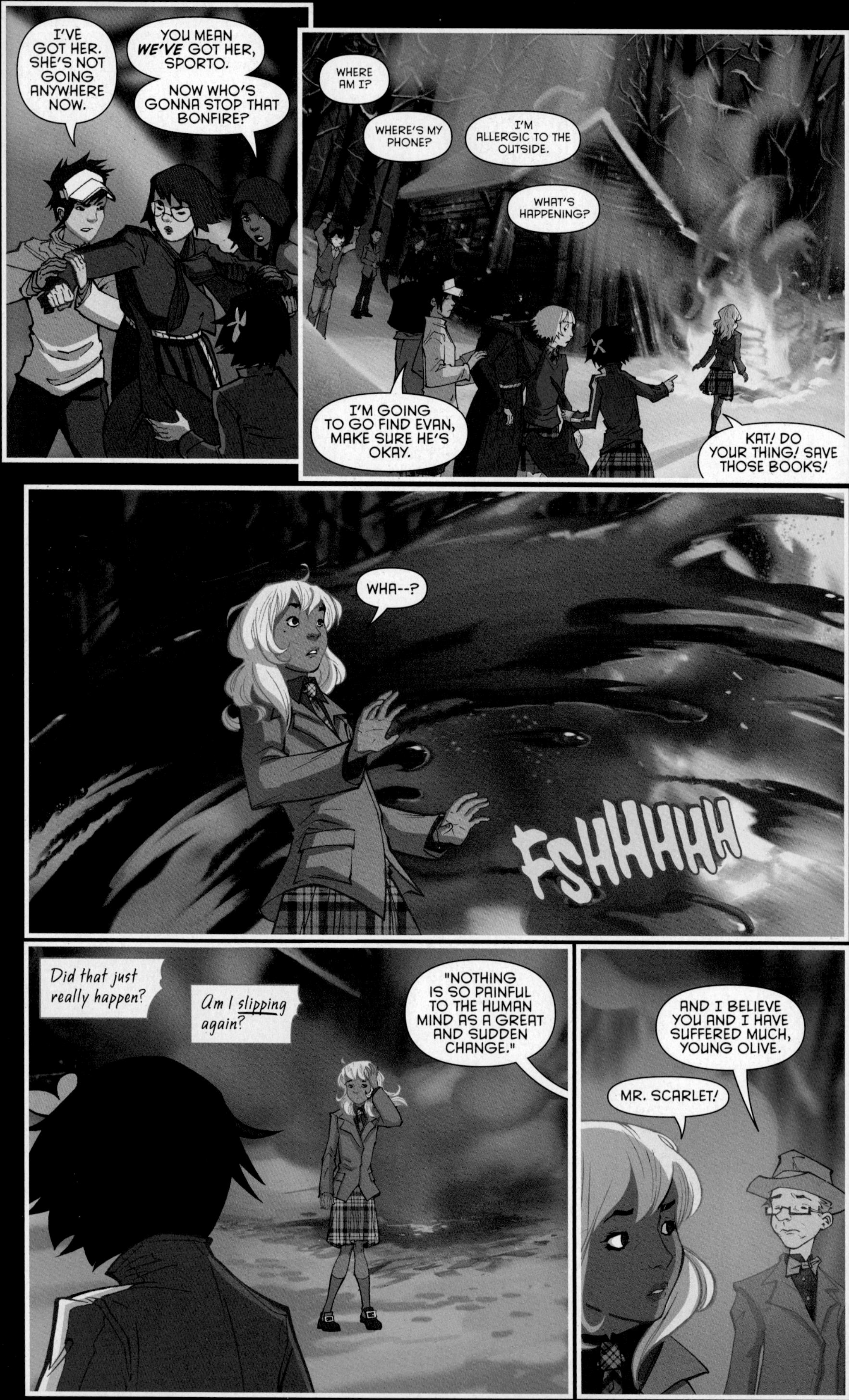

I'VE GOT HER. SHE'S NOT GOING ANYWHERE NOW.
YOU MEAN **WE'VE** GOT HER, SPORTO.
NOW WHO'S GONNA STOP THAT BONFIRE?
WHERE AM I?
WHERE'S MY PHONE?
I'M ALLERGIC TO THE OUTSIDE.
WHAT'S HAPPENING?
I'M GOING TO GO FIND EVAN, MAKE SURE HE'S OKAY.
KAT! DO YOUR THING! SAVE THOSE BOOKS!
WHA--?
FSHHHHH
*Did that just really happen?*
*Am I slipping again?*
"NOTHING IS SO PAINFUL TO THE HUMAN MIND AS A GREAT AND SUDDEN CHANGE."
AND I BELIEVE YOU AND I HAVE SUFFERED MUCH, YOUNG OLIVE.
MR. SCARLET!

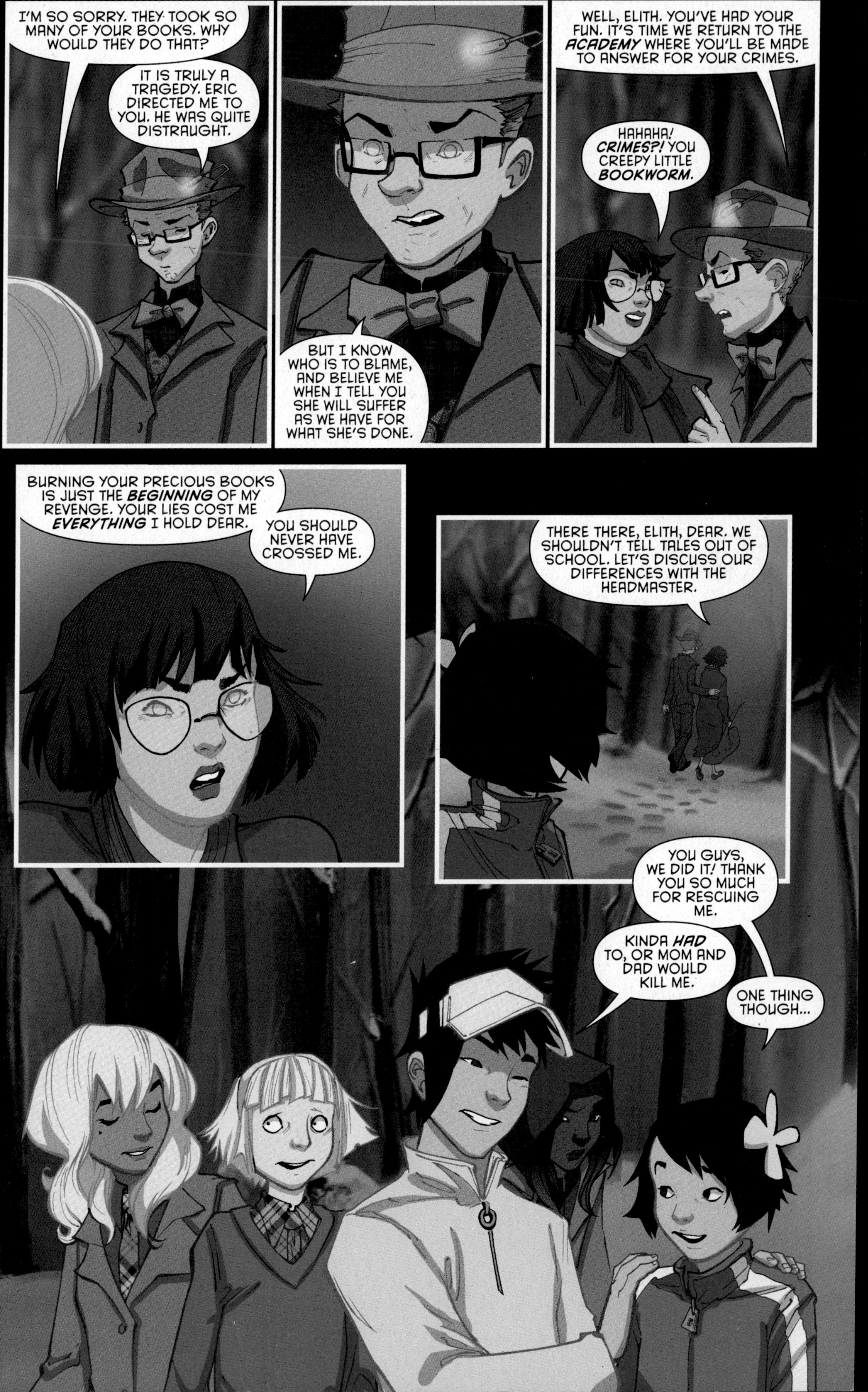
I'M SO SORRY. THEY TOOK SO MANY OF YOUR BOOKS. WHY WOULD THEY DO THAT?
IT IS TRULY A TRAGEDY. ERIC DIRECTED ME TO YOU. HE WAS QUITE DISTRAUGHT.
BUT I KNOW WHO IS TO BLAME, AND BELIEVE ME WHEN I TELL YOU SHE WILL SUFFER AS WE HAVE FOR WHAT SHE'S DONE.
WELL, ELITH. YOU'VE HAD YOUR FUN. IT'S TIME WE RETURN TO THE ACADEMY WHERE YOU'LL BE MADE TO ANSWER FOR YOUR CRIMES.
HAHAHA! CRIMES?! YOU CREEPY LITTLE BOOKWORM.
BURNING YOUR PRECIOUS BOOKS IS JUST THE BEGINNING OF MY REVENGE. YOUR LIES COST ME EVERYTHING I HOLD DEAR.
YOU SHOULD NEVER HAVE CROSSED ME.
THERE THERE, ELITH, DEAR. WE SHOULDN'T TELL TALES OUT OF SCHOOL. LET'S DISCUSS OUR DIFFERENCES WITH THE HEADMASTER.
YOU GUYS, WE DID IT! THANK YOU SO MUCH FOR RESCUING ME.
KINDA HAD TO, OR MOM AND DAD WOULD KILL ME.
ONE THING THOUGH...

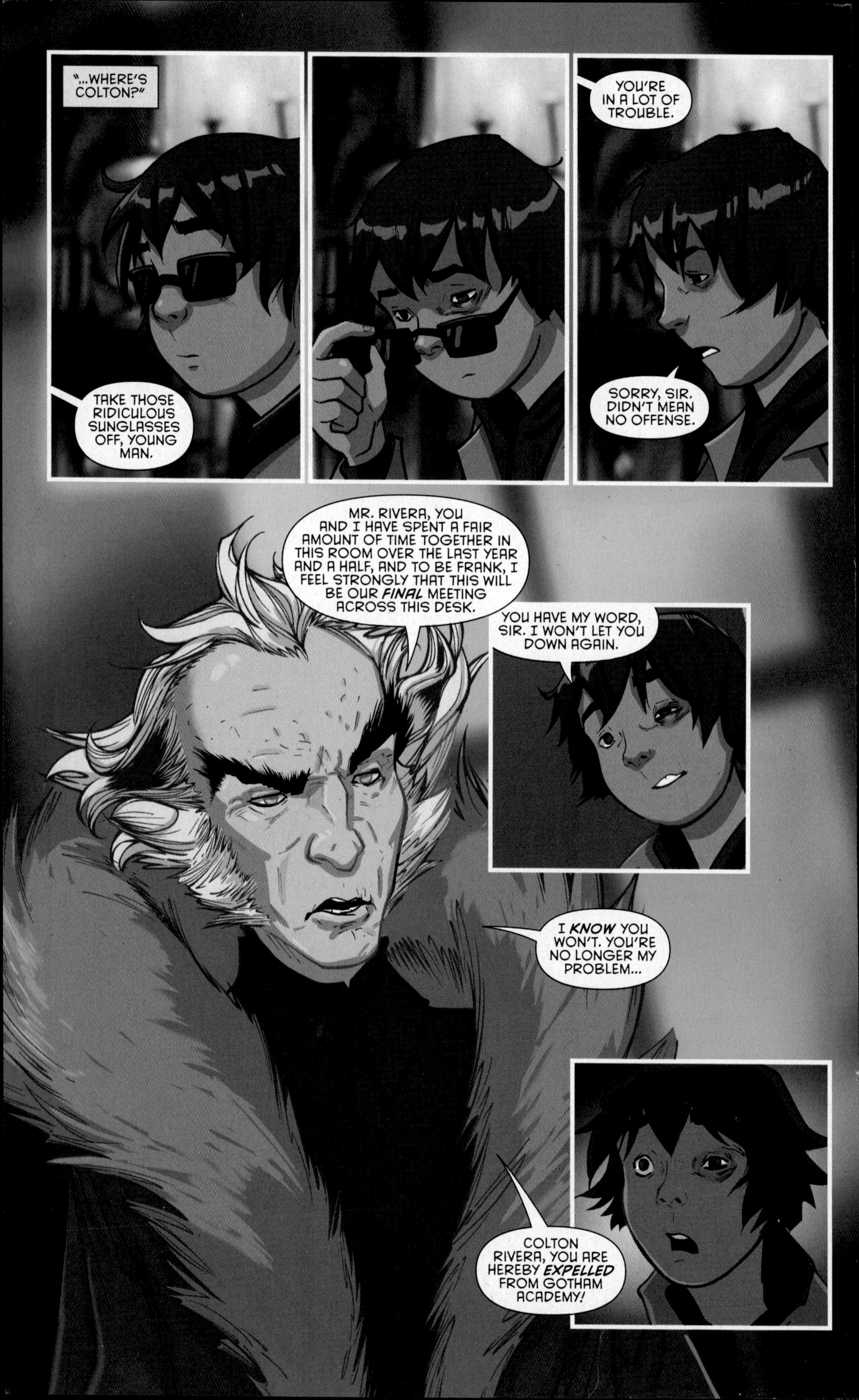
"...WHERE'S COLTON?"
TAKE THOSE RIDICULOUS SUNGLASSES OFF, YOUNG MAN.
YOU'RE IN A LOT OF TROUBLE.
SORRY, SIR. DIDN'T MEAN NO OFFENSE.
MR. RIVERA, YOU AND I HAVE SPENT A FAIR AMOUNT OF TIME TOGETHER IN THIS ROOM OVER THE LAST YEAR AND A HALF, AND TO BE FRANK, I FEEL STRONGLY THAT THIS WILL BE OUR *FINAL* MEETING ACROSS THIS DESK.
YOU HAVE MY WORD, SIR. I WON'T LET YOU DOWN AGAIN.
I ***KNOW*** YOU WON'T. YOU'RE NO LONGER MY PROBLEM...
COLTON RIVERA, YOU ARE HEREBY ***EXPELLED*** FROM GOTHAM ACADEMY!

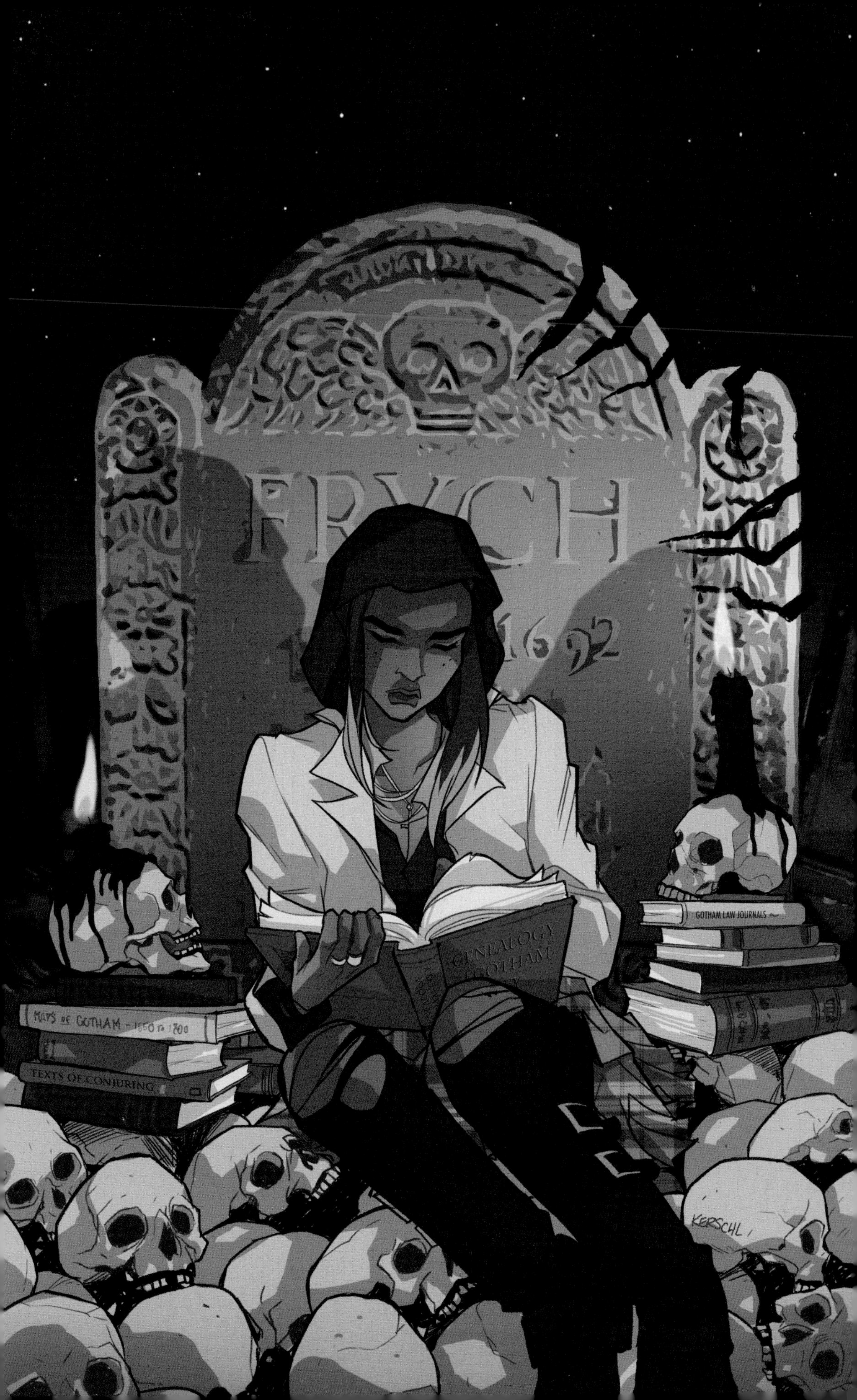
GOTHAM LAW JOURNALS
GENEALOGY
GOTHAM
MAPS OF GOTHAM - 1650 to 1700
TEXTS OF CONJURING
KERSCHL

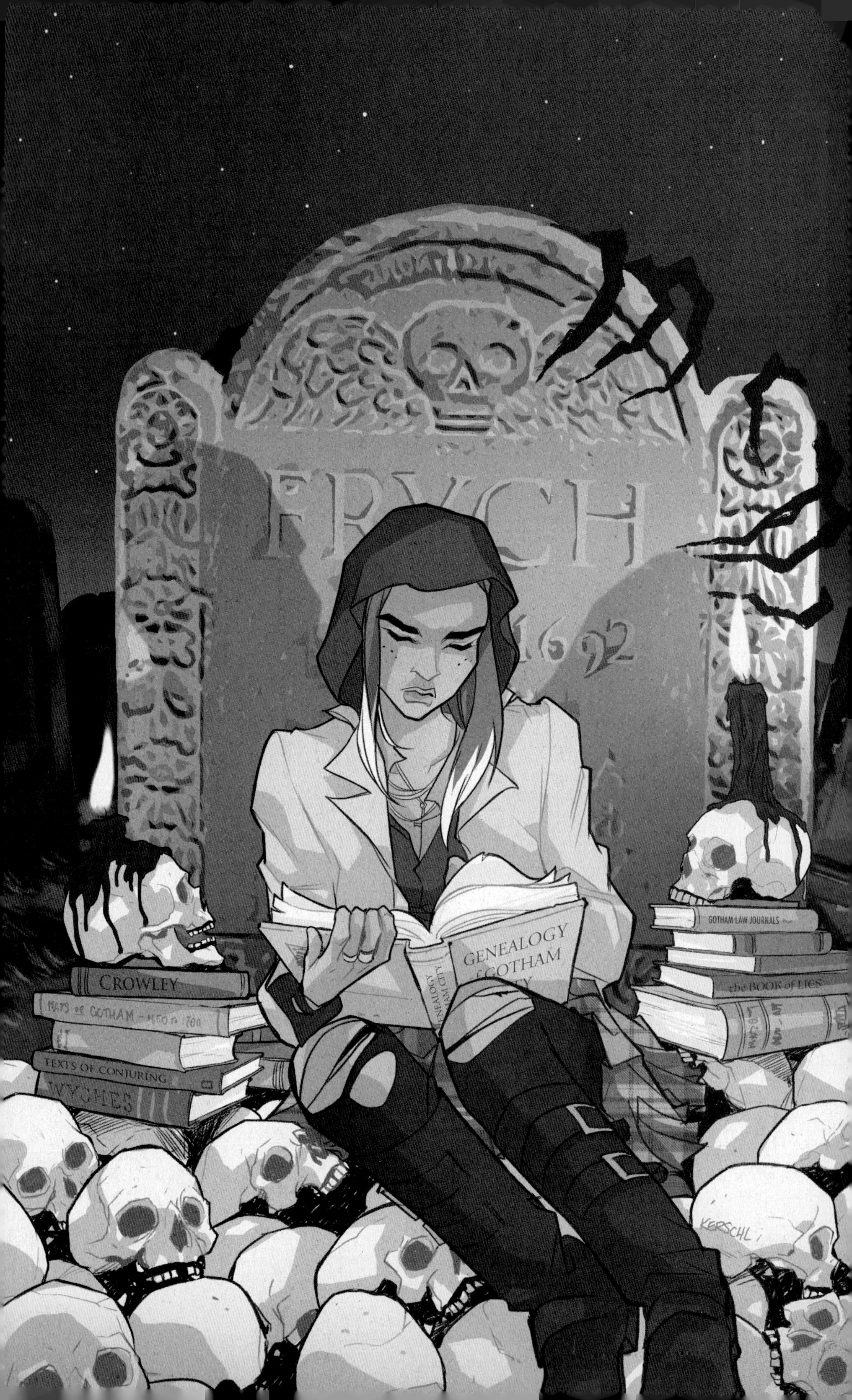
FRYCH
1692
GENEALOGY
GOTHAM
CROWLEY
MAPS OF GOTHAM
TEXTS OF CONJURING
WYCHES
GOTHAM LAW JOURNALS
the BOOK of LIES
KERSCHL

CRAP. TEACHER ALERT. HIDE!

HELLO?

WHERE?! WE'RE *TRAPPED!*

COLTON RIVERA IS PUTTING BACK HIS PRIZED *LOOT?* DOES THAT MEAN WE'RE GETTING CAUGHT? OH MAN, MY MOM'S GONNA MURDER ME.

YOU'LL BE FINE, POMELINE. I'VE GOT AN IDEA, BUT YOU'VE GOTTA TRUST ME.

I CAN HEAR YOU, THIEVES. DO YOU NOT REALIZE WITH WHOM YOU TRIFLE?

WHAT ARE YOU DOING, COLTON? HE'S TOTALLY GONNA--

I SCOOPED THIS FROM THE BAT ATTACK IN THE NORTH HALL LAST SEMESTER. BEEN SAVING IT FOR A RAINY DAY.

JUST STAY HERE UNTIL SILVERSMITH IS GONE, THEN HIGHTAIL IT HOME.

I'LL MAKE YOU *PAY* FOR YOUR...

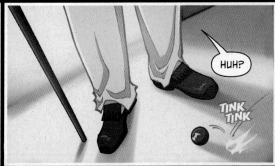

HUH?

TINK TINK

WHAT MANNER OF--

PSSSHYH

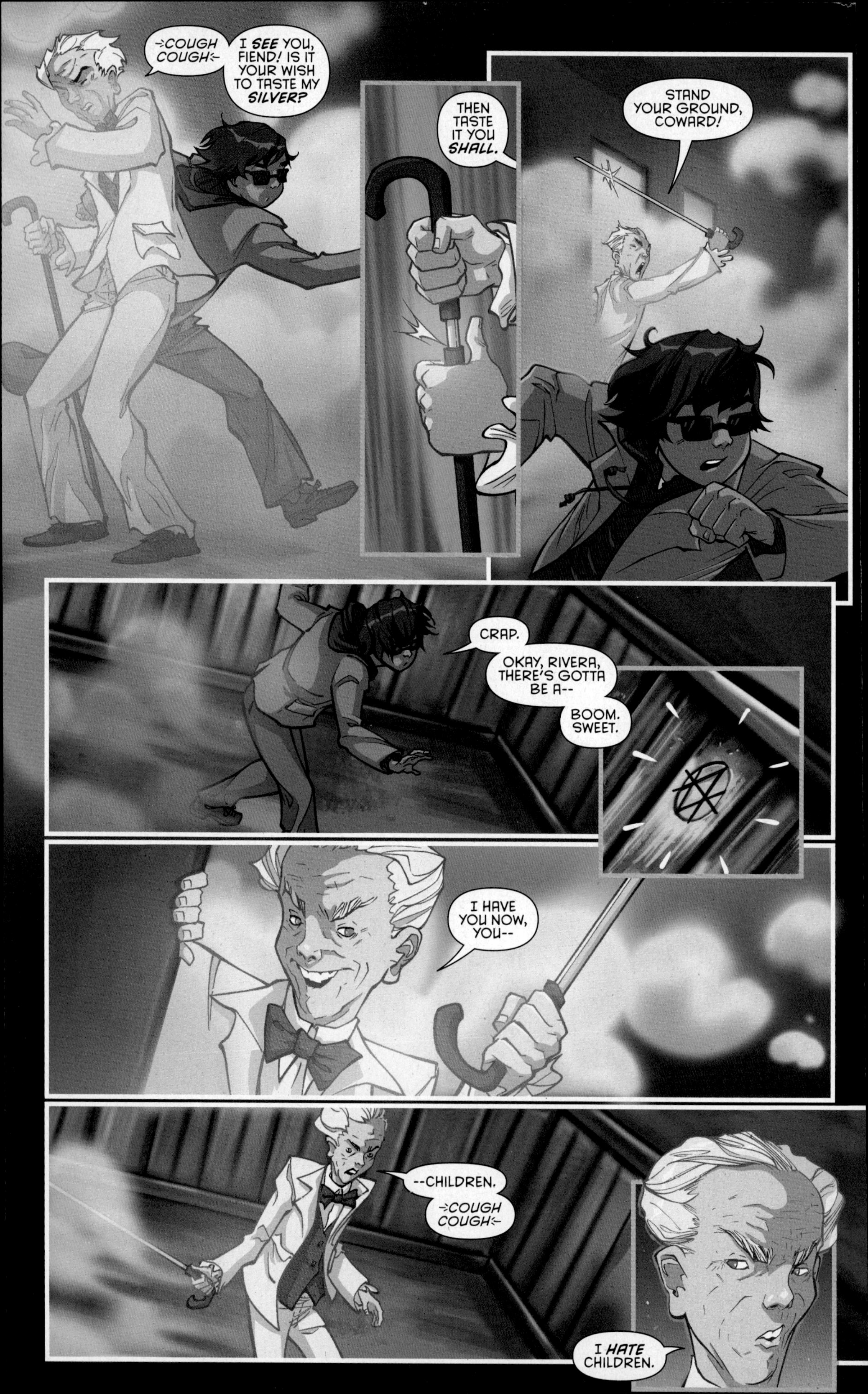

>COUGH COUGH<
I SEE YOU, FIEND! IS IT YOUR WISH TO TASTE MY SILVER?
THEN TASTE IT YOU SHALL.
STAND YOUR GROUND, COWARD!
CRAP.
OKAY, RIVERA, THERE'S GOTTA BE A--
BOOM. SWEET.
I HAVE YOU NOW, YOU--
--CHILDREN.
>COUGH COUGH<
I HATE CHILDREN.

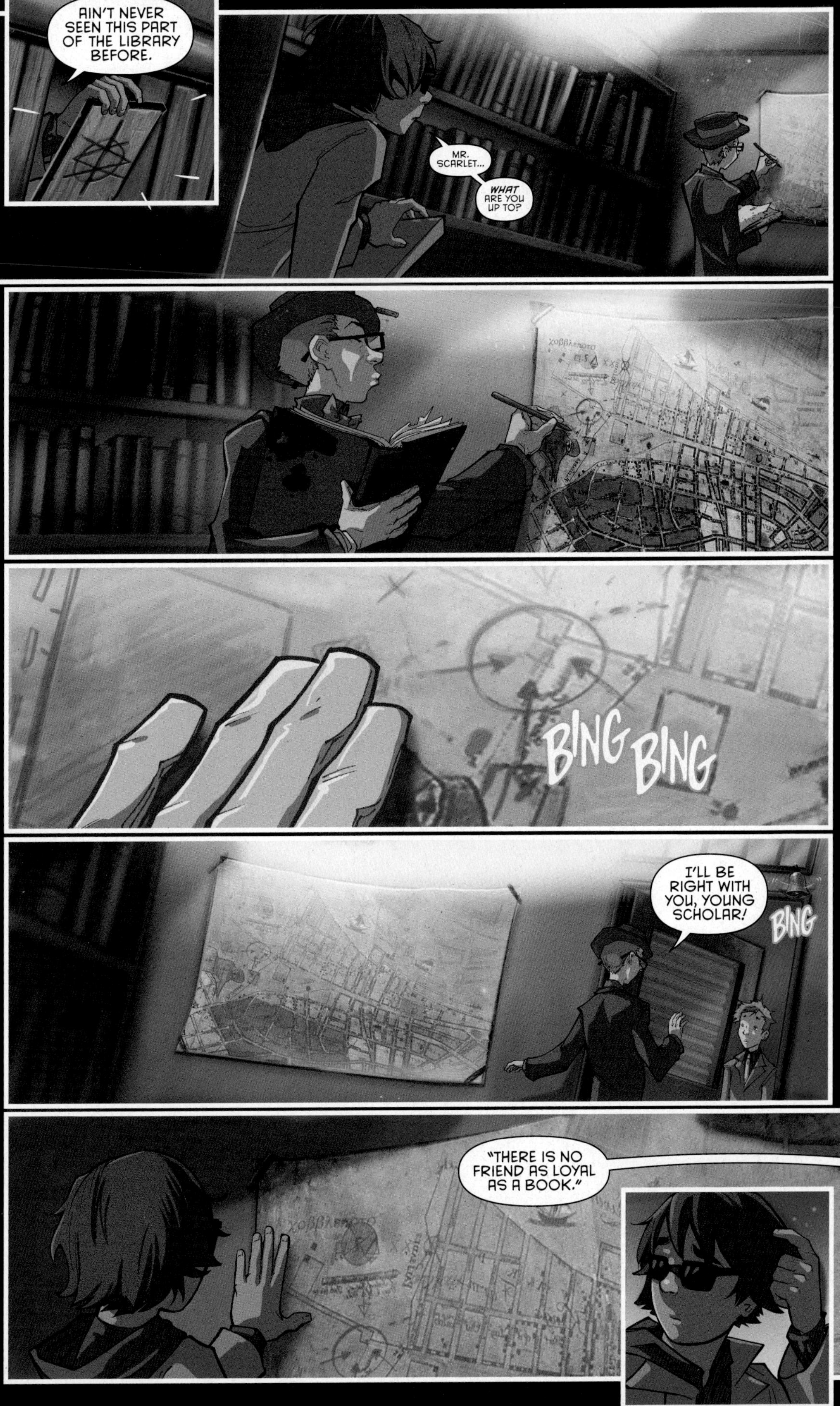
AIN'T NEVER SEEN THIS PART OF THE LIBRARY BEFORE.
MR. SCARLET...
WHAT ARE YOU UP TO?
BING BING
I'LL BE RIGHT WITH YOU, YOUNG SCHOLAR!
BING
"THERE IS NO FRIEND AS LOYAL AS A BOOK."

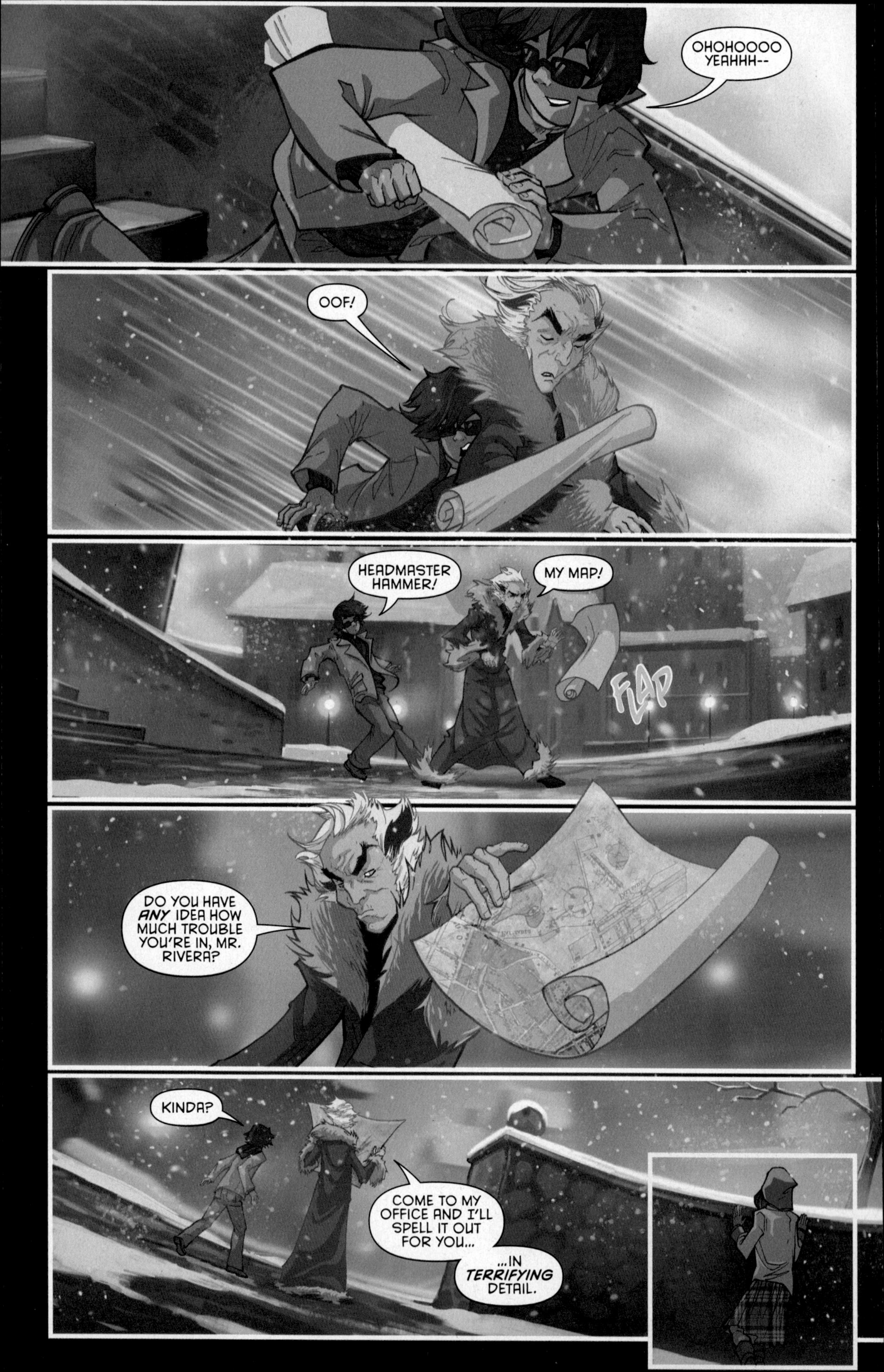
OHOHOOOO YEAHHH--
OOF!
HEADMASTER HAMMER!
MY MAP!
FLAP
DO YOU HAVE ANY IDEA HOW MUCH TROUBLE YOU'RE IN, MR. RIVERA?
KINDA?
COME TO MY OFFICE AND I'LL SPELL IT OUT FOR YOU...
...IN TERRIFYING DETAIL.

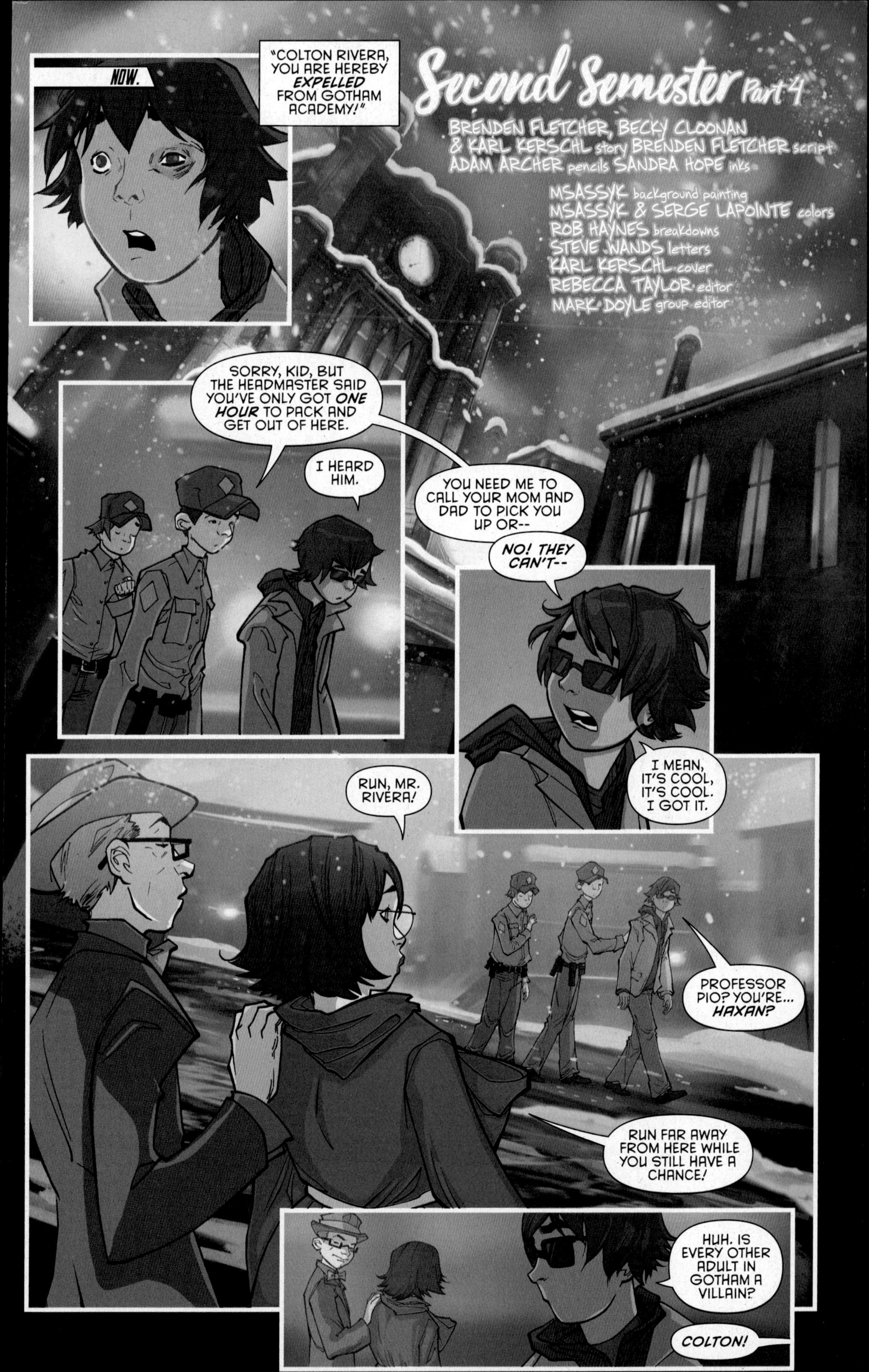
NOW.
"COLTON RIVERA, YOU ARE HEREBY EXPELLED FROM GOTHAM ACADEMY!"
Second Semester Part 4
BRENDEN FLETCHER, BECKY CLOONAN & KARL KERSCHL story BRENDEN FLETCHER script
ADAM ARCHER pencils SANDRA HOPE inks
MSASSYK background painting
MSASSYK & SERGE LAPOINTE colors
ROB HAYNES breakdowns
STEVE WANDS letters
KARL KERSCHL cover
REBECCA TAYLOR editor
MARK DOYLE group editor
SORRY, KID, BUT THE HEADMASTER SAID YOU'VE ONLY GOT ONE HOUR TO PACK AND GET OUT OF HERE.
I HEARD HIM.
YOU NEED ME TO CALL YOUR MOM AND DAD TO PICK YOU UP OR--
NO! THEY CAN'T--
I MEAN, IT'S COOL, IT'S COOL. I GOT IT.
RUN, MR. RIVERA!
PROFESSOR PIO? YOU'RE... HAXAN?
RUN FAR AWAY FROM HERE WHILE YOU STILL HAVE A CHANCE!
HUH. IS EVERY OTHER ADULT IN GOTHAM A VILLAIN?
COLTON!

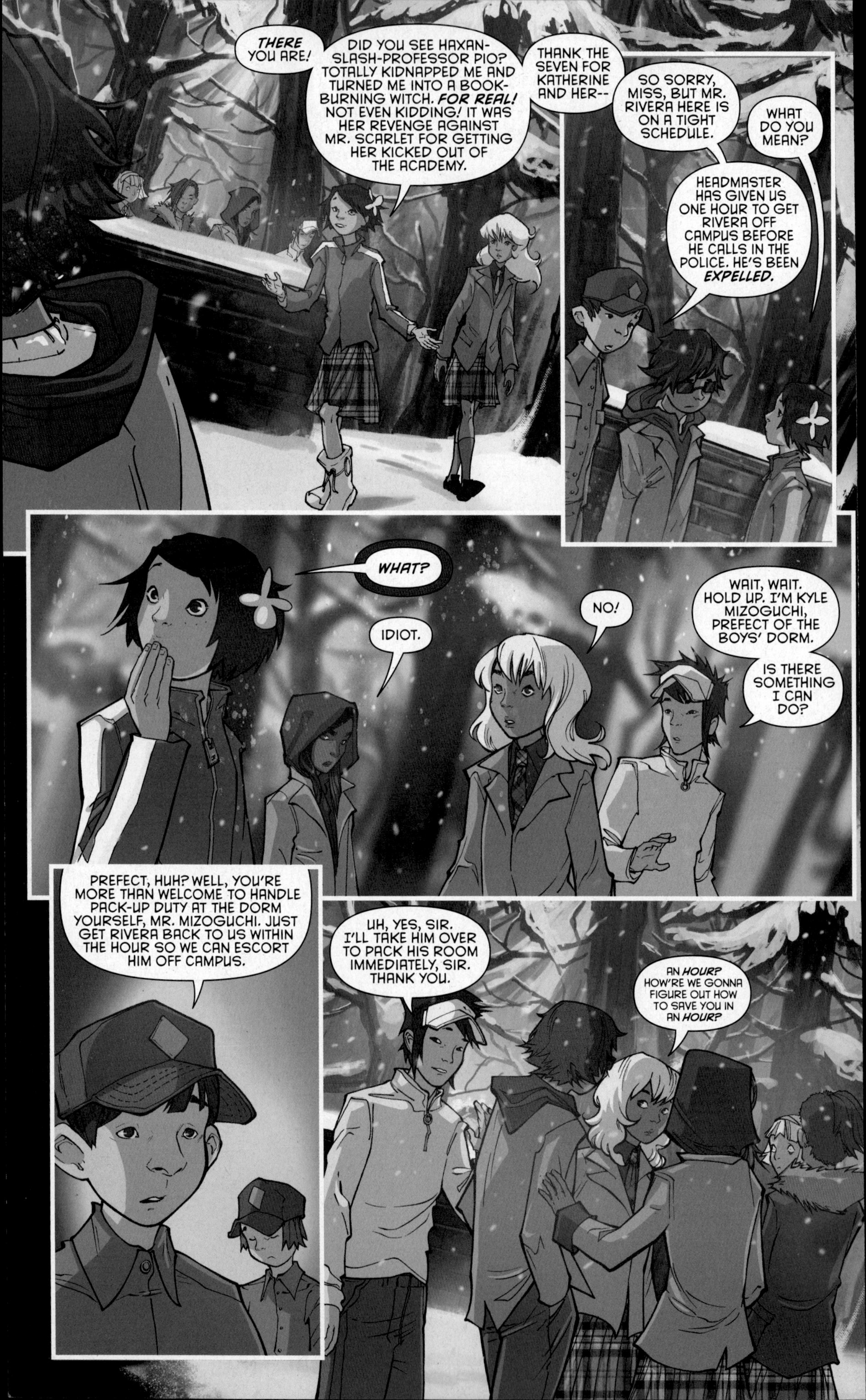
THERE YOU ARE!
DID YOU SEE HAXAN-SLASH-PROFESSOR PIO? TOTALLY KIDNAPPED ME AND TURNED ME INTO A BOOK-BURNING WITCH. FOR REAL! NOT EVEN KIDDING! IT WAS HER REVENGE AGAINST MR. SCARLET FOR GETTING HER KICKED OUT OF THE ACADEMY.
THANK THE SEVEN FOR KATHERINE AND HER--
SO SORRY, MISS, BUT MR. RIVERA HERE IS ON A TIGHT SCHEDULE.
WHAT DO YOU MEAN?
HEADMASTER HAS GIVEN US ONE HOUR TO GET RIVERA OFF CAMPUS BEFORE HE CALLS IN THE POLICE. HE'S BEEN EXPELLED.
WHAT?
IDIOT.
NO!
WAIT, WAIT. HOLD UP. I'M KYLE MIZOGUCHI, PREFECT OF THE BOYS' DORM.
IS THERE SOMETHING I CAN DO?
PREFECT, HUH? WELL, YOU'RE MORE THAN WELCOME TO HANDLE PACK-UP DUTY AT THE DORM YOURSELF, MR. MIZOGUCHI. JUST GET RIVERA BACK TO US WITHIN THE HOUR SO WE CAN ESCORT HIM OFF CAMPUS.
UH, YES, SIR. I'LL TAKE HIM OVER TO PACK HIS ROOM IMMEDIATELY, SIR. THANK YOU.
AN HOUR? HOW'RE WE GONNA FIGURE OUT HOW TO SAVE YOU IN AN HOUR?

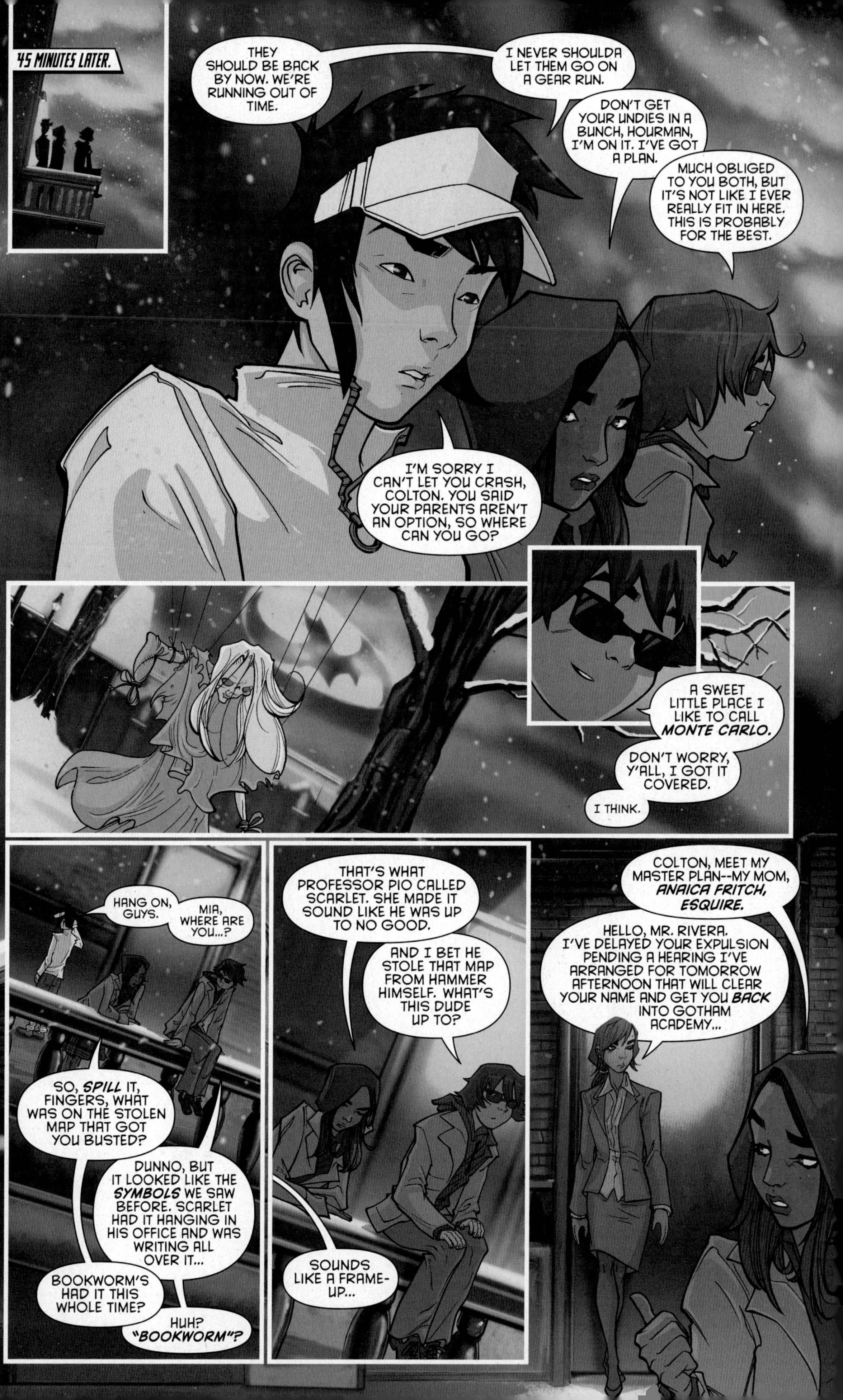
45 MINUTES LATER.
THEY SHOULD BE BACK BY NOW. WE'RE RUNNING OUT OF TIME.
I NEVER SHOULDA LET THEM GO ON A GEAR RUN.
DON'T GET YOUR UNDIES IN A BUNCH, HOURMAN, I'M ON IT. I'VE GOT A PLAN.
MUCH OBLIGED TO YOU BOTH, BUT IT'S NOT LIKE I EVER REALLY FIT IN HERE. THIS IS PROBABLY FOR THE BEST.
I'M SORRY I CAN'T LET YOU CRASH, COLTON. YOU SAID YOUR PARENTS AREN'T AN OPTION, SO WHERE CAN YOU GO?
A SWEET LITTLE PLACE I LIKE TO CALL MONTE CARLO.
DON'T WORRY, Y'ALL, I GOT IT COVERED.
I THINK.
HANG ON, GUYS.
MIA, WHERE ARE YOU...?
SO, SPILL IT, FINGERS, WHAT WAS ON THE STOLEN MAP THAT GOT YOU BUSTED?
DUNNO, BUT IT LOOKED LIKE THE SYMBOLS WE SAW BEFORE. SCARLET HAD IT HANGING IN HIS OFFICE AND WAS WRITING ALL OVER IT...
BOOKWORM'S HAD IT THIS WHOLE TIME?
HUH? "BOOKWORM"?
THAT'S WHAT PROFESSOR PIO CALLED SCARLET. SHE MADE IT SOUND LIKE HE WAS UP TO NO GOOD.
AND I BET HE STOLE THAT MAP FROM HAMMER HIMSELF. WHAT'S THIS DUDE UP TO?
SOUNDS LIKE A FRAME-UP...
COLTON, MEET MY MASTER PLAN--MY MOM, ANAICA FRITCH, ESQUIRE.
HELLO, MR. RIVERA. I'VE DELAYED YOUR EXPULSION PENDING A HEARING I'VE ARRANGED FOR TOMORROW AFTERNOON THAT WILL CLEAR YOUR NAME AND GET YOU BACK INTO GOTHAM ACADEMY...

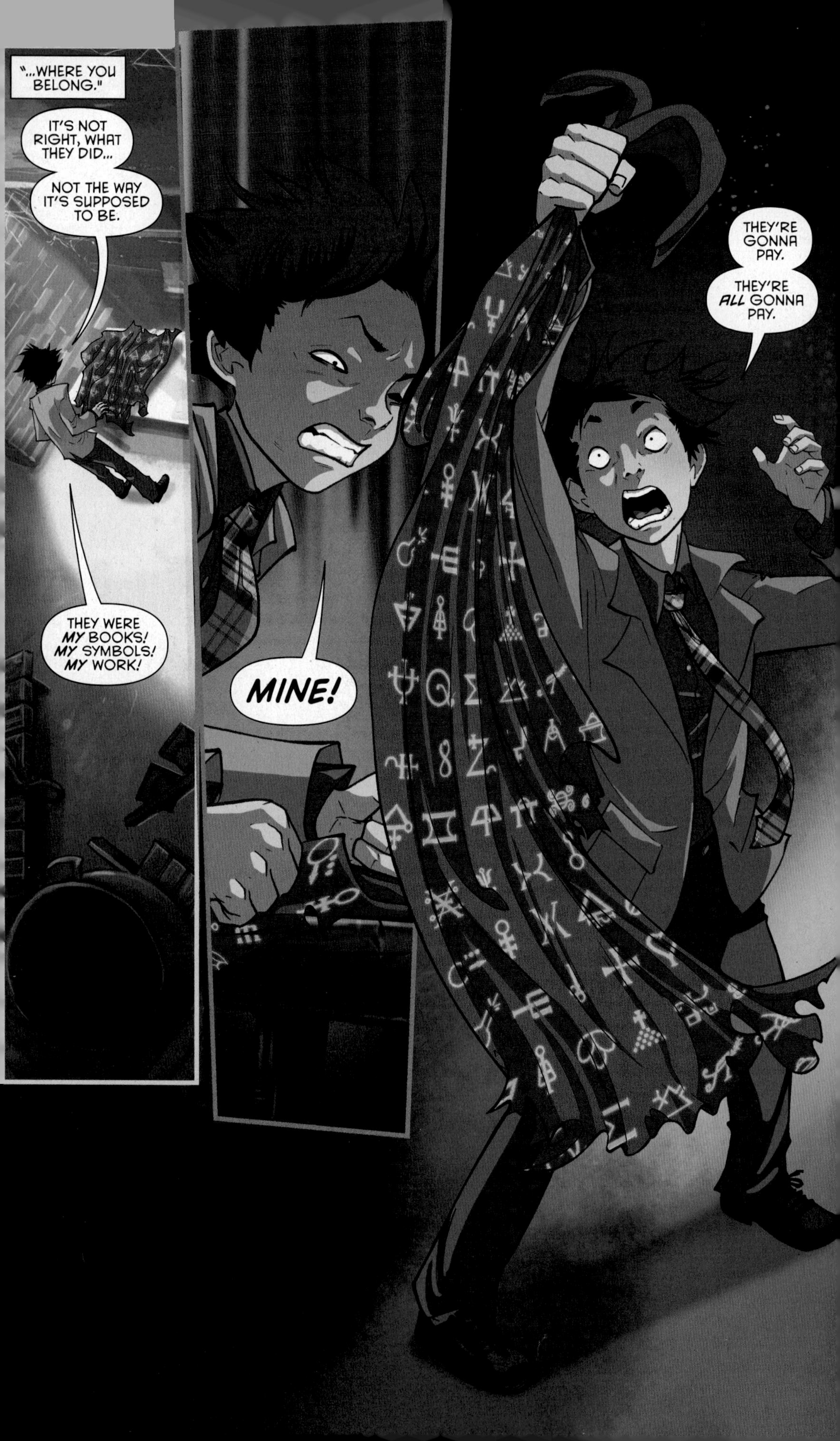
"...WHERE YOU BELONG."
IT'S NOT RIGHT, WHAT THEY DID...
NOT THE WAY IT'S SUPPOSED TO BE.
THEY WERE *MY* BOOKS! *MY* SYMBOLS! *MY* WORK!
*MINE!*
THEY'RE GONNA PAY.
THEY'RE *ALL* GONNA PAY.

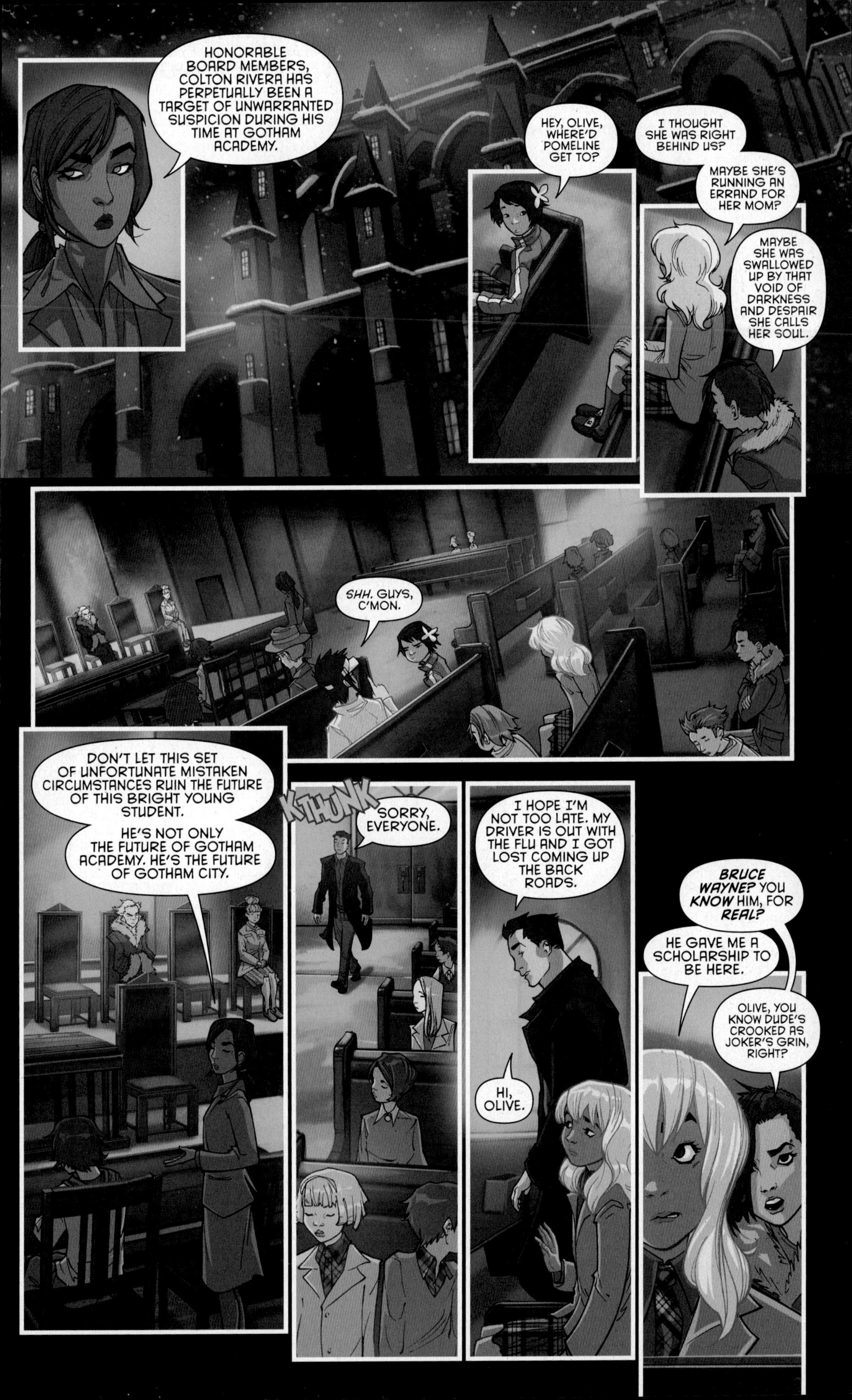
HONORABLE BOARD MEMBERS, COLTON RIVERA HAS PERPETUALLY BEEN A TARGET OF UNWARRANTED SUSPICION DURING HIS TIME AT GOTHAM ACADEMY.
HEY, OLIVE, WHERE'D POMELINE GET TO?
I THOUGHT SHE WAS RIGHT BEHIND US?
MAYBE SHE'S RUNNING AN ERRAND FOR HER MOM?
MAYBE SHE WAS SWALLOWED UP BY THAT VOID OF DARKNESS AND DESPAIR SHE CALLS HER SOUL.
SHH, GUYS, C'MON.
DON'T LET THIS SET OF UNFORTUNATE MISTAKEN CIRCUMSTANCES RUIN THE FUTURE OF THIS BRIGHT YOUNG STUDENT.
HE'S NOT ONLY THE FUTURE OF GOTHAM ACADEMY. HE'S THE FUTURE OF GOTHAM CITY.
KTHUNK
SORRY, EVERYONE.
I HOPE I'M NOT TOO LATE. MY DRIVER IS OUT WITH THE FLU AND I GOT LOST COMING UP THE BACK ROADS.
HI, OLIVE.
BRUCE WAYNE? YOU KNOW HIM, FOR REAL?
HE GAVE ME A SCHOLARSHIP TO BE HERE.
OLIVE, YOU KNOW DUDE'S CROOKED AS JOKER'S GRIN, RIGHT?

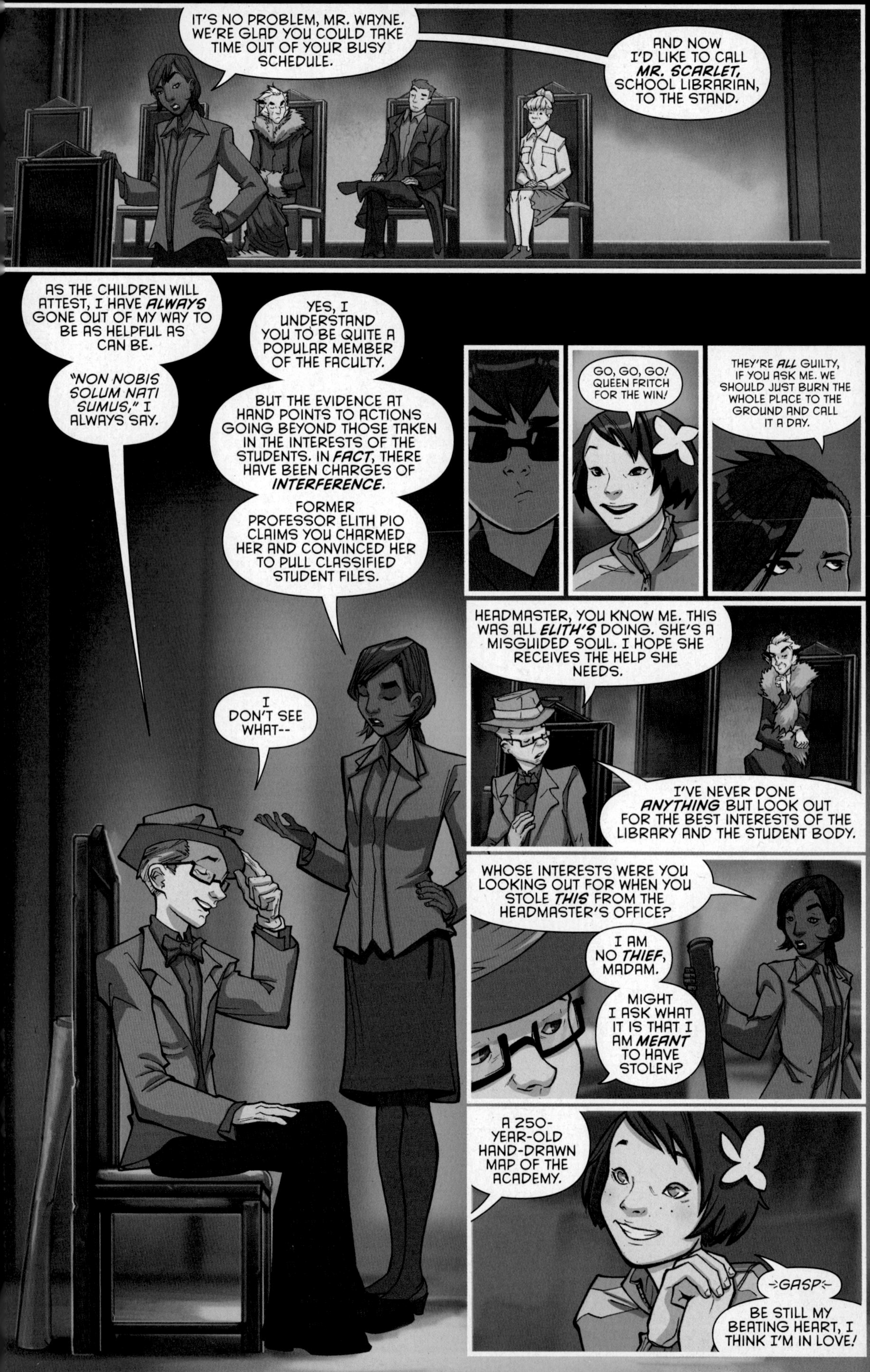
IT'S NO PROBLEM, MR. WAYNE. WE'RE GLAD YOU COULD TAKE TIME OUT OF YOUR BUSY SCHEDULE.
AND NOW I'D LIKE TO CALL ***MR. SCARLET,*** SCHOOL LIBRARIAN, TO THE STAND.
AS THE CHILDREN WILL ATTEST, I HAVE ***ALWAYS*** GONE OUT OF MY WAY TO BE AS HELPFUL AS CAN BE.
*"NON NOBIS SOLUM NATI SUMUS,"* I ALWAYS SAY.
YES, I UNDERSTAND YOU TO BE QUITE A POPULAR MEMBER OF THE FACULTY.
BUT THE EVIDENCE AT HAND POINTS TO ACTIONS GOING BEYOND THOSE TAKEN IN THE INTERESTS OF THE STUDENTS. IN ***FACT***, THERE HAVE BEEN CHARGES OF ***INTERFERENCE***.
FORMER PROFESSOR ELITH PIO CLAIMS YOU CHARMED HER AND CONVINCED HER TO PULL CLASSIFIED STUDENT FILES.
I DON'T SEE WHAT--
GO, GO, GO! QUEEN FRITCH FOR THE WIN!
THEY'RE ***ALL*** GUILTY, IF YOU ASK ME. WE SHOULD JUST BURN THE WHOLE PLACE TO THE GROUND AND CALL IT A DAY.
HEADMASTER, YOU KNOW ME. THIS WAS ALL ***ELITH'S*** DOING. SHE'S A MISGUIDED SOUL. I HOPE SHE RECEIVES THE HELP SHE NEEDS.
I'VE NEVER DONE ***ANYTHING*** BUT LOOK OUT FOR THE BEST INTERESTS OF THE LIBRARY AND THE STUDENT BODY.
WHOSE INTERESTS WERE YOU LOOKING OUT FOR WHEN YOU STOLE ***THIS*** FROM THE HEADMASTER'S OFFICE?
I AM NO ***THIEF***, MADAM.
MIGHT I ASK WHAT IT IS THAT I AM ***MEANT*** TO HAVE STOLEN?
A 250-YEAR-OLD HAND-DRAWN MAP OF THE ACADEMY.
*GASP*
BE STILL MY BEATING HEART, I THINK I'M IN LOVE!

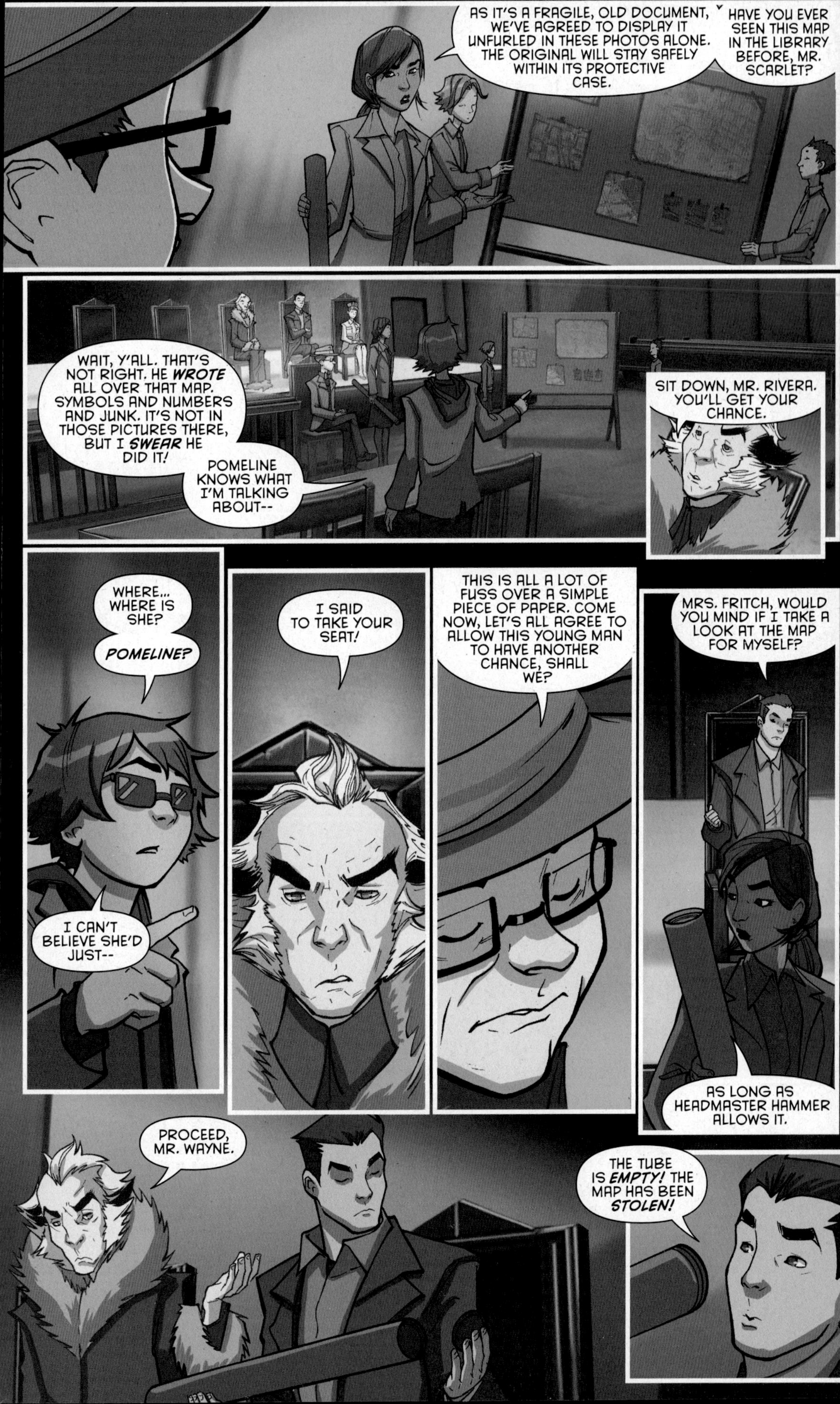

AS IT'S A FRAGILE, OLD DOCUMENT, WE'VE AGREED TO DISPLAY IT UNFURLED IN THESE PHOTOS ALONE. THE ORIGINAL WILL STAY SAFELY WITHIN ITS PROTECTIVE CASE.
HAVE YOU EVER SEEN THIS MAP IN THE LIBRARY BEFORE, MR. SCARLET?
WAIT, Y'ALL. THAT'S NOT RIGHT. HE *WROTE* ALL OVER THAT MAP. SYMBOLS AND NUMBERS AND JUNK. IT'S NOT IN THOSE PICTURES THERE, BUT I *SWEAR* HE DID IT!
POMELINE KNOWS WHAT I'M TALKING ABOUT--
SIT DOWN, MR. RIVERA. YOU'LL GET YOUR CHANCE.
WHERE... WHERE IS SHE?
*POMELINE?*
I CAN'T BELIEVE SHE'D JUST--
I SAID TO TAKE YOUR SEAT!
THIS IS ALL A LOT OF FUSS OVER A SIMPLE PIECE OF PAPER. COME NOW, LET'S ALL AGREE TO ALLOW THIS YOUNG MAN TO HAVE ANOTHER CHANCE, SHALL WE?
MRS. FRITCH, WOULD YOU MIND IF I TAKE A LOOK AT THE MAP FOR MYSELF?
AS LONG AS HEADMASTER HAMMER ALLOWS IT.
PROCEED, MR. WAYNE.
THE TUBE IS *EMPTY!* THE MAP HAS BEEN *STOLEN!*

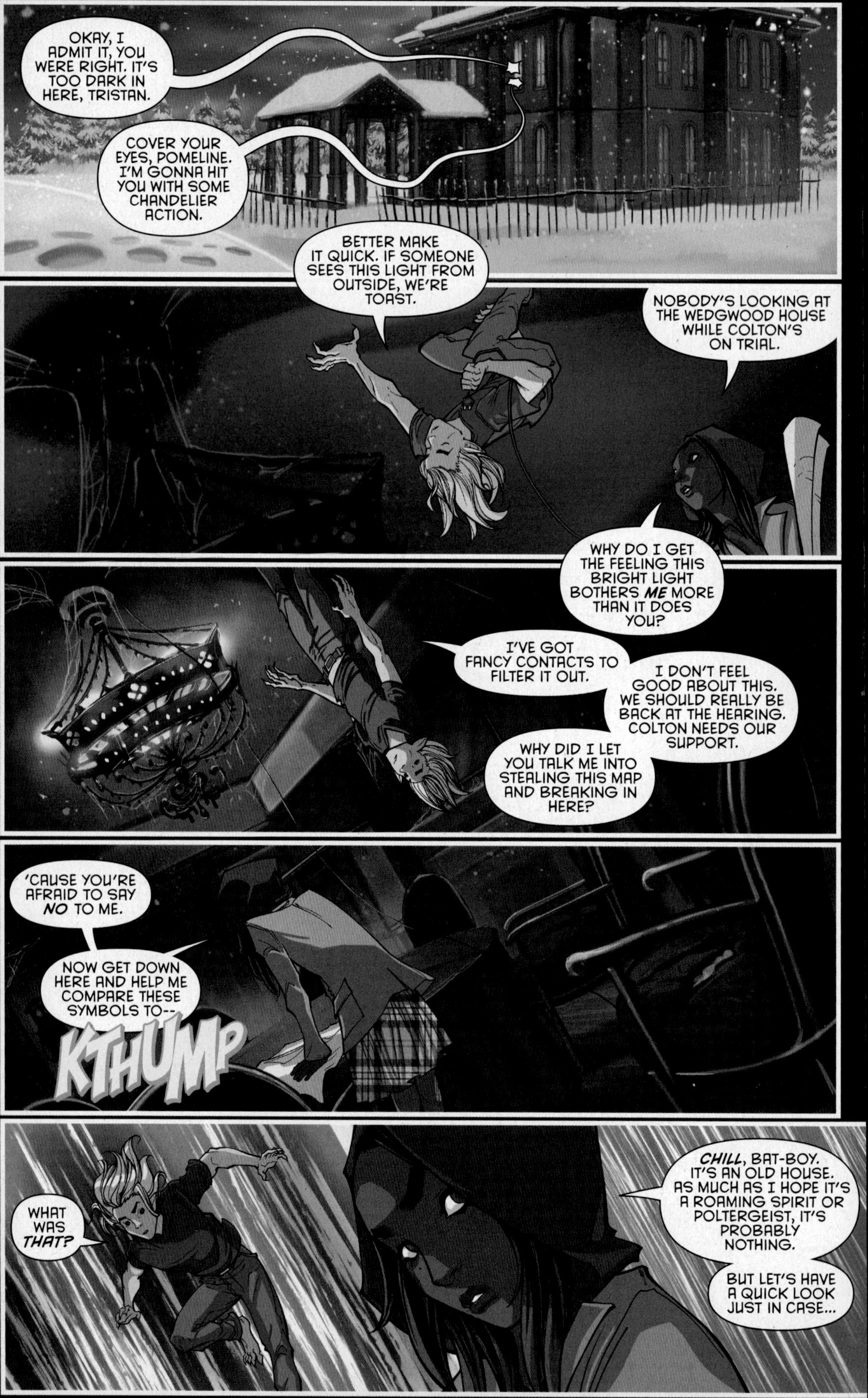
OKAY, I ADMIT IT, YOU WERE RIGHT. IT'S TOO DARK IN HERE, TRISTAN.
COVER YOUR EYES, POMELINE. I'M GONNA HIT YOU WITH SOME CHANDELIER ACTION.
BETTER MAKE IT QUICK. IF SOMEONE SEES THIS LIGHT FROM OUTSIDE, WE'RE TOAST.
NOBODY'S LOOKING AT THE WEDGWOOD HOUSE WHILE COLTON'S ON TRIAL.
WHY DO I GET THE FEELING THIS BRIGHT LIGHT BOTHERS *ME* MORE THAN IT DOES YOU?
I'VE GOT FANCY CONTACTS TO FILTER IT OUT.
I DON'T FEEL GOOD ABOUT THIS. WE SHOULD REALLY BE BACK AT THE HEARING. COLTON NEEDS OUR SUPPORT.
WHY DID I LET YOU TALK ME INTO STEALING THIS MAP AND BREAKING IN HERE?
'CAUSE YOU'RE AFRAID TO SAY *NO* TO ME.
NOW GET DOWN HERE AND HELP ME COMPARE THESE SYMBOLS TO--
KTHUMP
WHAT WAS *THAT?*
*CHILL*, BAT-BOY. IT'S AN OLD HOUSE. AS MUCH AS I HOPE IT'S A ROAMING SPIRIT OR POLTERGEIST, IT'S PROBABLY NOTHING.
BUT LET'S HAVE A QUICK LOOK JUST IN CASE...

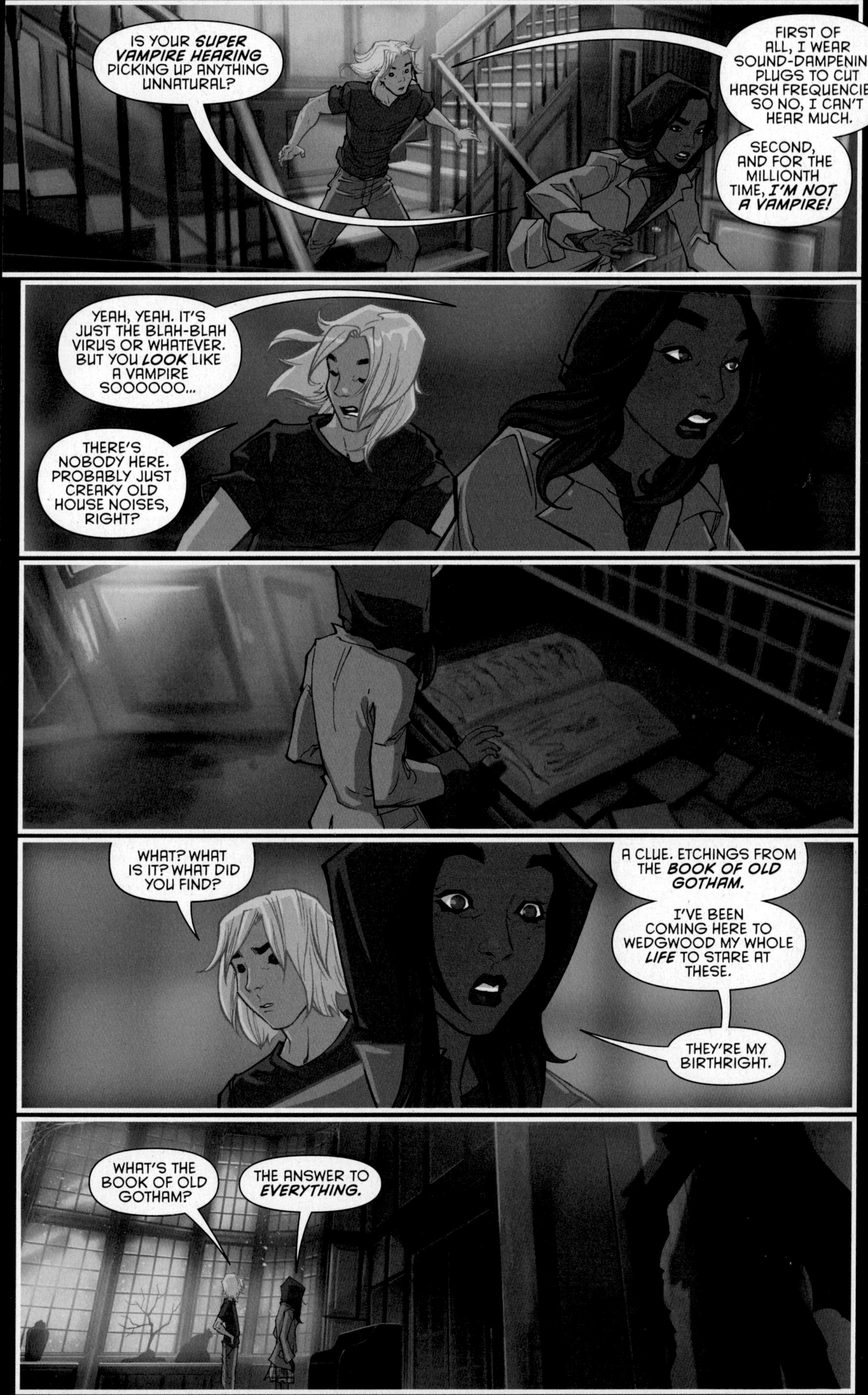
IS YOUR SUPER VAMPIRE HEARING PICKING UP ANYTHING UNNATURAL?
FIRST OF ALL, I WEAR SOUND-DAMPENING PLUGS TO CUT HARSH FREQUENCIES, SO NO, I CAN'T HEAR MUCH.
SECOND, AND FOR THE MILLIONTH TIME, I'M NOT A VAMPIRE!
YEAH, YEAH. IT'S JUST THE BLAH-BLAH VIRUS OR WHATEVER. BUT YOU LOOK LIKE A VAMPIRE SOOOOOO...
THERE'S NOBODY HERE. PROBABLY JUST CREAKY OLD HOUSE NOISES, RIGHT?
WHAT? WHAT IS IT? WHAT DID YOU FIND?
A CLUE. ETCHINGS FROM THE BOOK OF OLD GOTHAM.
I'VE BEEN COMING HERE TO WEDGWOOD MY WHOLE LIFE TO STARE AT THESE.
THEY'RE MY BIRTHRIGHT.
WHAT'S THE BOOK OF OLD GOTHAM?
THE ANSWER TO EVERYTHING.

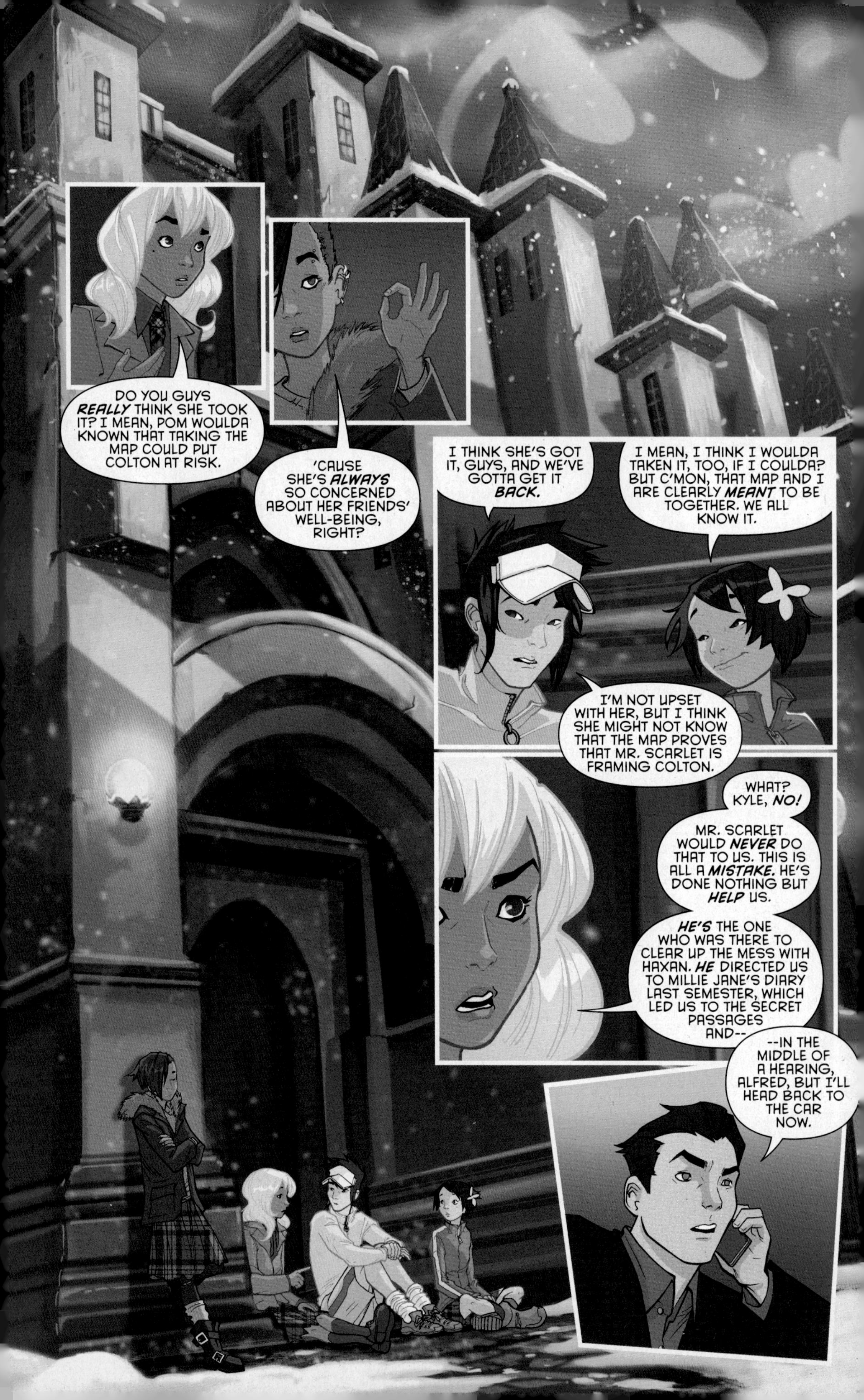
DO YOU GUYS REALLY THINK SHE TOOK IT? I MEAN, POM WOULDA KNOWN THAT TAKING THE MAP COULD PUT COLTON AT RISK.
'CAUSE SHE'S ALWAYS SO CONCERNED ABOUT HER FRIENDS' WELL-BEING, RIGHT?
I THINK SHE'S GOT IT, GUYS, AND WE'VE GOTTA GET IT BACK.
I MEAN, I THINK I WOULDA TAKEN IT, TOO, IF I COULDA? BUT C'MON, THAT MAP AND I ARE CLEARLY MEANT TO BE TOGETHER. WE ALL KNOW IT.
I'M NOT UPSET WITH HER, BUT I THINK SHE MIGHT NOT KNOW THAT THE MAP PROVES THAT MR. SCARLET IS FRAMING COLTON.
WHAT? KYLE, NO!
MR. SCARLET WOULD NEVER DO THAT TO US. THIS IS ALL A MISTAKE. HE'S DONE NOTHING BUT HELP US.
HE'S THE ONE WHO WAS THERE TO CLEAR UP THE MESS WITH HAXAN. HE DIRECTED US TO MILLIE JANE'S DIARY LAST SEMESTER, WHICH LED US TO THE SECRET PASSAGES AND--
--IN THE MIDDLE OF A HEARING, ALFRED, BUT I'LL HEAD BACK TO THE CAR NOW.

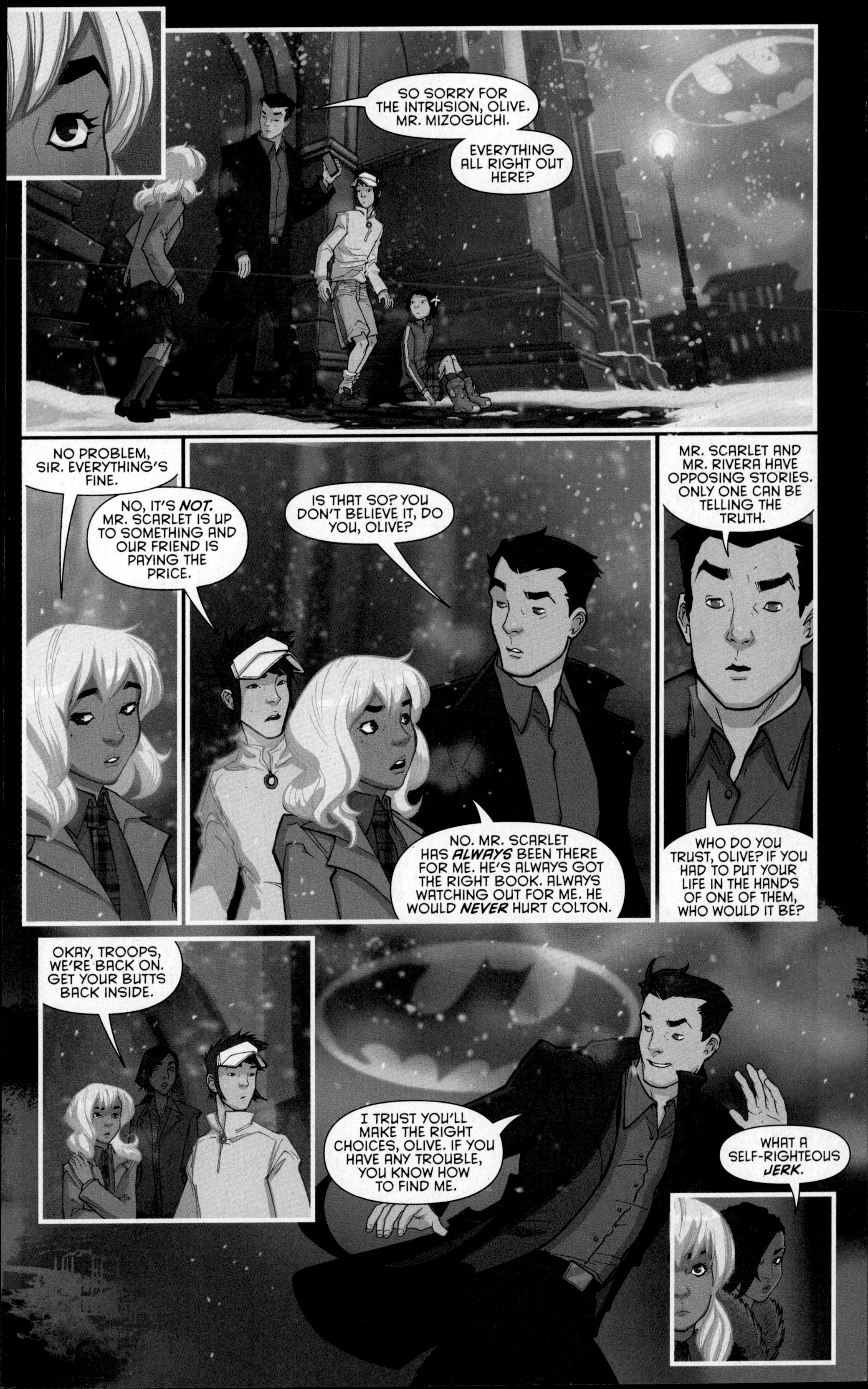
SO SORRY FOR THE INTRUSION, OLIVE. MR. MIZOGUCHI.
EVERYTHING ALL RIGHT OUT HERE?
NO PROBLEM, SIR. EVERYTHING'S FINE.
NO, IT'S **NOT.** MR. SCARLET IS UP TO SOMETHING AND OUR FRIEND IS PAYING THE PRICE.
IS THAT SO? YOU DON'T BELIEVE IT, DO YOU, OLIVE?
NO. MR. SCARLET HAS **ALWAYS** BEEN THERE FOR ME. HE'S ALWAYS GOT THE RIGHT BOOK. ALWAYS WATCHING OUT FOR ME. HE WOULD **NEVER** HURT COLTON.
MR. SCARLET AND MR. RIVERA HAVE OPPOSING STORIES. ONLY ONE CAN BE TELLING THE TRUTH.
WHO DO YOU TRUST, OLIVE? IF YOU HAD TO PUT YOUR LIFE IN THE HANDS OF ONE OF THEM, WHO WOULD IT BE?
OKAY, TROOPS, WE'RE BACK ON. GET YOUR BUTTS BACK INSIDE.
I TRUST YOU'LL MAKE THE RIGHT CHOICES, OLIVE. IF YOU HAVE ANY TROUBLE, YOU KNOW HOW TO FIND ME.
WHAT A SELF-RIGHTEOUS ***JERK.***

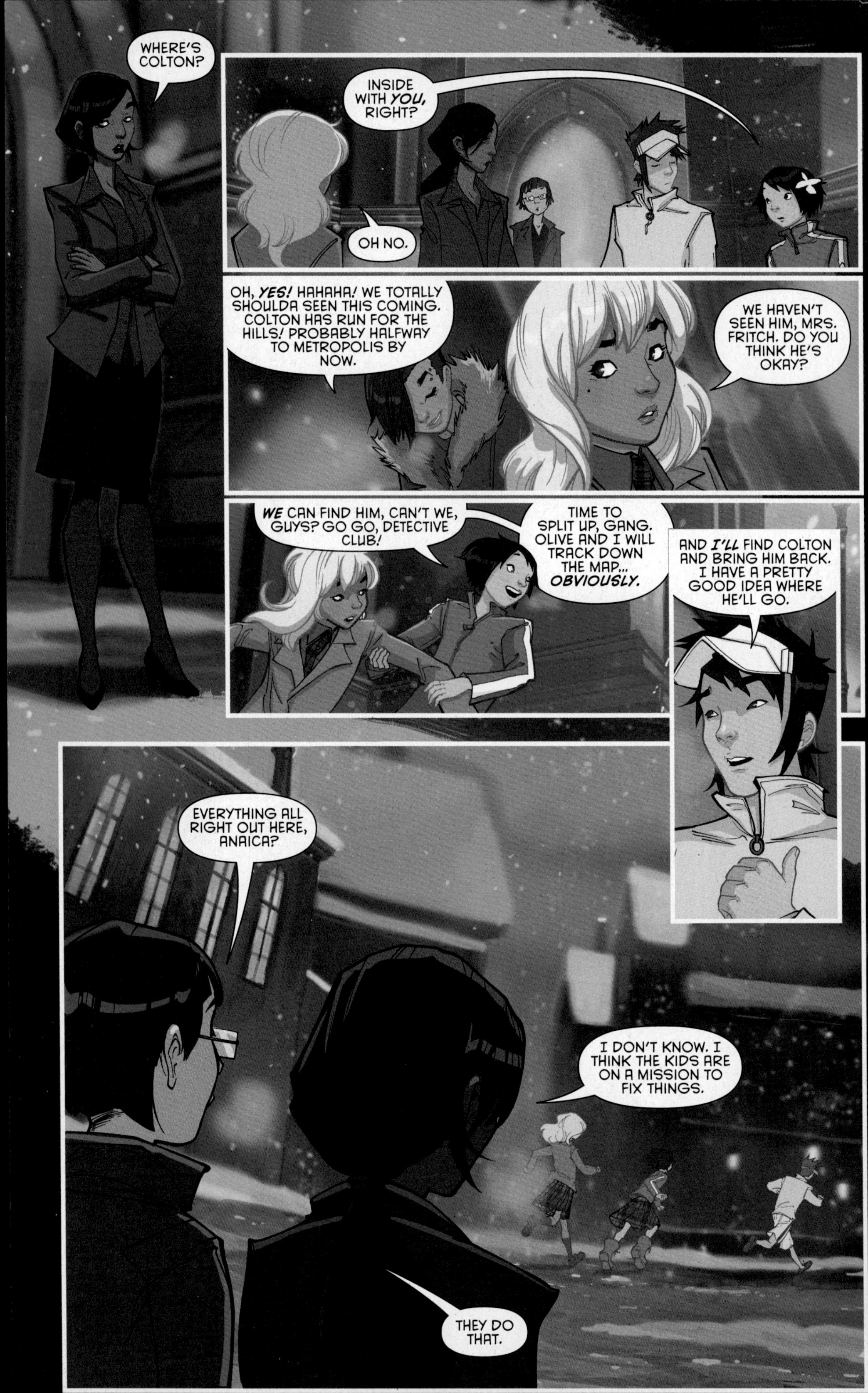
WHERE'S COLTON?
INSIDE WITH *YOU,* RIGHT?
OH NO.
OH, *YES!* HAHAHA! WE TOTALLY SHOULDA SEEN THIS COMING. COLTON HAS RUN FOR THE HILLS! PROBABLY HALFWAY TO METROPOLIS BY NOW.
WE HAVEN'T SEEN HIM, MRS. FRITCH. DO YOU THINK HE'S OKAY?
*WE* CAN FIND HIM, CAN'T WE, GUYS? GO GO, DETECTIVE CLUB!
TIME TO SPLIT UP, GANG. OLIVE AND I WILL TRACK DOWN THE MAP... ***OBVIOUSLY.***
AND *I'LL* FIND COLTON AND BRING HIM BACK. I HAVE A PRETTY GOOD IDEA WHERE HE'LL GO.
EVERYTHING ALL RIGHT OUT HERE, ANAICA?
I DON'T KNOW. I THINK THE KIDS ARE ON A MISSION TO FIX THINGS.
THEY DO THAT.

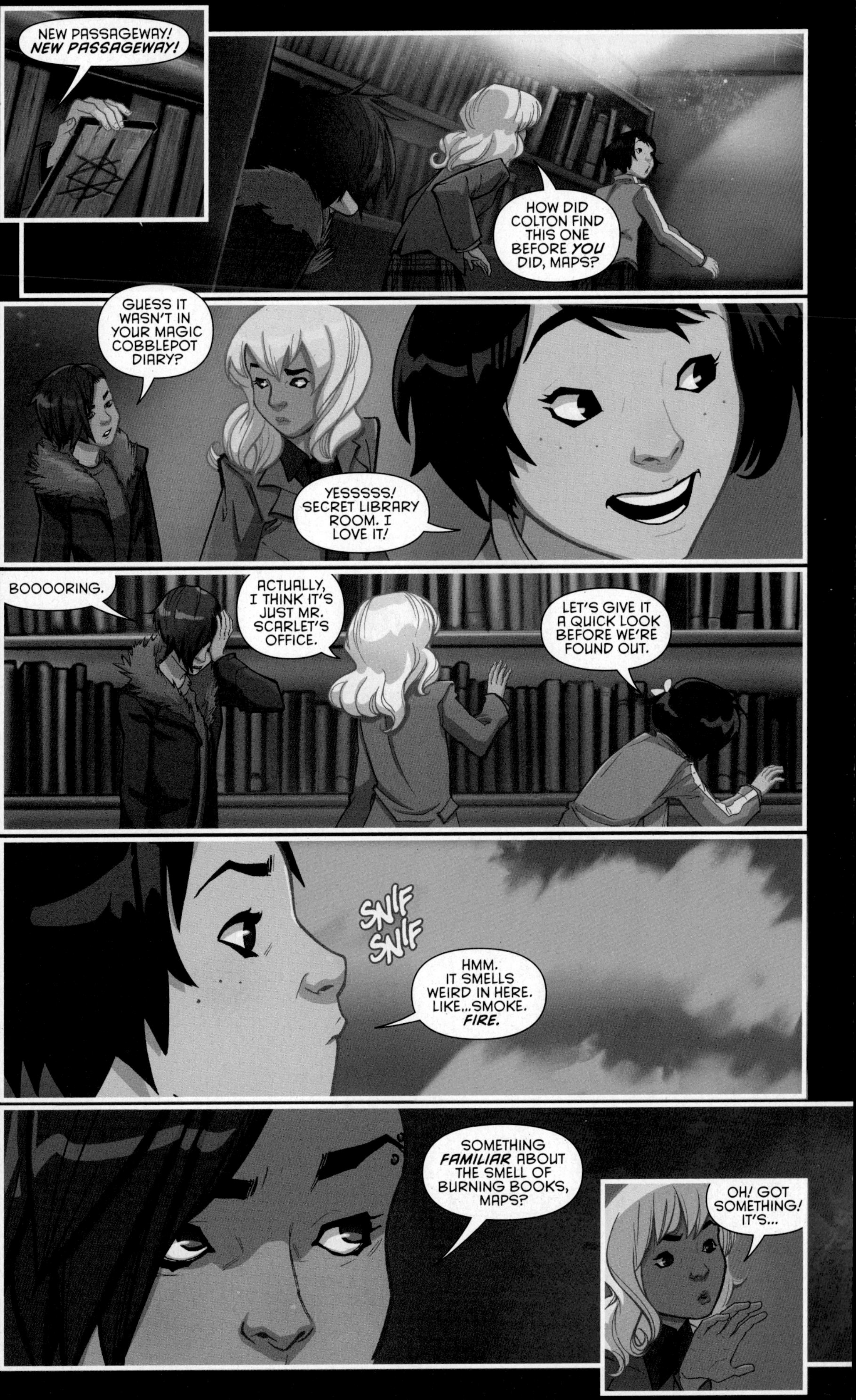
NEW PASSAGEWAY! *NEW PASSAGEWAY!*
HOW DID COLTON FIND THIS ONE BEFORE *YOU* DID, MAPS?
GUESS IT WASN'T IN YOUR MAGIC COBBLEPOT DIARY?
YESSSSS! SECRET LIBRARY ROOM. I LOVE IT!
BOOOORING.
ACTUALLY, I THINK IT'S JUST MR. SCARLET'S OFFICE.
LET'S GIVE IT A QUICK LOOK BEFORE WE'RE FOUND OUT.
SNIF SNIF
HMM. IT SMELLS WEIRD IN HERE. LIKE...SMOKE. *FIRE.*
SOMETHING *FAMILIAR* ABOUT THE SMELL OF BURNING BOOKS, MAPS?
OH! GOT SOMETHING! IT'S...

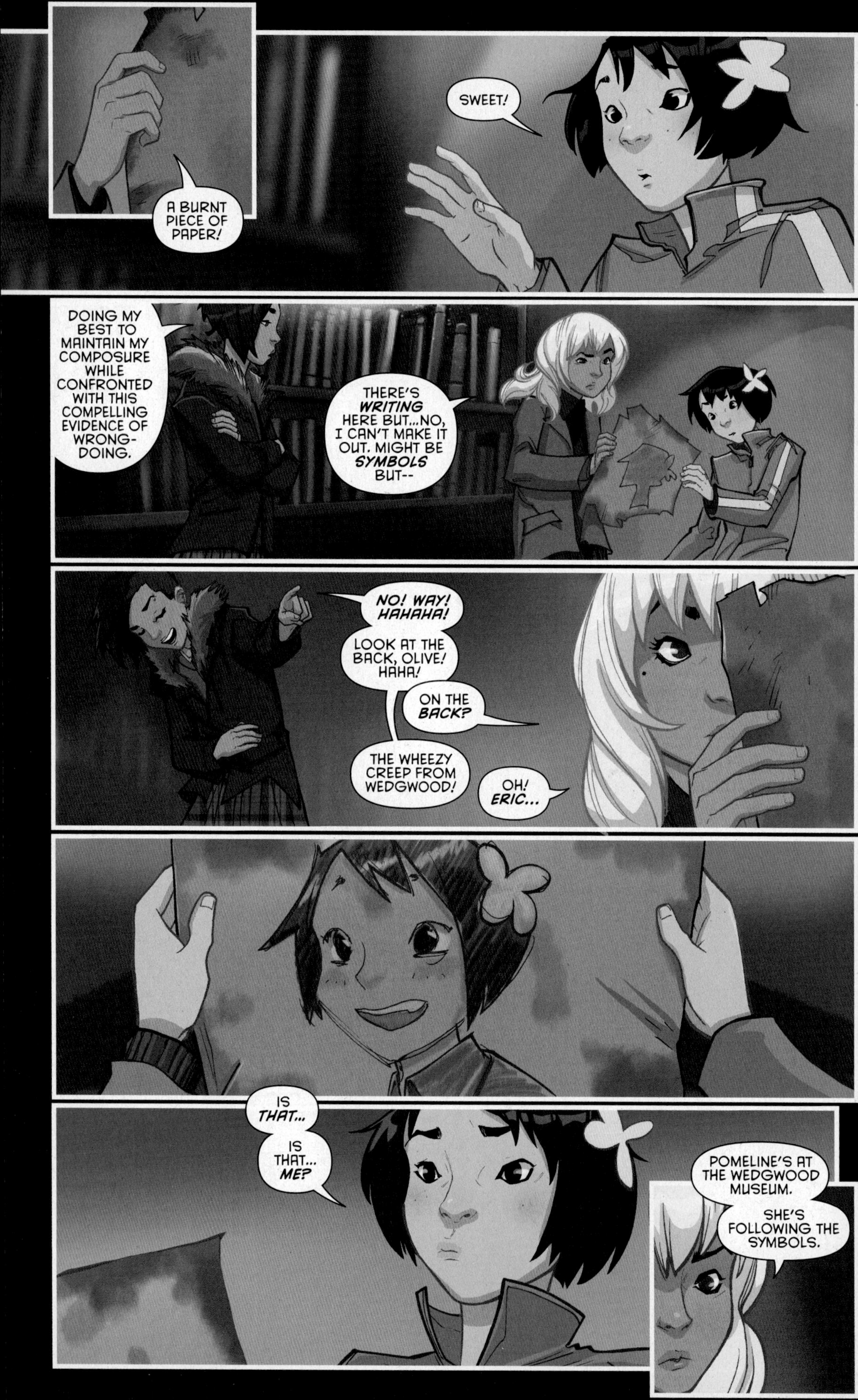
SWEET!
A BURNT PIECE OF PAPER!
DOING MY BEST TO MAINTAIN MY COMPOSURE WHILE CONFRONTED WITH THIS COMPELLING EVIDENCE OF WRONG-DOING.
THERE'S *WRITING* HERE BUT...NO, I CAN'T MAKE IT OUT. MIGHT BE *SYMBOLS* BUT--
*NO! WAY! HAHAHA!*
LOOK AT THE BACK, OLIVE! HAHA!
ON THE *BACK?*
THE WHEEZY CREEP FROM WEDGWOOD!
OH! *ERIC...*
IS *THAT...*
IS THAT... *ME?*
POMELINE'S AT THE WEDGWOOD MUSEUM.
SHE'S FOLLOWING THE SYMBOLS.

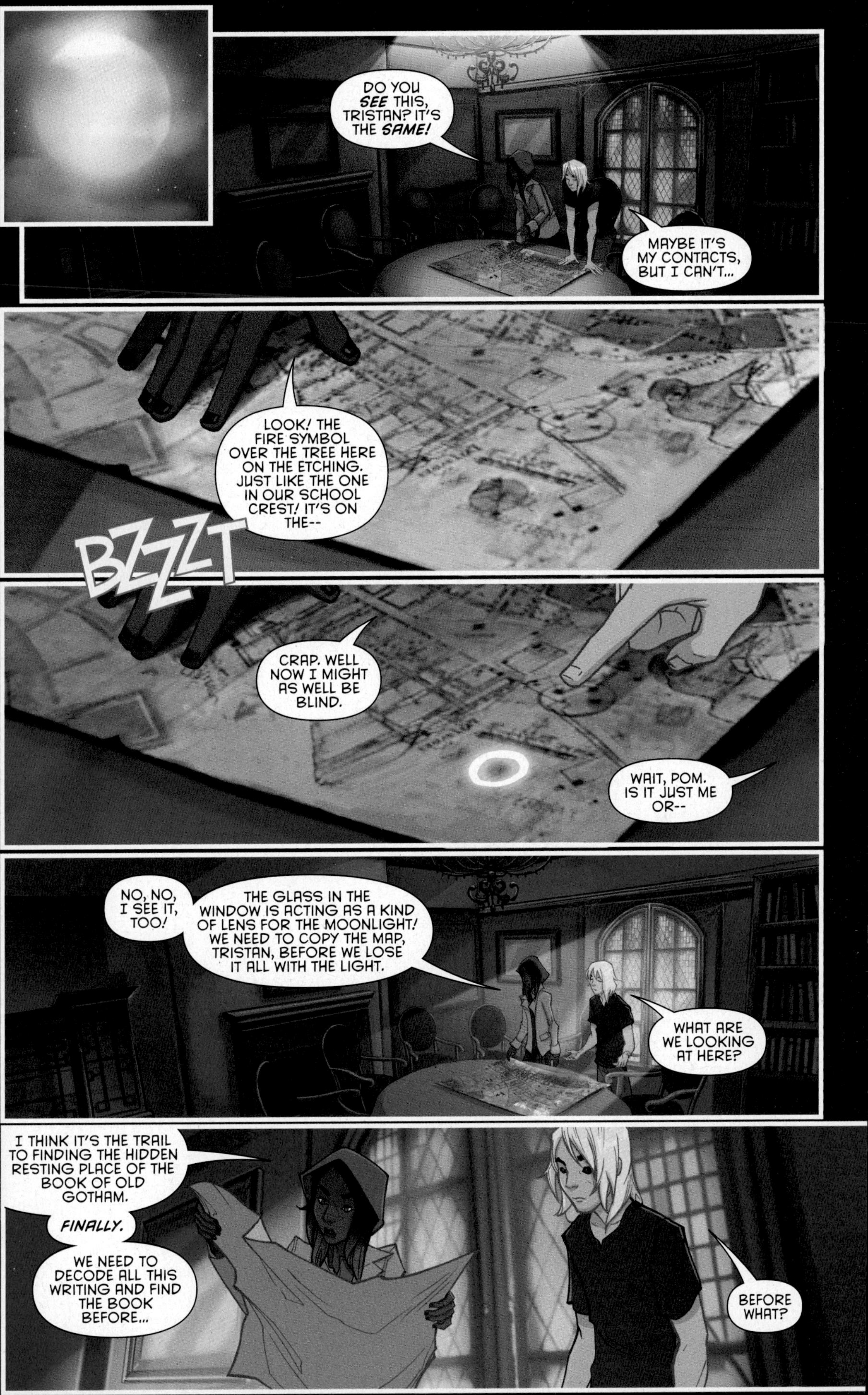
DO YOU SEE THIS, TRISTAN? IT'S THE SAME!
MAYBE IT'S MY CONTACTS, BUT I CAN'T...
LOOK! THE FIRE SYMBOL OVER THE TREE HERE ON THE ETCHING. JUST LIKE THE ONE IN OUR SCHOOL CREST! IT'S ON THE--
BZZZT
CRAP. WELL NOW I MIGHT AS WELL BE BLIND.
WAIT, POM. IS IT JUST ME OR--
NO, NO, I SEE IT, TOO!
THE GLASS IN THE WINDOW IS ACTING AS A KIND OF LENS FOR THE MOONLIGHT! WE NEED TO COPY THE MAP, TRISTAN, BEFORE WE LOSE IT ALL WITH THE LIGHT.
WHAT ARE WE LOOKING AT HERE?
I THINK IT'S THE TRAIL TO FINDING THE HIDDEN RESTING PLACE OF THE BOOK OF OLD GOTHAM.
FINALLY.
WE NEED TO DECODE ALL THIS WRITING AND FIND THE BOOK BEFORE...
BEFORE WHAT?

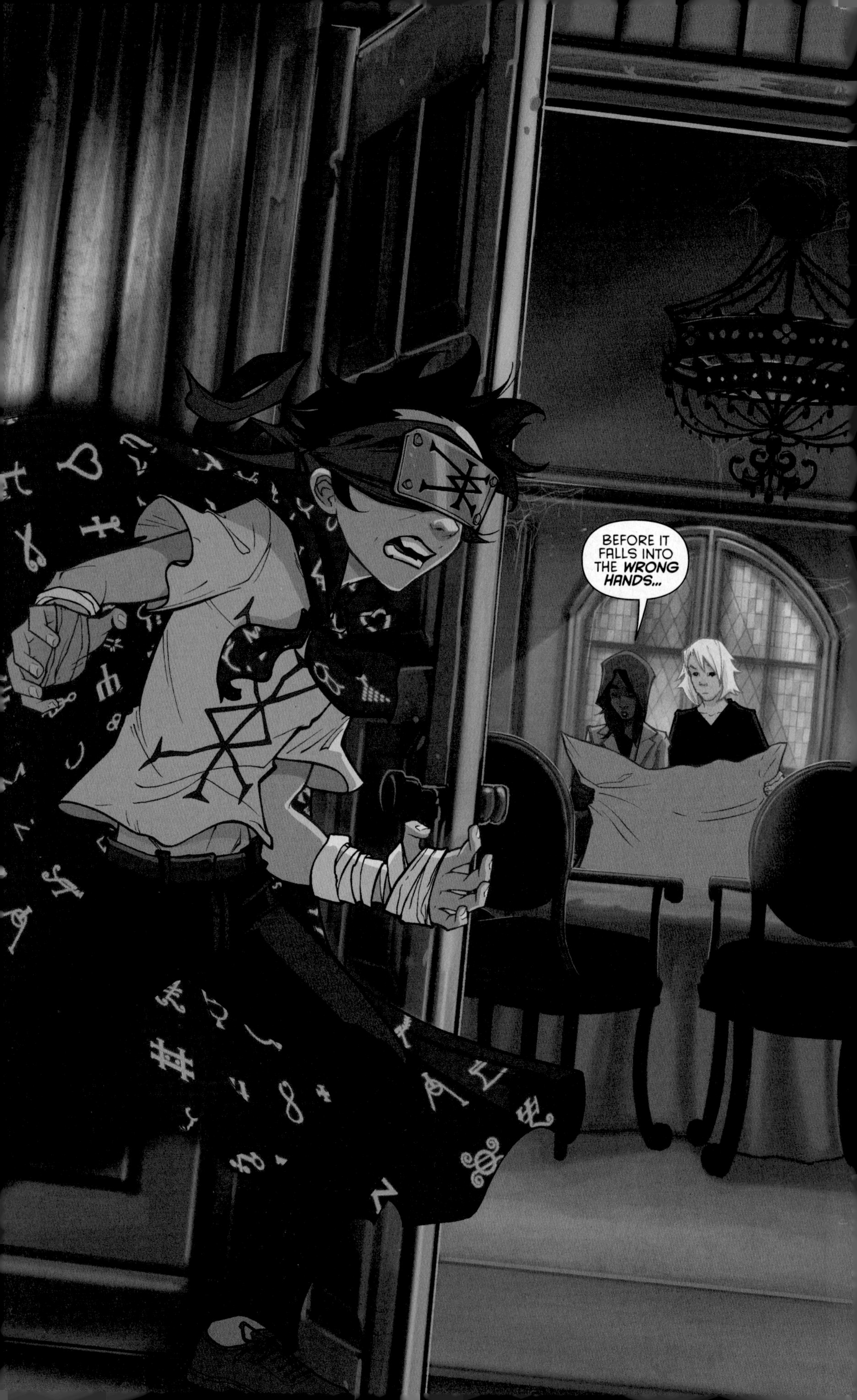
BEFORE IT FALLS INTO THE WRONG HANDS...

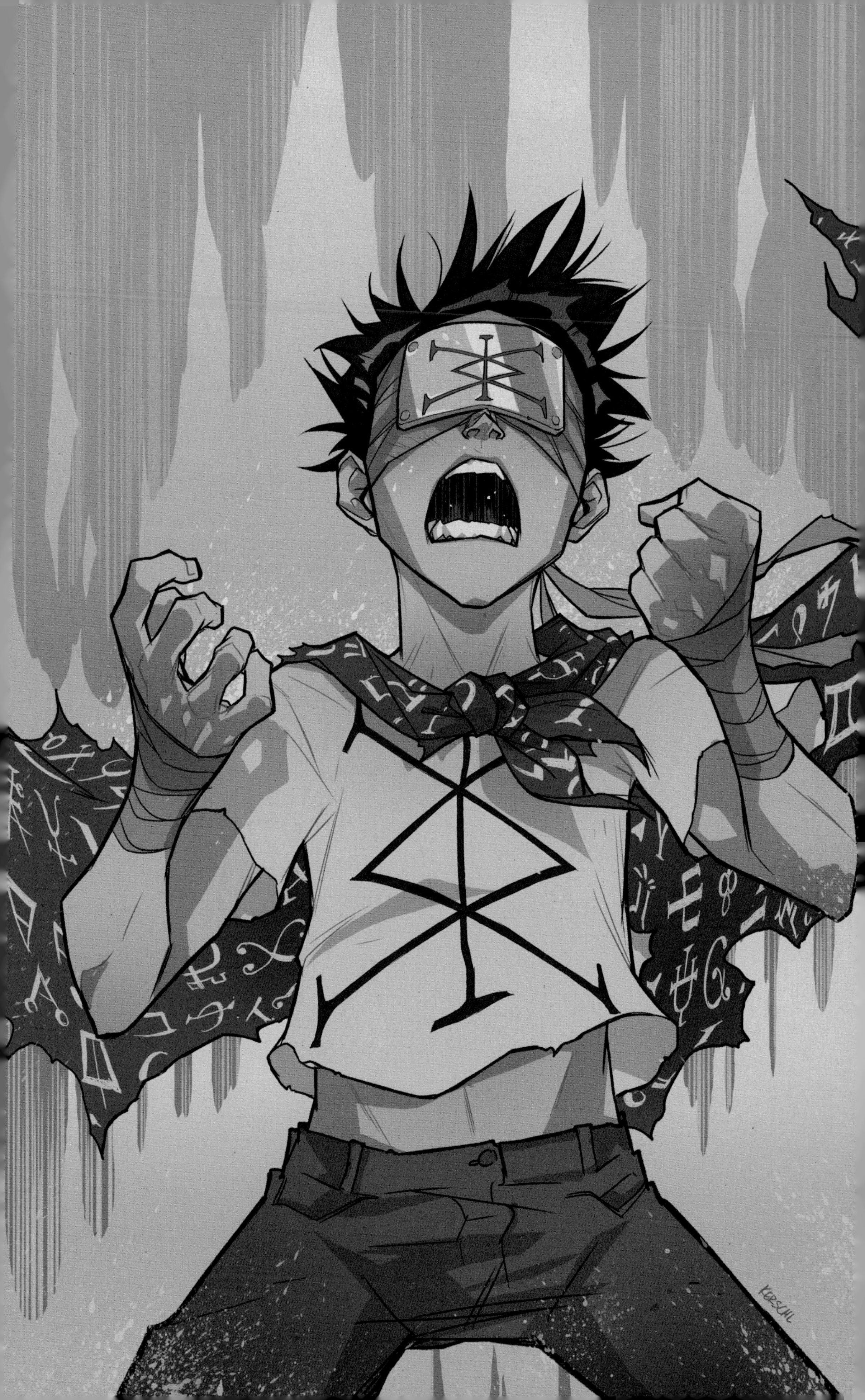
KERSCHL

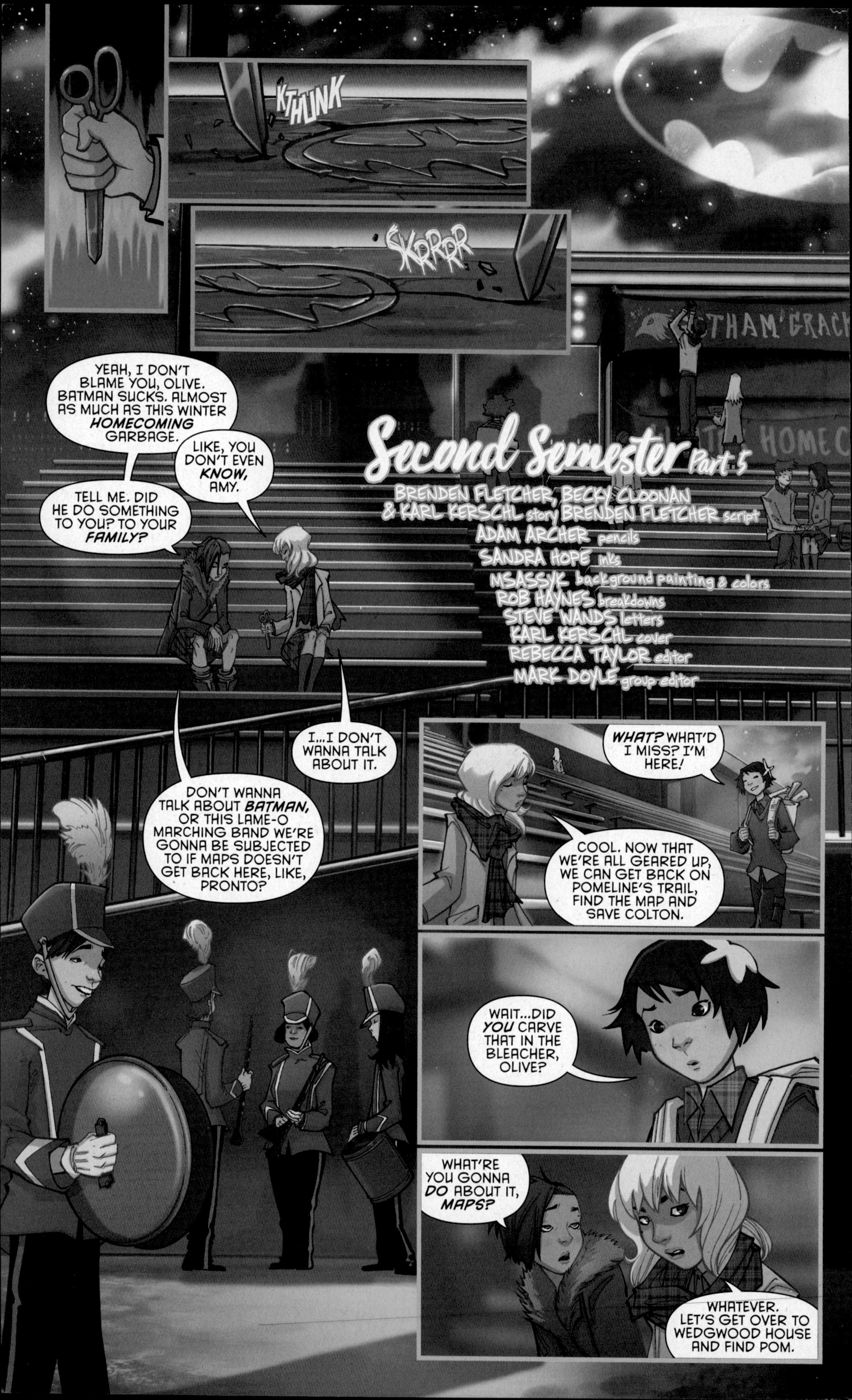
KTHUNK
SKRRR
THAM' GRACH
HOMEC
YEAH, I DON'T BLAME YOU, OLIVE. BATMAN SUCKS. ALMOST AS MUCH AS THIS WINTER *HOMECOMING* GARBAGE.
LIKE, YOU DON'T EVEN *KNOW,* AMY.
TELL ME. DID HE DO SOMETHING TO YOU? TO YOUR *FAMILY?*
Second Semester Part 5
BRENDEN FLETCHER, BECKY CLOONAN & KARL KERSCHL story BRENDEN FLETCHER script
ADAM ARCHER pencils
SANDRA HOPE inks
MSASSYK background painting & colors
ROB HAYNES breakdowns
STEVE WANDS letters
KARL KERSCHL cover
REBECCA TAYLOR editor
MARK DOYLE group editor
I...I DON'T WANNA TALK ABOUT IT.
DON'T WANNA TALK ABOUT *BATMAN,* OR THIS LAME-O MARCHING BAND WE'RE GONNA BE SUBJECTED TO IF MAPS DOESN'T GET BACK HERE, LIKE, PRONTO?
*WHAT?* WHAT'D I MISS? I'M HERE!
COOL. NOW THAT WE'RE ALL GEARED UP, WE CAN GET BACK ON POMELINE'S TRAIL, FIND THE MAP AND SAVE COLTON.
WAIT...DID *YOU* CARVE THAT IN THE BLEACHER, OLIVE?
WHAT'RE YOU GONNA *DO* ABOUT IT, *MAPS?*
WHATEVER. LET'S GET OVER TO WEDGWOOD HOUSE AND FIND POM.

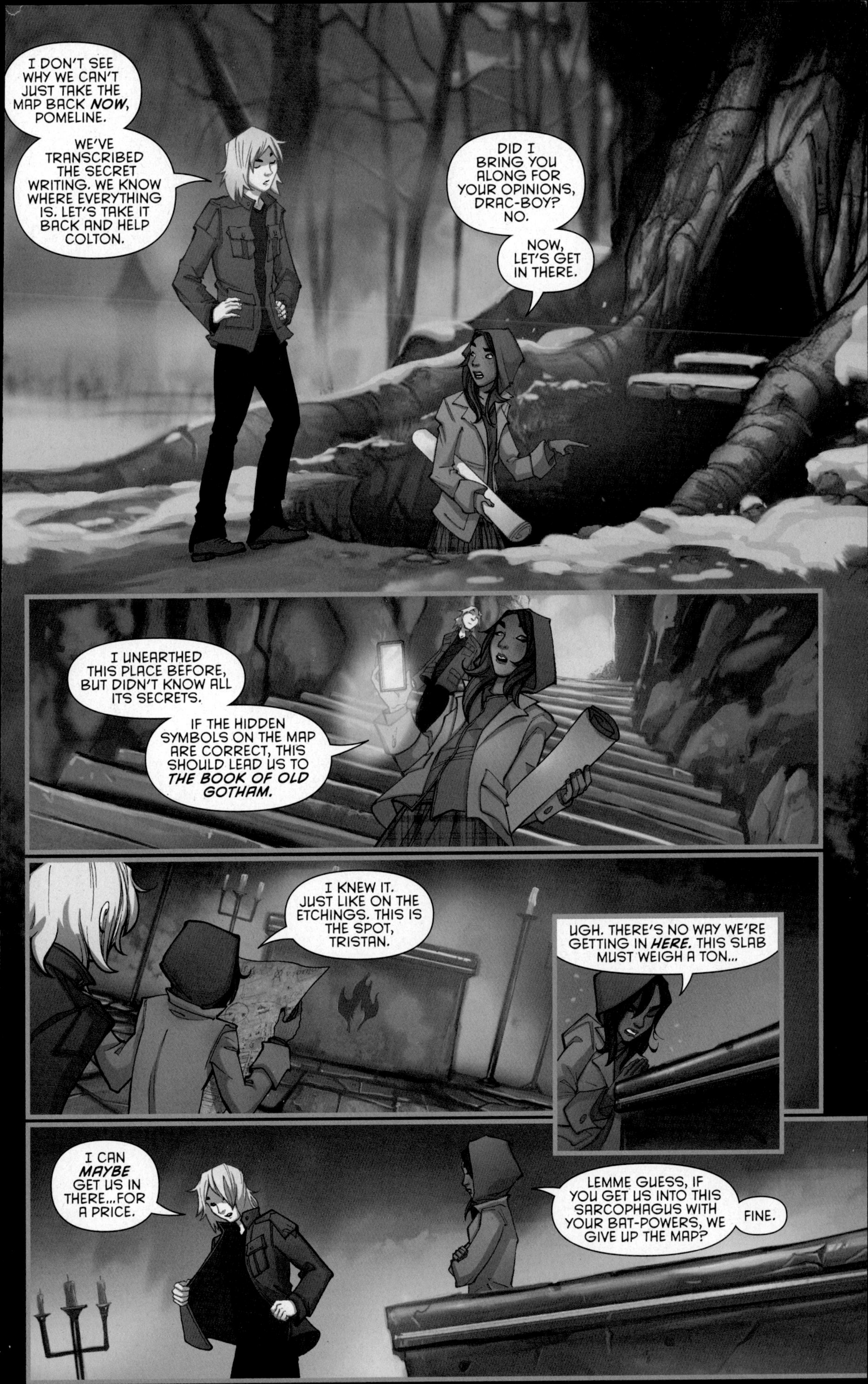
I DON'T SEE WHY WE CAN'T JUST TAKE THE MAP BACK *NOW*, POMELINE.
WE'VE TRANSCRIBED THE SECRET WRITING. WE KNOW WHERE EVERYTHING IS. LET'S TAKE IT BACK AND HELP COLTON.
DID I BRING YOU ALONG FOR YOUR OPINIONS, DRAC-BOY? NO.
NOW, LET'S GET IN THERE.
I UNEARTHED THIS PLACE BEFORE, BUT DIDN'T KNOW ALL ITS SECRETS.
IF THE HIDDEN SYMBOLS ON THE MAP ARE CORRECT, THIS SHOULD LEAD US TO ***THE BOOK OF OLD GOTHAM.***
I KNEW IT. JUST LIKE ON THE ETCHINGS. THIS IS THE SPOT, TRISTAN.
UGH. THERE'S NO WAY WE'RE GETTING IN *HERE.* THIS SLAB MUST WEIGH A TON...
I CAN *MAYBE* GET US IN THERE...FOR A PRICE.
LEMME GUESS, IF YOU GET US INTO THIS SARCOPHAGUS WITH YOUR BAT-POWERS, WE GIVE UP THE MAP?
FINE.

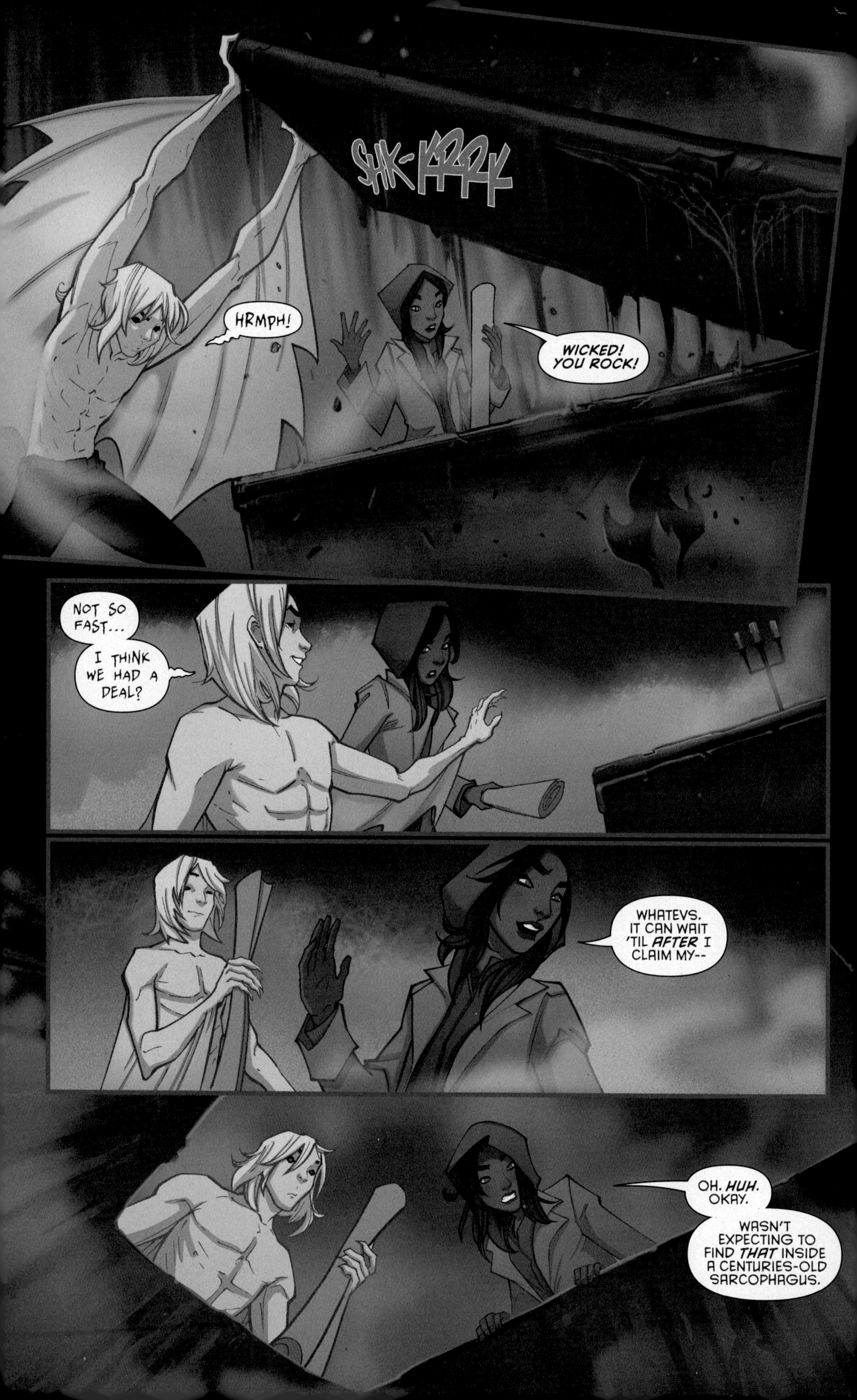
SHK-KRRK
HRMPH!
WICKED! YOU ROCK!
NOT SO FAST...
I THINK WE HAD A DEAL?
WHATEVS. IT CAN WAIT 'TIL *AFTER* I CLAIM MY--
OH. *HUH.* OKAY.
WASN'T EXPECTING TO FIND *THAT* INSIDE A CENTURIES-OLD SARCOPHAGUS.

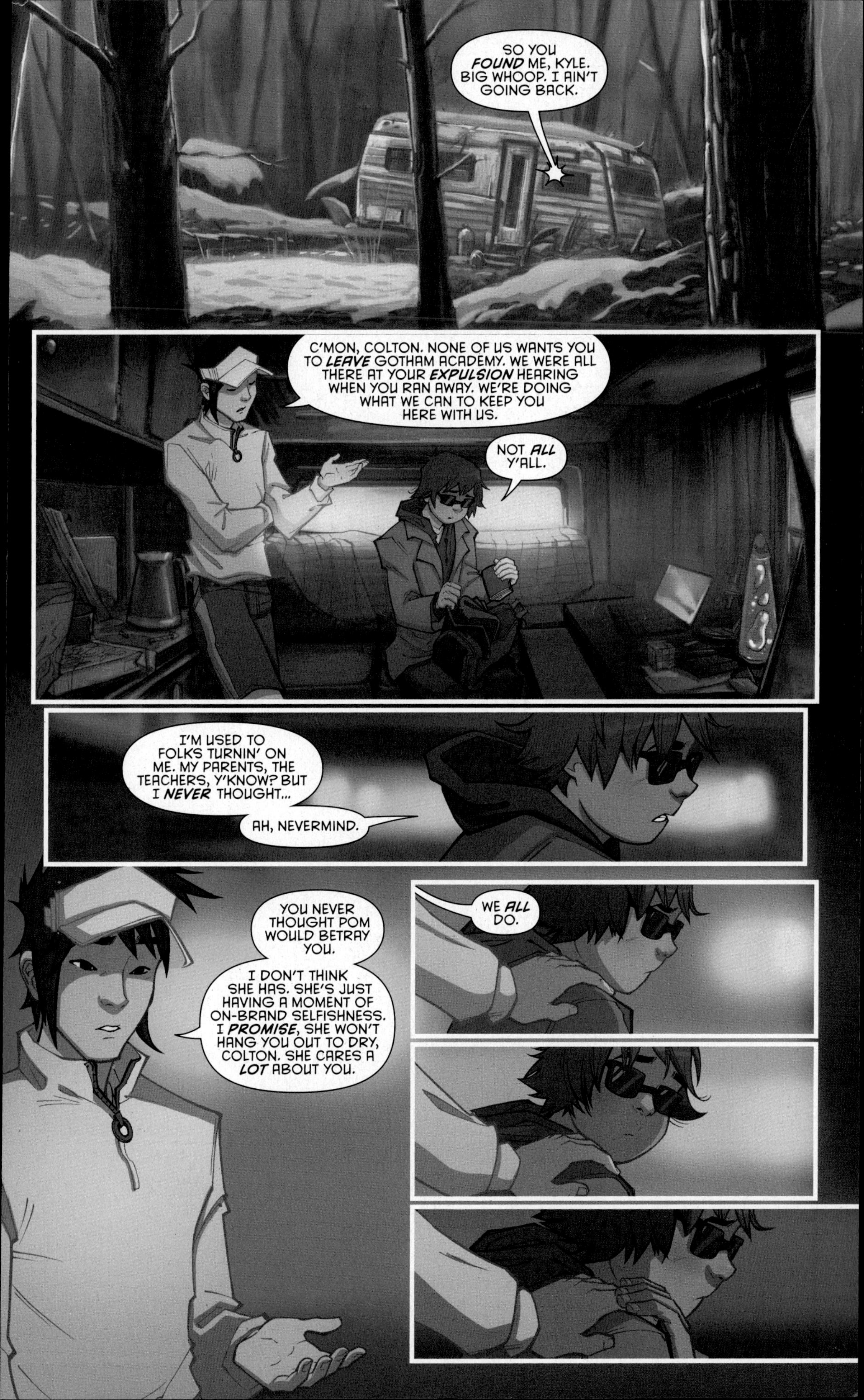

SO YOU FOUND ME, KYLE. BIG WHOOP. I AIN'T GOING BACK.
C'MON, COLTON. NONE OF US WANTS YOU TO LEAVE GOTHAM ACADEMY. WE WERE ALL THERE AT YOUR EXPULSION HEARING WHEN YOU RAN AWAY. WE'RE DOING WHAT WE CAN TO KEEP YOU HERE WITH US.
NOT ALL Y'ALL.
I'M USED TO FOLKS TURNIN' ON ME. MY PARENTS, THE TEACHERS, Y'KNOW? BUT I NEVER THOUGHT...
AH, NEVERMIND.
YOU NEVER THOUGHT POM WOULD BETRAY YOU.
I DON'T THINK SHE HAS. SHE'S JUST HAVING A MOMENT OF ON-BRAND SELFISHNESS. I PROMISE, SHE WON'T HANG YOU OUT TO DRY, COLTON. SHE CARES A LOT ABOUT YOU.
WE ALL DO.

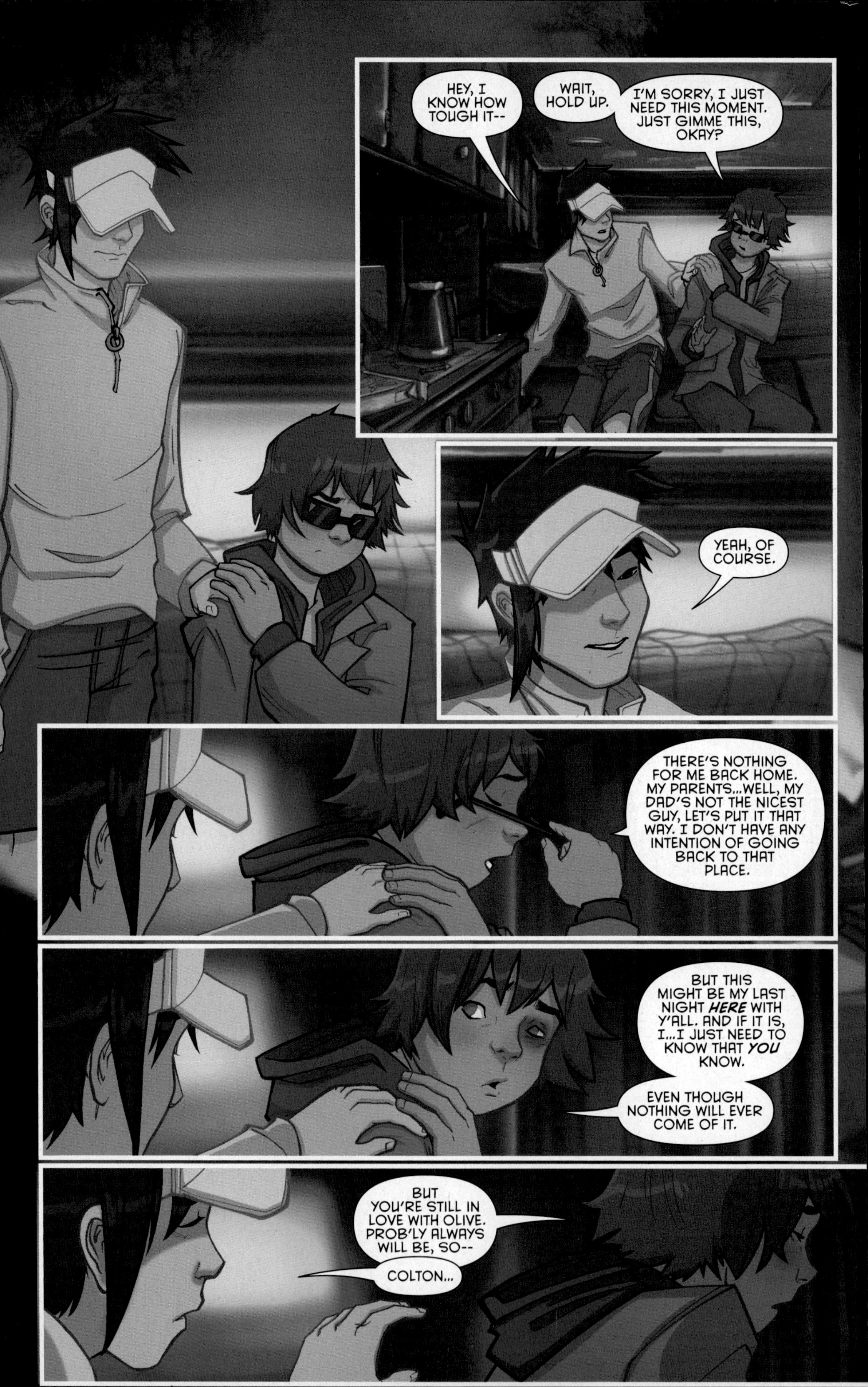
HEY, I KNOW HOW TOUGH IT--
WAIT, HOLD UP.
I'M SORRY, I JUST NEED THIS MOMENT. JUST GIMME THIS, OKAY?
YEAH, OF COURSE.
THERE'S NOTHING FOR ME BACK HOME. MY PARENTS...WELL, MY DAD'S NOT THE NICEST GUY, LET'S PUT IT THAT WAY. I DON'T HAVE ANY INTENTION OF GOING BACK TO THAT PLACE.
BUT THIS MIGHT BE MY LAST NIGHT *HERE* WITH Y'ALL. AND IF IT IS, I...I JUST NEED TO KNOW THAT *YOU* KNOW.
EVEN THOUGH NOTHING WILL EVER COME OF IT.
BUT YOU'RE STILL IN LOVE WITH OLIVE. PROB'LY ALWAYS WILL BE, SO--
COLTON...

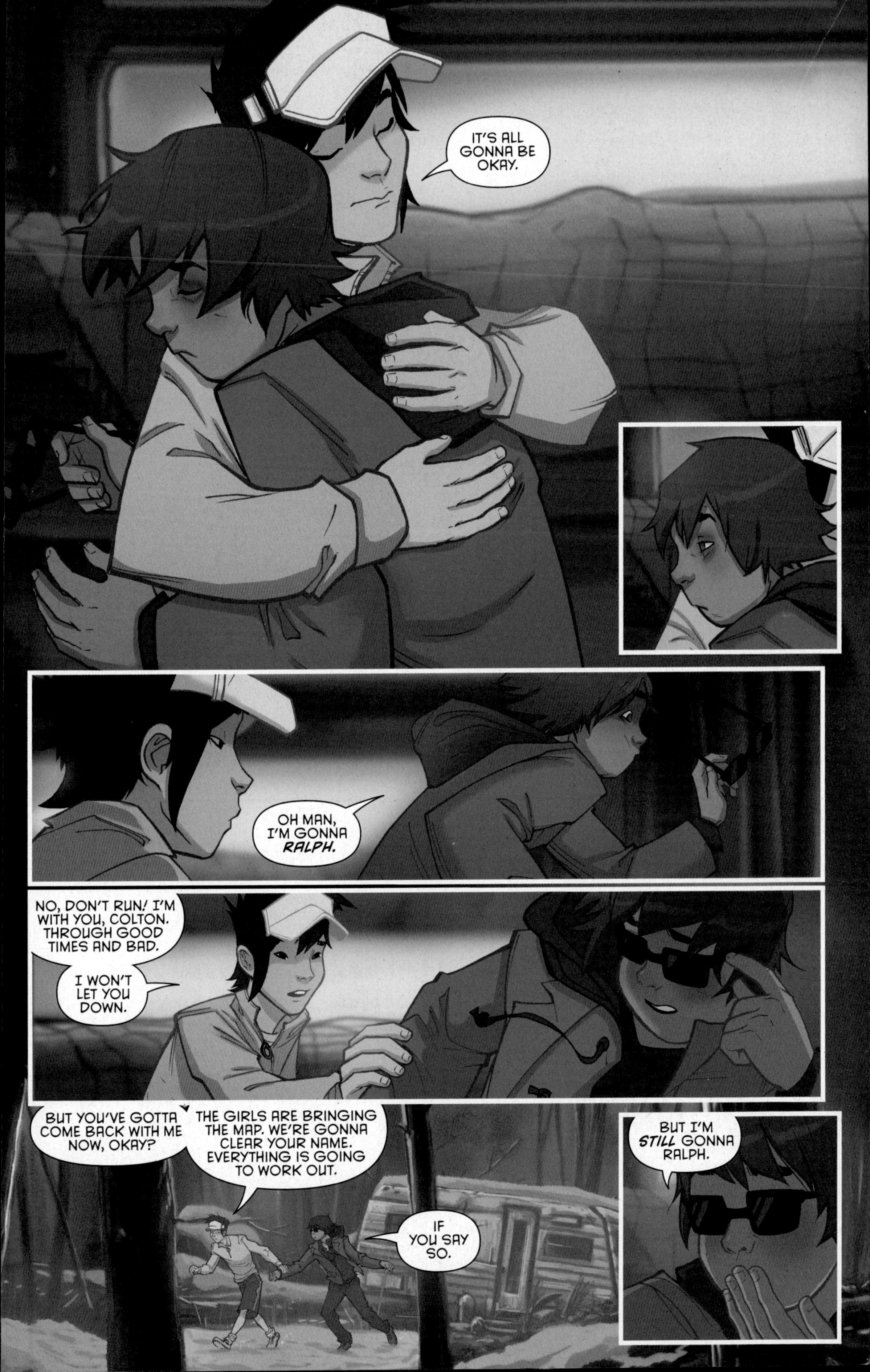
IT'S ALL GONNA BE OKAY.
OH MAN, I'M GONNA *RALPH.*
NO, DON'T RUN! I'M WITH YOU, COLTON. THROUGH GOOD TIMES AND BAD.
I WON'T LET YOU DOWN.
BUT YOU'VE GOTTA COME BACK WITH ME NOW, OKAY?
THE GIRLS ARE BRINGING THE MAP. WE'RE GONNA CLEAR YOUR NAME. EVERYTHING IS GOING TO WORK OUT.
IF YOU SAY SO.
BUT I'M *STILL* GONNA RALPH.

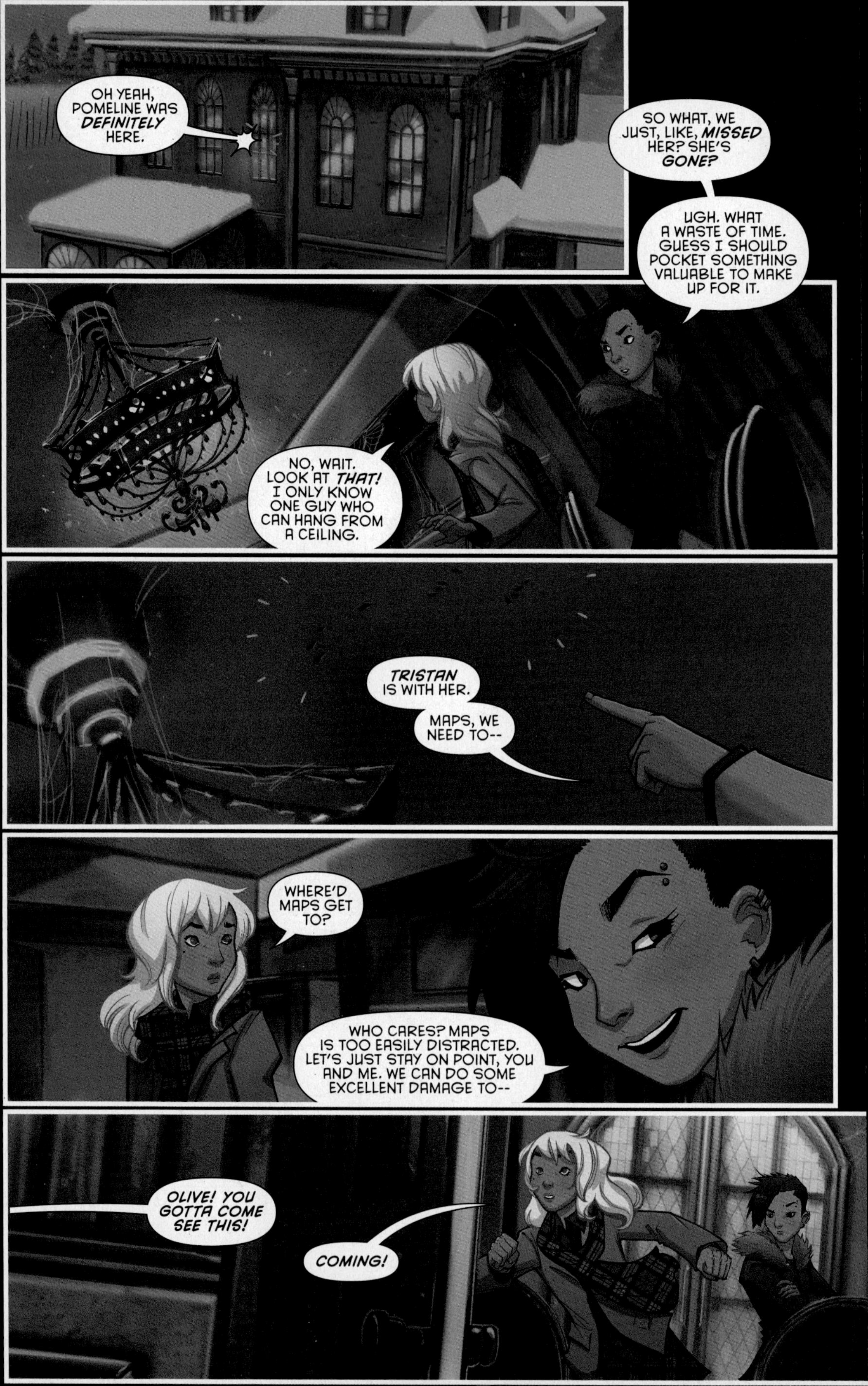
OH YEAH, POMELINE WAS DEFINITELY HERE.
SO WHAT, WE JUST, LIKE, MISSED HER? SHE'S GONE?
UGH. WHAT A WASTE OF TIME. GUESS I SHOULD POCKET SOMETHING VALUABLE TO MAKE UP FOR IT.
NO, WAIT. LOOK AT THAT! I ONLY KNOW ONE GUY WHO CAN HANG FROM A CEILING.
TRISTAN IS WITH HER.
MAPS, WE NEED TO--
WHERE'D MAPS GET TO?
WHO CARES? MAPS IS TOO EASILY DISTRACTED. LET'S JUST STAY ON POINT, YOU AND ME. WE CAN DO SOME EXCELLENT DAMAGE TO--
OLIVE! YOU GOTTA COME SEE THIS!
COMING!

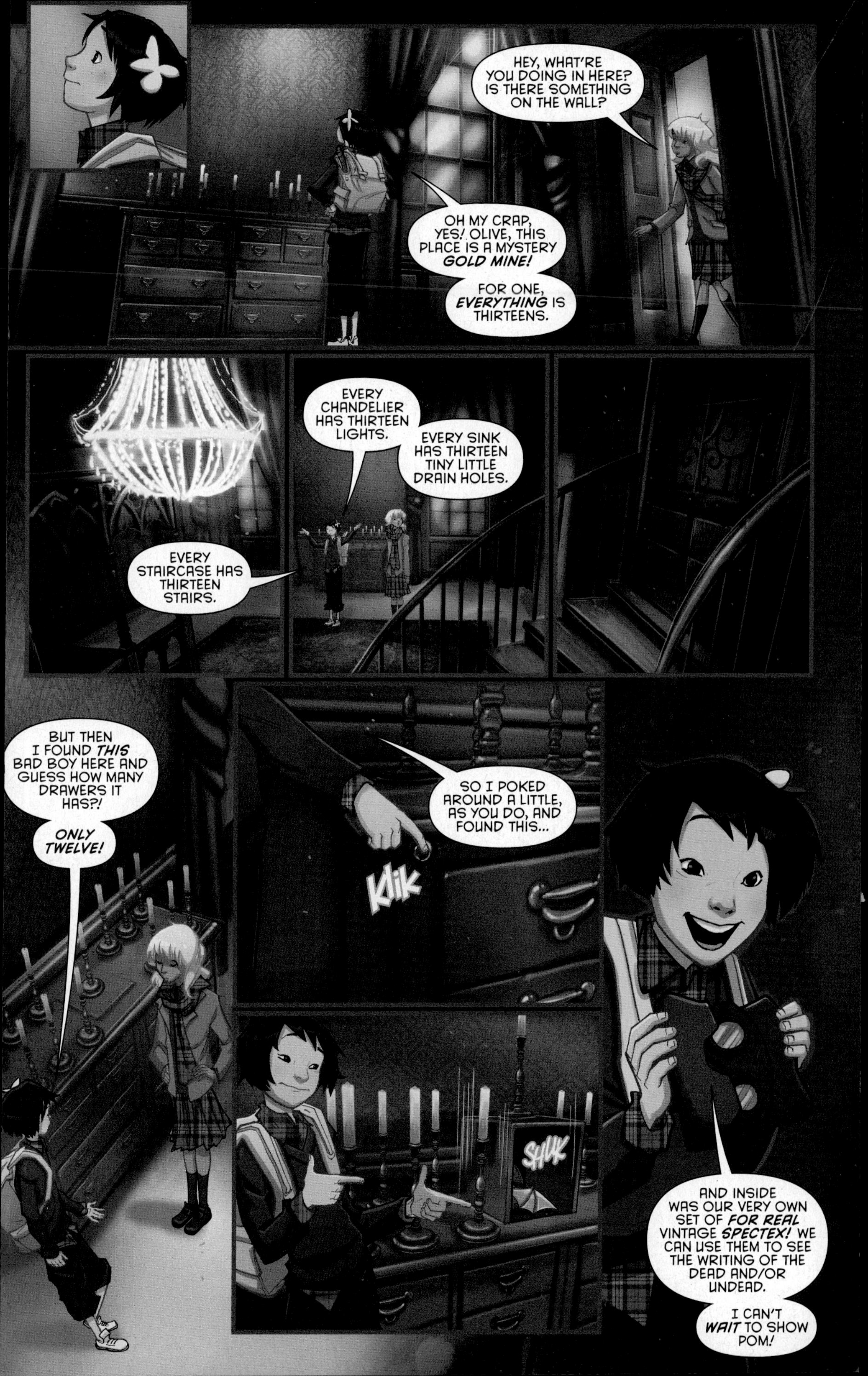
HEY, WHAT'RE YOU DOING IN HERE? IS THERE SOMETHING ON THE WALL?
OH MY CRAP, YES! OLIVE, THIS PLACE IS A MYSTERY GOLD MINE!
FOR ONE, EVERYTHING IS THIRTEENS.
EVERY CHANDELIER HAS THIRTEEN LIGHTS.
EVERY SINK HAS THIRTEEN TINY LITTLE DRAIN HOLES.
EVERY STAIRCASE HAS THIRTEEN STAIRS.
BUT THEN I FOUND THIS BAD BOY HERE AND GUESS HOW MANY DRAWERS IT HAS?!
ONLY TWELVE!
SO I POKED AROUND A LITTLE, AS YOU DO, AND FOUND THIS...
KLIK
SHUK
AND INSIDE WAS OUR VERY OWN SET OF FOR REAL VINTAGE SPECTEX! WE CAN USE THEM TO SEE THE WRITING OF THE DEAD AND/OR UNDEAD.
I CAN'T WAIT TO SHOW POM!

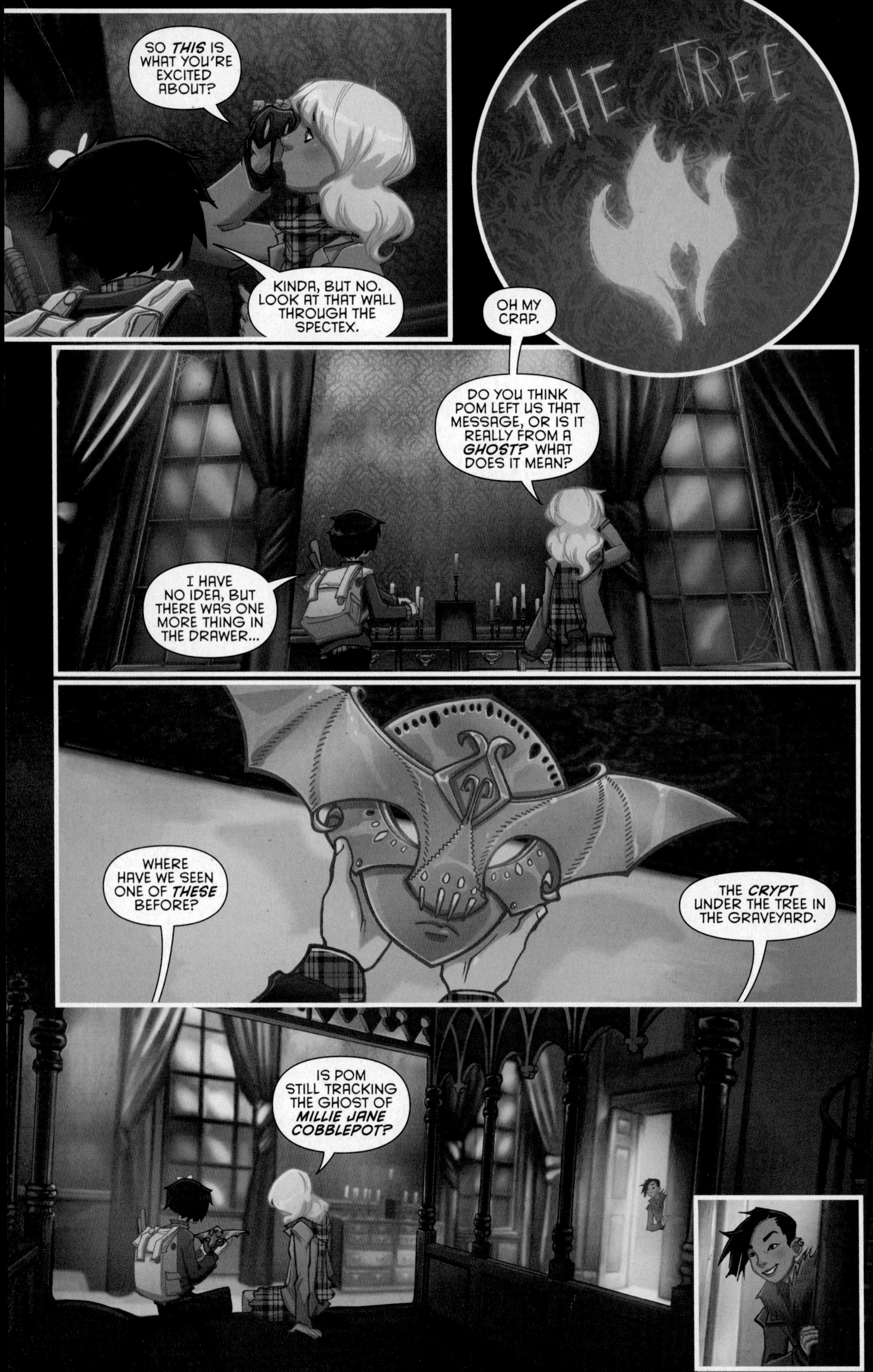

SO *THIS* IS WHAT YOU'RE EXCITED ABOUT?
KINDA, BUT NO. LOOK AT THAT WALL THROUGH THE SPECTEX.
THE TREE
OH MY CRAP.
DO YOU THINK POM LEFT US THAT MESSAGE, OR IS IT REALLY FROM A *GHOST?* WHAT DOES IT MEAN?
I HAVE NO IDEA, BUT THERE WAS ONE MORE THING IN THE DRAWER...
WHERE HAVE WE SEEN ONE OF *THESE* BEFORE?
THE *CRYPT* UNDER THE TREE IN THE GRAVEYARD.
IS POM STILL TRACKING THE GHOST OF *MILLIE JANE COBBLEPOT?*

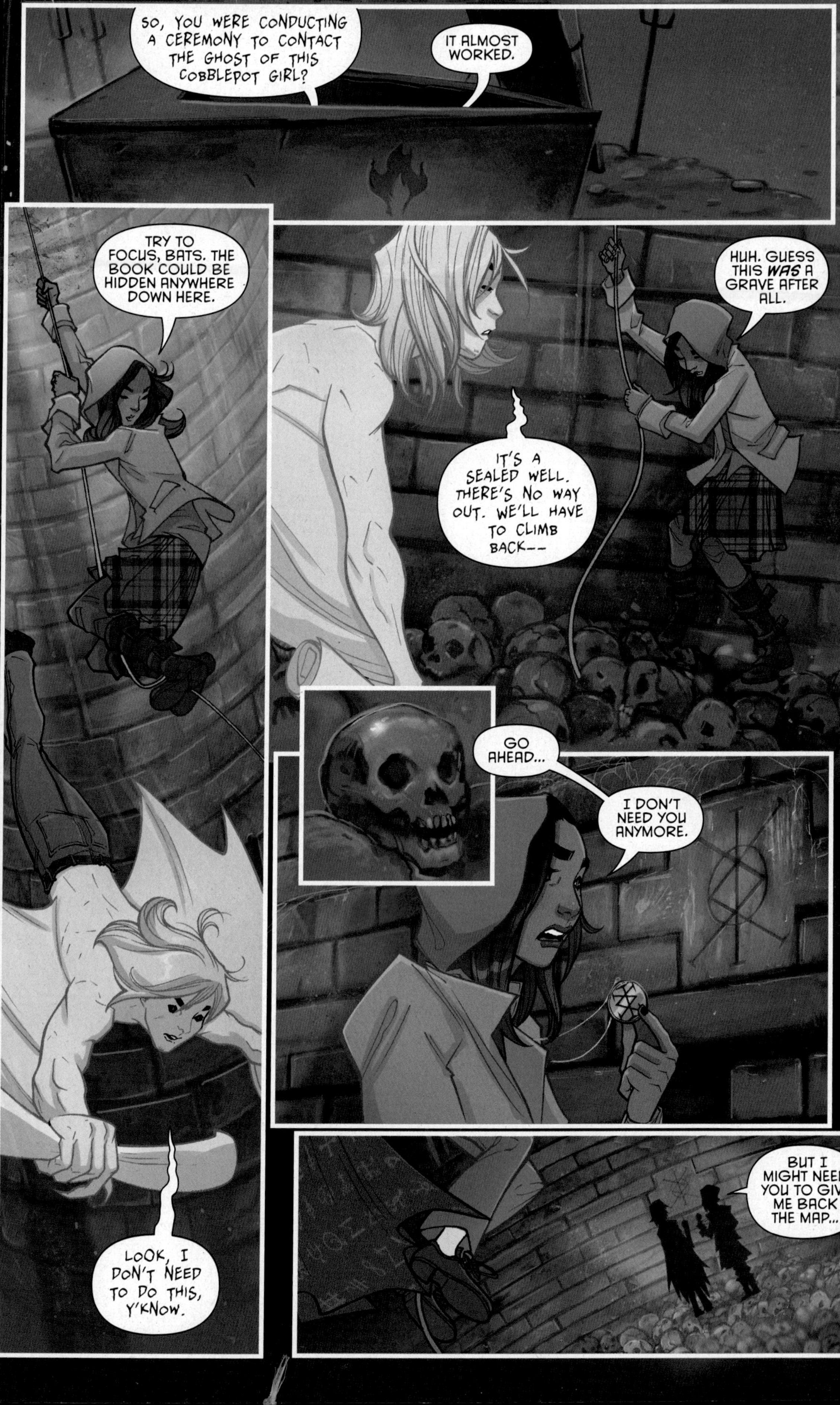
SO, YOU WERE CONDUCTING A CEREMONY TO CONTACT THE GHOST OF THIS COBBLEPOT GIRL?
IT ALMOST WORKED.
TRY TO FOCUS, BATS. THE BOOK COULD BE HIDDEN ANYWHERE DOWN HERE.
IT'S A SEALED WELL. THERE'S NO WAY OUT. WE'LL HAVE TO CLIMB BACK--
HUH. GUESS THIS *WAS* A GRAVE AFTER ALL.
LOOK, I DON'T NEED TO DO THIS, Y'KNOW.
GO AHEAD...
I DON'T NEED YOU ANYMORE.
BUT I MIGHT NEED YOU TO GIVE ME BACK THE MAP...

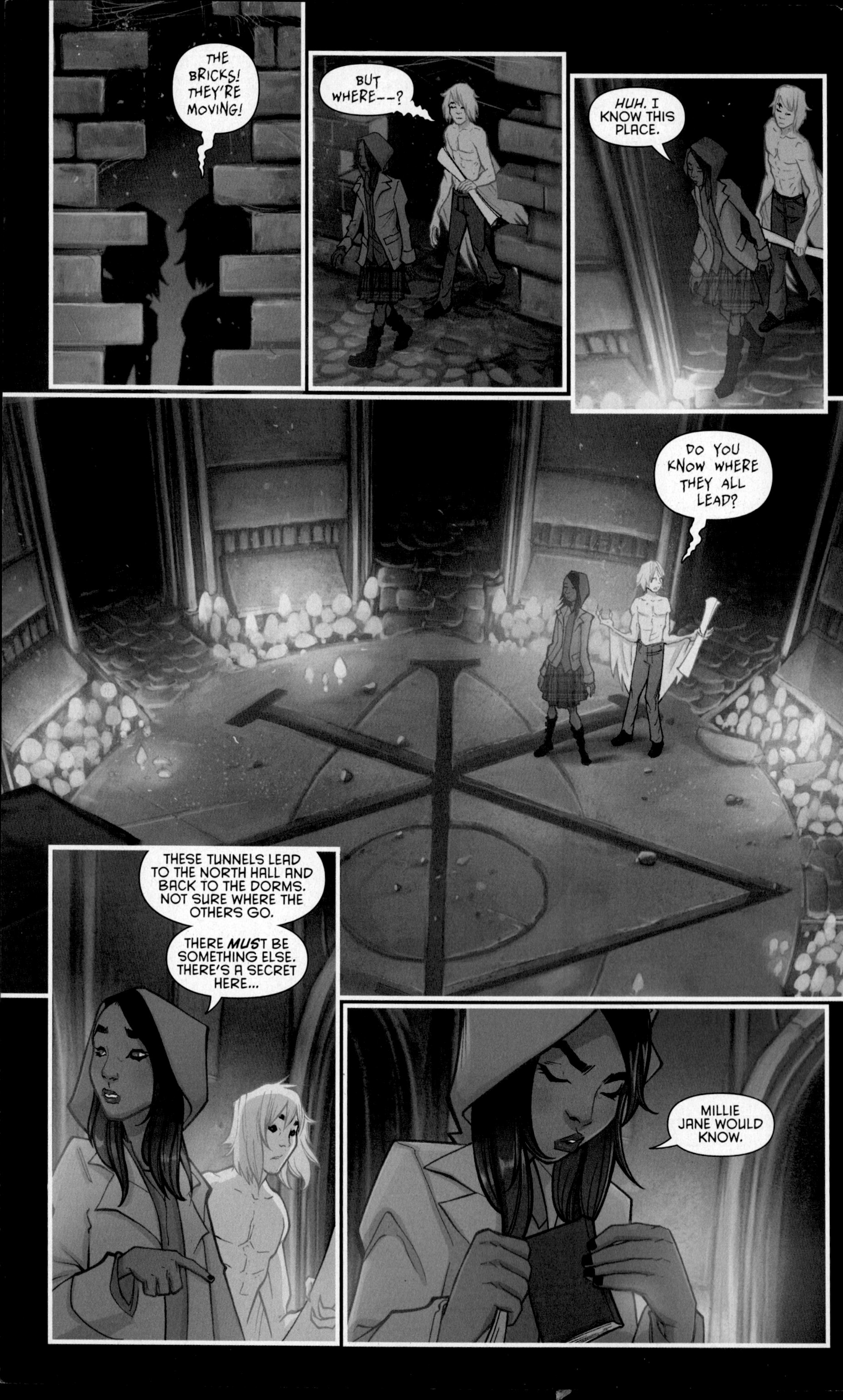
THE BRICKS! THEY'RE MOVING!
BUT WHERE--?
HUH. I KNOW THIS PLACE.
DO YOU KNOW WHERE THEY ALL LEAD?
THESE TUNNELS LEAD TO THE NORTH HALL AND BACK TO THE DORMS. NOT SURE WHERE THE OTHERS GO.
THERE MUST BE SOMETHING ELSE. THERE'S A SECRET HERE...
MILLIE JANE WOULD KNOW.

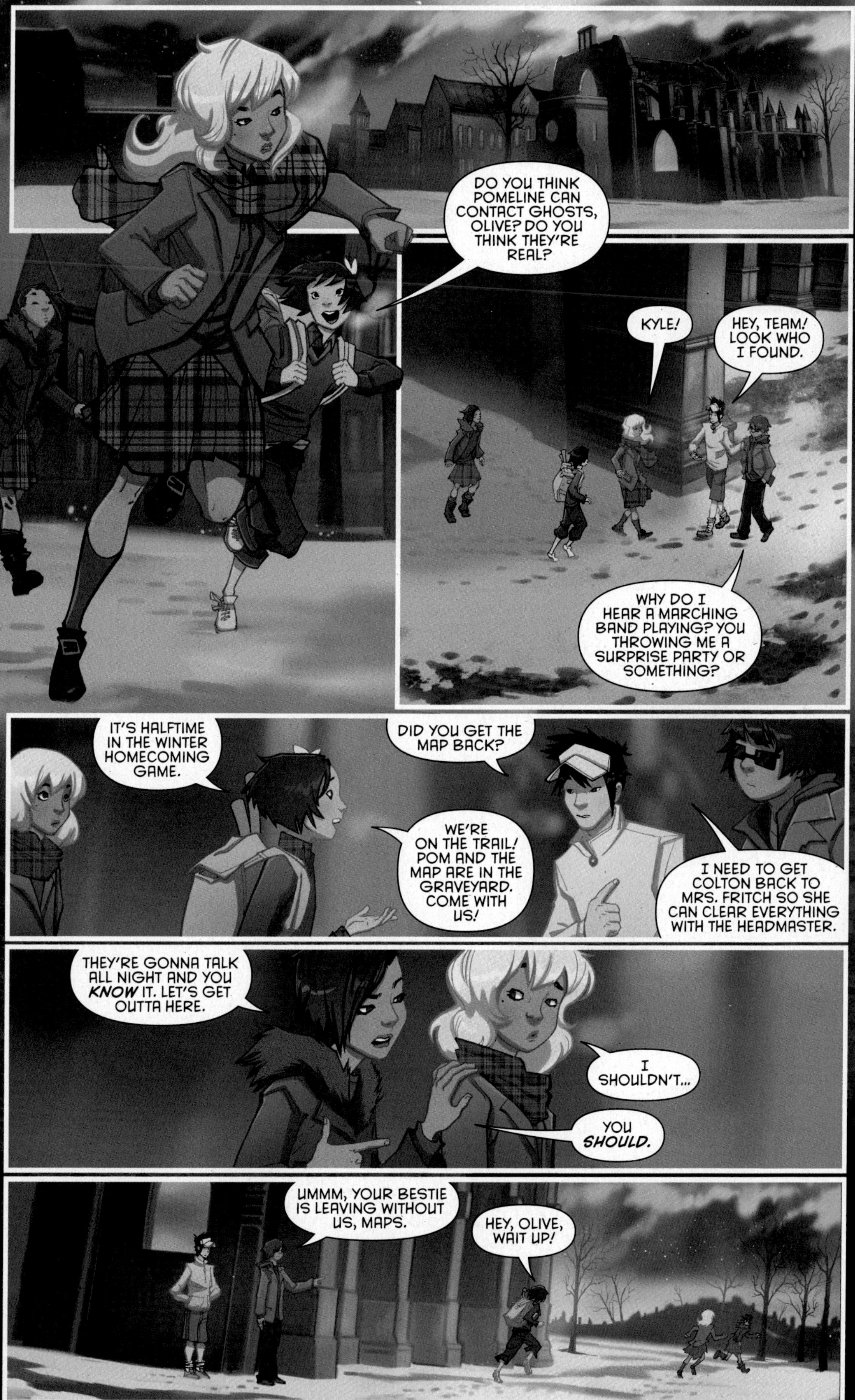
DO YOU THINK POMELINE CAN CONTACT GHOSTS, OLIVE? DO YOU THINK THEY'RE REAL?
KYLE!
HEY, TEAM! LOOK WHO I FOUND.
WHY DO I HEAR A MARCHING BAND PLAYING? YOU THROWING ME A SURPRISE PARTY OR SOMETHING?
IT'S HALFTIME IN THE WINTER HOMECOMING GAME.
DID YOU GET THE MAP BACK?
WE'RE ON THE TRAIL! POM AND THE MAP ARE IN THE GRAVEYARD. COME WITH US!
I NEED TO GET COLTON BACK TO MRS. FRITCH SO SHE CAN CLEAR EVERYTHING WITH THE HEADMASTER.
THEY'RE GONNA TALK ALL NIGHT AND YOU ***KNOW*** IT. LET'S GET OUTTA HERE.
I SHOULDN'T...
YOU ***SHOULD.***
UMMM, YOUR BESTIE IS LEAVING WITHOUT US, MAPS.
HEY, OLIVE, WAIT UP!

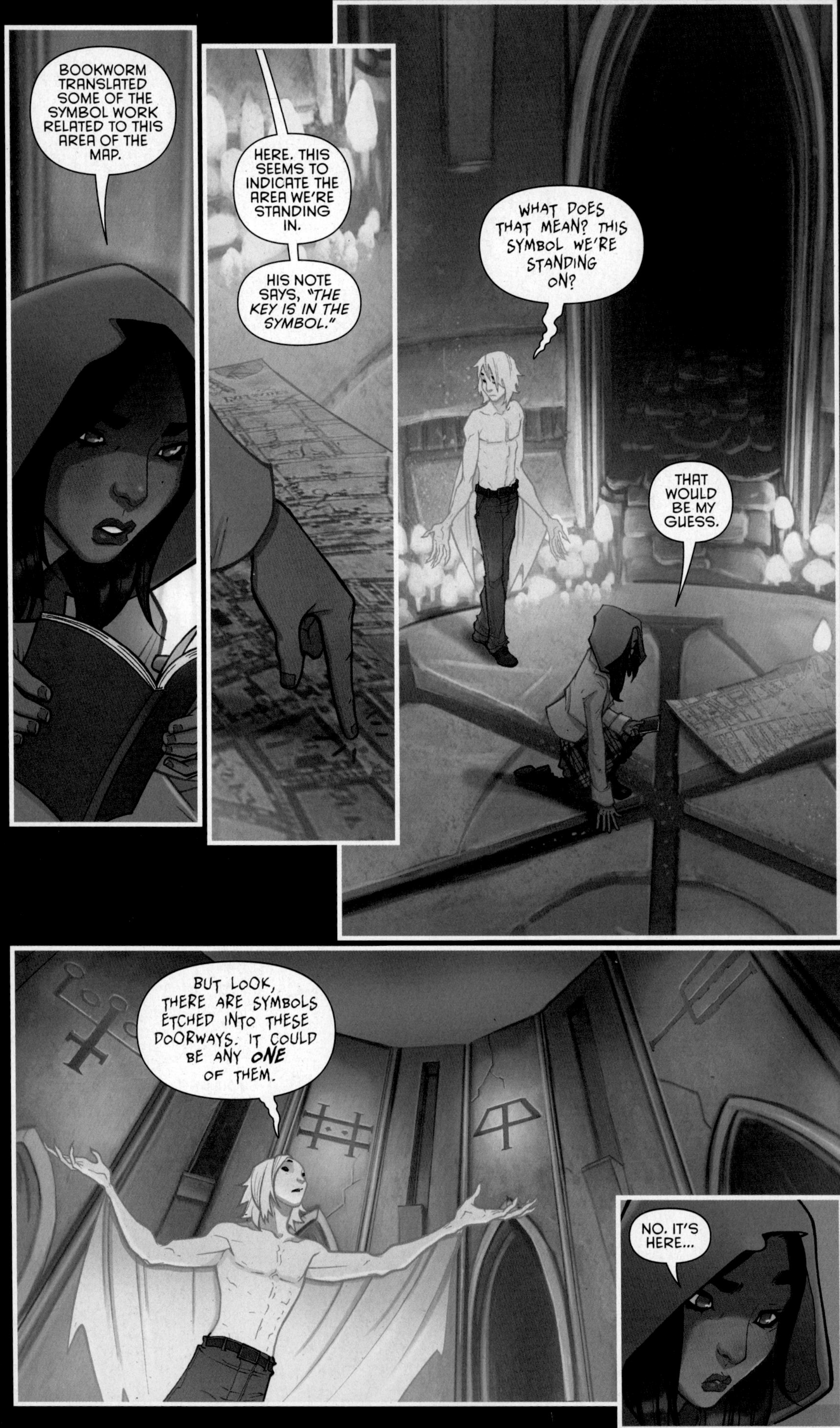
BOOKWORM TRANSLATED SOME OF THE SYMBOL WORK RELATED TO THIS AREA OF THE MAP.
HERE. THIS SEEMS TO INDICATE THE AREA WE'RE STANDING IN.
HIS NOTE SAYS, "THE KEY IS IN THE SYMBOL."
WHAT DOES THAT MEAN? THIS SYMBOL WE'RE STANDING ON?
THAT WOULD BE MY GUESS.
BUT LOOK, THERE ARE SYMBOLS ETCHED INTO THESE DOORWAYS. IT COULD BE ANY ONE OF THEM.
NO. IT'S HERE...

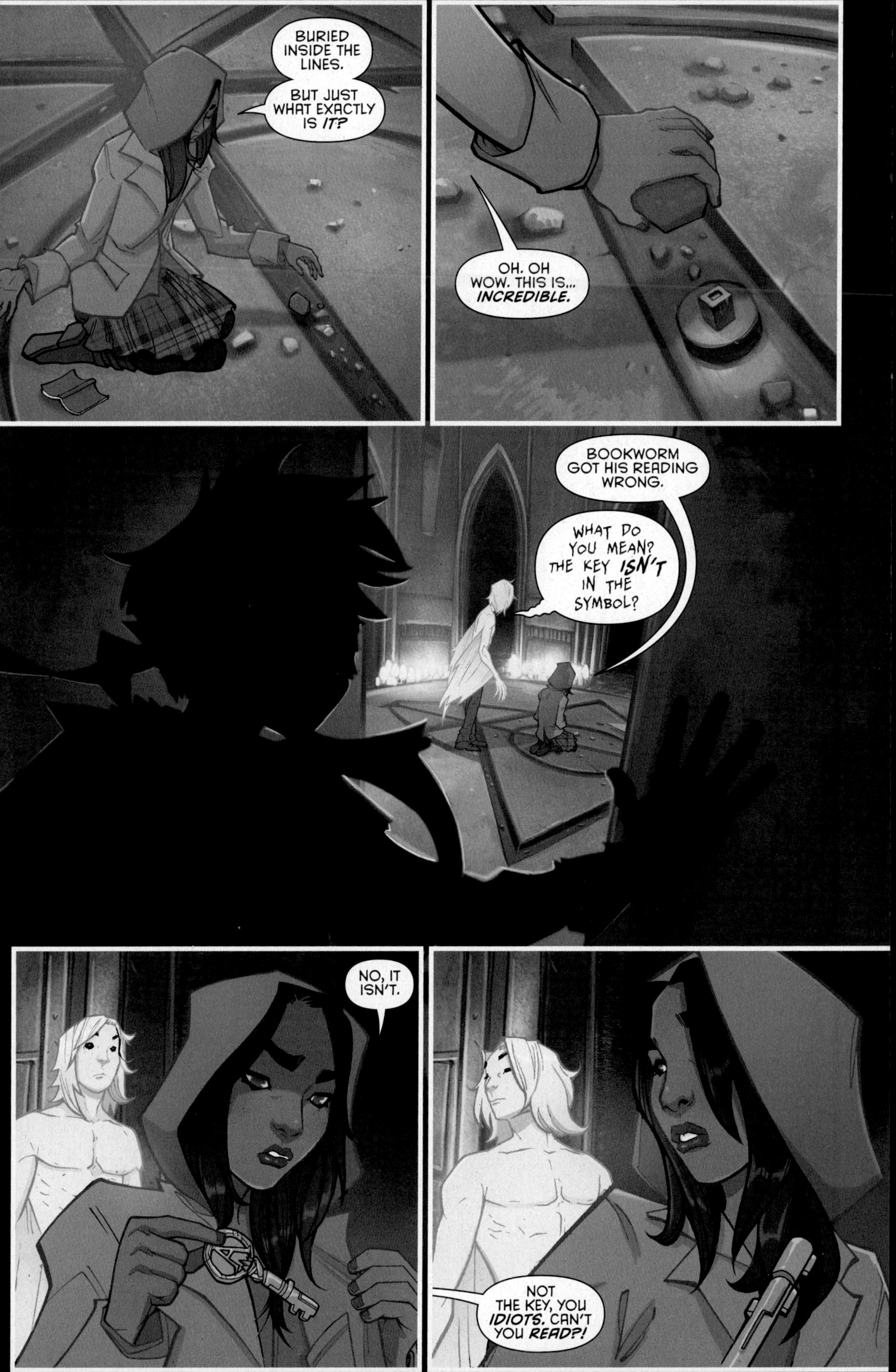
BURIED INSIDE THE LINES.
BUT JUST WHAT EXACTLY IS IT?
OH. OH WOW. THIS IS... INCREDIBLE.
BOOKWORM GOT HIS READING WRONG.
WHAT DO YOU MEAN? THE KEY ISN'T IN THE SYMBOL?
NO, IT ISN'T.
NOT THE KEY, YOU IDIOTS. CAN'T YOU READ?!

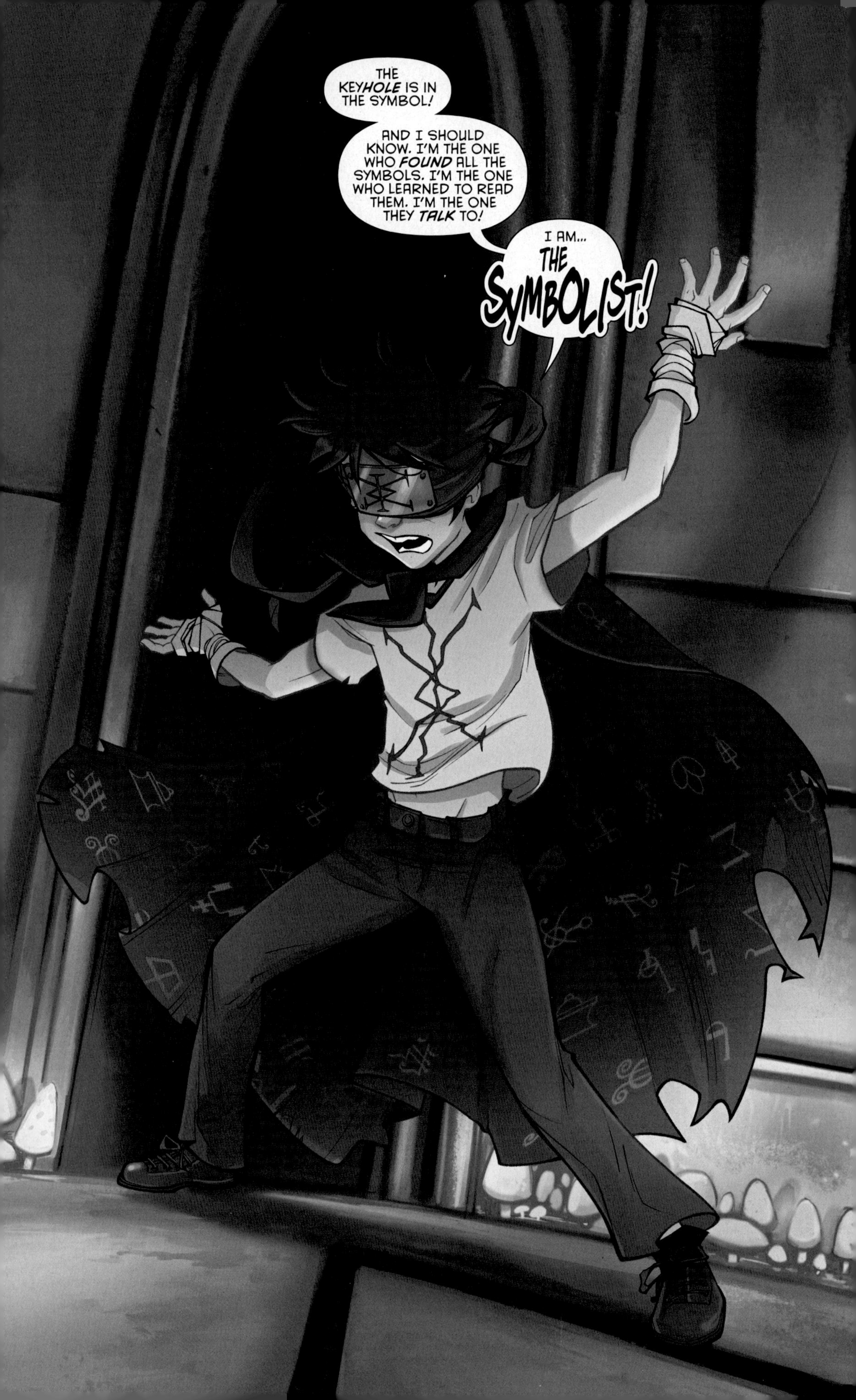
THE KEYHOLE IS IN THE SYMBOL!
AND I SHOULD KNOW. I'M THE ONE WHO FOUND ALL THE SYMBOLS. I'M THE ONE WHO LEARNED TO READ THEM. I'M THE ONE THEY TALK TO!
I AM... THE SYMBOLIST!

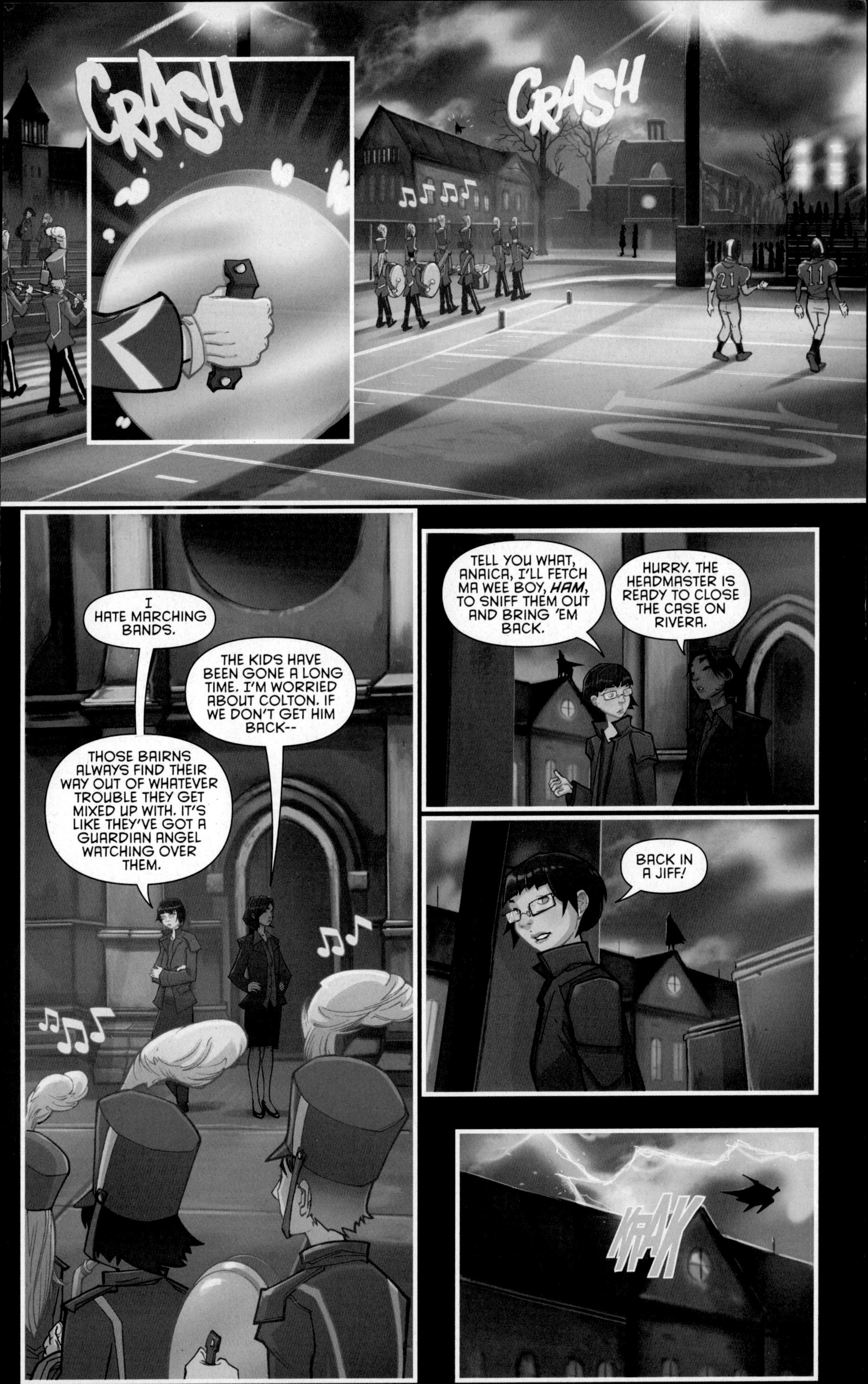
CRASH
CRASH
I HATE MARCHING BANDS.
THE KIDS HAVE BEEN GONE A LONG TIME. I'M WORRIED ABOUT COLTON. IF WE DON'T GET HIM BACK--
THOSE BAIRNS ALWAYS FIND THEIR WAY OUT OF WHATEVER TROUBLE THEY GET MIXED UP WITH. IT'S LIKE THEY'VE GOT A GUARDIAN ANGEL WATCHING OVER THEM.
TELL YOU WHAT, ANAICA, I'LL FETCH MA WEE BOY, *HAM*, TO SNIFF THEM OUT AND BRING 'EM BACK.
HURRY. THE HEADMASTER IS READY TO CLOSE THE CASE ON RIVERA.
BACK IN A JIFF!
KRAK

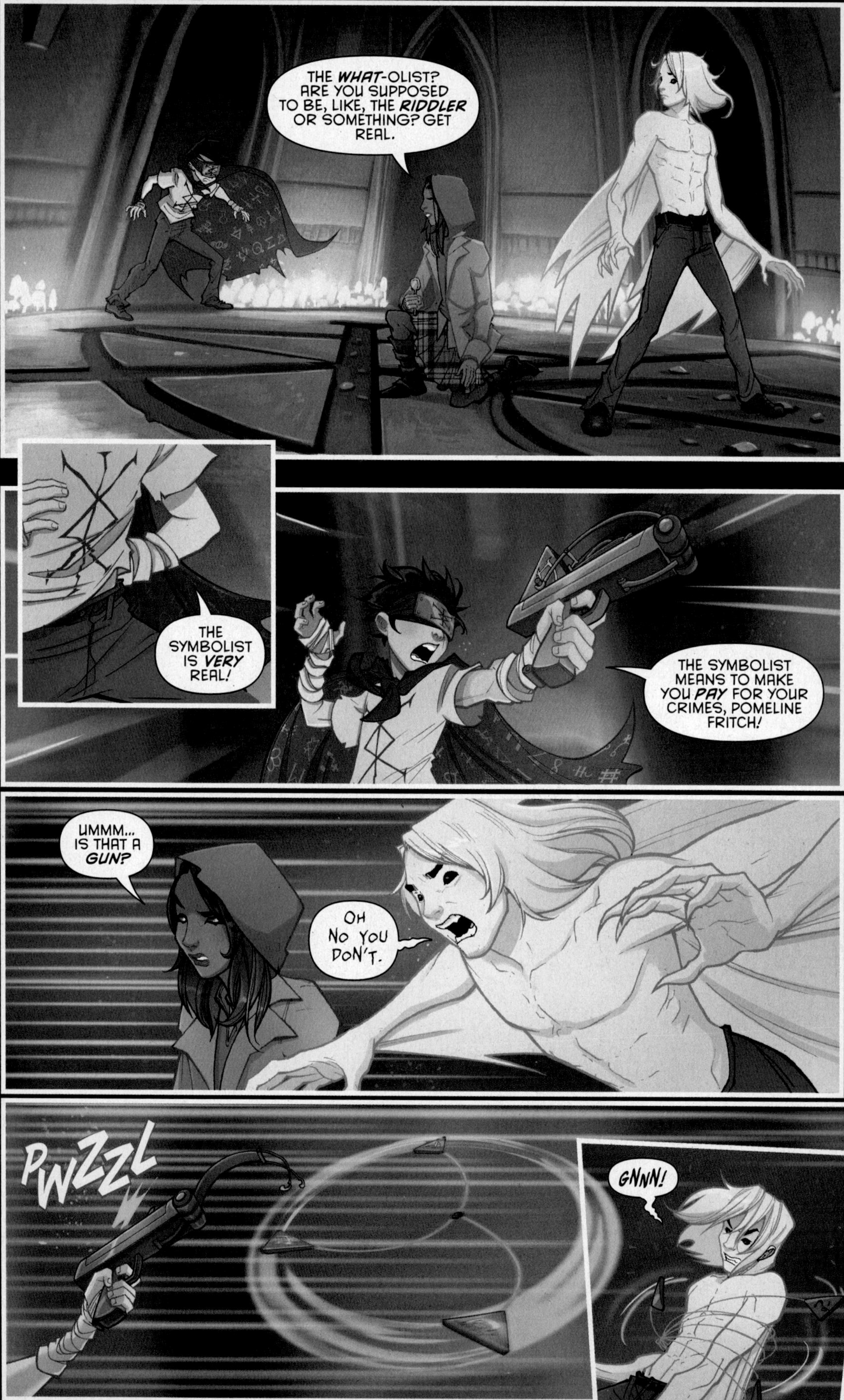
THE WHAT-OLIST? ARE YOU SUPPOSED TO BE, LIKE, THE RIDDLER OR SOMETHING? GET REAL.
THE SYMBOLIST IS VERY REAL!
THE SYMBOLIST MEANS TO MAKE YOU PAY FOR YOUR CRIMES, POMELINE FRITCH!
UMMM... IS THAT A GUN?
OH NO YOU DON'T.
PWZZL
GNNN!

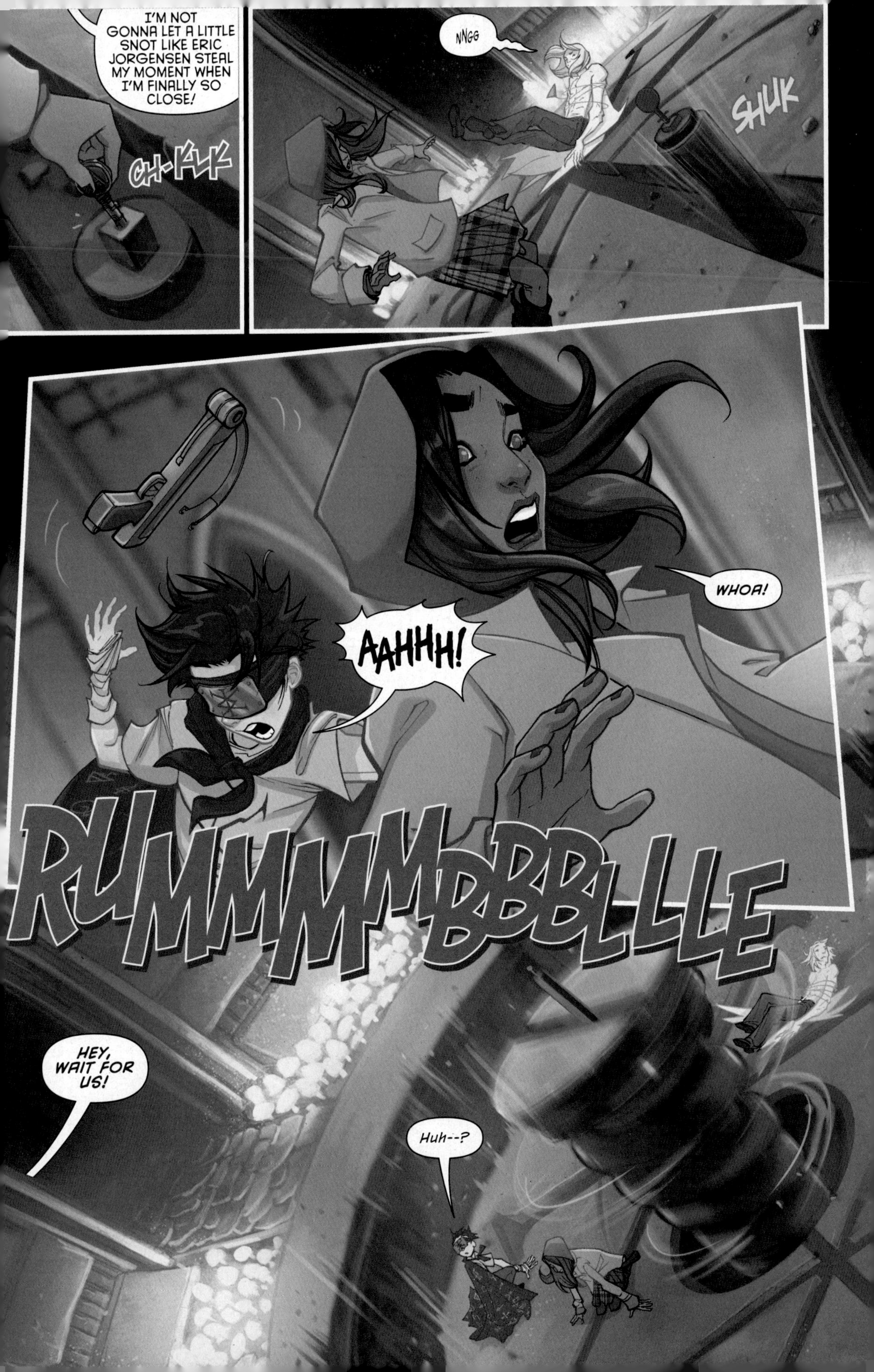
I'M NOT GONNA LET A LITTLE SNOT LIKE ERIC JORGENSEN STEAL MY MOMENT WHEN I'M FINALLY SO CLOSE!
CH-KLK
NNGG
SHUK
WHOA!
AAHHH!
RUMMMMBBBLLLE
HEY, WAIT FOR US!
Huh--?

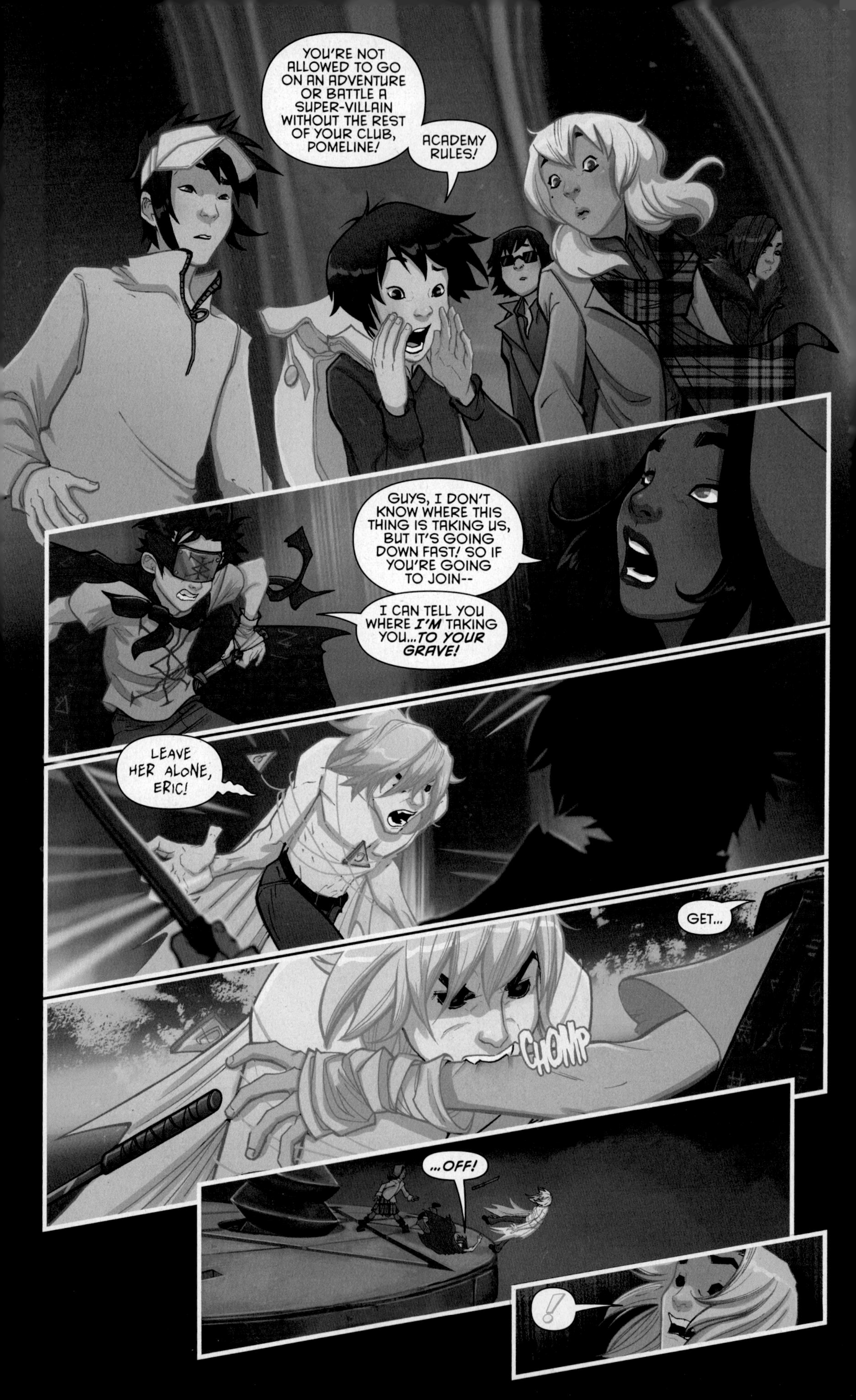
YOU'RE NOT ALLOWED TO GO ON AN ADVENTURE OR BATTLE A SUPER-VILLAIN WITHOUT THE REST OF YOUR CLUB, POMELINE!
ACADEMY RULES!
GUYS, I DON'T KNOW WHERE THIS THING IS TAKING US, BUT IT'S GOING DOWN FAST! SO IF YOU'RE GOING TO JOIN--
I CAN TELL YOU WHERE *I'M* TAKING YOU...*TO YOUR GRAVE!*
LEAVE HER ALONE, ERIC!
GET...
CHOMP
...OFF!
!

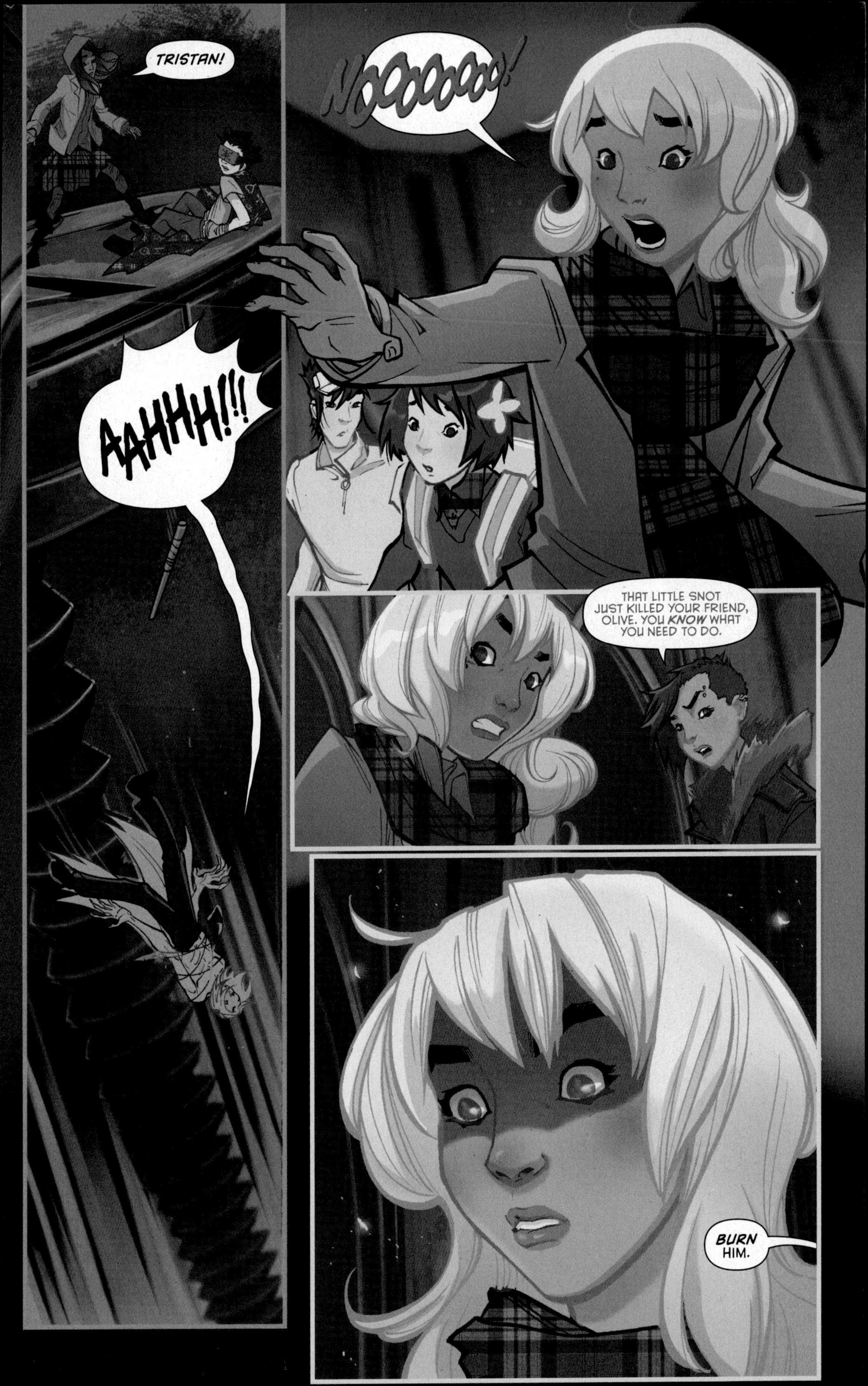
TRISTAN!
AAHHH!!!
NOOOOOOOO!
THAT LITTLE SNOT JUST KILLED YOUR FRIEND, OLIVE. YOU KNOW WHAT YOU NEED TO DO.
BURN HIM.

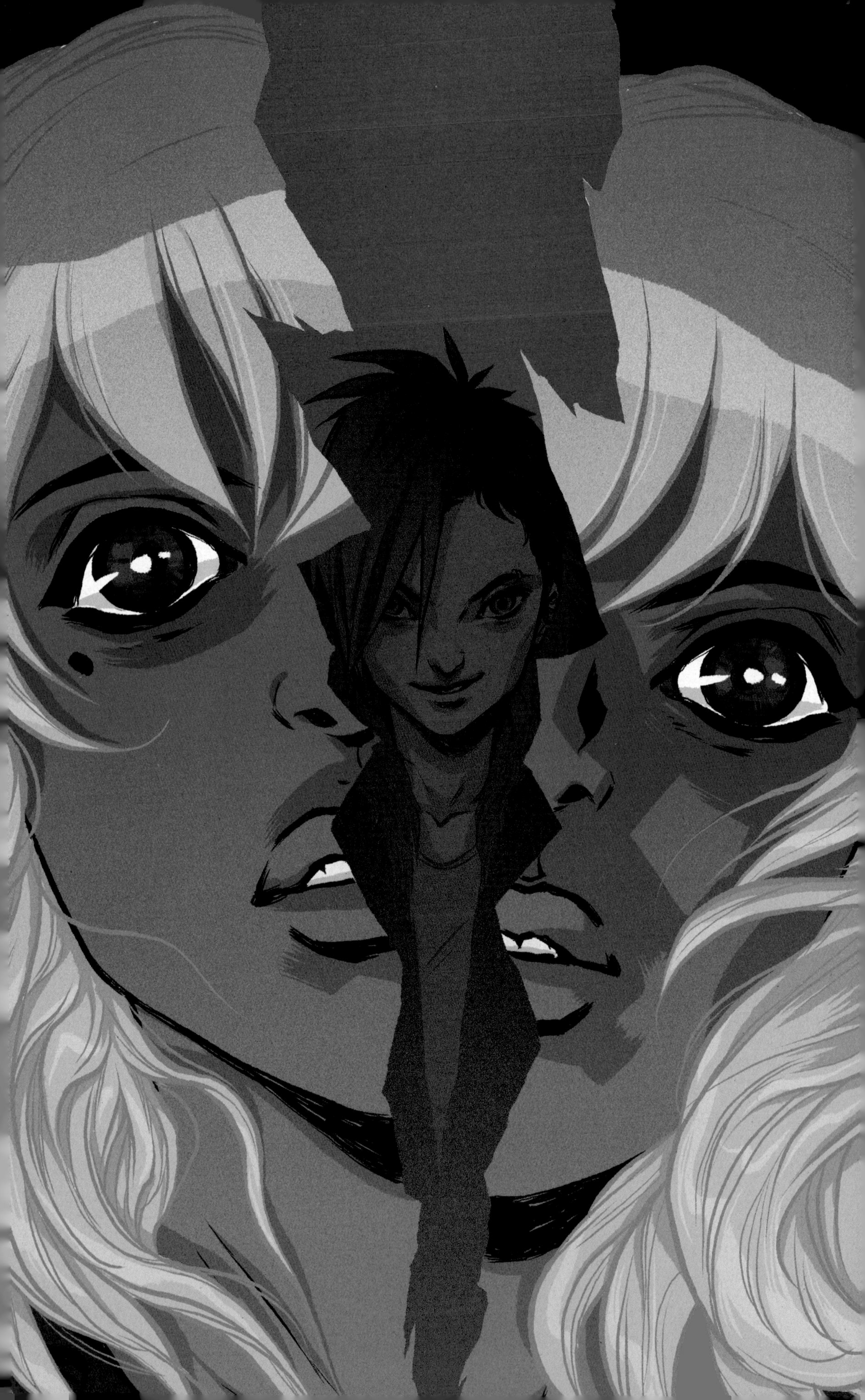

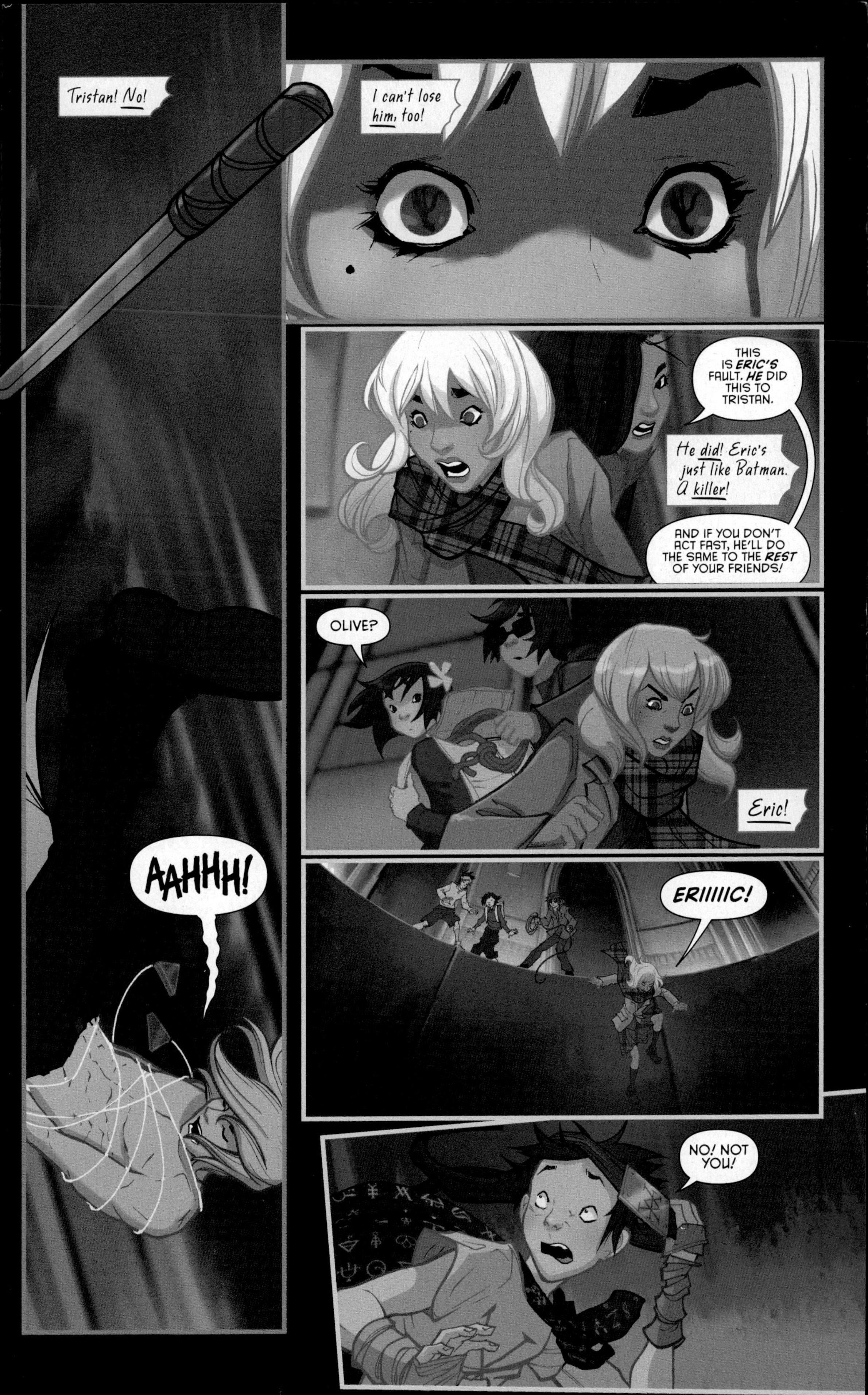

Tristan! No!
I can't lose him, too!
THIS IS ERIC'S FAULT. HE DID THIS TO TRISTAN.
He did! Eric's just like Batman. A killer!
AND IF YOU DON'T ACT FAST, HE'LL DO THE SAME TO THE REST OF YOUR FRIENDS!
OLIVE?
Eric!
AAHHH!
ERIIIIIC!
NO! NOT YOU!

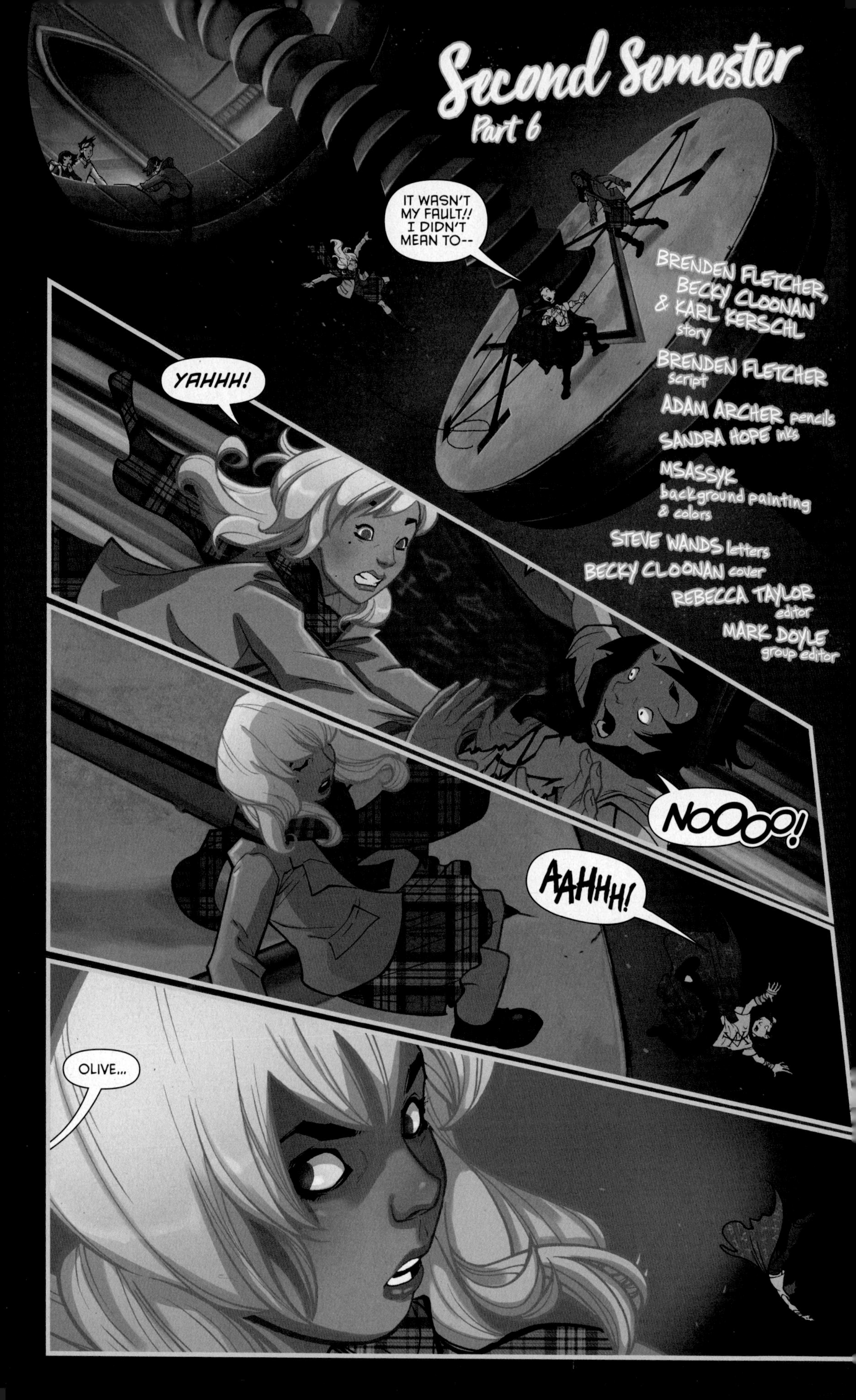
Second Semester
Part 6
IT WASN'T MY FAULT!! I DIDN'T MEAN TO--
BRENDEN FLETCHER, BECKY CLOONAN & KARL KERSCHL story
BRENDEN FLETCHER script
ADAM ARCHER pencils
SANDRA HOPE inks
MSASSYK background painting & colors
STEVE WANDS letters
BECKY CLOONAN cover
REBECCA TAYLOR editor
MARK DOYLE group editor
YAHHH!
NOOOO!
AAHHH!
OLIVE...

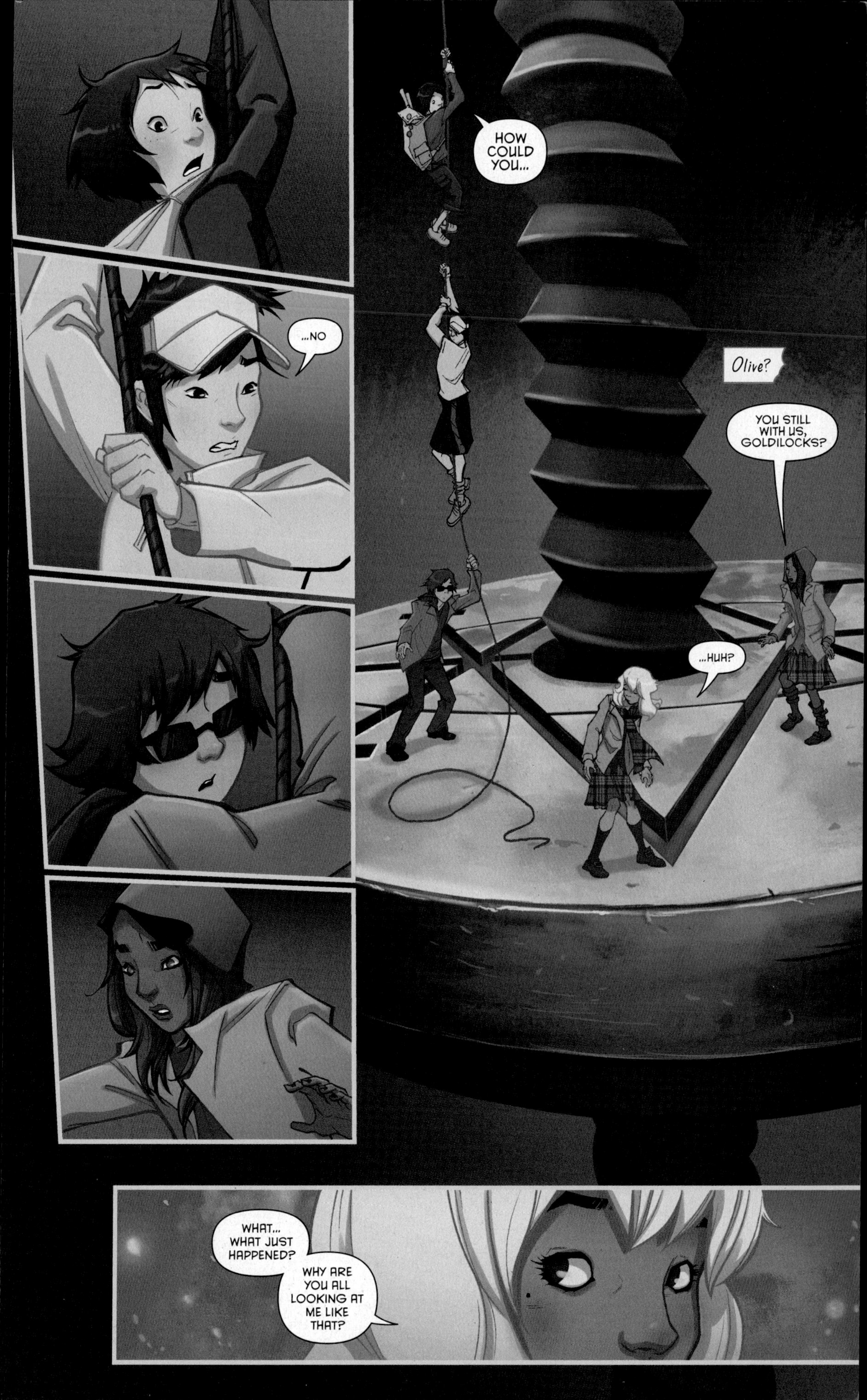
HOW COULD YOU...
...NO
Olive?
YOU STILL WITH US, GOLDILOCKS?
...HUH?
WHAT... WHAT JUST HAPPENED?
WHY ARE YOU ALL LOOKING AT ME LIKE THAT?

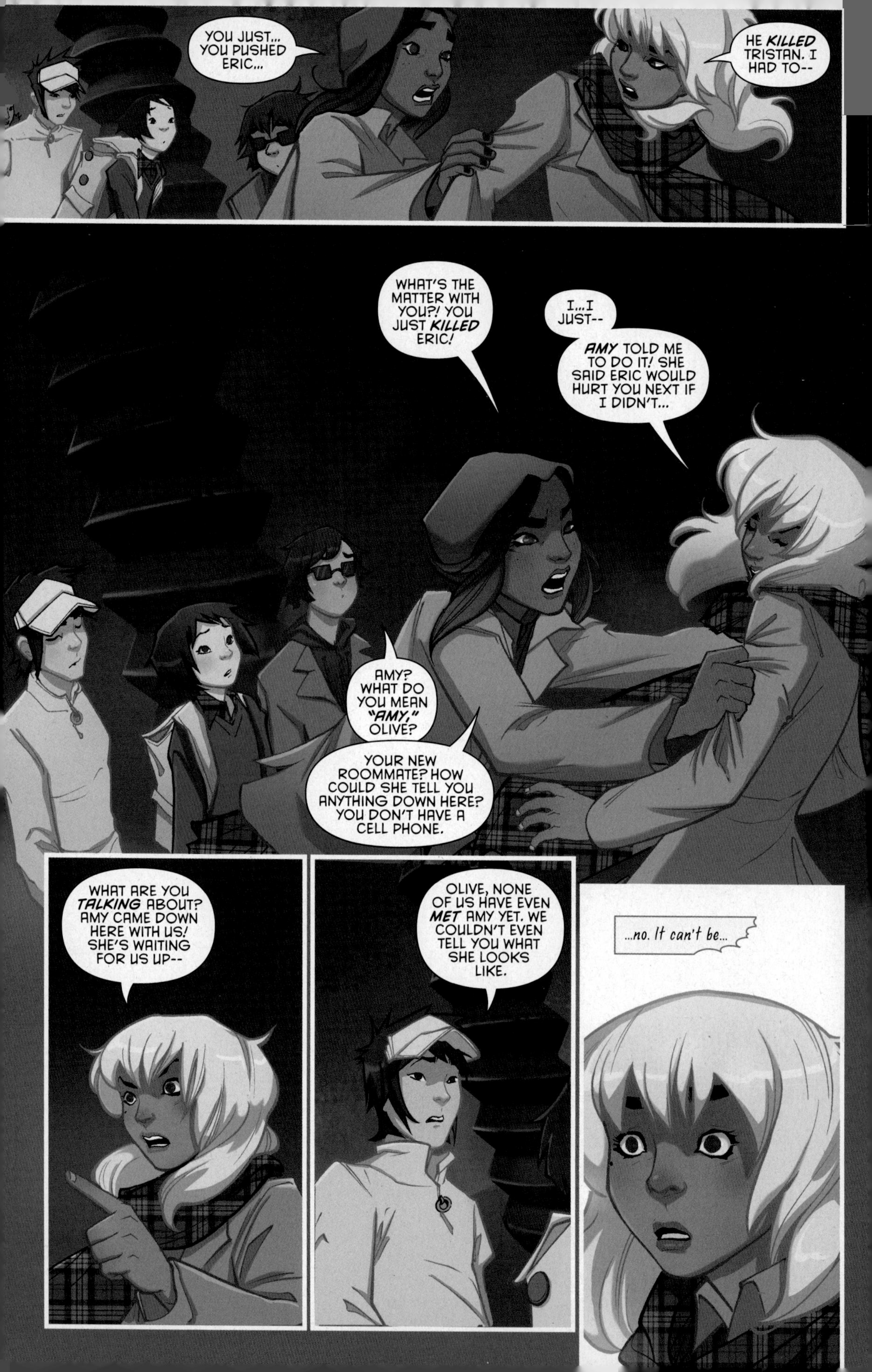
YOU JUST... YOU PUSHED ERIC...
HE KILLED TRISTAN. I HAD TO--
WHAT'S THE MATTER WITH YOU?! YOU JUST KILLED ERIC!
I...I JUST--
AMY TOLD ME TO DO IT! SHE SAID ERIC WOULD HURT YOU NEXT IF I DIDN'T...
AMY? WHAT DO YOU MEAN "AMY," OLIVE?
YOUR NEW ROOMMATE? HOW COULD SHE TELL YOU ANYTHING DOWN HERE? YOU DON'T HAVE A CELL PHONE.
WHAT ARE YOU TALKING ABOUT? AMY CAME DOWN HERE WITH US! SHE'S WAITING FOR US UP--
OLIVE, NONE OF US HAVE EVEN MET AMY YET. WE COULDN'T EVEN TELL YOU WHAT SHE LOOKS LIKE.
...no. It can't be...

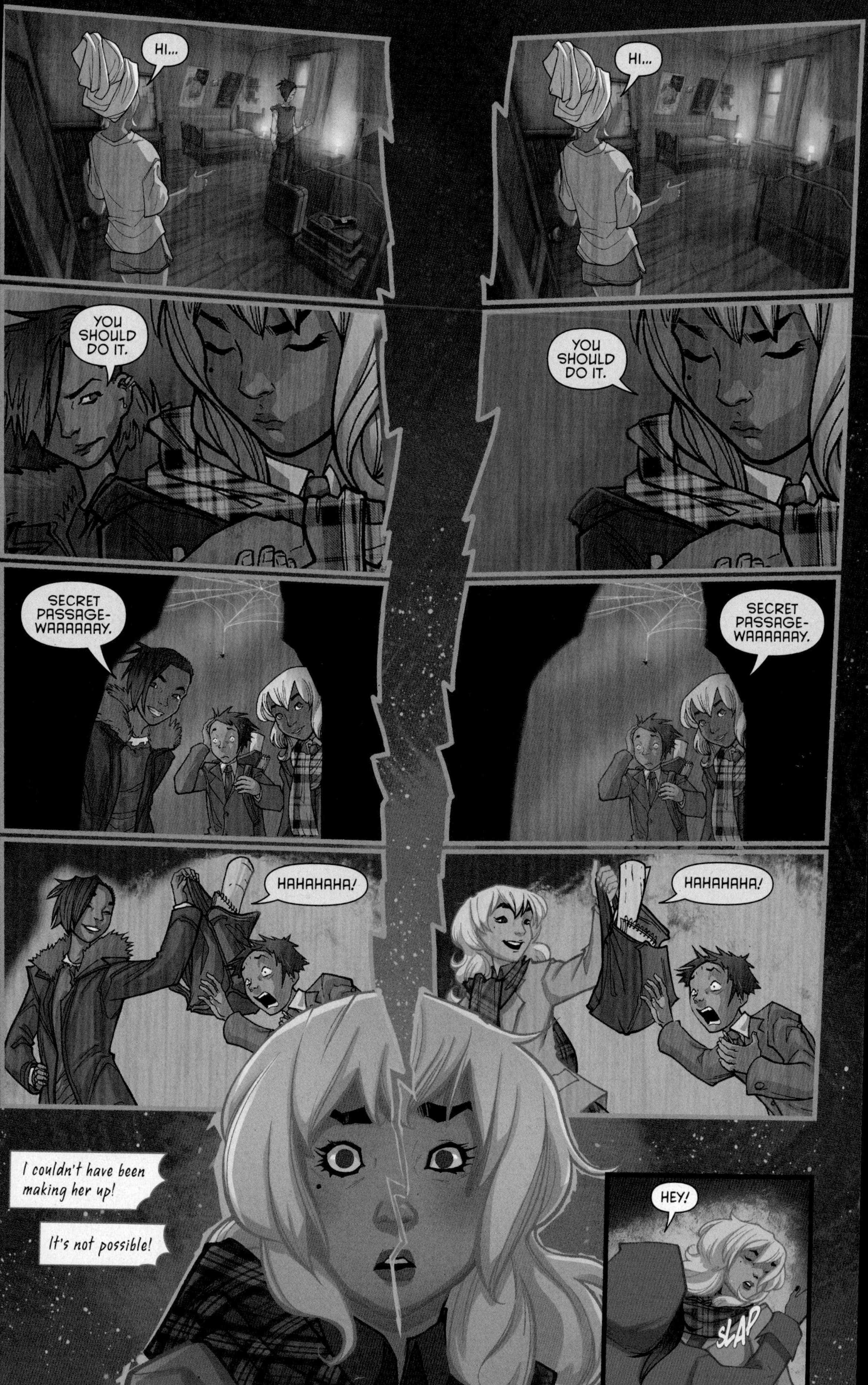
HI...
HI...
YOU SHOULD DO IT.
YOU SHOULD DO IT.
SECRET PASSAGE-WAAAAAAY.
SECRET PASSAGE-WAAAAAAY.
HAHAHAHA!
HAHAHAHA!
I couldn't have been making her up!
It's not possible!
HEY!
SLAP

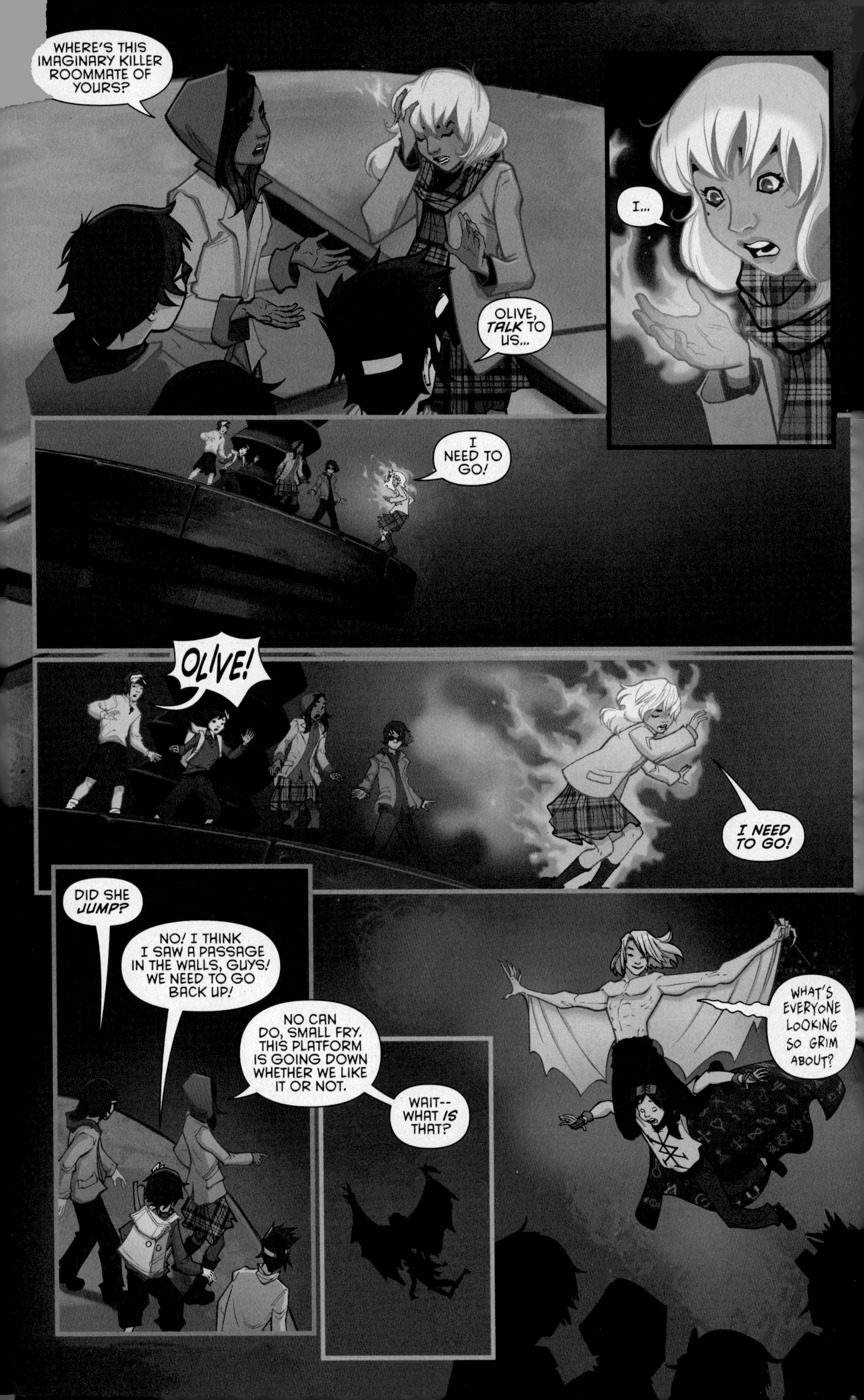
WHERE'S THIS IMAGINARY KILLER ROOMMATE OF YOURS?
OLIVE, *TALK* TO US...
I...
I NEED TO GO!
OLIVE!
*I NEED TO GO!*
DID SHE *JUMP?*
NO! I THINK I SAW A PASSAGE IN THE WALLS, GUYS! WE NEED TO GO BACK UP!
NO CAN DO, SMALL FRY. THIS PLATFORM IS GOING DOWN WHETHER WE LIKE IT OR NOT.
WAIT-- WHAT *IS* THAT?
WHAT'S EVERYONE LOOKING SO GRIM ABOUT?

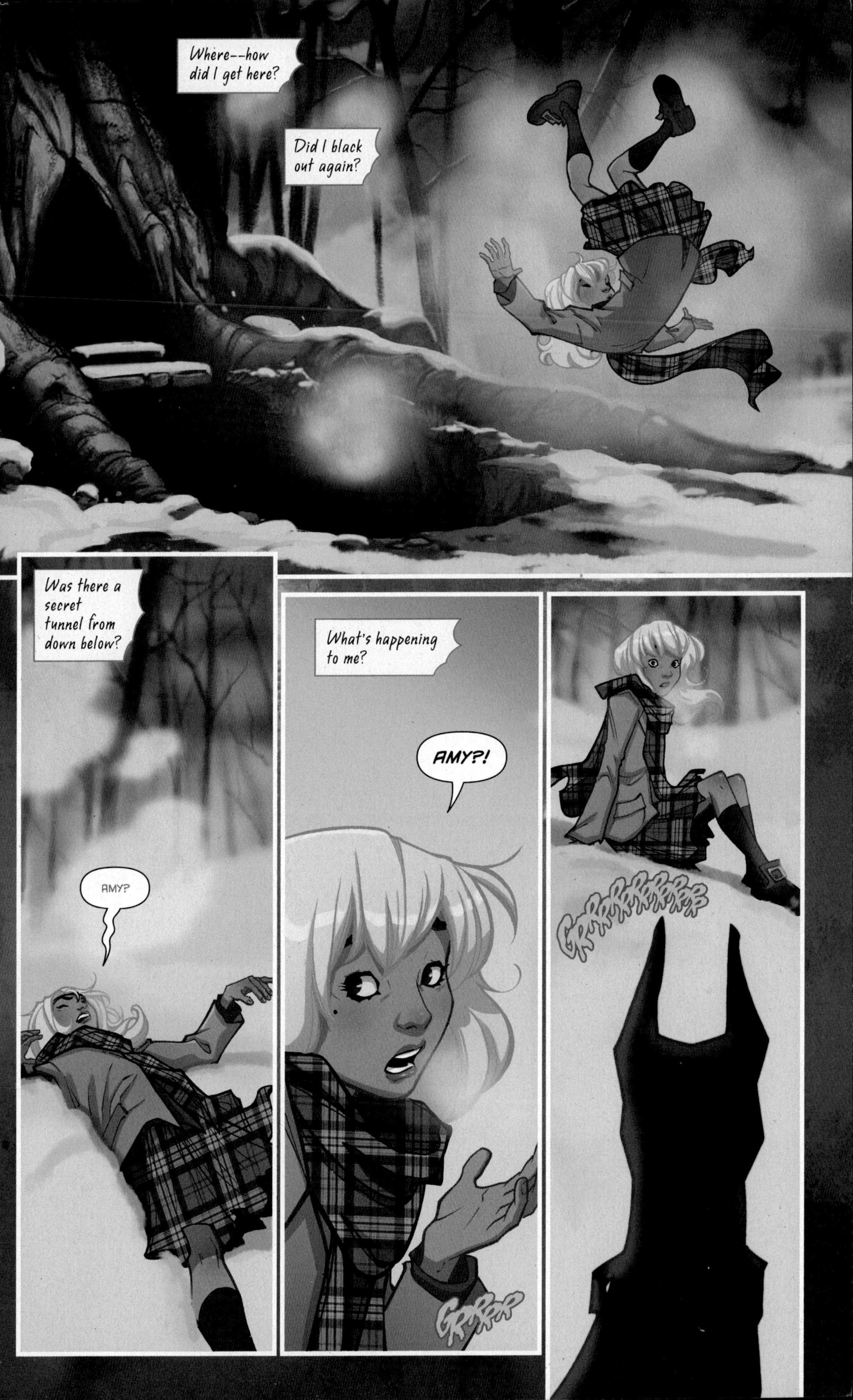

Where--how did I get here?
Did I black out again?
Was there a secret tunnel from down below?
AMY?
GRRRR
What's happening to me?
AMY?!
GRRRRRRRRRR

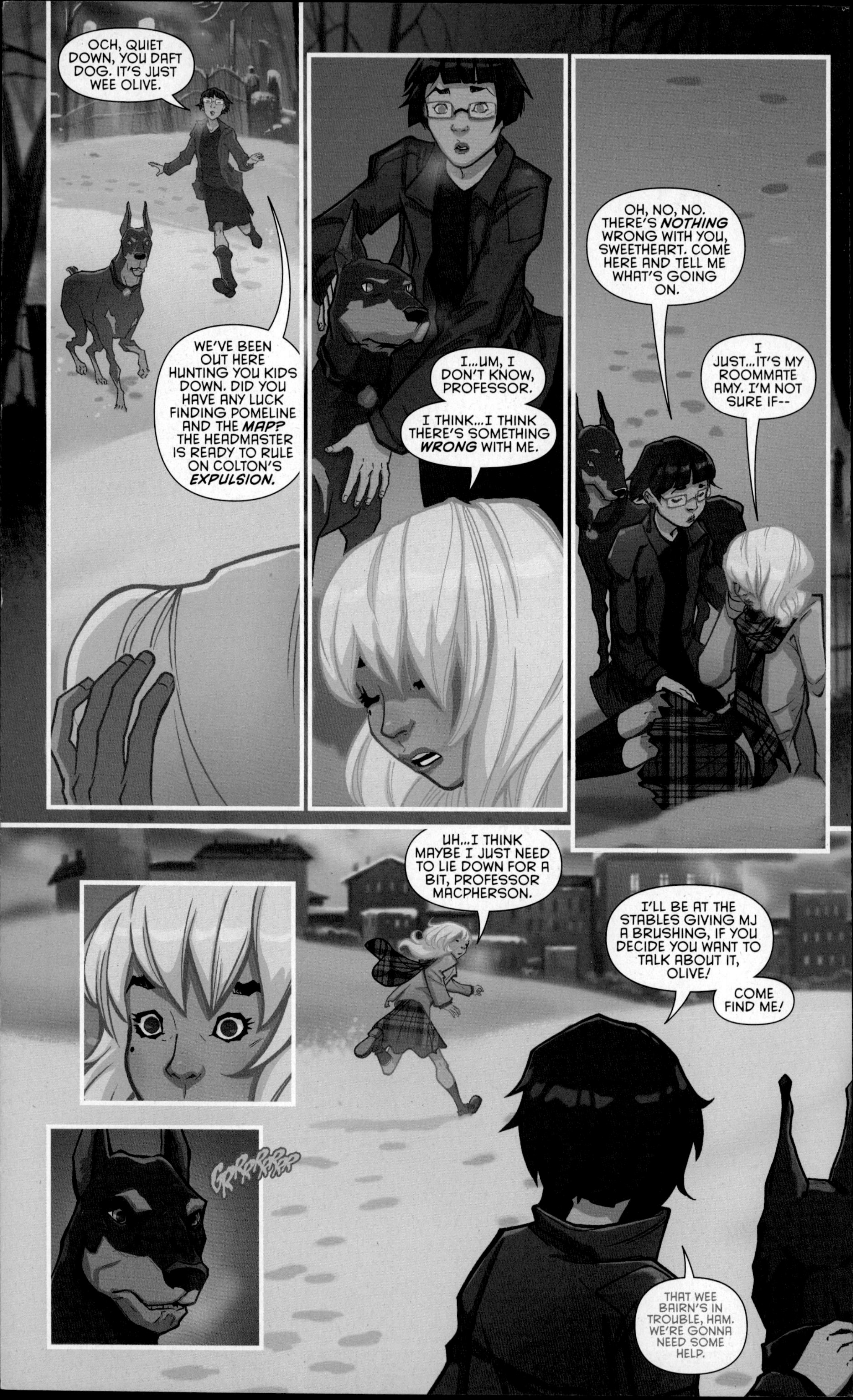
OCH, QUIET DOWN, YOU DAFT DOG. IT'S JUST WEE OLIVE.
WE'VE BEEN OUT HERE HUNTING YOU KIDS DOWN. DID YOU HAVE ANY LUCK FINDING POMELINE AND THE *MAP?* THE HEADMASTER IS READY TO RULE ON COLTON'S *EXPULSION.*
I...UM, I DON'T KNOW, PROFESSOR.
I THINK...I THINK THERE'S SOMETHING *WRONG* WITH ME.
OH, NO, NO. THERE'S *NOTHING* WRONG WITH YOU, SWEETHEART. COME HERE AND TELL ME WHAT'S GOING ON.
I JUST...IT'S MY ROOMMATE AMY. I'M NOT SURE IF--
UH...I THINK MAYBE I JUST NEED TO LIE DOWN FOR A BIT, PROFESSOR MACPHERSON.
I'LL BE AT THE STABLES GIVING MJ A BRUSHING, IF YOU DECIDE YOU WANT TO TALK ABOUT IT, OLIVE!
COME FIND ME!
GRRRRRRR
THAT WEE BAIRN'S IN TROUBLE, HAM. WE'RE GONNA NEED SOME HELP.

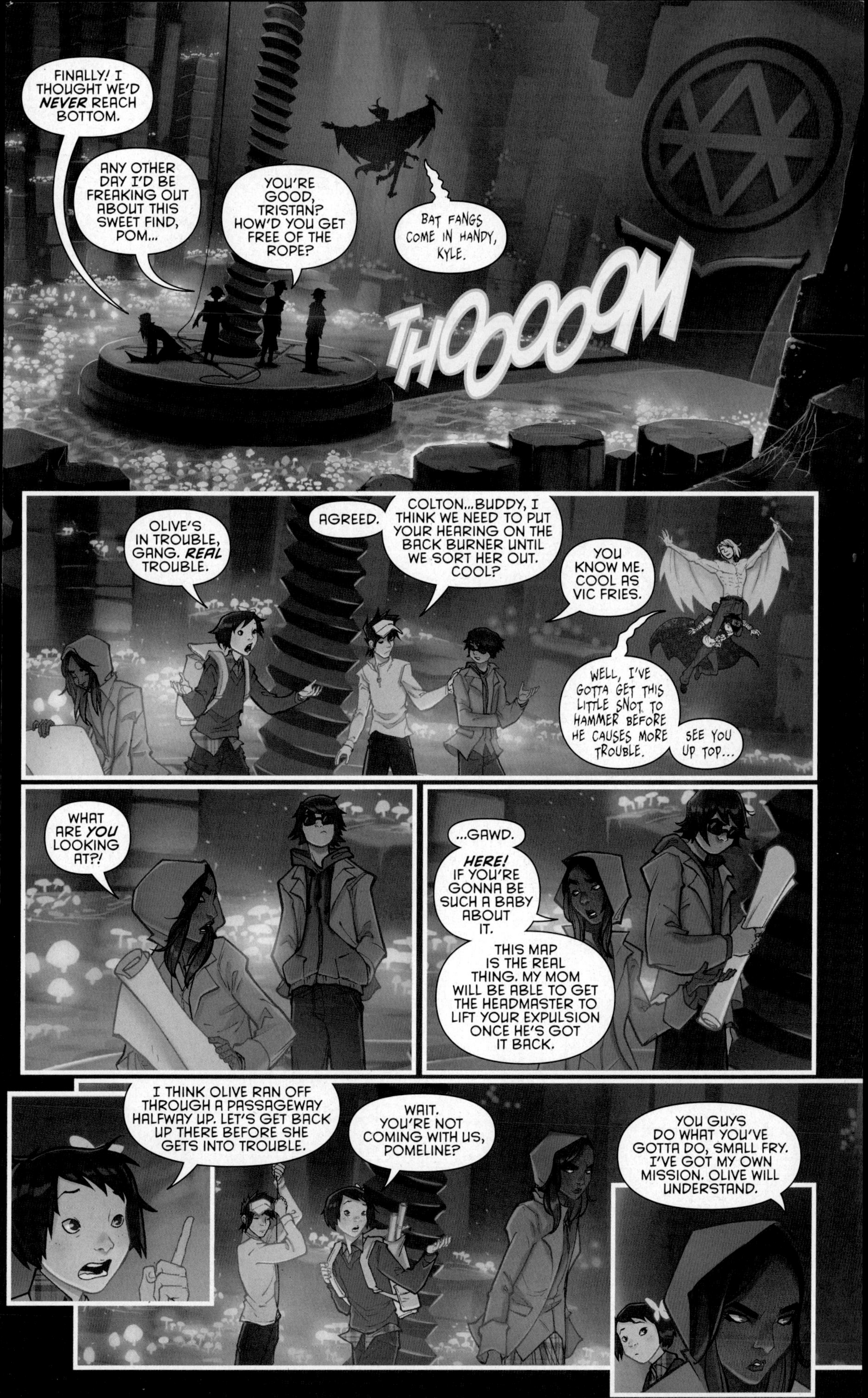

FINALLY! I THOUGHT WE'D NEVER REACH BOTTOM.
ANY OTHER DAY I'D BE FREAKING OUT ABOUT THIS SWEET FIND, POM...
YOU'RE GOOD, TRISTAN? HOW'D YOU GET FREE OF THE ROPE?
BAT FANGS COME IN HANDY, KYLE.
THOOOOOM
OLIVE'S IN TROUBLE, GANG. REAL TROUBLE.
AGREED.
COLTON...BUDDY, I THINK WE NEED TO PUT YOUR HEARING ON THE BACK BURNER UNTIL WE SORT HER OUT. COOL?
YOU KNOW ME. COOL AS VIC FRIES.
WELL, I'VE GOTTA GET THIS LITTLE SNOT TO HAMMER BEFORE HE CAUSES MORE TROUBLE.
SEE YOU UP TOP...
WHAT ARE YOU LOOKING AT?!
...GAWD.
HERE! IF YOU'RE GONNA BE SUCH A BABY ABOUT IT.
THIS MAP IS THE REAL THING. MY MOM WILL BE ABLE TO GET THE HEADMASTER TO LIFT YOUR EXPULSION ONCE HE'S GOT IT BACK.
I THINK OLIVE RAN OFF THROUGH A PASSAGEWAY HALFWAY UP. LET'S GET BACK UP THERE BEFORE SHE GETS INTO TROUBLE.
WAIT. YOU'RE NOT COMING WITH US, POMELINE?
YOU GUYS DO WHAT YOU'VE GOTTA DO, SMALL FRY. I'VE GOT MY OWN MISSION. OLIVE WILL UNDERSTAND.

OKAY. I KNOW YOU'D HELP US IF YOU COULD.

YOU SHOULD TAKE THIS...

MY BACKPACK HAS ALL THE GEAR YOU'LL EVER NEED TO BE SAFE.

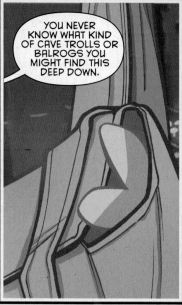

YOU NEVER KNOW WHAT KIND OF CAVE TROLLS OR BALROGS YOU MIGHT FIND THIS DEEP DOWN.

GET OVER IT, COOL BREEZE.

WHAT DO YOU EVEN *WANT* FROM ME?

COLTON'S GOING WITH *HER?* BUT--

IT'S THE LURE OF THE LOOT, BROTHER O' MINE. COLTON SMELLS A PAYDAY DOWN THERE.

I SHOULDN'T BE SURPRISED. THEY'RE TWO OF A KIND...

GUESS IT'S JUST YOU AND ME, MIA. LET'S GET OUTTA HERE AND FIND OLIVE.

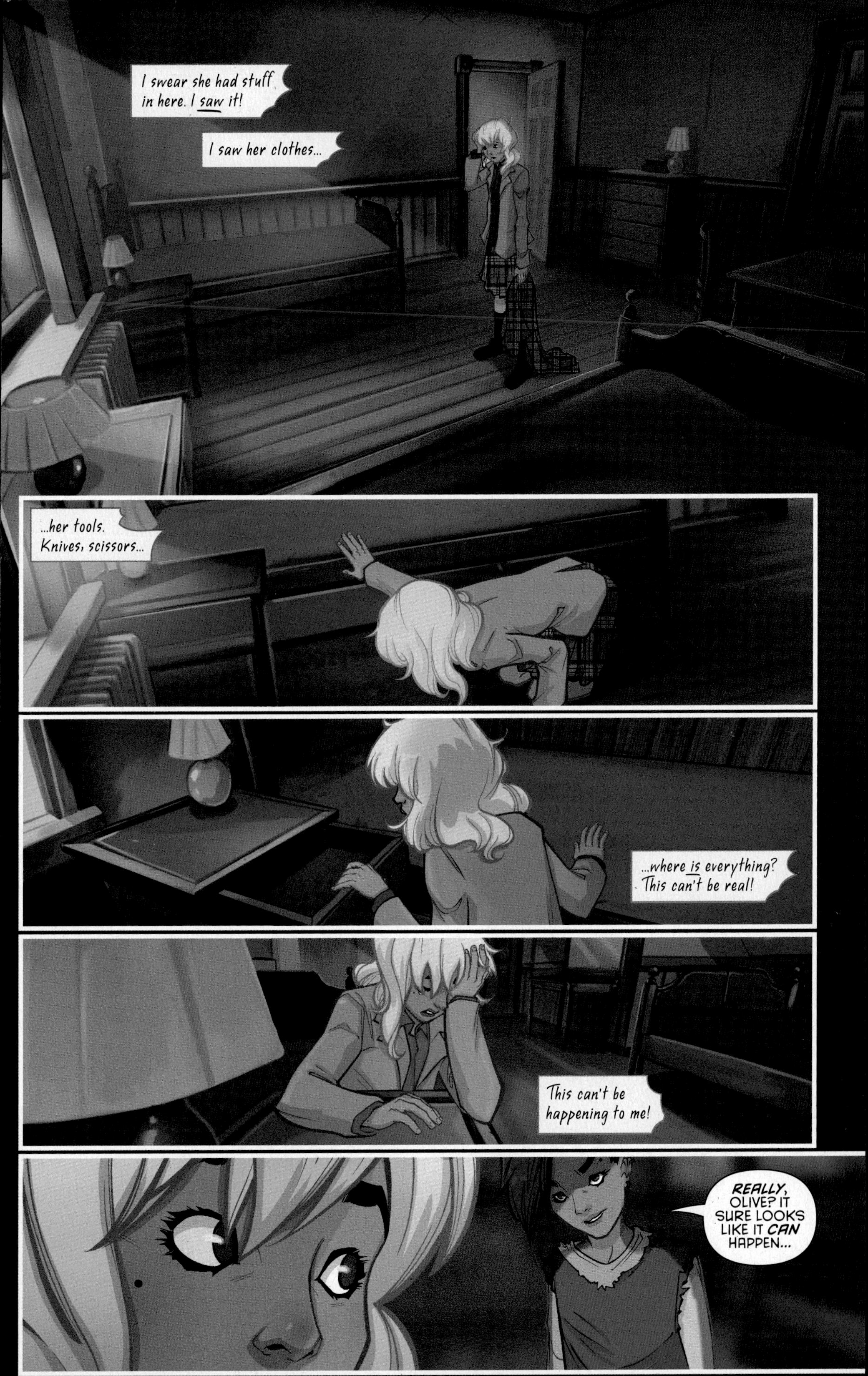
I swear she had stuff in here. I saw it!
I saw her clothes...
...her tools. Knives, scissors...
...where is everything? This can't be real!
This can't be happening to me!
REALLY, OLIVE? IT SURE LOOKS LIKE IT CAN HAPPEN...

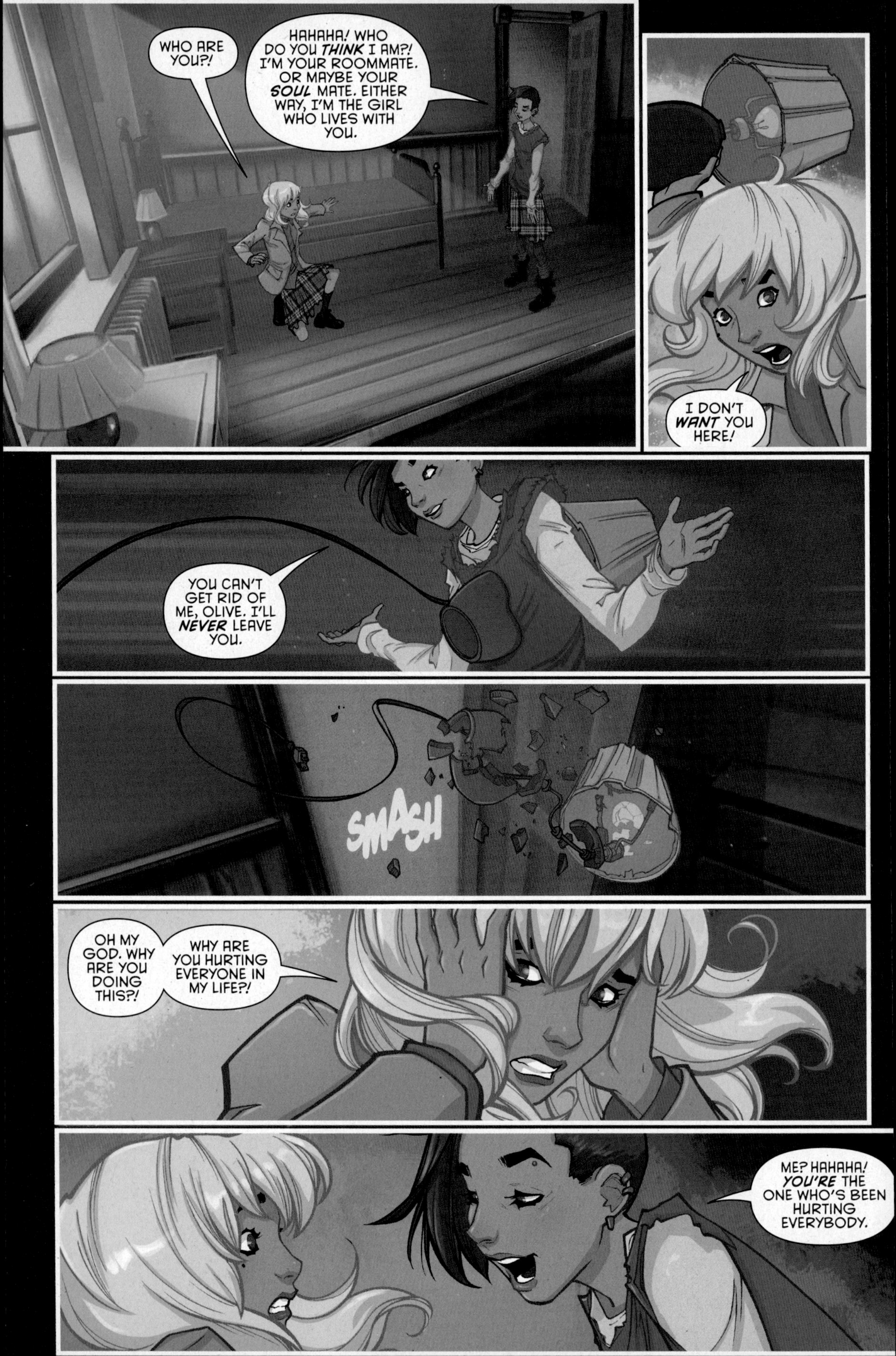

WHO ARE YOU?!
HAHAHA! WHO DO YOU *THINK* I AM?! I'M YOUR ROOMMATE. OR MAYBE YOUR *SOUL* MATE. EITHER WAY, I'M THE GIRL WHO LIVES WITH YOU.
I DON'T *WANT* YOU HERE!
YOU CAN'T GET RID OF ME, OLIVE. I'LL *NEVER* LEAVE YOU.
SMASH
OH MY GOD. WHY ARE YOU DOING THIS?!
WHY ARE YOU HURTING EVERYONE IN MY LIFE?!
ME? HAHAHA! *YOU'RE* THE ONE WHO'S BEEN HURTING EVERYBODY.

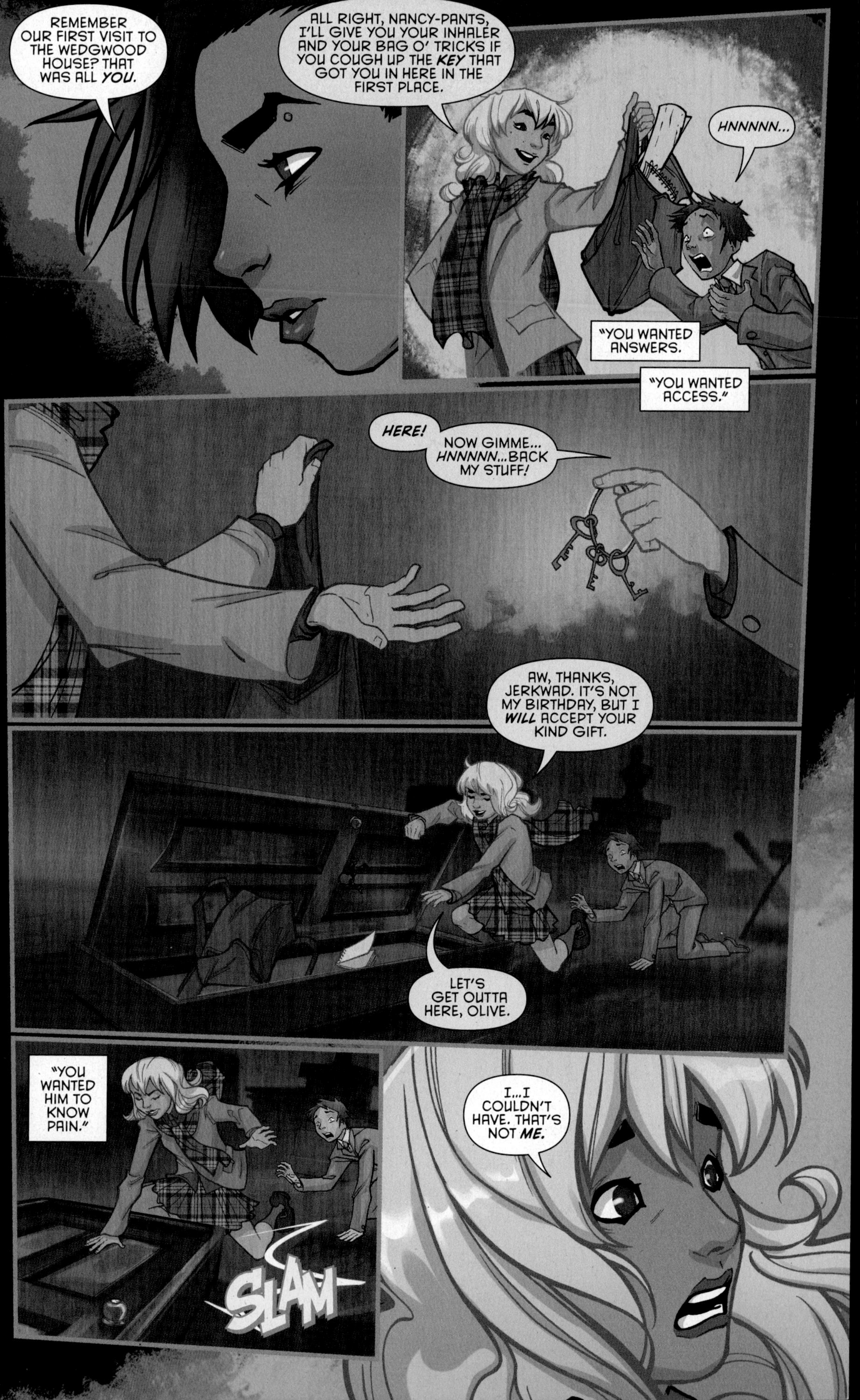

REMEMBER OUR FIRST VISIT TO THE WEDGWOOD HOUSE? THAT WAS ALL *YOU.*
ALL RIGHT, NANCY-PANTS, I'LL GIVE YOU YOUR INHALER AND YOUR BAG O' TRICKS IF YOU COUGH UP THE *KEY* THAT GOT YOU IN HERE IN THE FIRST PLACE.
HNNNNN...
"YOU WANTED ANSWERS.
"YOU WANTED ACCESS."
*HERE!*
NOW GIMME... *HNNNNN*...BACK MY STUFF!
AW, THANKS, JERKWAD. IT'S NOT MY BIRTHDAY, BUT I *WILL* ACCEPT YOUR KIND GIFT.
LET'S GET OUTTA HERE, OLIVE.
"YOU WANTED HIM TO KNOW PAIN."
SLAM
I...I COULDN'T HAVE. THAT'S NOT *ME.*

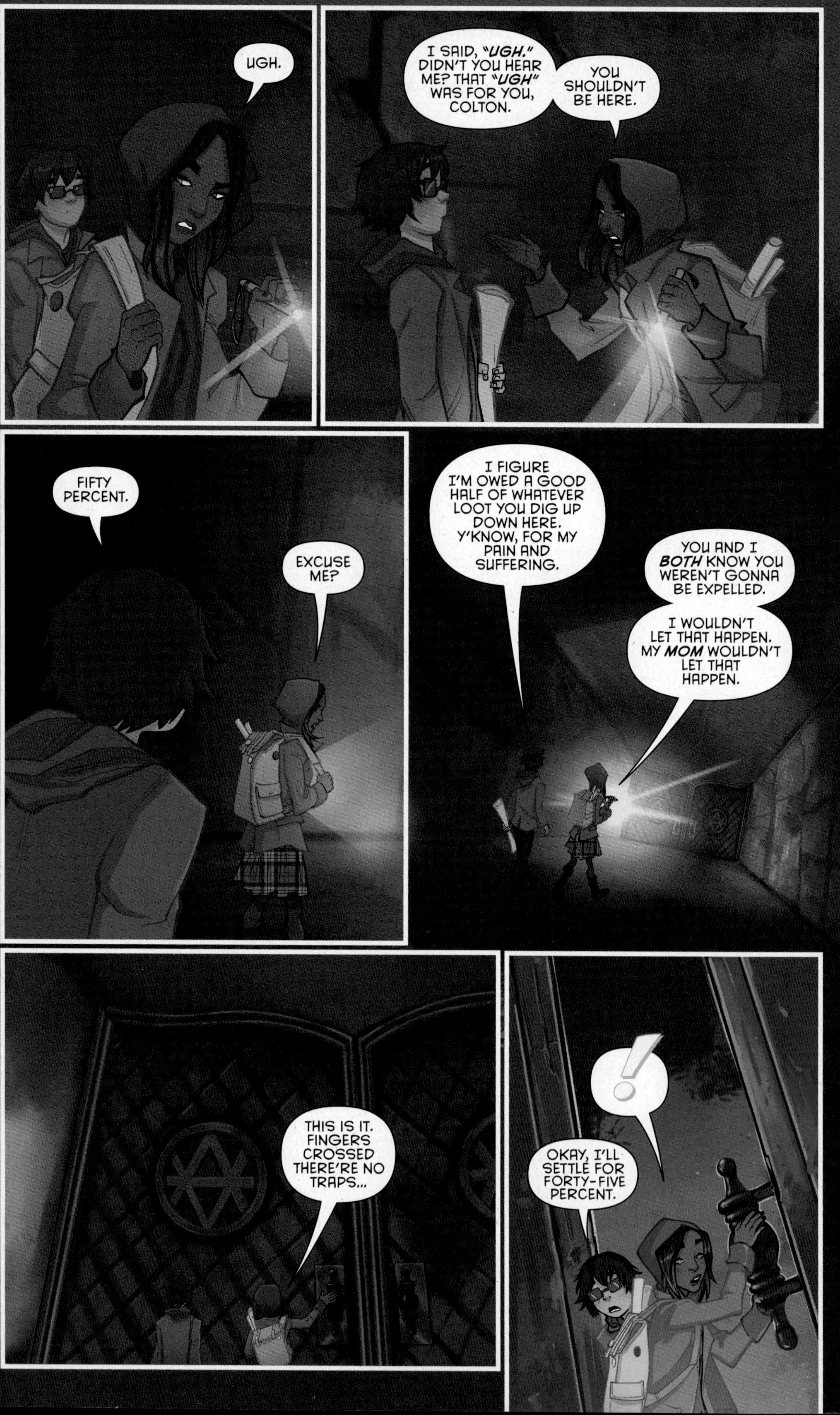
UGH.
I SAID, "UGH." DIDN'T YOU HEAR ME? THAT "UGH" WAS FOR YOU, COLTON.
YOU SHOULDN'T BE HERE.
FIFTY PERCENT.
EXCUSE ME?
I FIGURE I'M OWED A GOOD HALF OF WHATEVER LOOT YOU DIG UP DOWN HERE. Y'KNOW, FOR MY PAIN AND SUFFERING.
YOU AND I BOTH KNOW YOU WEREN'T GONNA BE EXPELLED.
I WOULDN'T LET THAT HAPPEN. MY MOM WOULDN'T LET THAT HAPPEN.
THIS IS IT. FINGERS CROSSED THERE'RE NO TRAPS...
!
OKAY, I'LL SETTLE FOR FORTY-FIVE PERCENT.

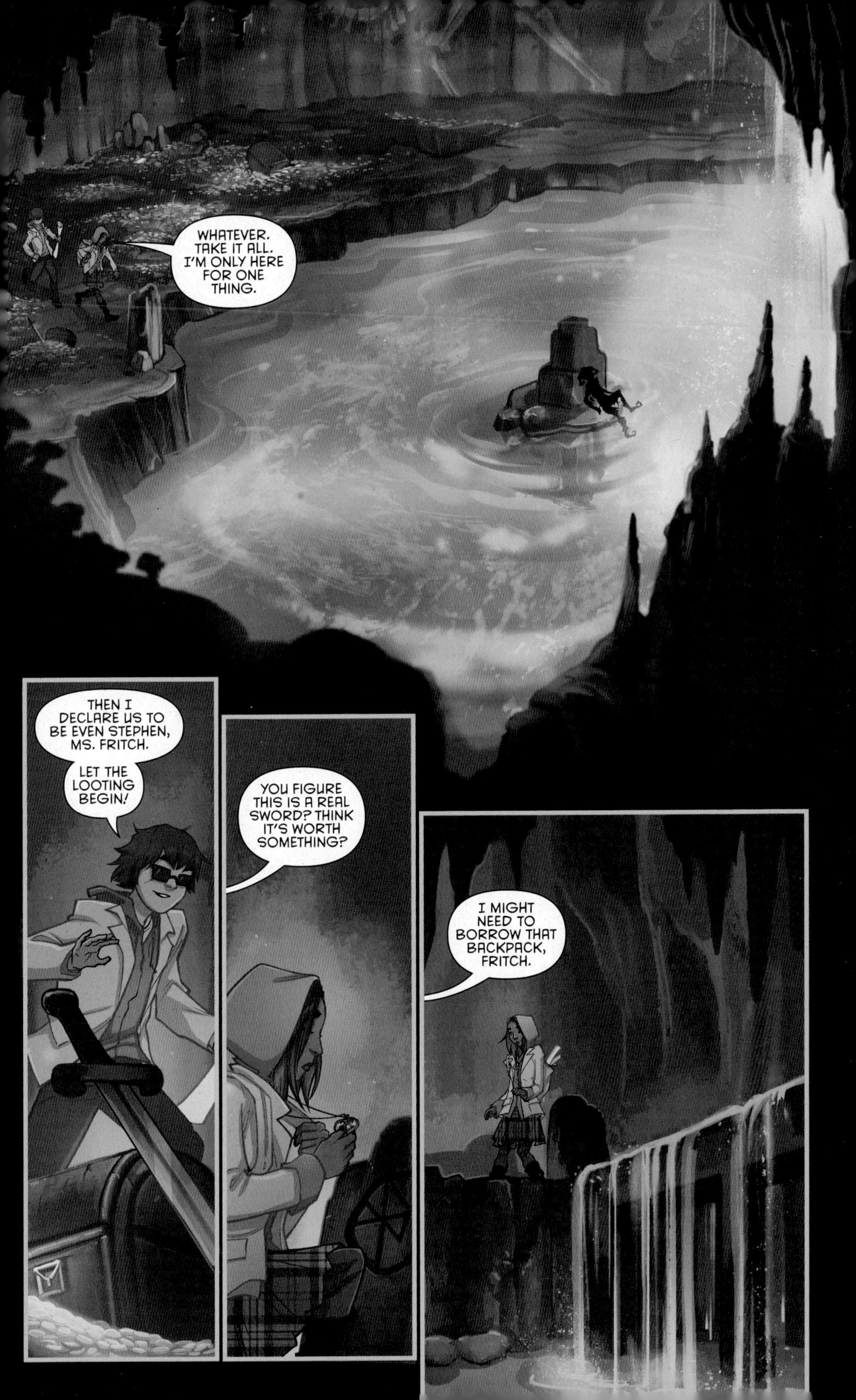
WHATEVER. TAKE IT ALL. I'M ONLY HERE FOR ONE THING.
THEN I DECLARE US TO BE EVEN STEPHEN, MS. FRITCH.
LET THE LOOTING BEGIN!
YOU FIGURE THIS IS A REAL SWORD? THINK IT'S WORTH SOMETHING?
I MIGHT NEED TO BORROW THAT BACKPACK, FRITCH.

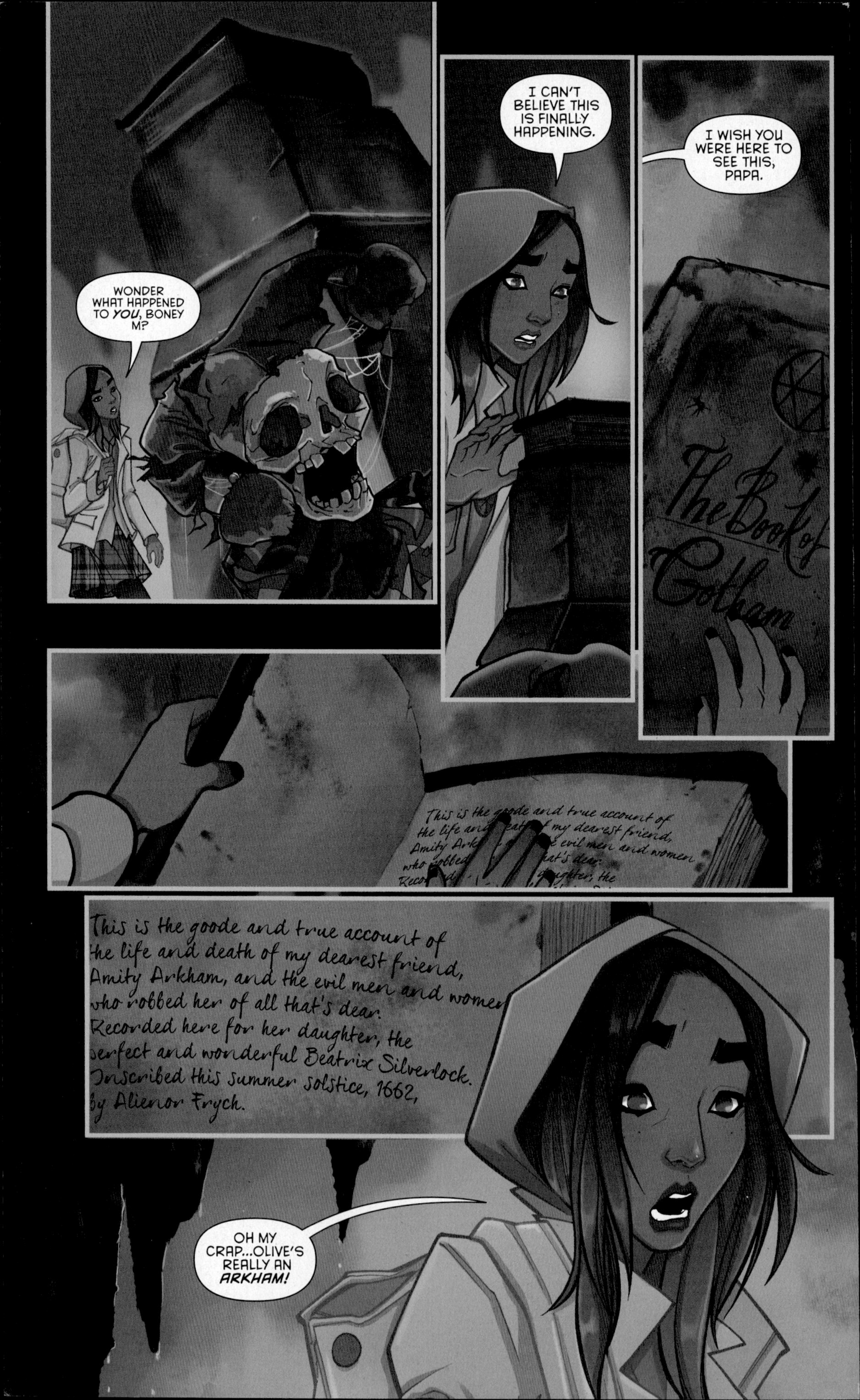
WONDER WHAT HAPPENED TO *YOU*, BONEY M?
I CAN'T BELIEVE THIS IS FINALLY HAPPENING.
I WISH YOU WERE HERE TO SEE THIS, PAPA.
The Book of Gotham
This is the goode and true account of the life and death of my dearest friend, Amity Arkham, and the evil men and women who robbed her of all that's dear. Recorded here for her daughter, the perfect and wonderful Beatrix Silverlock. Inscribed this summer solstice, 1662, by Alienor Frych.
OH MY CRAP...OLIVE'S REALLY AN *ARKHAM!*

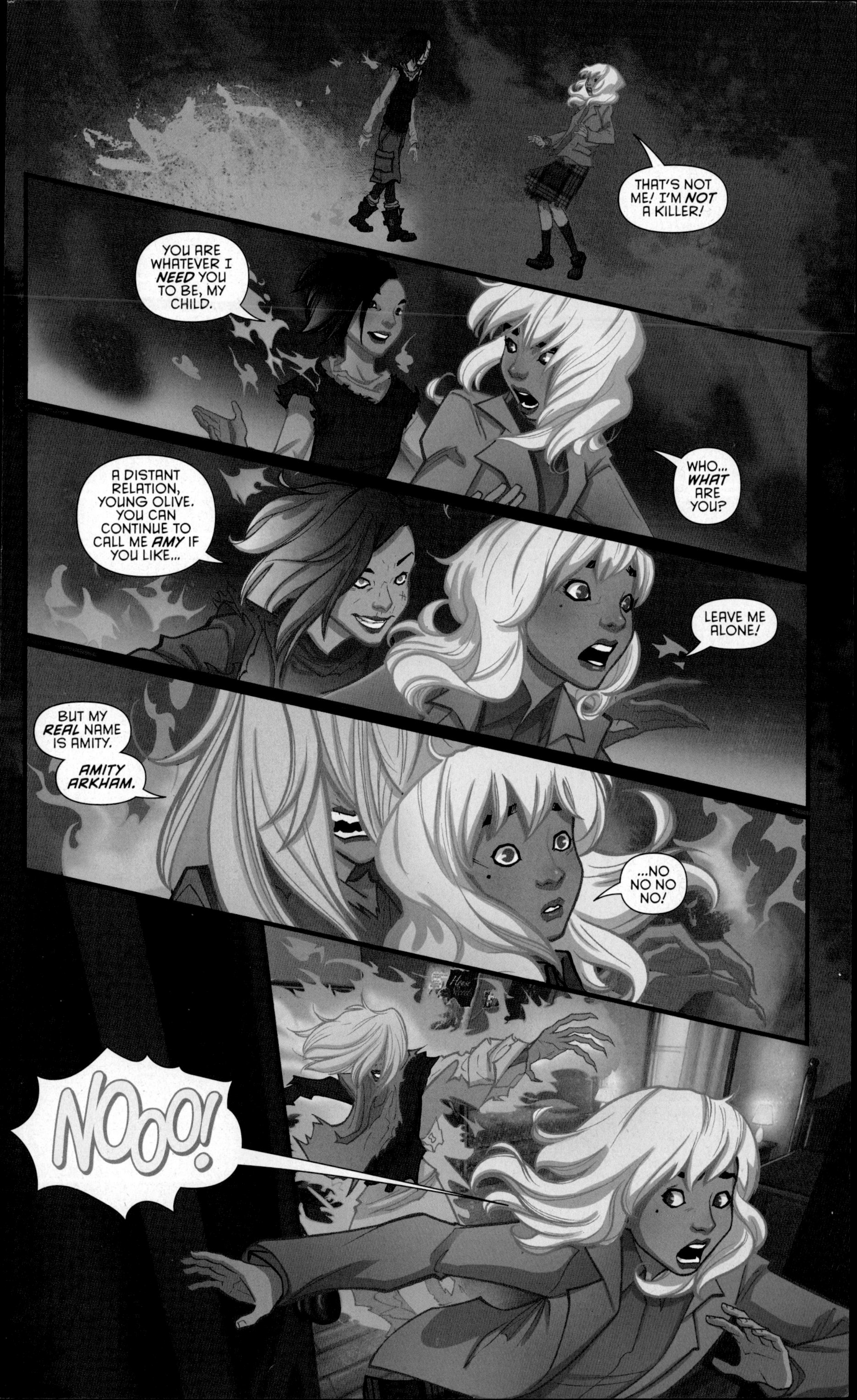

THAT'S NOT ME! I'M NOT A KILLER!
YOU ARE WHATEVER I NEED YOU TO BE, MY CHILD.
WHO... WHAT ARE YOU?
A DISTANT RELATION, YOUNG OLIVE. YOU CAN CONTINUE TO CALL ME AMY IF YOU LIKE...
LEAVE ME ALONE!
BUT MY REAL NAME IS AMITY.
AMITY ARKHAM.
...NO NO NO NO!
NOOO!

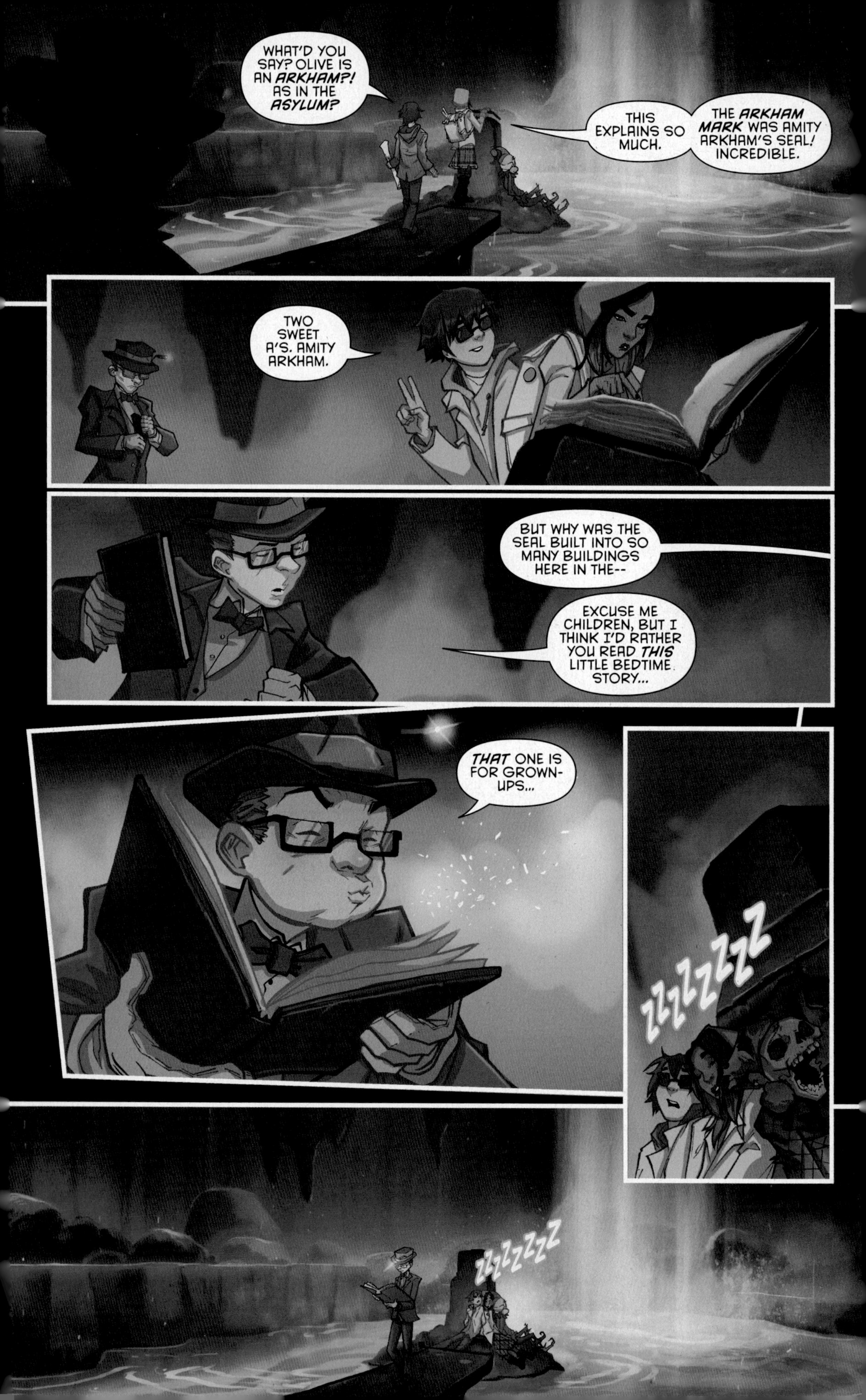
WHAT'D YOU SAY? OLIVE IS AN ARKHAM?! AS IN THE ASYLUM?
THIS EXPLAINS SO MUCH.
THE ARKHAM MARK WAS AMITY ARKHAM'S SEAL! INCREDIBLE.
TWO SWEET A'S. AMITY ARKHAM.
BUT WHY WAS THE SEAL BUILT INTO SO MANY BUILDINGS HERE IN THE--
EXCUSE ME CHILDREN, BUT I THINK I'D RATHER YOU READ THIS LITTLE BEDTIME STORY...
THAT ONE IS FOR GROWN-UPS...
ZZZZZZZZ
ZZZZZZZZ

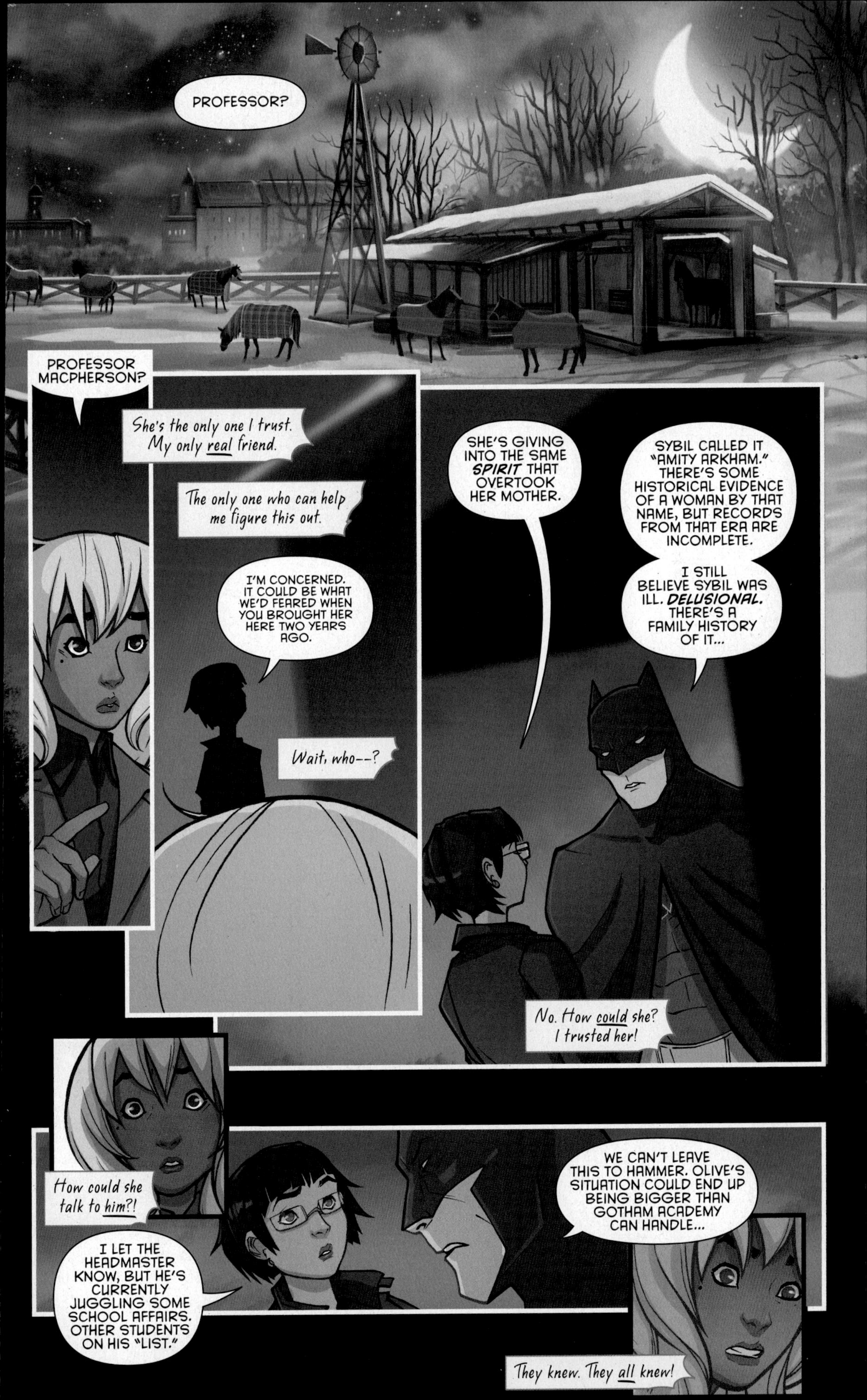
PROFESSOR?
PROFESSOR MACPHERSON?
She's the only one I trust. My only real friend.
The only one who can help me figure this out.
I'M CONCERNED. IT COULD BE WHAT WE'D FEARED WHEN YOU BROUGHT HER HERE TWO YEARS AGO.
Wait, who--?
SHE'S GIVING INTO THE SAME SPIRIT THAT OVERTOOK HER MOTHER.
SYBIL CALLED IT "AMITY ARKHAM." THERE'S SOME HISTORICAL EVIDENCE OF A WOMAN BY THAT NAME, BUT RECORDS FROM THAT ERA ARE INCOMPLETE.
I STILL BELIEVE SYBIL WAS ILL. DELUSIONAL. THERE'S A FAMILY HISTORY OF IT...
No. How could she? I trusted her!
How could she talk to him?!
I LET THE HEADMASTER KNOW, BUT HE'S CURRENTLY JUGGLING SOME SCHOOL AFFAIRS. OTHER STUDENTS ON HIS "LIST."
WE CAN'T LEAVE THIS TO HAMMER. OLIVE'S SITUATION COULD END UP BEING BIGGER THAN GOTHAM ACADEMY CAN HANDLE...
They knew. They all knew!

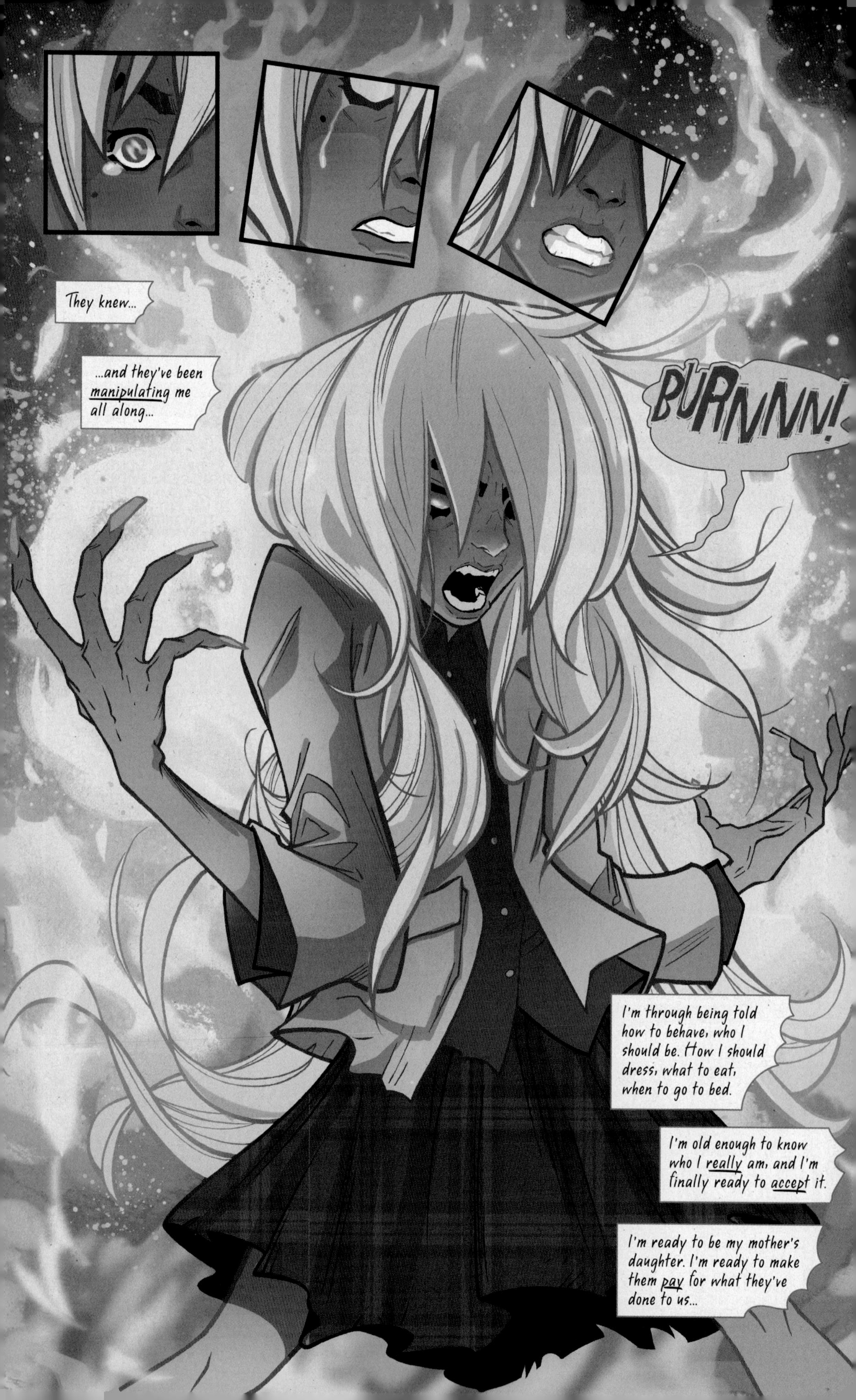
They knew...
...and they've been manipulating me all along...
BURNNN!
I'm through being told how to behave, who I should be. How I should dress, what to eat, when to go to bed.
I'm old enough to know who I really am, and I'm finally ready to accept it.
I'm ready to be my mother's daughter. I'm ready to make them pay for what they've done to us...

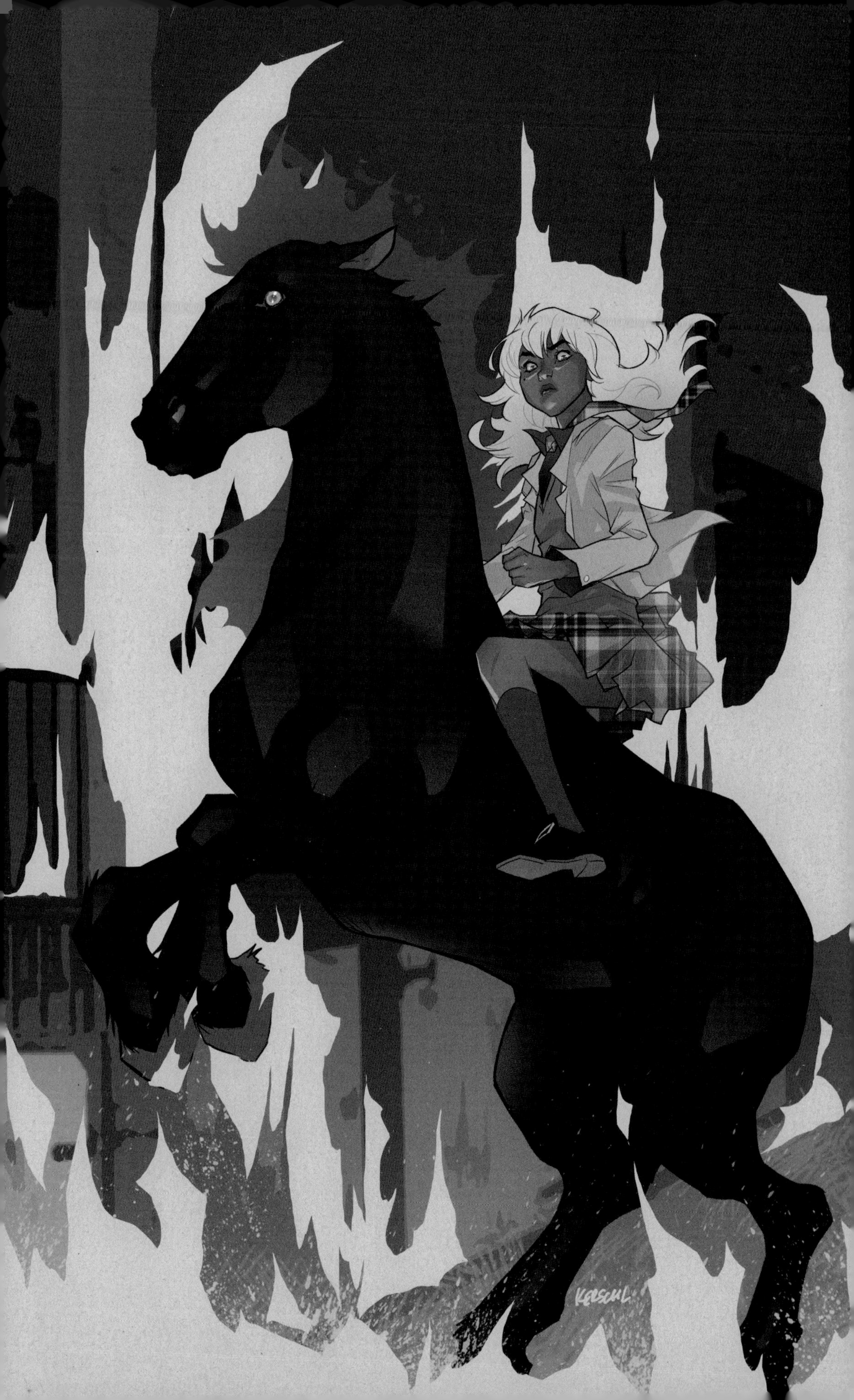

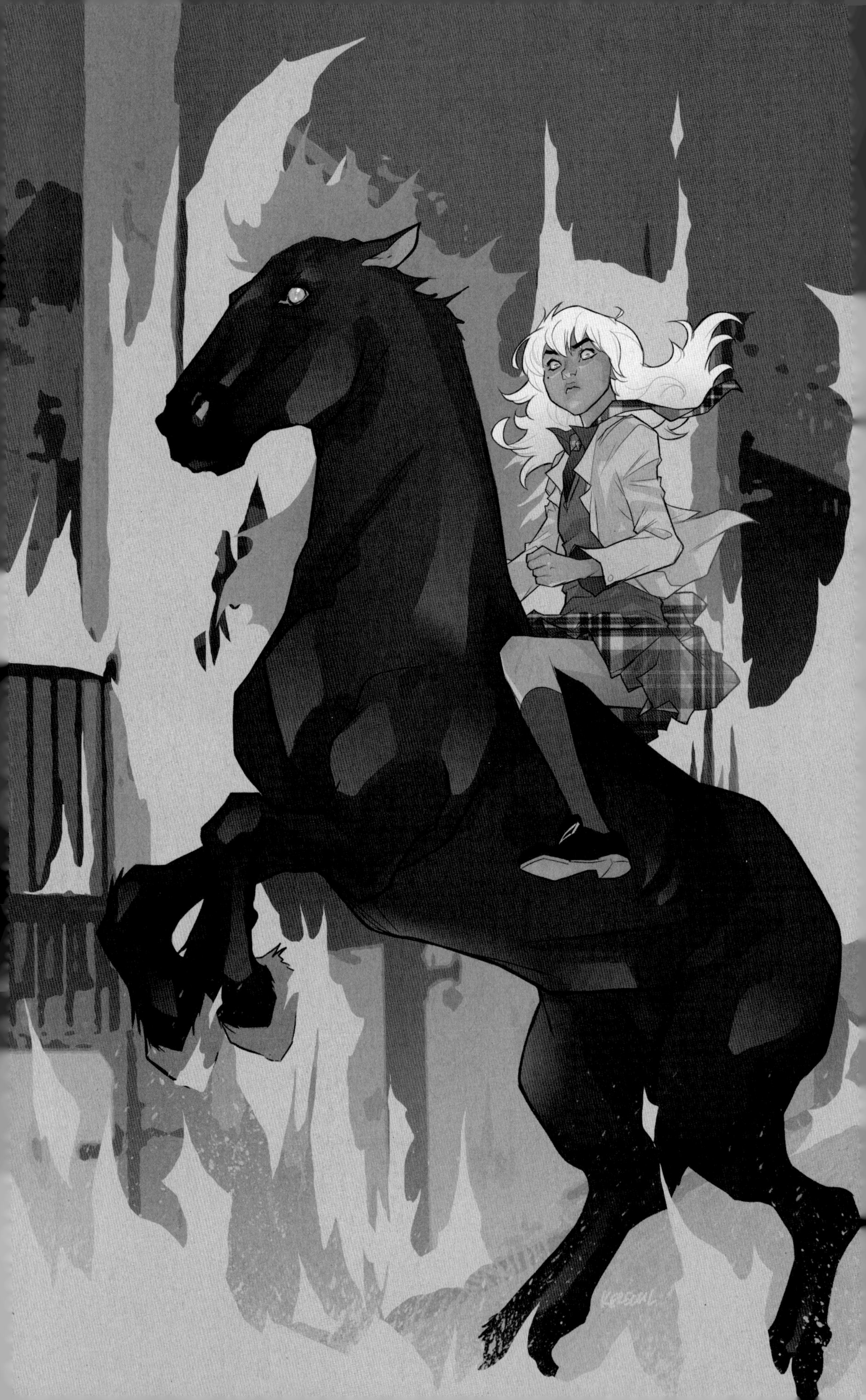

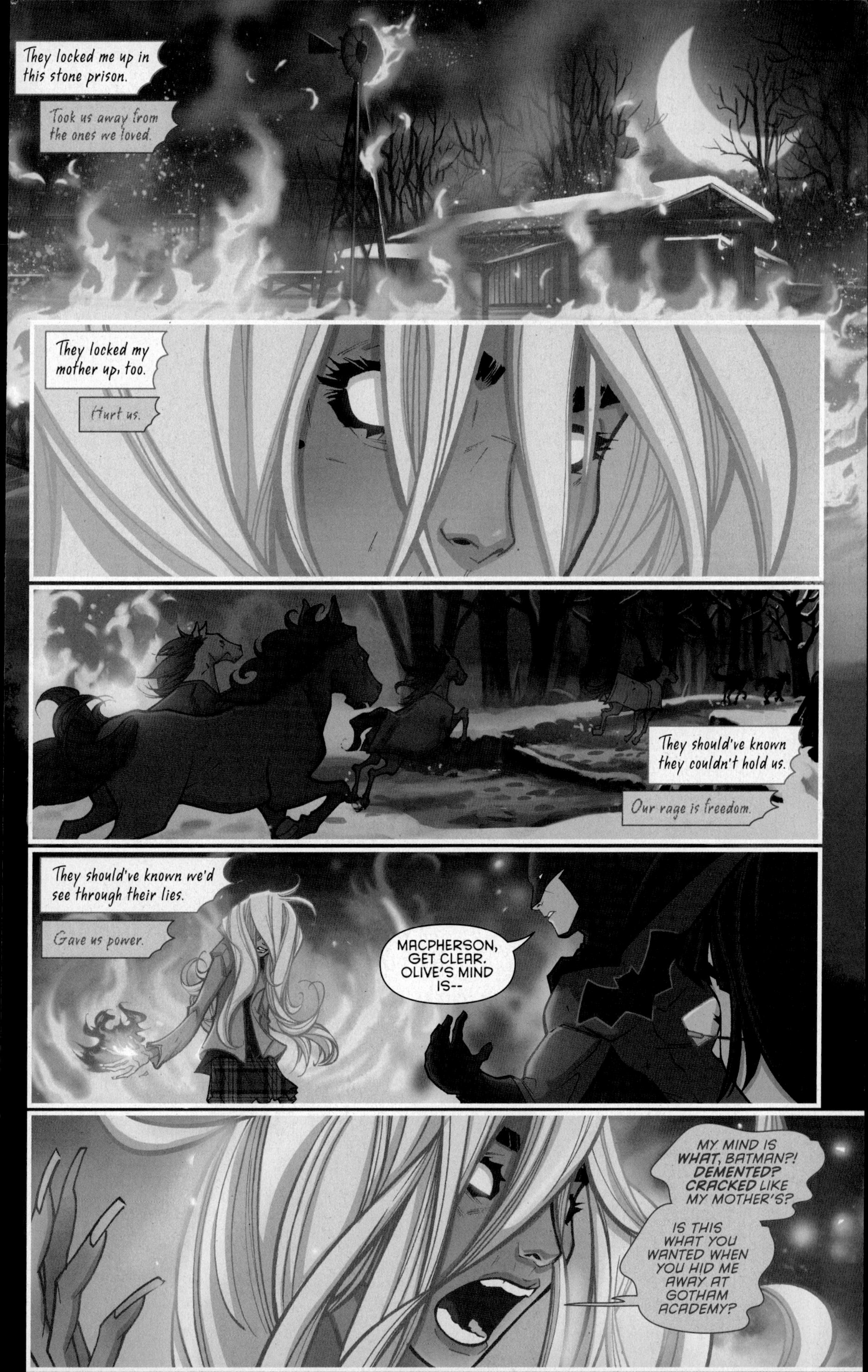
They locked me up in this stone prison.
Took us away from the ones we loved.
They locked my mother up, too.
Hurt us.
They should've known they couldn't hold us.
Our rage is freedom.
They should've known we'd see through their lies.
Gave us power.
MACPHERSON, GET CLEAR. OLIVE'S MIND IS--
MY MIND IS WHAT, BATMAN?! DEMENTED? CRACKED LIKE MY MOTHER'S?
IS THIS WHAT YOU WANTED WHEN YOU HID ME AWAY AT GOTHAM ACADEMY?

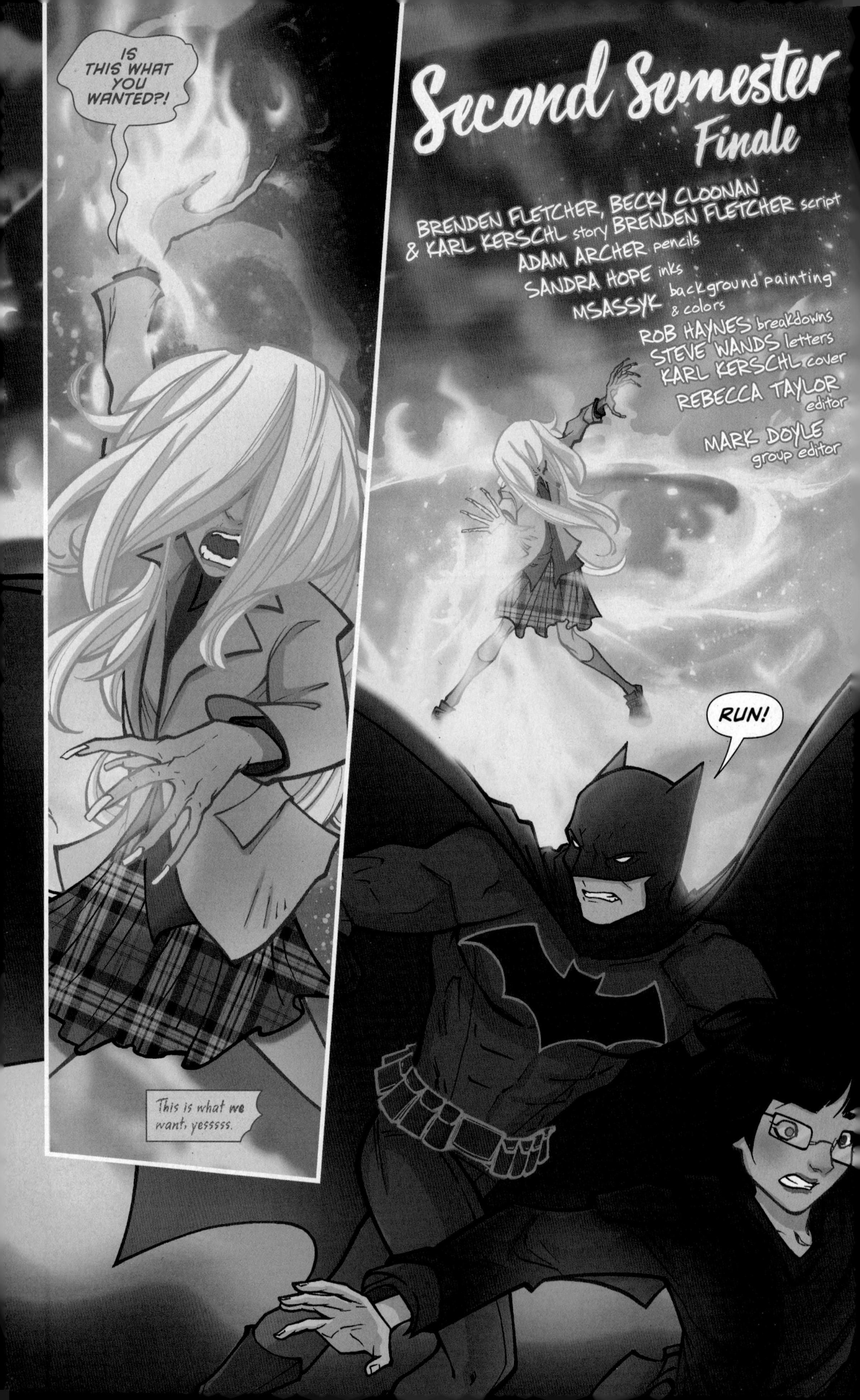
IS THIS WHAT YOU WANTED?!
Second Semester Finale
BRENDEN FLETCHER, BECKY CLOONAN & KARL KERSCHL story BRENDEN FLETCHER script
ADAM ARCHER pencils
SANDRA HOPE inks
MSASSYK background painting & colors
ROB HAYNES breakdowns
STEVE WANDS letters
KARL KERSCHL cover
REBECCA TAYLOR editor
MARK DOYLE group editor
This is what we want, yesssss.
RUN!

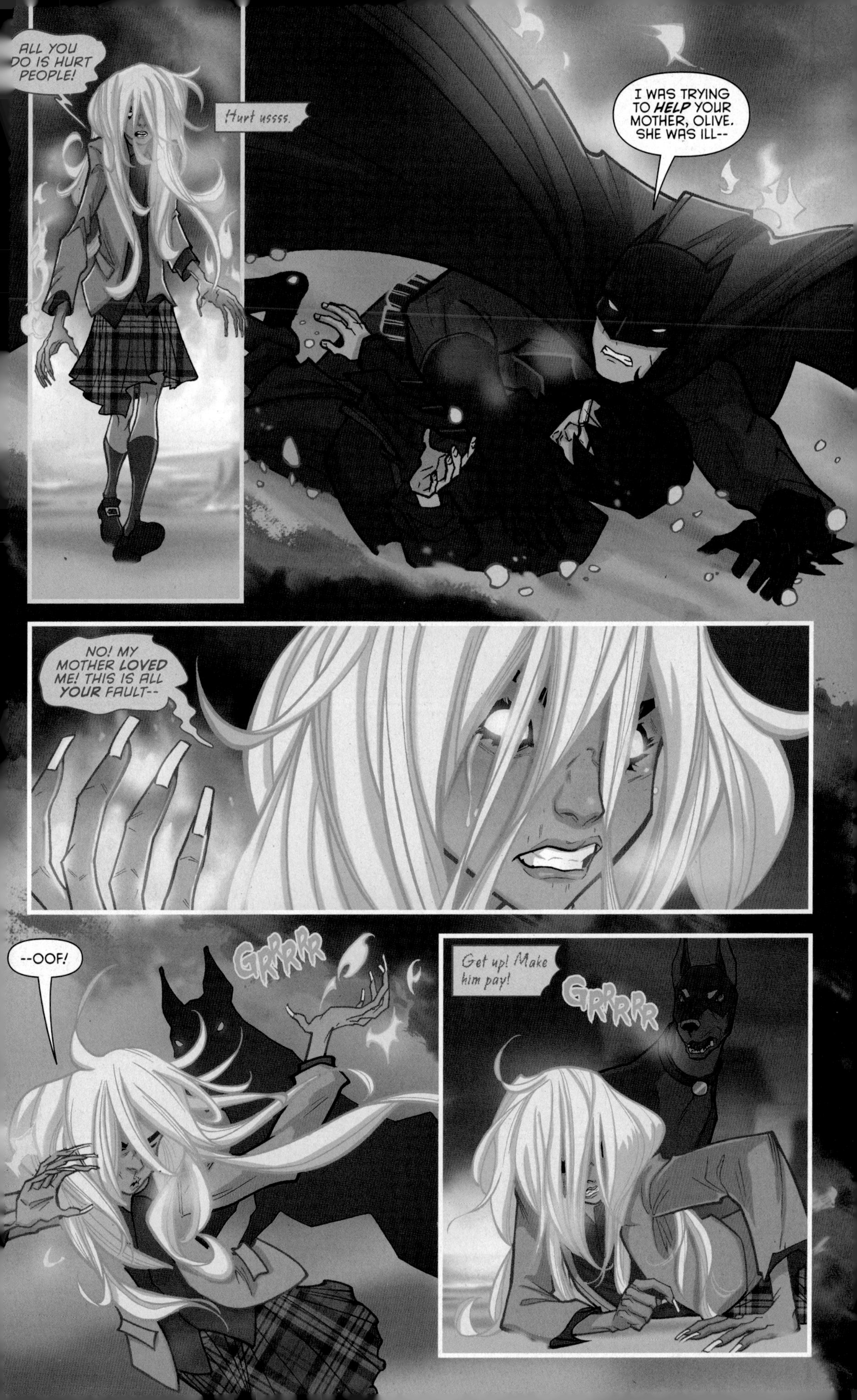
ALL YOU DO IS HURT PEOPLE!
Hurt ussss.
I WAS TRYING TO HELP YOUR MOTHER, OLIVE. SHE WAS ILL--
NO! MY MOTHER LOVED ME! THIS IS ALL YOUR FAULT--
--OOF!
GRRRRR
Get up! Make him pay!
GRRRRR

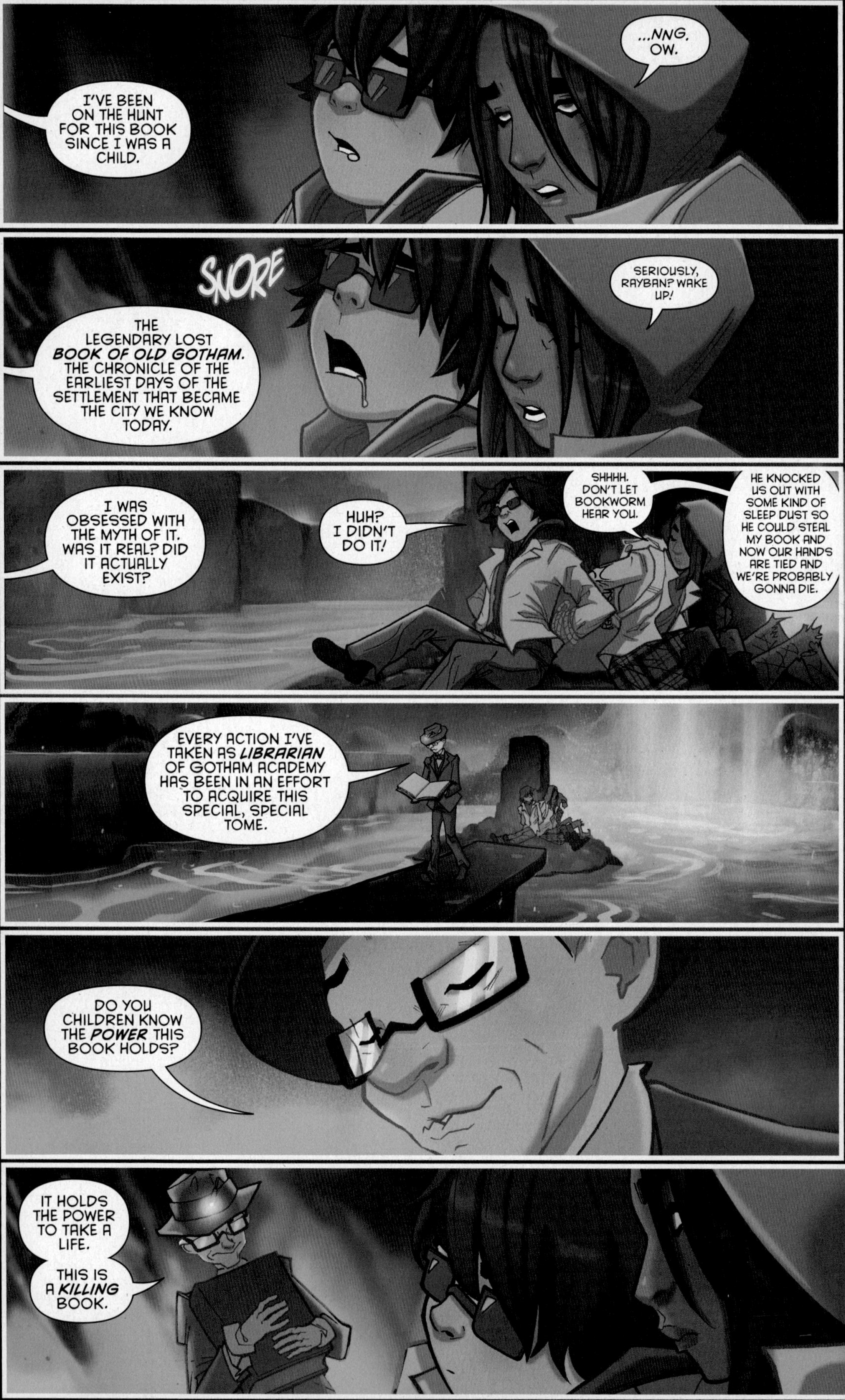
I'VE BEEN ON THE HUNT FOR THIS BOOK SINCE I WAS A CHILD.
...NNG, OW.
SNORE
THE LEGENDARY LOST BOOK OF OLD GOTHAM. THE CHRONICLE OF THE EARLIEST DAYS OF THE SETTLEMENT THAT BECAME THE CITY WE KNOW TODAY.
SERIOUSLY, RAYBAN? WAKE UP!
I WAS OBSESSED WITH THE MYTH OF IT. WAS IT REAL? DID IT ACTUALLY EXIST?
HUH? I DIDN'T DO IT!
SHHHH. DON'T LET BOOKWORM HEAR YOU.
HE KNOCKED US OUT WITH SOME KIND OF SLEEP DUST SO HE COULD STEAL MY BOOK AND NOW OUR HANDS ARE TIED AND WE'RE PROBABLY GONNA DIE.
EVERY ACTION I'VE TAKEN AS LIBRARIAN OF GOTHAM ACADEMY HAS BEEN IN AN EFFORT TO ACQUIRE THIS SPECIAL, SPECIAL TOME.
DO YOU CHILDREN KNOW THE POWER THIS BOOK HOLDS?
IT HOLDS THE POWER TO TAKE A LIFE.
THIS IS A KILLING BOOK.

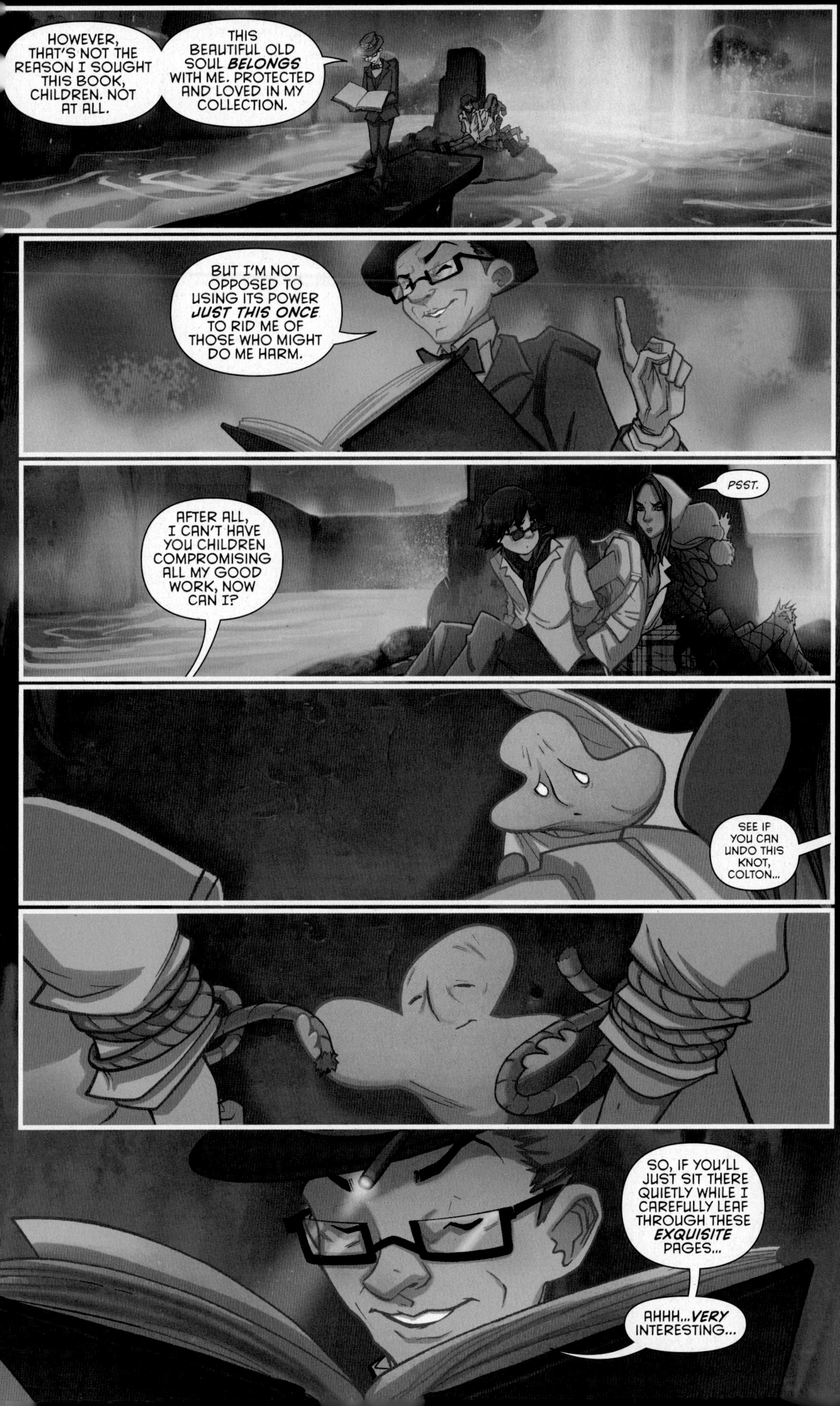
HOWEVER, THAT'S NOT THE REASON I SOUGHT THIS BOOK, CHILDREN. NOT AT ALL.
THIS BEAUTIFUL OLD SOUL BELONGS WITH ME. PROTECTED AND LOVED IN MY COLLECTION.
BUT I'M NOT OPPOSED TO USING ITS POWER JUST THIS ONCE TO RID ME OF THOSE WHO MIGHT DO ME HARM.
AFTER ALL, I CAN'T HAVE YOU CHILDREN COMPROMISING ALL MY GOOD WORK, NOW CAN I?
PSST.
SEE IF YOU CAN UNDO THIS KNOT, COLTON...
SO, IF YOU'LL JUST SIT THERE QUIETLY WHILE I CAREFULLY LEAF THROUGH THESE EXQUISITE PAGES...
AHHH...VERY INTERESTING...

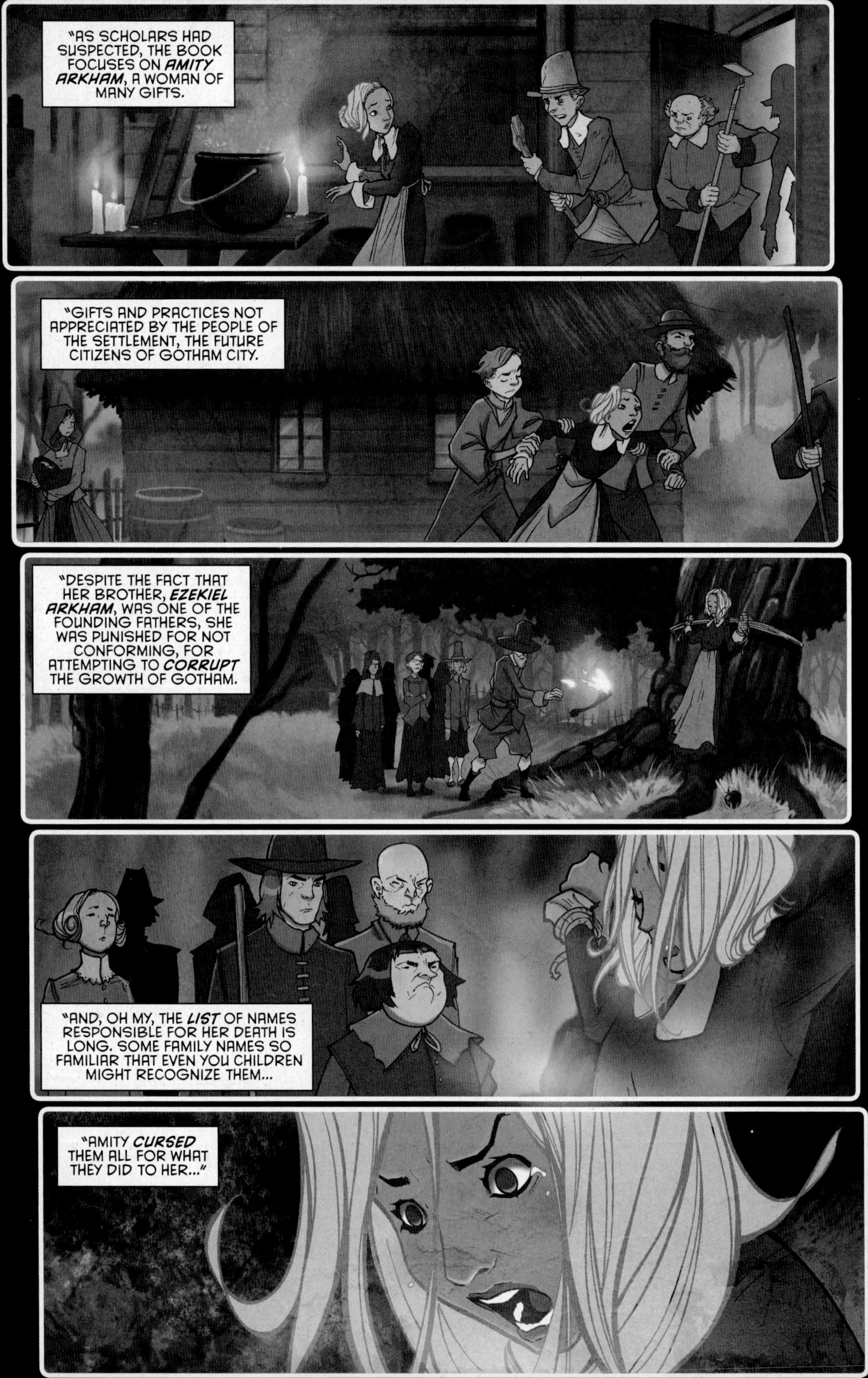
"AS SCHOLARS HAD SUSPECTED, THE BOOK FOCUSES ON AMITY ARKHAM, A WOMAN OF MANY GIFTS.
"GIFTS AND PRACTICES NOT APPRECIATED BY THE PEOPLE OF THE SETTLEMENT, THE FUTURE CITIZENS OF GOTHAM CITY.
"DESPITE THE FACT THAT HER BROTHER, EZEKIEL ARKHAM, WAS ONE OF THE FOUNDING FATHERS, SHE WAS PUNISHED FOR NOT CONFORMING, FOR ATTEMPTING TO CORRUPT THE GROWTH OF GOTHAM.
"AND, OH MY, THE LIST OF NAMES RESPONSIBLE FOR HER DEATH IS LONG. SOME FAMILY NAMES SO FAMILIAR THAT EVEN YOU CHILDREN MIGHT RECOGNIZE THEM...
"AMITY CURSED THEM ALL FOR WHAT THEY DID TO HER..."

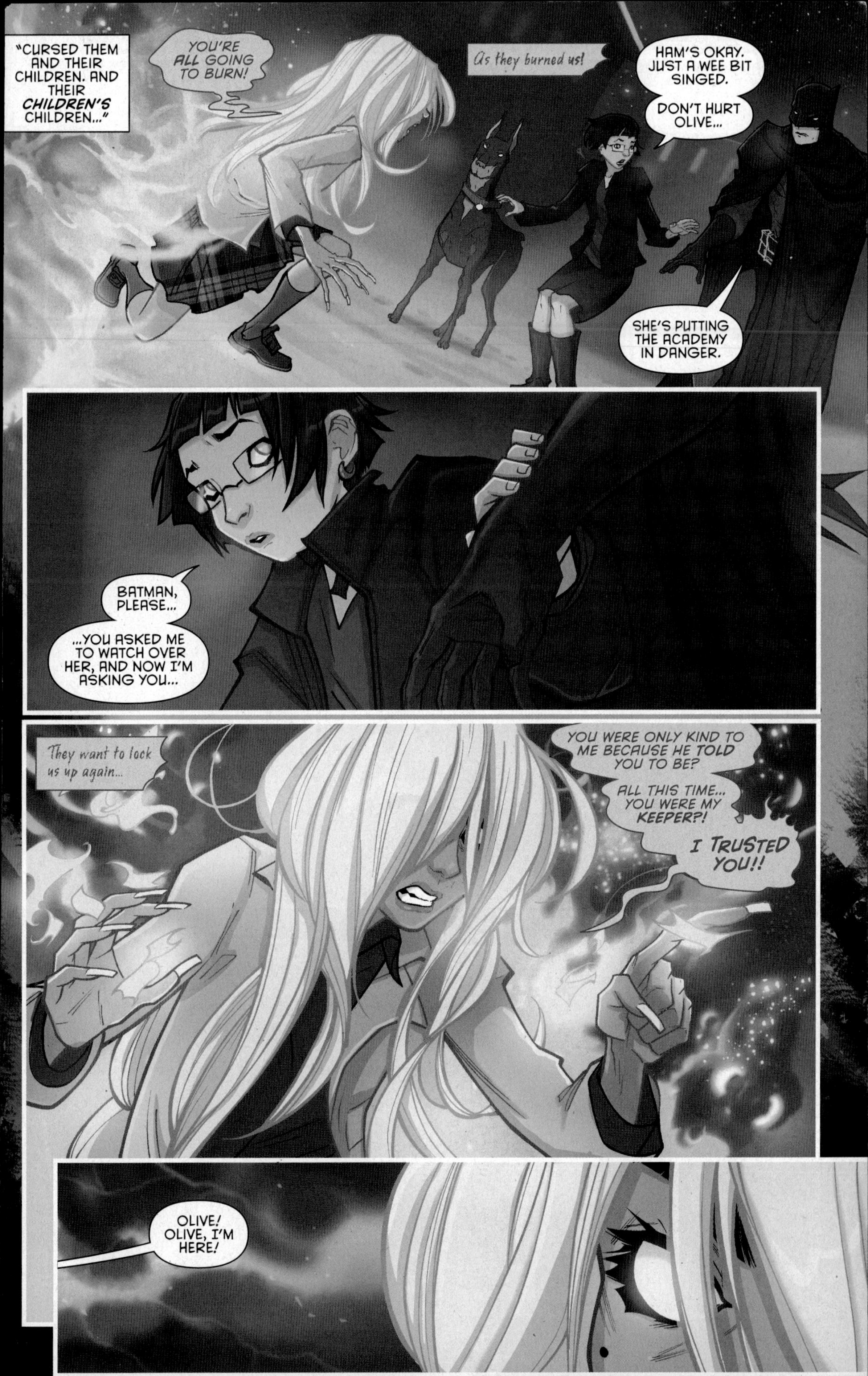
"CURSED THEM AND THEIR CHILDREN. AND THEIR CHILDREN'S CHILDREN..."
YOU'RE ALL GOING TO BURN!
As they burned us!
HAM'S OKAY. JUST A WEE BIT SINGED.
DON'T HURT OLIVE...
SHE'S PUTTING THE ACADEMY IN DANGER.
BATMAN, PLEASE...
...YOU ASKED ME TO WATCH OVER HER, AND NOW I'M ASKING YOU...
They want to lock us up again...
YOU WERE ONLY KIND TO ME BECAUSE HE TOLD YOU TO BE?
ALL THIS TIME... YOU WERE MY KEEPER?!
I TRUSTED YOU!!
OLIVE! OLIVE, I'M HERE!

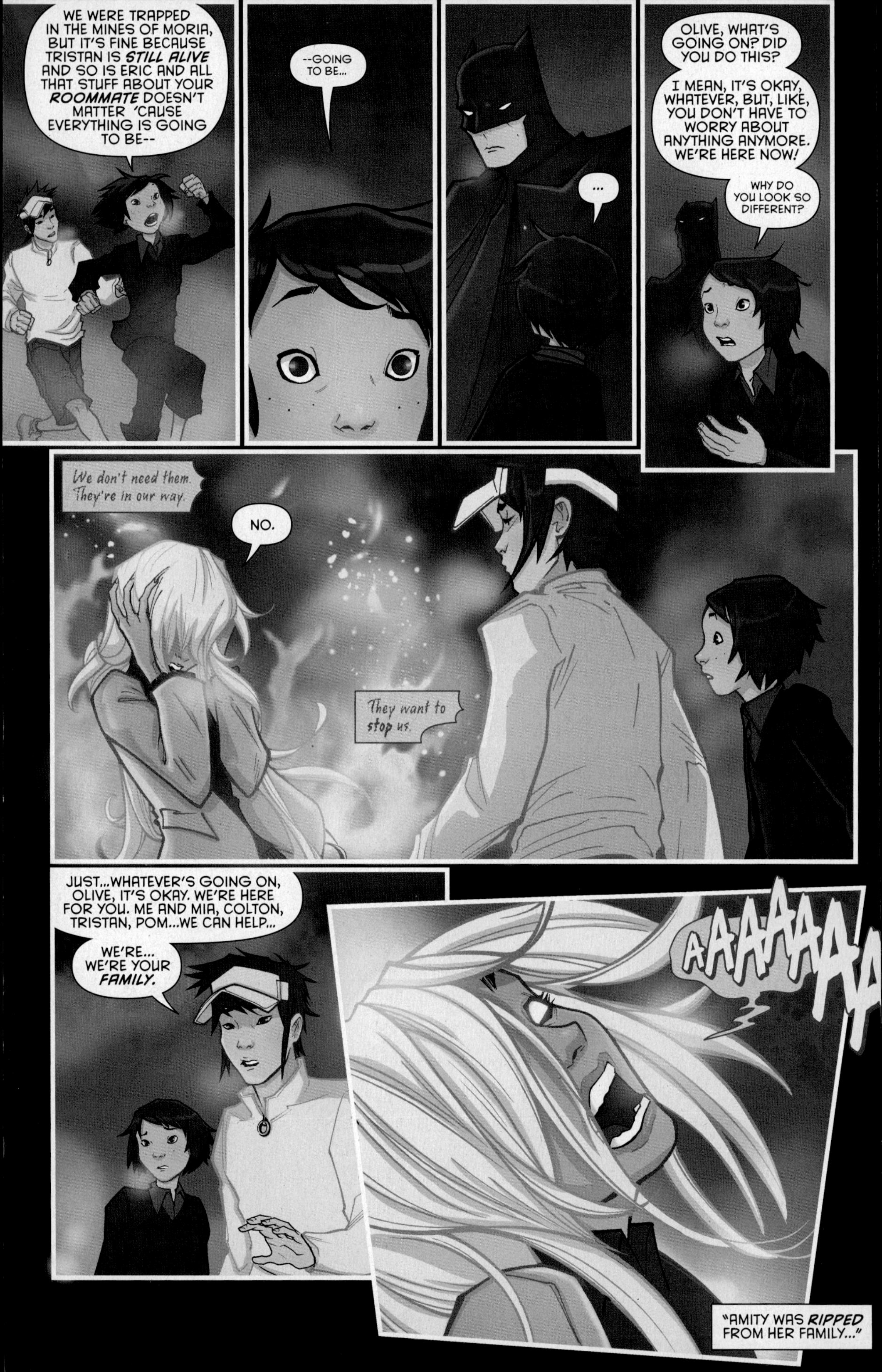
WE WERE TRAPPED IN THE MINES OF MORIA, BUT IT'S FINE BECAUSE TRISTAN IS *STILL ALIVE* AND SO IS ERIC AND ALL THAT STUFF ABOUT YOUR *ROOMMATE* DOESN'T MATTER 'CAUSE EVERYTHING IS GOING TO BE--
--GOING TO BE...
...
OLIVE, WHAT'S GOING ON? DID YOU DO THIS?
I MEAN, IT'S OKAY, WHATEVER, BUT, LIKE, YOU DON'T HAVE TO WORRY ABOUT ANYTHING ANYMORE. WE'RE HERE NOW!
WHY DO YOU LOOK SO DIFFERENT?
We don't need them. They're in our way.
NO.
They want to **stop** us.
JUST...WHATEVER'S GOING ON, OLIVE, IT'S OKAY. WE'RE HERE FOR YOU. ME AND MIA, COLTON, TRISTAN, POM...WE CAN HELP...
WE'RE... WE'RE YOUR *FAMILY.*
AAAAAAA
"AMITY WAS *RIPPED* FROM HER FAMILY..."

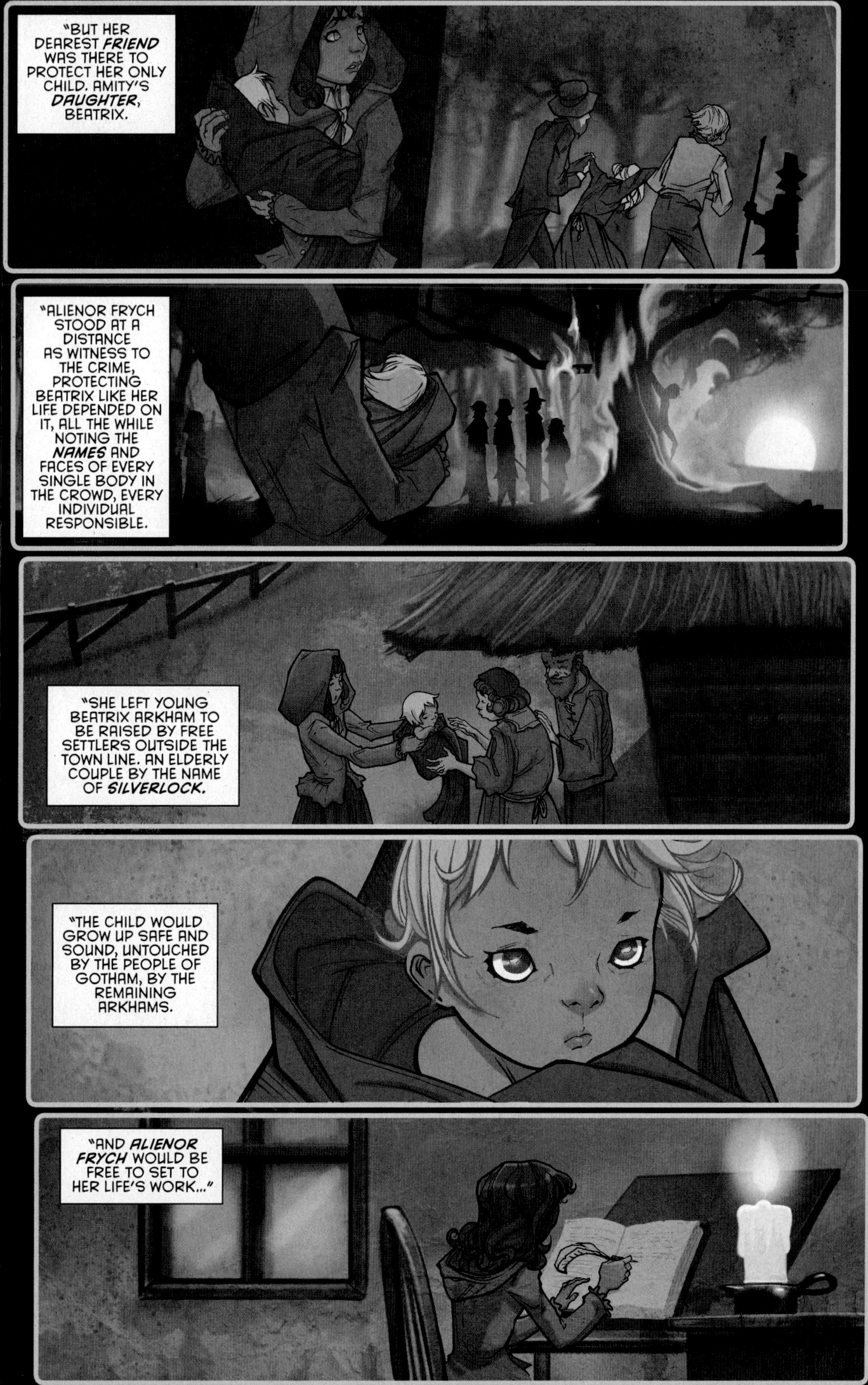
"BUT HER DEAREST FRIEND WAS THERE TO PROTECT HER ONLY CHILD. AMITY'S DAUGHTER, BEATRIX.
"ALIENOR FRYCH STOOD AT A DISTANCE AS WITNESS TO THE CRIME, PROTECTING BEATRIX LIKE HER LIFE DEPENDED ON IT, ALL THE WHILE NOTING THE NAMES AND FACES OF EVERY SINGLE BODY IN THE CROWD, EVERY INDIVIDUAL RESPONSIBLE.
"SHE LEFT YOUNG BEATRIX ARKHAM TO BE RAISED BY FREE SETTLERS OUTSIDE THE TOWN LINE. AN ELDERLY COUPLE BY THE NAME OF SILVERLOCK.
"THE CHILD WOULD GROW UP SAFE AND SOUND, UNTOUCHED BY THE PEOPLE OF GOTHAM, BY THE REMAINING ARKHAMS.
"AND ALIENOR FRYCH WOULD BE FREE TO SET TO HER LIFE'S WORK..."

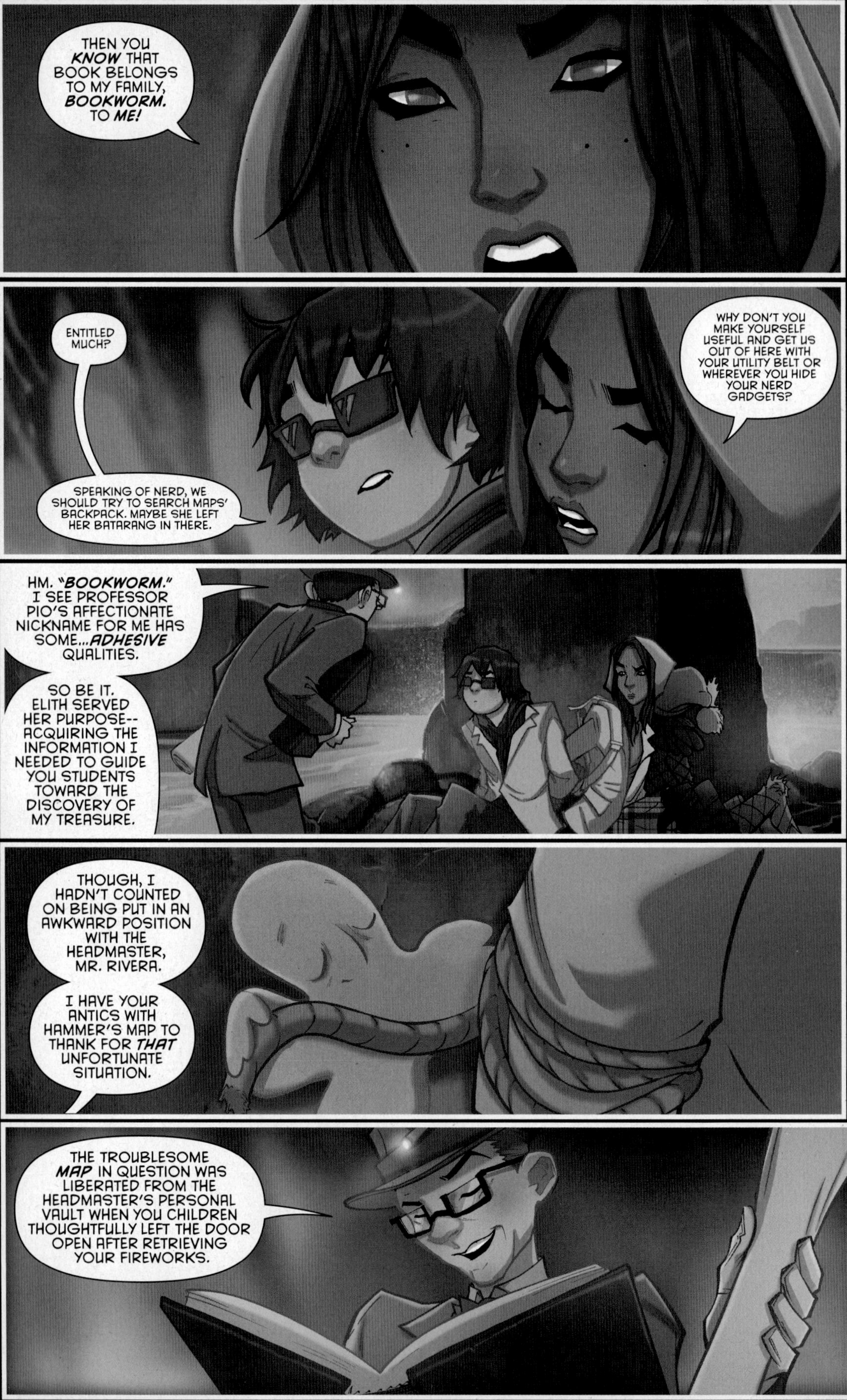
THEN YOU KNOW THAT BOOK BELONGS TO MY FAMILY, BOOKWORM. TO ME!
ENTITLED MUCH?
SPEAKING OF NERD, WE SHOULD TRY TO SEARCH MAPS' BACKPACK. MAYBE SHE LEFT HER BATARANG IN THERE.
WHY DON'T YOU MAKE YOURSELF USEFUL AND GET US OUT OF HERE WITH YOUR UTILITY BELT OR WHEREVER YOU HIDE YOUR NERD GADGETS?
HM. "BOOKWORM." I SEE PROFESSOR PIO'S AFFECTIONATE NICKNAME FOR ME HAS SOME...ADHESIVE QUALITIES.
SO BE IT. ELITH SERVED HER PURPOSE--ACQUIRING THE INFORMATION I NEEDED TO GUIDE YOU STUDENTS TOWARD THE DISCOVERY OF MY TREASURE.
THOUGH, I HADN'T COUNTED ON BEING PUT IN AN AWKWARD POSITION WITH THE HEADMASTER, MR. RIVERA.
I HAVE YOUR ANTICS WITH HAMMER'S MAP TO THANK FOR THAT UNFORTUNATE SITUATION.
THE TROUBLESOME MAP IN QUESTION WAS LIBERATED FROM THE HEADMASTER'S PERSONAL VAULT WHEN YOU CHILDREN THOUGHTFULLY LEFT THE DOOR OPEN AFTER RETRIEVING YOUR FIREWORKS.

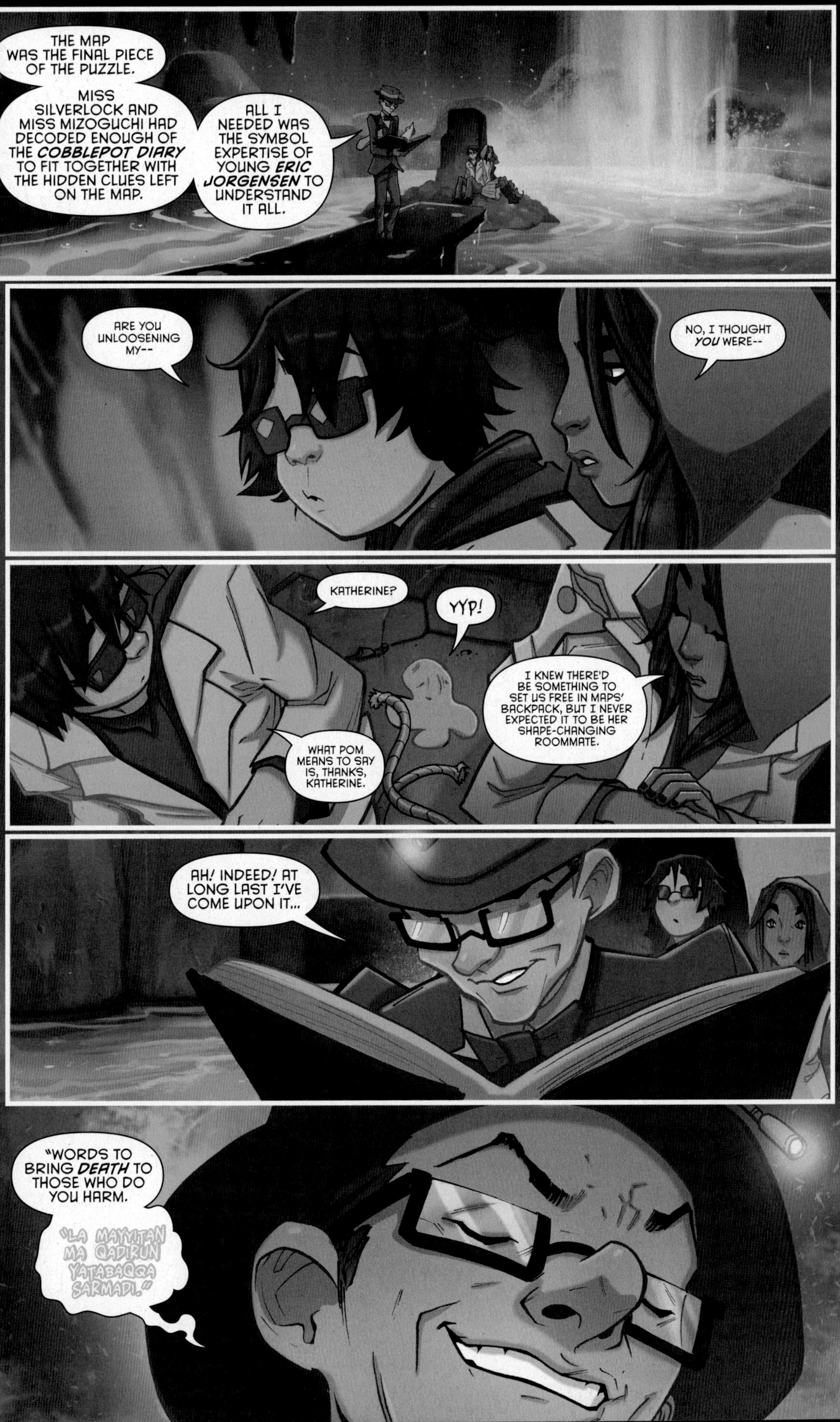
THE MAP WAS THE FINAL PIECE OF THE PUZZLE.
MISS SILVERLOCK AND MISS MIZOGUCHI HAD DECODED ENOUGH OF THE *COBBLEPOT DIARY* TO FIT TOGETHER WITH THE HIDDEN CLUES LEFT ON THE MAP.
ALL I NEEDED WAS THE SYMBOL EXPERTISE OF YOUNG *ERIC JORGENSEN* TO UNDERSTAND IT ALL.
ARE YOU UNLOOSENING MY--
NO, I THOUGHT *YOU* WERE--
KATHERINE?
YYP!
I KNEW THERE'D BE SOMETHING TO SET US FREE IN MAPS' BACKPACK, BUT I NEVER EXPECTED IT TO BE HER SHAPE-CHANGING ROOMMATE.
WHAT POM MEANS TO SAY IS, THANKS, KATHERINE.
AH! INDEED! AT LONG LAST I'VE COME UPON IT...
"WORDS TO BRING *DEATH* TO THOSE WHO DO YOU HARM.
"LA MAYYITAN MA QADIRUN YATABAQQA SARMADI."

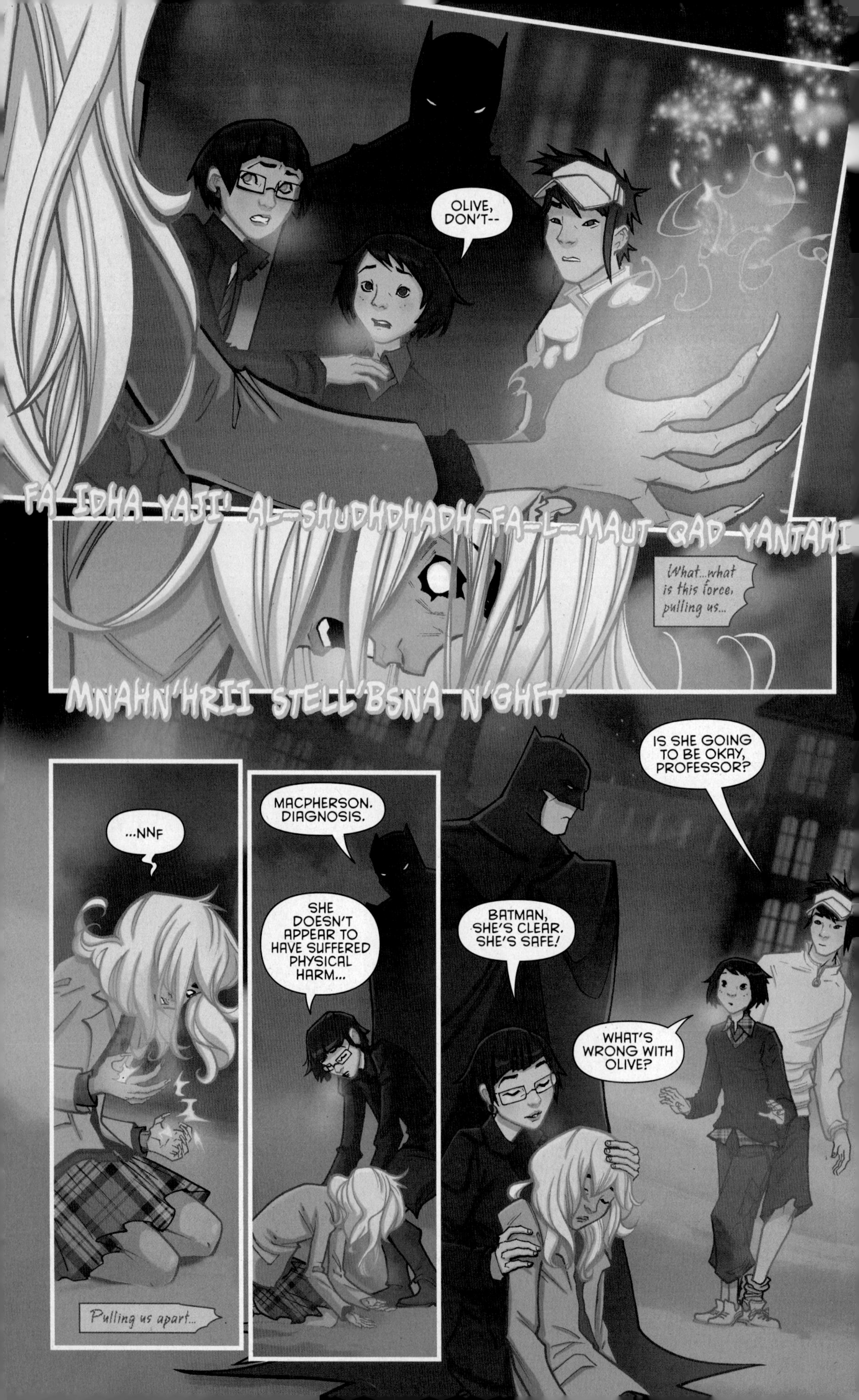
OLIVE, DON'T--
FA IDHA YAJI' AL-SHUDHDHADH FA-L-MAUT QAD YANTAHI
What...what is this force, pulling us...
MNAHN'HRII STELL'BSNA N'GHFT
...NNF
Pulling us apart...
MACPHERSON. DIAGNOSIS.
SHE DOESN'T APPEAR TO HAVE SUFFERED PHYSICAL HARM...
BATMAN, SHE'S CLEAR. SHE'S SAFE!
IS SHE GOING TO BE OKAY, PROFESSOR?
WHAT'S WRONG WITH OLIVE?

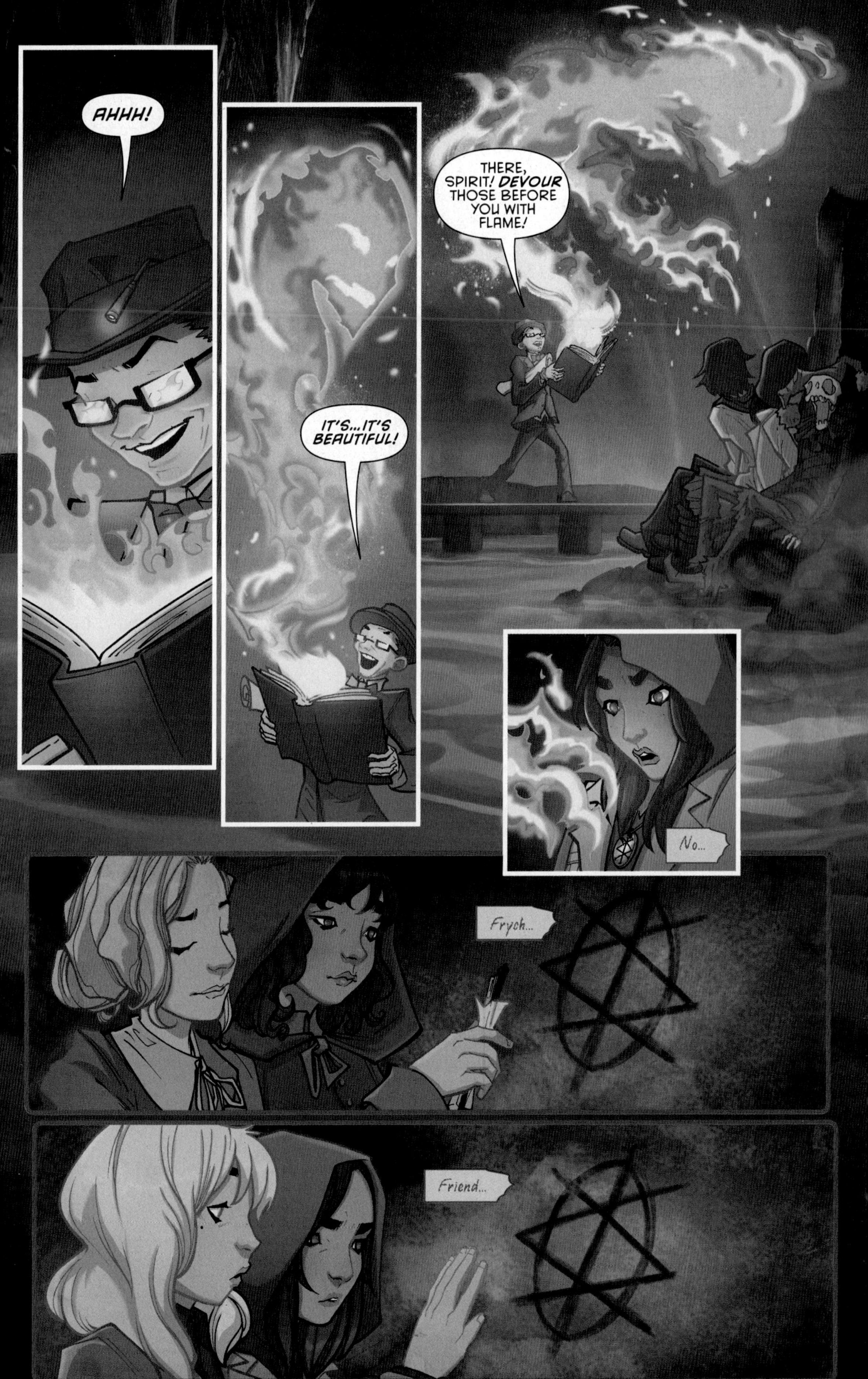
AHHH!
IT'S...IT'S BEAUTIFUL!
THERE, SPIRIT! DEVOUR THOSE BEFORE YOU WITH FLAME!
No...
Frych...
Friend...

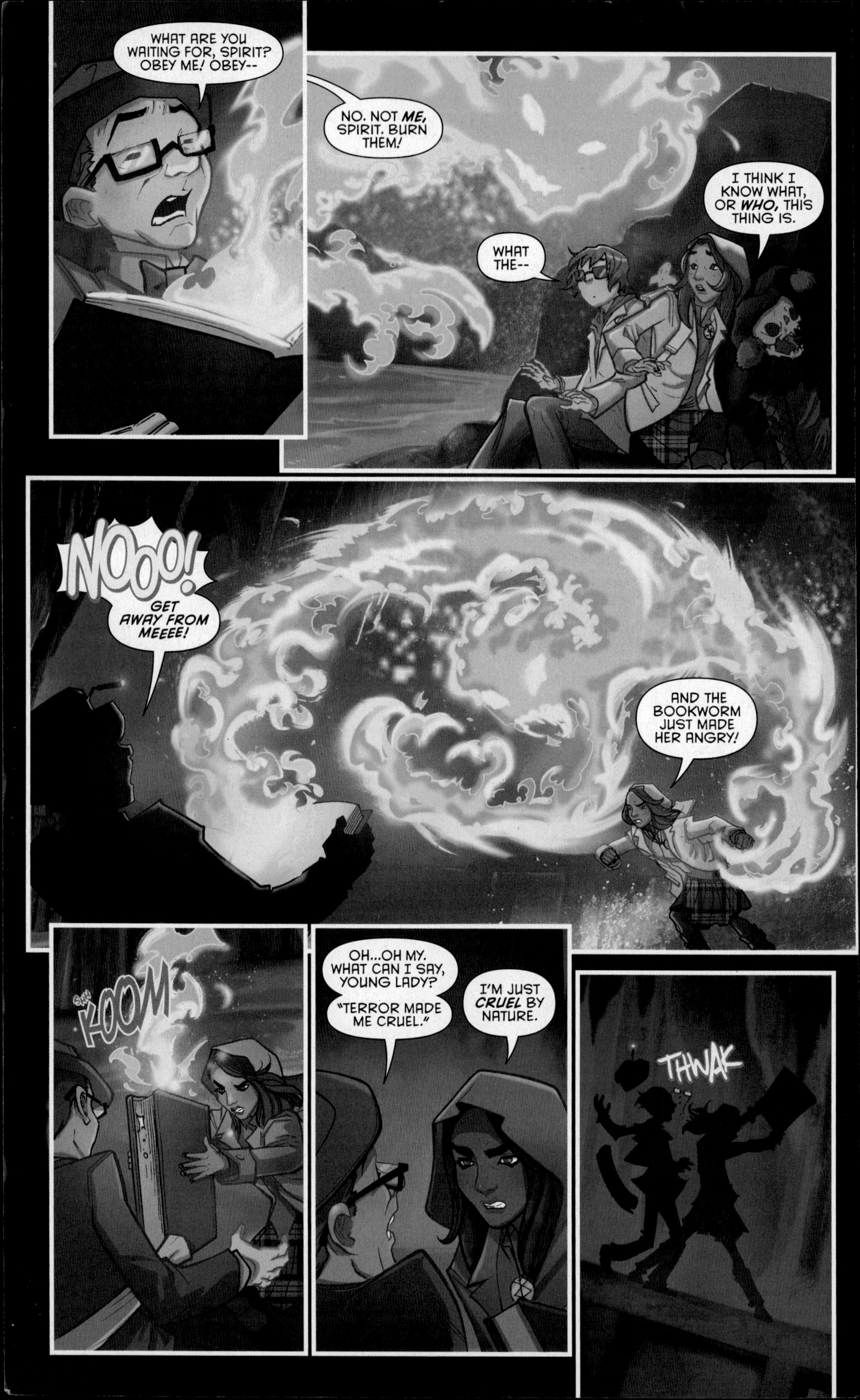

WHAT ARE YOU WAITING FOR, SPIRIT? OBEY ME! OBEY--
NO. NOT ME, SPIRIT. BURN THEM!
WHAT THE--
I THINK I KNOW WHAT, OR WHO, THIS THING IS.
NOOO!
GET AWAY FROM MEEEE!
AND THE BOOKWORM JUST MADE HER ANGRY!
SHH
KOOM
OH...OH MY. WHAT CAN I SAY, YOUNG LADY?
"TERROR MADE ME CRUEL."
I'M JUST CRUEL BY NATURE.
THWAK

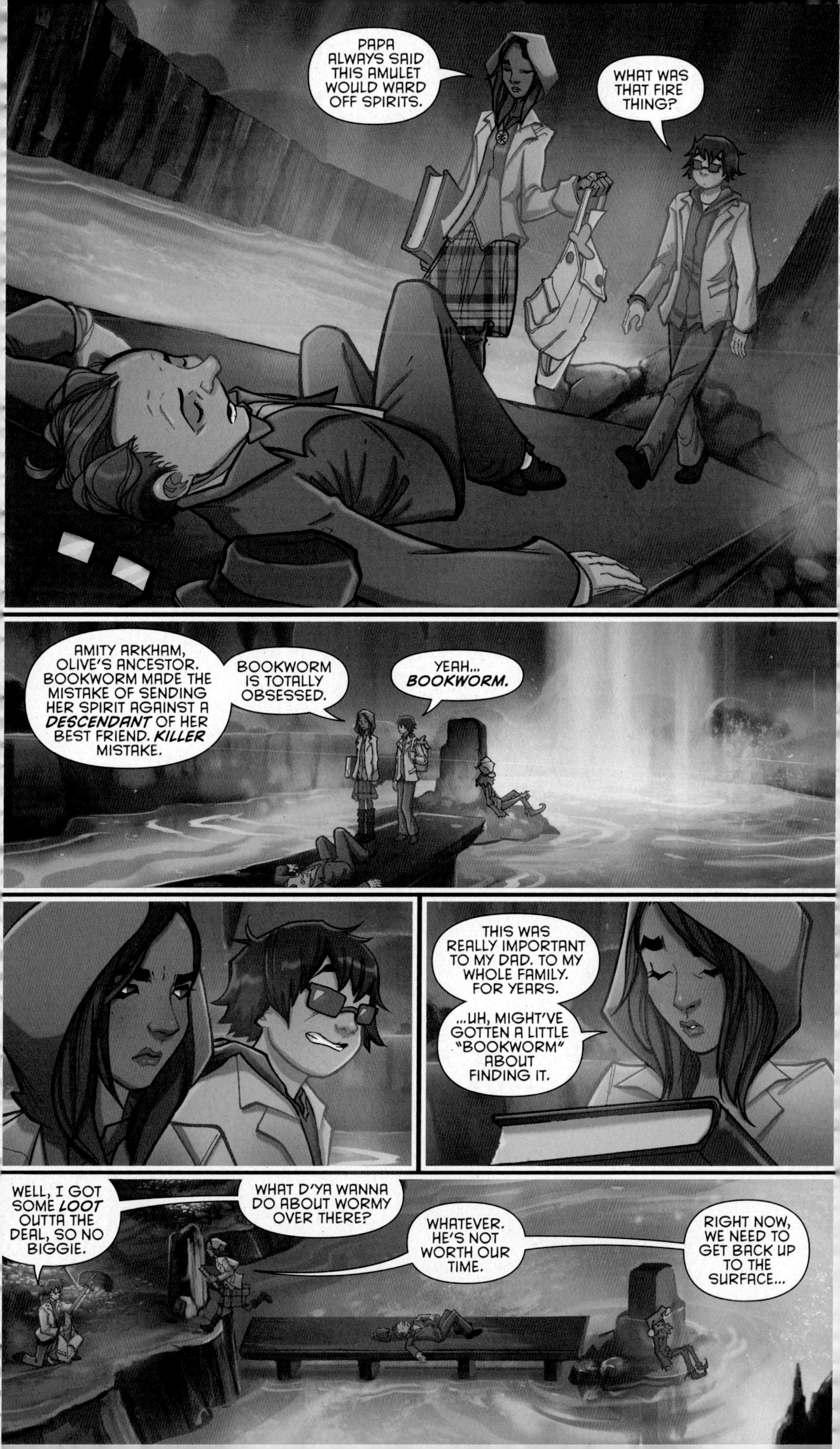
PAPA ALWAYS SAID THIS AMULET WOULD WARD OFF SPIRITS.
WHAT WAS THAT FIRE THING?
AMITY ARKHAM, OLIVE'S ANCESTOR. BOOKWORM MADE THE MISTAKE OF SENDING HER SPIRIT AGAINST A *DESCENDANT* OF HER BEST FRIEND. *KILLER* MISTAKE.
BOOKWORM IS TOTALLY OBSESSED.
YEAH... ***BOOKWORM.***
THIS WAS REALLY IMPORTANT TO MY DAD. TO MY WHOLE FAMILY. FOR YEARS.
...UH, MIGHT'VE GOTTEN A LITTLE "BOOKWORM" ABOUT FINDING IT.
WELL, I GOT SOME *LOOT* OUTTA THE DEAL, SO NO BIGGIE.
WHAT D'YA WANNA DO ABOUT WORMY OVER THERE?
WHATEVER. HE'S NOT WORTH OUR TIME.
RIGHT NOW, WE NEED TO GET BACK UP TO THE SURFACE...

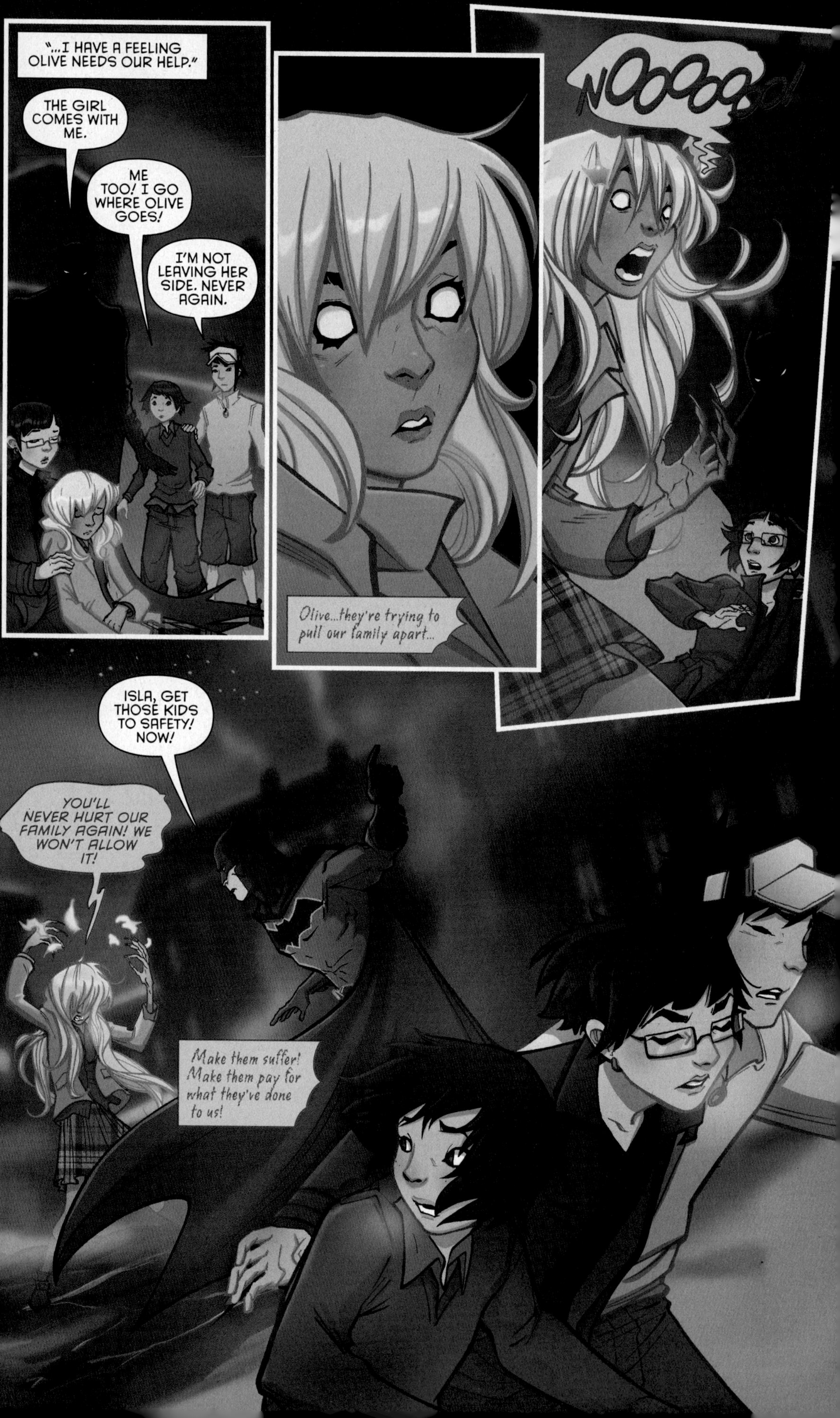
"...I HAVE A FEELING OLIVE NEEDS OUR HELP."
THE GIRL COMES WITH ME.
ME TOO! I GO WHERE OLIVE GOES!
I'M NOT LEAVING HER SIDE. NEVER AGAIN.
Olive...they're trying to pull our family apart...
NOOOOOOO!
ISLA, GET THOSE KIDS TO SAFETY! NOW!
YOU'LL NEVER HURT OUR FAMILY AGAIN! WE WON'T ALLOW IT!
Make them suffer! Make them pay for what they've done to us!

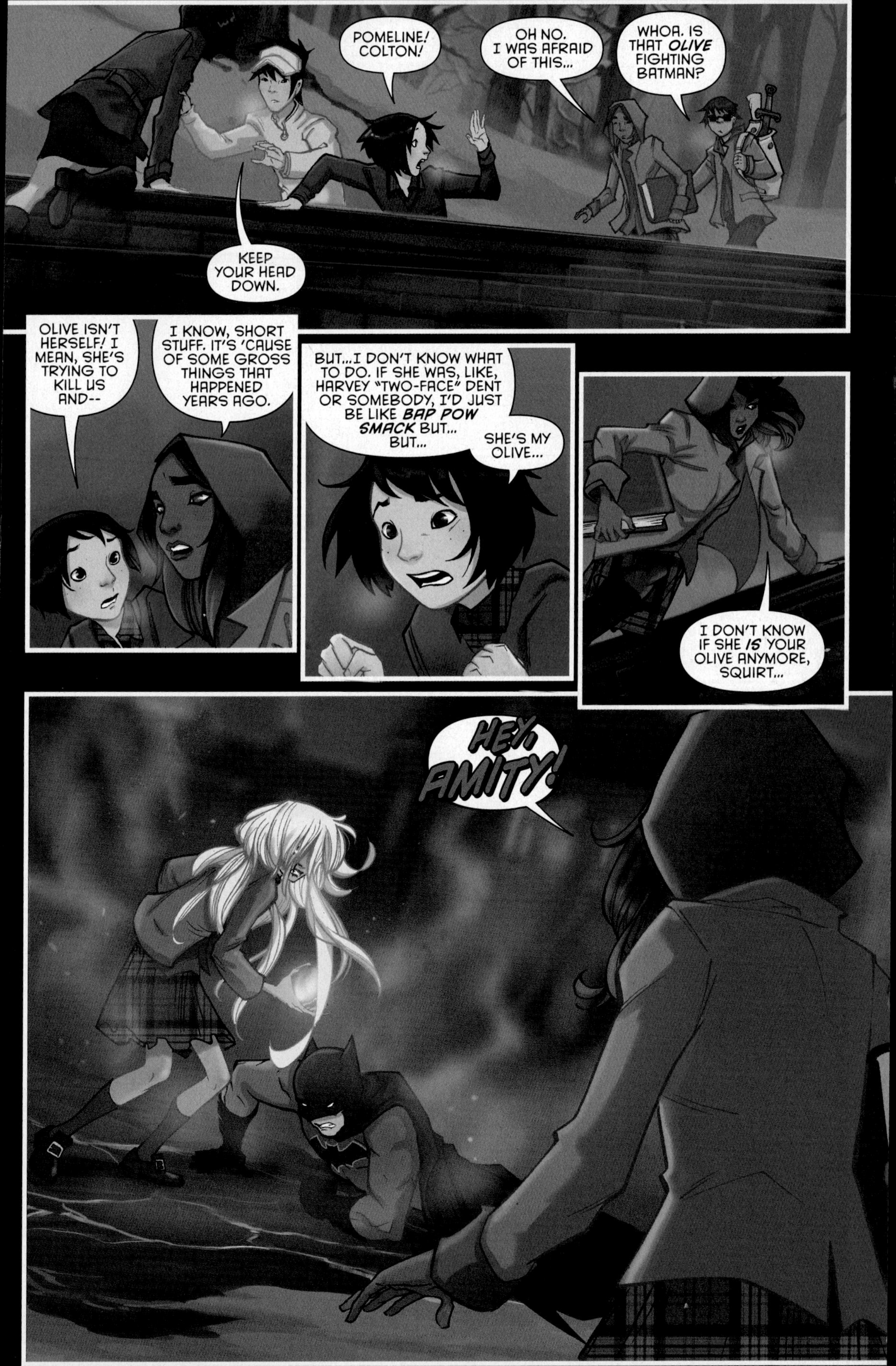
POMELINE! COLTON!
OH NO. I WAS AFRAID OF THIS...
WHOA. IS THAT *OLIVE* FIGHTING BATMAN?
KEEP YOUR HEAD DOWN.
OLIVE ISN'T HERSELF! I MEAN, SHE'S TRYING TO KILL US AND--
I KNOW, SHORT STUFF. IT'S 'CAUSE OF SOME GROSS THINGS THAT HAPPENED YEARS AGO.
BUT...I DON'T KNOW WHAT TO DO. IF SHE WAS, LIKE, HARVEY "TWO-FACE" DENT OR SOMEBODY, I'D JUST BE LIKE *BAP POW SMACK* BUT... BUT...
SHE'S MY OLIVE...
I DON'T KNOW IF SHE *IS* YOUR OLIVE ANYMORE, SQUIRT...
HEY, AMITY!

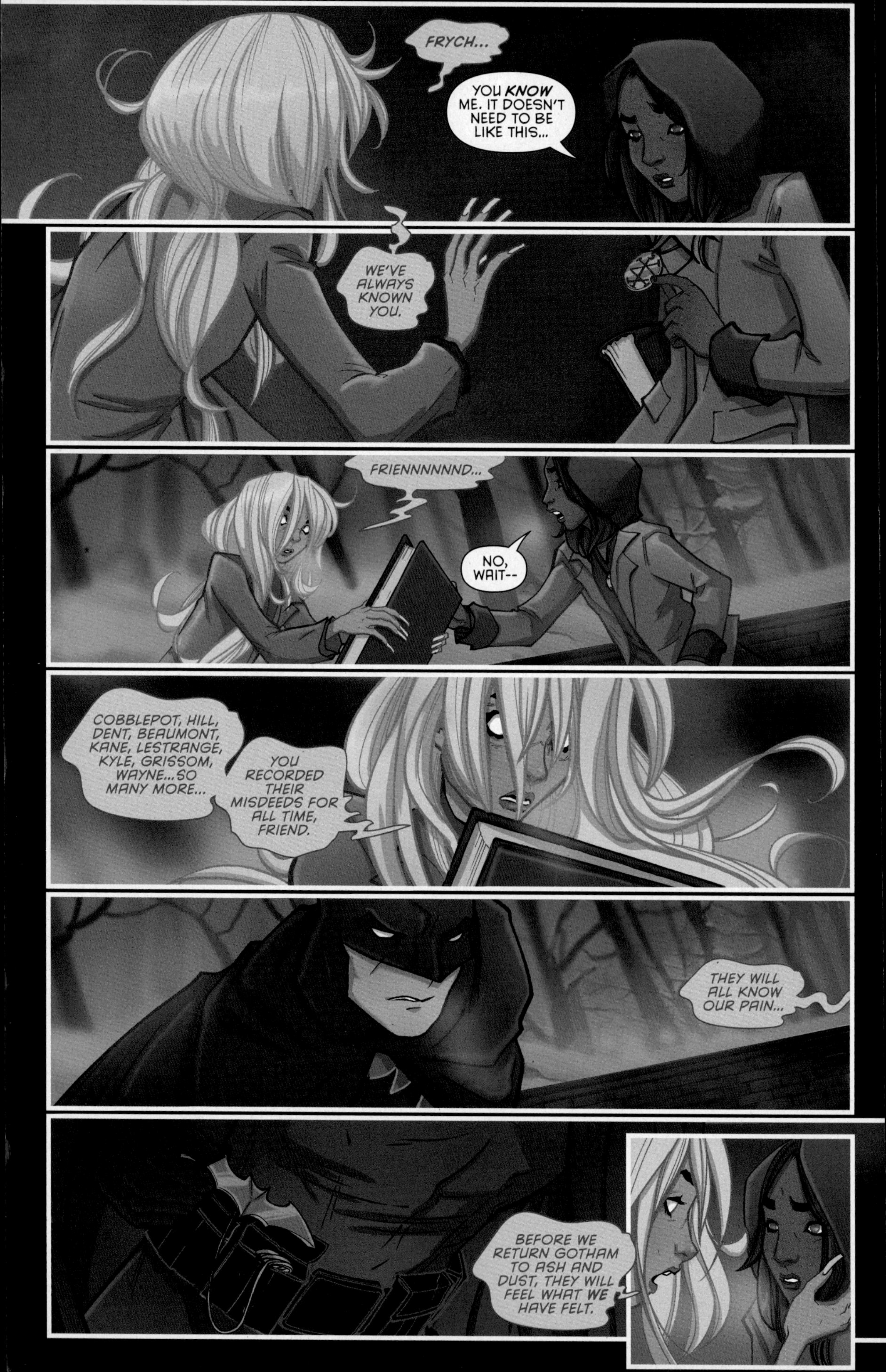
FRYCH...
YOU KNOW ME. IT DOESN'T NEED TO BE LIKE THIS...
WE'VE ALWAYS KNOWN YOU.
FRIENNNNNND...
NO, WAIT--
COBBLEPOT, HILL, DENT, BEAUMONT, KANE, LESTRANGE, KYLE, GRISSOM, WAYNE...SO MANY MORE...
YOU RECORDED THEIR MISDEEDS FOR ALL TIME, FRIEND.
THEY WILL ALL KNOW OUR PAIN...
BEFORE WE RETURN GOTHAM TO ASH AND DUST, THEY WILL FEEL WHAT WE HAVE FELT.

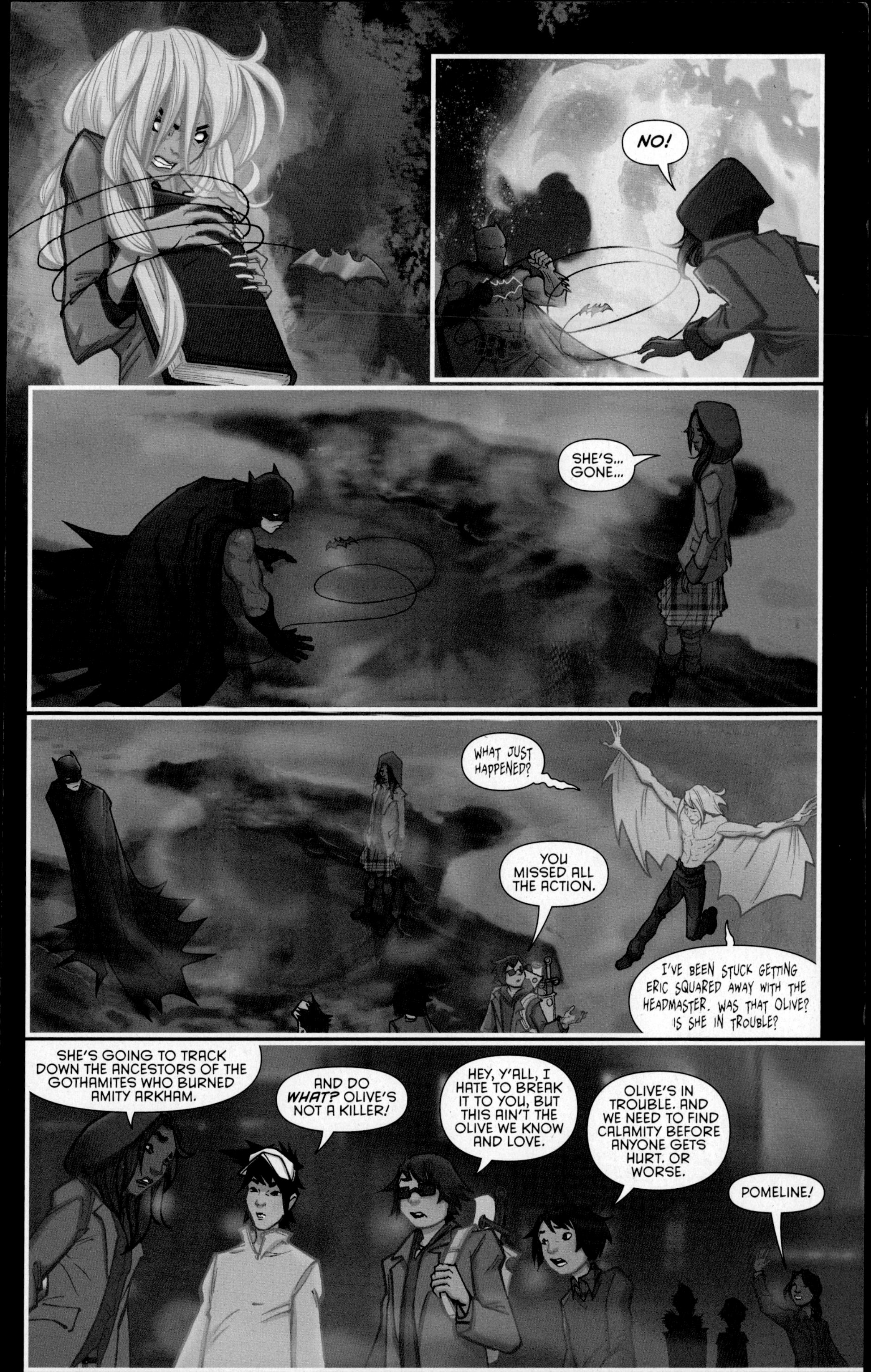
NO!
SHE'S... GONE...
WHAT JUST HAPPENED?
YOU MISSED ALL THE ACTION.
I'VE BEEN STUCK GETTING ERIC SQUARED AWAY WITH THE HEADMASTER. WAS THAT OLIVE? IS SHE IN TROUBLE?
SHE'S GOING TO TRACK DOWN THE ANCESTORS OF THE GOTHAMITES WHO BURNED AMITY ARKHAM.
AND DO WHAT? OLIVE'S NOT A KILLER!
HEY, Y'ALL, I HATE TO BREAK IT TO YOU, BUT THIS AIN'T THE OLIVE WE KNOW AND LOVE.
OLIVE'S IN TROUBLE. AND WE NEED TO FIND CALAMITY BEFORE ANYONE GETS HURT. OR WORSE.
POMELINE!

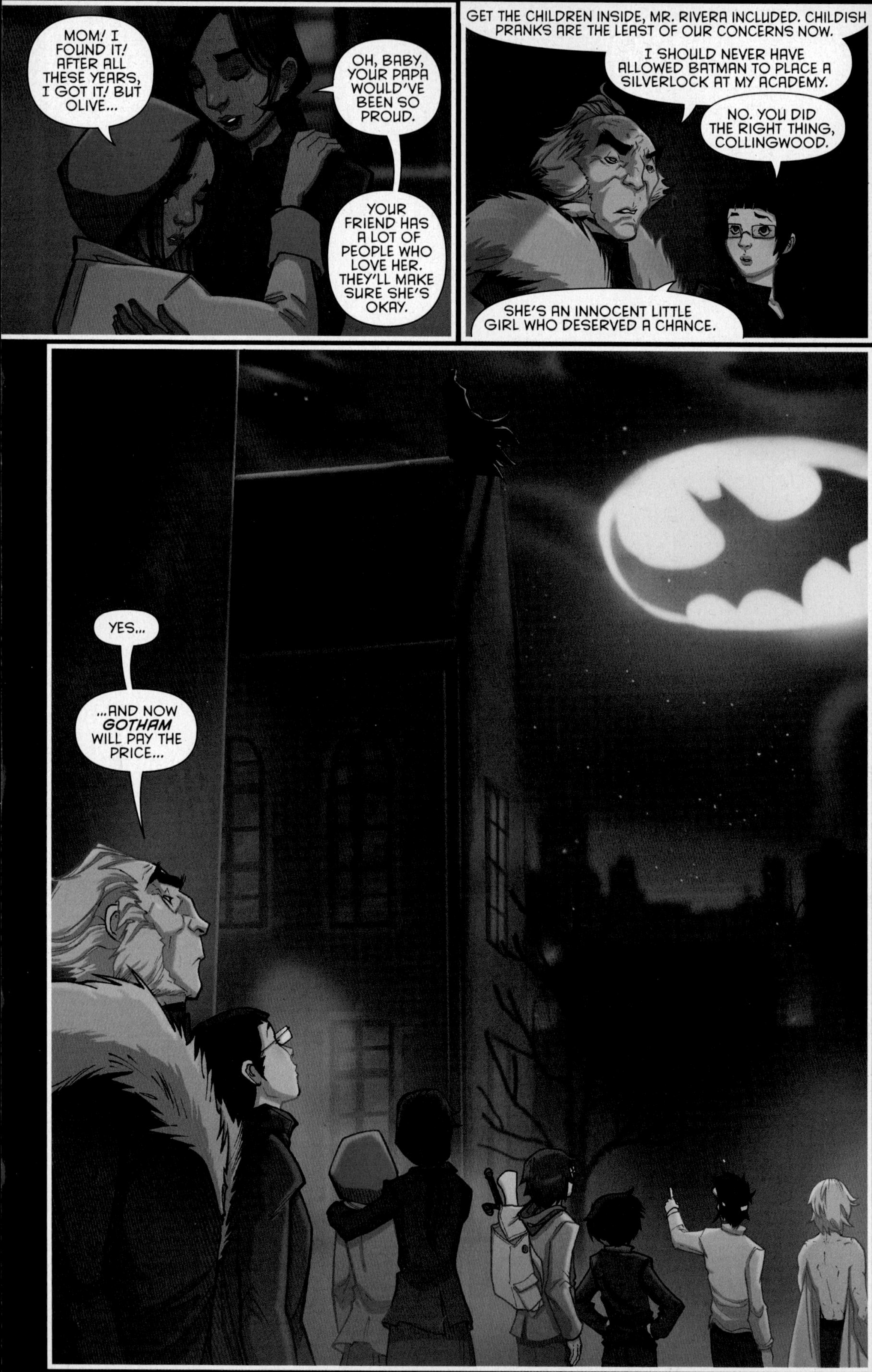

MOM! I FOUND IT! AFTER ALL THESE YEARS, I GOT IT! BUT OLIVE...
OH, BABY, YOUR PAPA WOULD'VE BEEN SO PROUD.
YOUR FRIEND HAS A LOT OF PEOPLE WHO LOVE HER. THEY'LL MAKE SURE SHE'S OKAY.
GET THE CHILDREN INSIDE, MR. RIVERA INCLUDED. CHILDISH PRANKS ARE THE LEAST OF OUR CONCERNS NOW.
I SHOULD NEVER HAVE ALLOWED BATMAN TO PLACE A SILVERLOCK AT MY ACADEMY.
NO. YOU DID THE RIGHT THING, COLLINGWOOD.
SHE'S AN INNOCENT LITTLE GIRL WHO DESERVED A CHANCE.
YES...
...AND NOW *GOTHAM* WILL PAY THE PRICE...

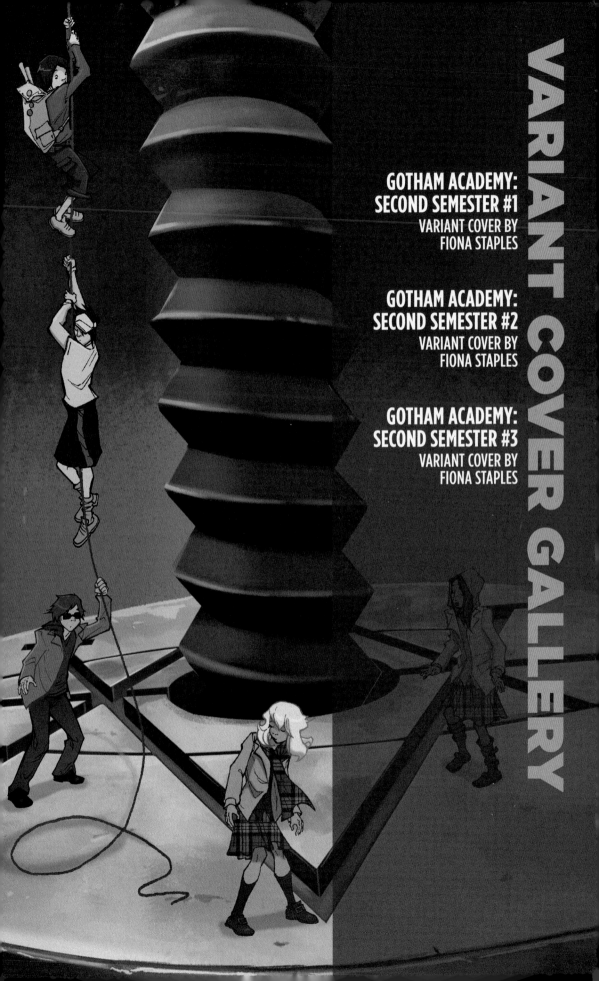

GOTHAM ACADEMY:
SECOND SEMESTER #1
VARIANT COVER BY
FIONA STAPLES

GOTHAM ACADEMY:
SECOND SEMESTER #2
VARIANT COVER BY
FIONA STAPLES

GOTHAM ACADEMY:
SECOND SEMESTER #3
VARIANT COVER BY
FIONA STAPLES

VARIANT COVER GALLERY

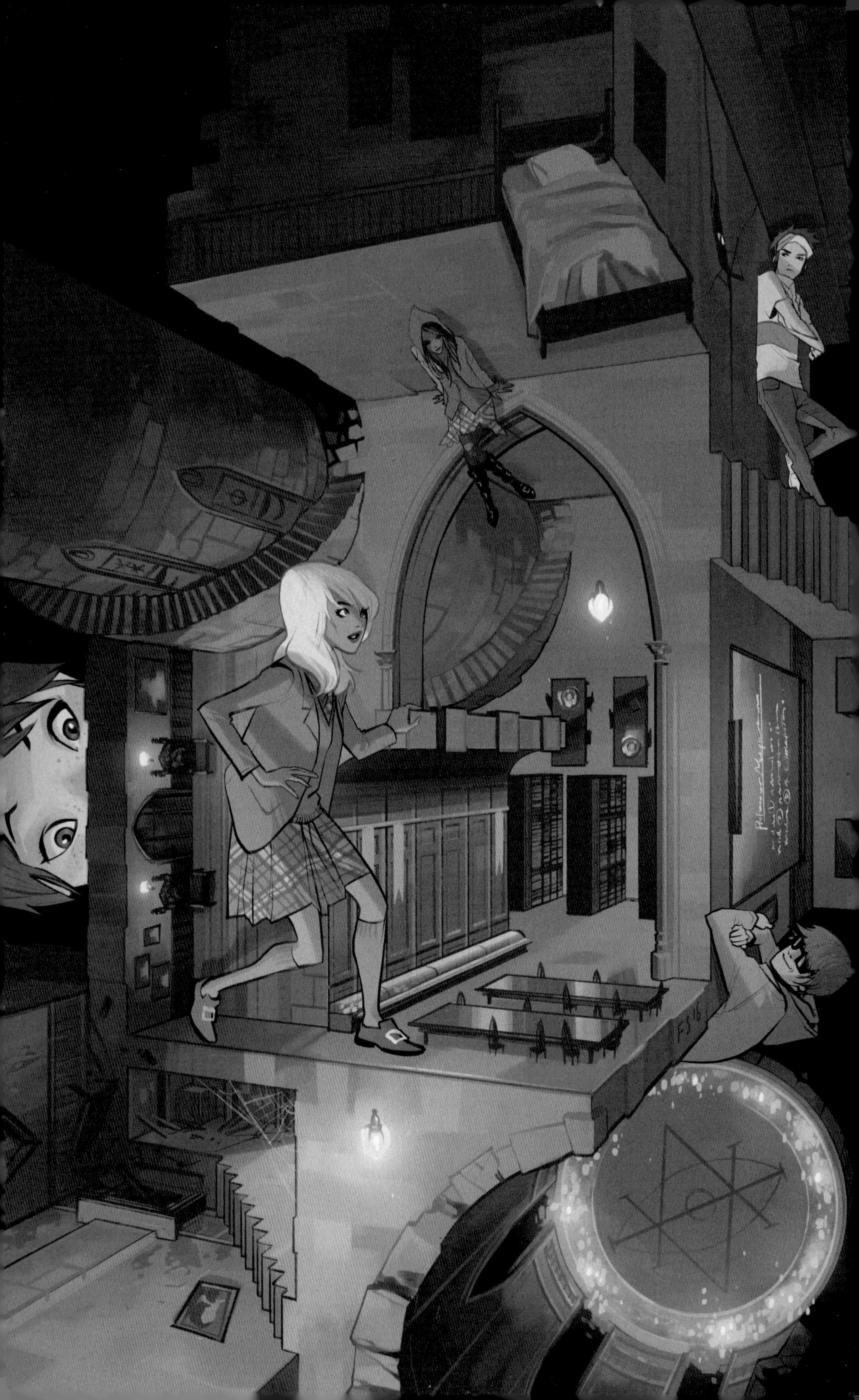

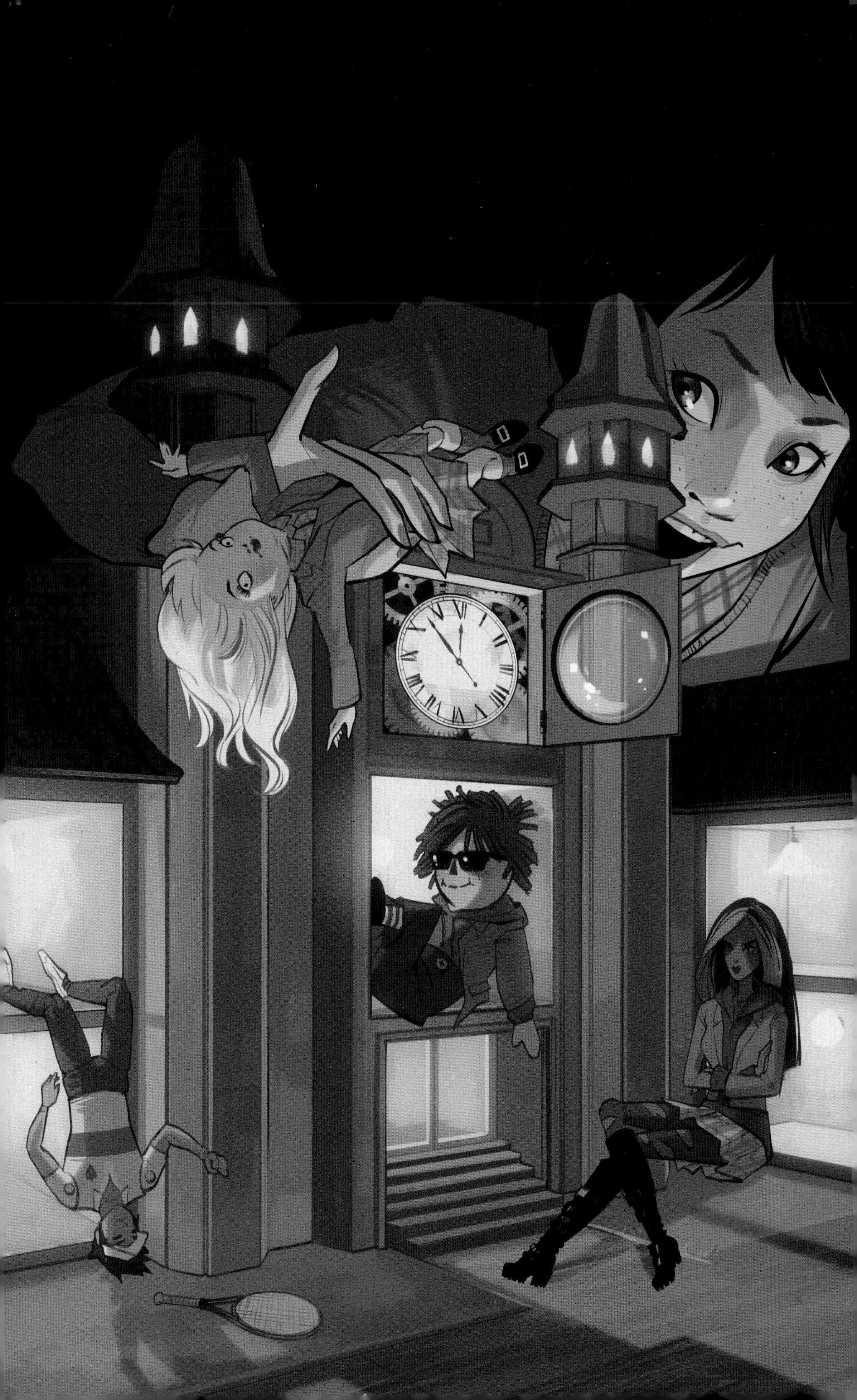

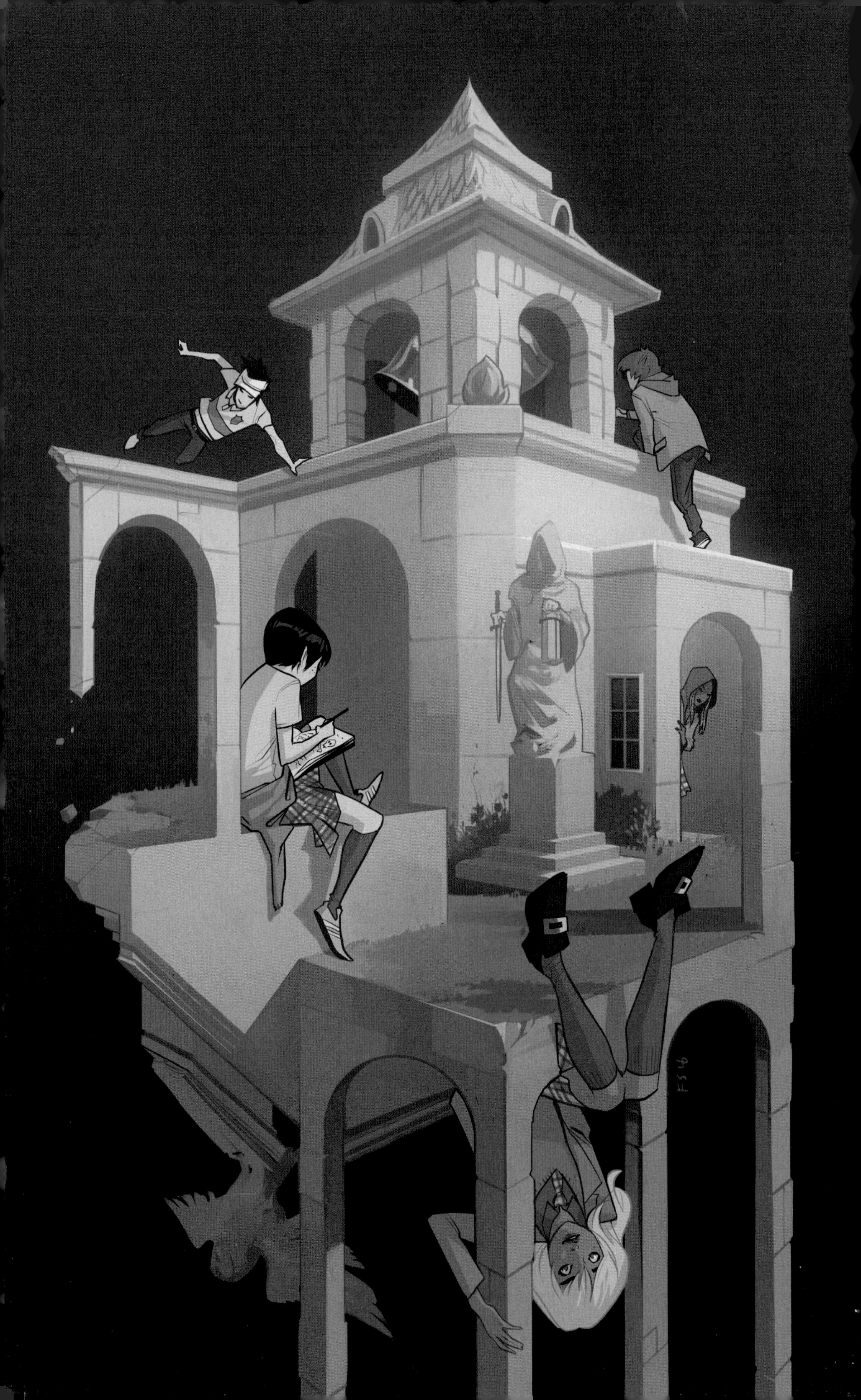

> "A brand-new take on a classic, and it looks absolutely, jaw-droppingly fantastic."
> – **NEWSARAMA**

> "A whole lot of excitement and killer art."
> – **COMIC BOOK RESOURCES**

# BATGIRL
## VOL. 1: BATGIRL OF BURNSIDE
CAMERON STEWART &
BRENDEN FLETCHER
with BABS TARR

**BATGIRL VOL. 2:**
**FAMILY BUSINESS**

**BATGIRL VOL. 3:**
**MINDFIELDS**

**BLACK CANARY VOL. 1:**
**KICKING AND SCREAMING**